Deploying Chromebooks in the Classroom

Planning, Installing, and Managing Chromebooks in Schools and Colleges

Guy Hart-Davis

Apress®

Deploying Chromebooks in the Classroom: Planning, Installing, and Managing Chromebooks in Schools and Colleges

Guy Hart-Davis
County Durham, United Kingdom

ISBN-13 (pbk): 978-1-4842-3765-6
https://doi.org/10.1007/978-1-4842-3766-3

ISBN-13 (electronic): 978-1-4842-3766-3

Library of Congress Control Number: 2018955242

Managing Director, Apress Media LLC: Welmoed Spahr
Acquisitions Editor: Aaron Black
Development Editor: James Markham
Coordinating Editor: Jessica Vakili

Cover designed by eStudioCalamar

Cover image designed by Freepik (www.freepik.com)

Distributed to the book trade worldwide by Springer Science+Business Media New York, 233 Spring Street, 6th Floor, New York, NY 10013. Phone 1-800-SPRINGER, fax (201) 348-4505, email orders-ny@springer-sbm.com, or visit www.springeronline.com. Apress Media, LLC is a California LLC, and the sole member (owner) is Springer Science + Business Media Finance Inc (SSBM Finance Inc). SSBM Finance Inc is a Delaware corporation.

For information on translations, please email rights@apress.com or visit http://www.apress.com/rights-permissions.

Apress titles may be purchased in bulk for academic, corporate, or promotional use. eBook versions and licenses are also available for most titles. For more information, reference our Print and eBook Bulk Sales web page at http://www.apress.com/bulk-sales.

Any source code or other supplementary material referenced by the author in this book is available to readers on GitHub via the book's product page, located at www.apress.com/978-1-4842-3765-6. For more detailed information, please visit http://www.apress.com/source-code.

Printed on acid-free paper

Table of Contents

About the Author

Guy Hart-Davis is the author of more than 140 computer books, including several from Apress—among them *Deploying iPads in the Classroom, Deploying Raspberry Pi in the Classroom,* and *Pro Office for iPad.*

CHAPTER 1

Planning Your Deployment of Chromebooks in the Classroom

In this chapter, we will discuss how to plan your deployment of Chromebooks in the classroom. We will start with a quick reality check about your school's plans to add computers to the classroom and then move along to practical matters. We will then make sure you know the capabilities of Chromebooks and how they compare—both favorably and unfavorably—to alternatives, such as other laptop-style computers and tablet computers. We will then go through what you will need to do to plan the deployment: choose a deployment model, decide how to manage the Chromebooks, and ensure that your school's network and Internet connection have enough bandwidth to handle the additional traffic that the Chromebooks will generate.

One crucial decision this chapter will not cover is how to select the right Chromebook model or models for your school's students and teachers. Chapter 2 will cover this topic in depth.

© Guy Hart-Davis 2018
G. Hart-Davis, *Deploying Chromebooks in the Classroom*,
https://doi.org/10.1007/978-1-4842-3766-3_1

Making the Decision to Computerize Classrooms or Classes

To deploy Chromebooks or other computers successfully in your school, you should have the agreement and cooperation of your colleagues, your students, and perhaps also the students' parents. While it is certainly possible to make the decision to computerize alone and then impose the decision on others, you will typically get much better results by involving each group in making the decision and supporting its implementation.

Given that you are reading this book, you have likely progressed past this stage in the planning process. If this is the case, skip ahead to the next section, "Understanding Chromebook Capabilities." If not, you will probably want to take the following steps, not necessarily in this exact order:

- Research the costs and benefits of computerizing one or more classrooms or classes.

- Convince your colleagues of the merits of adding the computers.

- Get input from the students.

- Build a budget for a pilot scheme and get it approved.

- Select a classroom or a class for the pilot scheme.

- Run the pilot scheme.

- Review the success or otherwise of the pilot scheme and the feedback you get from it.

- Scale up your pilot scheme for what the full deployment will need.

- Create a budget for the full deployment.

- Execute the full deployment.

- Build in a review cycle to gauge successes, failures, and improvements needed.

DEVELOPING A FAQ AND ACCEPTABLE-USE POLICIES

As you plan and build out your deployment, develop a FAQ—a list of frequently asked questions—that you can make available on your school's website as an information resource for students, parents, teachers, and support staff.

The FAQ needs to cover everything from the school's purpose in deploying the Chromebooks; through straightforward issues such as startup, login, and basic skills, such as running apps and accessing resources; to more advanced topics such as understanding the restrictions the school has applied to the Chromebooks and the ways in which the school can monitor Chromebook usage. Make sure to publicize the FAQ in the school, and also provide an easy-to-use mechanism for users to submit questions to be added to the FAQ. Add a shortcut to the FAQ to each Chromebook's desktop to encourage students and teachers to use it.

You will also need to create two acceptable-use policies. The first policy should explain the rules under which students use the Chromebooks, what they are allowed to do, what is not permitted—and who is responsible for lost or broken Chromebooks. The second policy should do likewise for teachers. Students and teachers should sign the acceptable-use policies to confirm that they accept the rules. For younger students and for one-to-one deployments (in which the students typically take the Chromebooks home), the students' parents should also sign the policies.

Understanding the Chromebook's Capabilities

The Chromebook is a thin-client laptop computer concept developed by Google. Chromebooks are built by various hardware companies, including major computer manufacturers such as (in alphabetical order) Acer, Asus, Dell, HP, Lenovo, Samsung, and Toshiba. Some high-end Chromebooks, such as the Pixelbook, bear the Google brand, but the vast majority are built and sold by other manufacturers.

The following subsections will make sure you know the essentials of Chromebooks.

General Characteristics of Chromebooks

Like a typical laptop, a Chromebook is a complete computer with a built-in screen, a keyboard, and a touchpad pointing device. Most Chromebooks also include small speakers for audio output and a webcam for video conferencing. Figure 1-1 shows a Chromebook made by Asus.

Figure 1-1. *A Chromebook is a laptop computer that runs a lightweight operating system called Chrome OS*

Many different Chromebook models are available, varying considerably in size, varying greatly in power, and spanning a large range in price. We will look at the specific features of Chromebooks in detail in Chapter 2.

Typical screen sizes range from 10 inches to 15.6 inches, with the Chromebooks' body sizes varying accordingly. Some Chromebook models are ruggedized, designed for use in high-impact situations (such as schools). Chromebook weights mostly fall into the two-to-four-pound range, making the computers easily portable.

Chrome OS and Chrome Apps

Chromebooks run Chrome OS, an operating system developed by Google. Chrome OS is based on the kernel—the core part—of the Linux operating system and has an interface built around Chrome, Google's widely popular web browser. Chrome OS is a lightweight operating system that runs quickly, even on hardware that is fairly modest by today's standards. Figure 1-2 shows the Chrome OS desktop with two windows open.

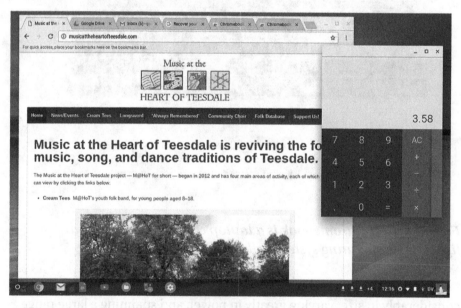

Figure 1-2. *Chrome OS performs many operations in the Chrome browser but also has several local apps, such as the Calculator app shown here*

Chrome OS is designed to store most of its data online rather than on a local drive (as most personal computers usually do). Storing data online reduces the need for storage on the Chromebook itself, so most Chromebooks have modest-size solid-state devices (SSDs) rather than spinning hard disks.

Chromebooks run Chrome apps—apps designed to run on Chrome OS. Many actions for which you would use apps on other operating systems (such as Windows) take place in the Chrome browser on Chromebooks.

Many recent Chromebook models can also run apps built for the Android operating system, which is widely used on smartphones and tablets.

Google Accounts

Chromebooks are designed to work with Google accounts, and each person who uses a Chromebook regularly needs a Google account. A Google account is free to set up and comes with 15 GB of data storage, which is enough for typical usage. Users with heavy needs can pay for extra storage—for example, 100 GB costs $1.99 per month, and 1 TB costs $9.99 per month—up to 30 TB.

Note   If someone needs to use a Chromebook temporarily for browsing, you can let her use the Guest login instead of adding a user profile for her. A guest user cannot create or edit documents stored in a Google account.

Once the user has logged in to her Google account, the Chrome apps automatically store data in the account. Because the data is stored online, by logging in to her Google account, the user can access her files using any Chromebook. This flexibility is great for schools that equip classes or classrooms with Chromebooks.

Note   The first person to set up a particular Chromebook becomes the "owner" of the Chromebook. Google ties the Chromebook to the owner's account so that only the owner can change important system settings on the Chromebook.

Chromebooks Support Multiple User Accounts

Like most modern computers, the Chromebook supports multiple user accounts, making Chromebooks good for use in families, businesses, and schools. Each account's data is kept separately, so no user can access another user's data.

Note   You can create up to 17 user profiles on a Chromebook, enabling up to 17 different users to each have their own space. Each user profile takes up some space on the Chromebook, so it is best not to add profiles unnecessarily so as to avoid running out of storage space.

The Chromebook Works as Both a Consumer Device and a Managed Device

The Chromebook works as both a consumer device and as a managed device. As a consumer device, the owner controls the Chromebook and is the only person who can change important system settings. As a managed device, the Chromebook can be managed using the Chrome Management tools in the Google Admin console. These tools give administrators close control over the Chromebooks.

> **Note**   In your school, you will almost certainly want to treat Chromebooks as managed devices. The only exception is if your school deploys only a handful of Chromebooks, in which case managing them manually may make sense.

Comparing Chromebooks to Laptops and Tablets

In this section, we will examine how Chromebooks compare to other devices you might want to deploy in your school's classrooms: first, laptops, and then tablets, such as iPads and Android tablets. As of this writing, manufacturers have begun to release Chrome tablets, touchscreen-driven devices running Chrome OS; however, this section focuses on conventional Chromebooks, which include keyboards.

> **Note**   Unlike Android tablets, on which you can set up multiple user accounts and switch freely among them, the iPad is designed as a single-user device; only a single user account can be set up on an iPad. However, Apple provides a feature called Shared iPad that enables schools and other institutions to share iPads among students who log on using Managed Apple IDs. Essentially, when a student logs on to a shared iPad, iOS downloads the user's files across the network and stores them on the iPad so that the user can work with them.

Understanding the Advantages of Chromebooks over Other Laptops

The following list explains the main advantages of Chromebooks over other laptops:

- *Automatic updates*: Chromebooks can automatically download operating-system updates when they are available. Installing updates on Chromebooks tends to be much faster than installing updates on Windows.

- *Few viruses:* Chrome OS is largely immune to viruses, unlike conventional operating systems, such as Windows or MacOS.

- *Online storage*: A Chromebook stores all the user's files online instead of storing them locally, so the files are accessible from anywhere that has an Internet connection.

- *The user can switch Chromebooks easily*: Having the files stored online means that a user can switch from one Chromebook to another, needing to do no more than log on to another Chromebook to have his files available and ready for use on it.

- *Easy to reset*: Because each user's files are stored online, you can reset a Chromebook without having to make backups of its contents beforehand and without having to restore that content afterward. This makes resetting a useful maneuver for recovering from configuration problems. Chrome OS also offers the Powerwash, a kind of super-reset that returns the Chromebook to its original factory condition.

- *Cost*: Chromebooks tend to be less expensive than full-fledged laptops. But because the success of inexpensive Chromebooks spurred PC manufacturers to release lower-cost Windows laptops, the price difference between Chromebooks and low-end Windows laptops is not dramatic. Apple's MacBook laptops remain vastly more expensive than most Chromebooks but arguably do not compete directly with them.

- *Google Apps are included*: Chromebooks give you access to the Google Apps suite—online apps for creating documents, spreadsheets, presentations, and other widely used file types. You do not need to get a separate app suite, such as Microsoft Office. When used in schools, Chromebooks can use Google's G Suite for Education, which comprises the Google Apps suite and extra apps.

- *Android apps*: Some Chromebooks can run Android apps. This means that a vast number of apps are available, including many games—something that may appeal to students more than to teachers!

Understanding the Disadvantages of Chromebooks Compared to Other Laptops

The following list discusses the main disadvantages of Chromebooks compared to other laptops:

- *Some major apps are not available*: Chrome OS has a relatively small number of apps available, most of which are implemented via the Web. Apart from the Android apps that some Chromebooks can run, you cannot install apps for other operating systems. For example, Chromebooks cannot run the full versions of Microsoft Office apps, such as Word and Excel. (Android versions of Microsoft Office apps have substantially fewer features than the full versions.)

- *Chromebooks require a constant Internet connection*: Because Chromebooks store all their files online, they normally need a constant Internet connection to function properly. (Chromebooks do enable the user to perform some computing offline, but being constantly online gives better results.)

- *Increased Internet traffic*: Because Chromebooks need a constant Internet connection, they cause a lot of traffic. You may need to upgrade your school's Internet connection to avoid its getting swamped by the extra traffic.

Understanding the Advantages of Chromebooks Compared to Tablets

The following list explores the main advantages of Chromebooks compared to tablet computers:

- *Keyboards*: Each Chromebook model has a hardware keyboard, enabling the user to enter text at his full speed and edit existing text easily. By contrast, it is hard to touch-type on the onscreen keyboards that most tablets provide. While you can add a keyboard to a tablet, doing so involves extra expense. You must also usually use Bluetooth, which often means connection headaches and laggy input.

- *Better for creating text-based content*: Related to the previous point about keyboards, Chromebooks are usually stronger tools for creating text-based content than tablets are.

- *Easier to manage centrally than Android tablets*: Chromebooks are easier to manage than Android tablets. For iPads, however, Apple and third-party companies provide powerful management tools that have similar capabilities to Google's tools for managing Chromebooks.

- *Less expensive than iPads*: Most Chromebooks designed for school use are considerably less expensive than iPads, especially if you have to add accessories (such as external keyboards) to the iPads. Android tablets vary greatly in cost, so Chromebooks do not necessarily have a cost advantage over them.

Understanding the Disadvantages of Chromebooks Compared to Tablets

The following list explains the two main disadvantages of Chromebooks compared to tablet computers:

- *Less easy to carry*: Because they include keyboards and touchpads, Chromebooks tend to be larger and heavier than tablets that have the same screen size.

- *Harder to use as a handheld device*: Tablet computers are—obviously enough—designed for handheld use. Chromebooks are designed for use as laptops, either on a surface (such as a table or a desk) or on the user's legs or lap. Even though some Chromebook models have

13

touchscreens and are convertible, changing into tablet mode by folding the keyboard back under the screen, they remain harder to use as handheld devices than pure tablets.

Also, just as when compared to laptops, Chromebooks have the disadvantage of requiring a constant Internet connection and causing increased Internet traffic.

Analyzing Your School's Needs and Making a Plan

Once you have decided that you will deploy Chromebooks rather than another technology, you will need to work out the best way to deploy them. In this section, we will discuss the main questions you should consider to establish your school's needs and to plan the deployment. These questions include the following:

- What deployment model will you use? Will you issue Chromebooks to individual students? Will you get Chromebooks to equip, say, a classroom or classbound computer carts? Will you get Chromebooks for teachers as well as for students?

- How many Chromebooks will your school get?

- Which Chromebook models will your school get?

- If you equip the teachers with Chromebooks, how will they use them?

- Will you need to train the teachers to use the Chromebooks? If so, what kind of training will you run?

- How will your school's students use the Chromebooks?

- How will you manage the Chromebooks?

- How will the Chromebooks fit into your school's IT system and connect to its resources?

- Does your school have adequate network and Internet bandwidth to handle the increased traffic that the Chromebooks will bring?

The following subsections will explore these questions in more detail but not in quite the same order.

What Deployment Model Will You Use?

Usually, your first decision is which deployment model to use for the Chromebooks. Typically, this means choosing between a one-to-one deployment model and a model based on classes or classrooms:

- *One-to-one*: In the one-to-one deployment model, you issue a Chromebook to each student in a class or other group. The student keeps that Chromebook and can store local copies of files on it for use when no Internet connection is available—for example, downloading PDF files of papers to read. Normally, the student gets to take the Chromebook home at the end of the school day so she can use it for homework and other study. However, in some cases, the Chromebook is restricted to the school's premises, so the student checks out the Chromebook at the beginning of the school day and checks it back in at the end.

- *Class or classroom*: In the class deployment model or the classroom deployment model, you outfit a class or a classroom with enough Chromebooks for the largest number of students the class or classroom will contain. ("Class" here refers to the group of students, whereas "classroom" refers to the room.) The teacher issues a Chromebook to each student at the beginning of a lesson, and the student logs in to the Chromebook using his Google account, which gives him access to all of the files he has stored in that account online. At the end of the lesson, the student logs out of his Google account and returns the Chromebook to the teacher. In this deployment model, the Chromebooks may live in the classroom or in another secure location, such as a charging and storage cart that you can move from one classroom to another as needed.

Whether you decide to issue Chromebooks to students or to classes (or classrooms), you will likely want teachers to use Chromebooks as well, especially if they are using Google Classroom to run lessons. (Chapter 8 will cover Google Classroom.) For each teacher who needs a Chromebook, you can choose between issuing a Chromebook on a permanent or semi-permanent basis and having the teacher use a Chromebook that's assigned to the class or classroom in which she will be teaching. There are good arguments for and against each approach, but issuing Chromebooks to teachers enables them to do much more with the Chromebooks and generally delivers greater value.

Note   If you decide to issue Chromebooks to teachers, you may want to issue the teachers with models that are more powerful or have larger screens—or both—than the Chromebooks that the students use. The teachers may also not need ruggedized Chromebooks.

How Many Chromebooks Will Your School Need?

After deciding which deployment model to use, you next need to establish roughly how many Chromebooks your school will need. You should be able to determine the number easily enough based on the deployment model you have chosen:

- *One-to-one deployment*: Plan to get one Chromebook for each student involved, plus Chromebooks for teachers or assistants, plus a reserve of extra Chromebooks for when students break their Chromebooks, leave them at home, or incapacitate them.

- *Class or classroom deployment*: Plan to get one Chromebook each for the maximum number of students who will be in the class or classroom, plus a Chromebook for each teacher or assistant who will lead the class. Again, you will want a reserve of Chromebooks to handle contingencies such as Chromebooks getting damaged or misconfigured, or visiting students or teachers requiring extra Chromebooks.

GETTING AND MAINTAINING YOUR RESERVE OF CHROMEBOOKS

How many Chromebooks do you need as a reserve? There is no hard-and-fast answer to this question because it depends on your situation and on your students, but between 10 percent and 20 percent of your base number generally seems to work well. For example, for a class of 30 students, a reserve of 3 to 6 Chromebooks would normally be enough to cover any Chromebooks that students have forgotten to bring and any damaged Chromebooks. But, as you might imagine, more would be better.

If money is tight, you may find it hard to get the budget for an adequate reserve of Chromebooks in your initial deployment. You may find that having the Chromebooks do double duty as teacher-training Chromebooks or instructor Chromebooks gets you further than simply calling them reserves.

You should also include at least some new Chromebooks in your IT budget each year. Assuming you can buy some new Chromebooks, you can then downgrade some of the surviving older Chromebooks to reserve status. This way, you can gradually build up enough of a reserve to handle extra demand when it occurs.

Which Models of Chromebooks Will Your School Get?

When it comes to choosing Chromebooks, you will need to choose from a vast selection of different models. We will defer this question until Chapter 2, which will dig into the factors you will likely find most important when choosing Chromebooks.

How Will Your School's Teachers Use the Chromebooks?

You will also need to consider how the teachers will use the Chromebooks. While there are many different ways of using a Chromebook for teaching, the following tend to be the main uses:

- *Use Google Classroom to lead lessons*: Google Classroom is designed to enable a teacher to organize and manage a class.

- *Demonstrating techniques*: The teacher can quickly demonstrate skills and gestures, app usage, and so on using her Chromebook to enable a student to perform these moves on his Chromebook.

- *Displaying information on a TV or monitor*: The teacher can share content from her Chromebook on a TV or monitor, enabling all the students to see the content.

- *Communicating with students*: The teacher can communicate with students via various means, ranging from communication within the Google Classroom app to standard instant messaging and email.

- *Collecting and grading papers and homework*: The teacher can collect work from students easily, grade it, and return it.

How Will Your School's Students Use the Chromebooks?

Students can use Chromebooks to perform a wide range of tasks both at school and (in a one-to-one deployment) outside it. The following list gives examples of typical tasks that students may perform using Chromebooks:

- *Reading textbooks*: Many textbooks are available in electronic formats, reducing the load that students need to carry to and from school.

- *Researching topics online*: Students can access a vast array of information resources on the Internet, depending on how much freedom your school gives them.

- *Viewing and editing photos*: Chromebook can access the Google Photos site for viewing photos and making minor edits to them. For more extensive editing of photos, more powerful apps are available.

- *Watching videos*: Chromebooks make it easy to watch videos on YouTube and other online sites.

- *Taking notes*: Chromebooks are great for taking notes and storing them online.

- *Creating and editing documents, spreadsheets, and presentations*: Each Chromebook has access to the Google Apps suite, so students can use Google Docs to create and edit documents, Google Sheets to build spreadsheets, and Google Slides to develop presentations.

- *Email and communication*: Chromebooks integrate seamlessly with Gmail for email. For chat, you can use apps such as Google Hangouts and Skype. For collaboration, you can use apps such as Slack.

- *Completing and submitting papers and homework*: Students can use Chromebooks to complete papers and homework and submit them to teachers for grading.

- *Social networking*: Social networking is notorious as a time-sink, but it can be useful for organizing and coordinating school-related events.

Once you have identified the tasks the teachers and students will perform on the Chromebooks, you should be in a good position to identify the apps they will need to perform those tasks.

Which Apps Will You Need to Get?

Chrome OS is designed to perform most tasks on the Web through the Chrome web browser rather than by using apps. For example, to create a word-processing document, you use Chrome to access the Google Docs website and create the document there rather than launching a local app such as Microsoft Word.

As a result, a typical Chromebook comes with only a few apps in the conventional sense. Many of the icons that appear on the shelf (the strip across the bottom of the desktop) and on the Launcher screen (shown in Figure 1-3) are simply shortcuts to the corresponding websites rather than apps themselves. For example, clicking the Gmail icon will open a Chrome tab to your email on the Gmail website (`mail.google.com`), and clicking the Drive icon will open a Chrome tab to the Google Drive website (`drive.google.com`). Other icons *are* for actual apps—for example, clicking the Camera icon will launch the Camera app, which runs locally and enables you to capture photos and videos using the Chromebook's built-in webcam.

Figure 1-3. *Many of the "apps" on the Launcher screen are website shortcuts rather than local apps*

Table 1-1 briefly summarizes the icons that typically appear in the Launcher on a Chromebook, presenting the icons in alphabetical order, saying which is an app and which is a shortcut, and giving the main uses of the app or the corresponding website.

Table 1-1. *Icons That Normally Appear in the Chrome OS Launcher*

Icon Name	Link or App	Uses
Gmail	Link	Communicating via email
Google Drive	Link	Storing files online
Web Store	Link	Browsing and installing apps
Chrome	App	Browsing the Web and running browser-based apps
Play Store	Link	Browsing and buying apps, music, videos, books, and more
Text	App	Creating text notes
YouTube	Link	Watching videos on YouTube site
Google Calendar	Link	Calendaring and scheduling
Google Maps	Link	Exploring places via map and getting directions
Docs	Link	Creating word-processing documents
Play Movies	Link	Watching movies and TV shows
Sheets	Link	Creating spreadsheet documents
Slides	Link	Creating presentations
Play Music	Link	Browsing, listening to, and buying music
Google Photos	Link	Viewing and editing photos
Play Games	Link	Browsing, buying, and playing games
Play Books	Link	Browsing, buying, and reading books
Files	App	Working with files stored on the Chromebook and in your Google account

(continued)

Table 1-1. (*continued*)

Icon Name	Link or App	Uses
Calculator	App	Performing calculations. At first, the window shows a simple interface. Maximize the window to reveal controls for mathematical and scientific calculations.
Camera	App	Taking photos and videos with the Chromebook's webcam
Google Keep	App	Taking written notes and voice notes

You can install other apps from the Chrome Web Store as needed. So, after making your list of tasks that users will perform with the Chromebooks, identify the tasks the built-in apps do not cover, and explore the Chrome Web Store to find apps that can handle those tasks.

Note   If the Chromebook you choose is one of the models capable of running Android apps, you can install Android apps from the Google Play Store. As of December 2017, more than 3.5 million apps were available in the Google Play Store, and the number continues to rise, so identifying the most suitable apps can be a daunting task.

UNDERSTANDING CHROME DESKTOP APPS AND PROGRESSIVE WEB APPS

In addition to implementing Chrome apps in Chrome OS, Google also implemented desktop versions of Chrome apps—apps you could run in the Chrome browser on Windows, MacOS, and Linux. These desktop Chrome apps worked fine but were used by only around one percent of Chrome desktop users, so Google ended support for them in December 2017.

As of this writing (Spring 2018), Google is moving to a new type of browser-based apps. These are called Progressive Web Apps (PWAs) and add some app features to websites that support them. For example, a PWA can run in a full-screen mode rather than being limited to the browser window, can install components (when the user clicks the appropriate button), can send push notifications, and can store data for offline use.

Unlike Chrome apps, PWAs are not limited to the Chrome browser. PWAs currently work in Firefox and Opera on standard Android, and on the Samsung browser (which is sometimes called "Internet" and sometimes called "Browser") on Samsung Android phones. Microsoft has announced that it will add PWAs to Windows 10, and Apple will support PWAs in Safari on MacOS.

Because Google is discontinuing desktop Chrome apps and transitioning to PWAs, some commentators suspect that Chrome apps on Chrome OS may eventually follow the same path—so you may eventually need to run PWAs rather than Chrome apps on your school's Chromebooks. As of this writing, however, Google has not announced such a move.

How Will You Manage Your School's Chromebooks?

If your school has a single-digit number of Chromebooks, you might want to consider managing them manually—individually setting up each Chromebook and manually applying the settings it needs.

If your school has ten or more Chromebooks, you will almost certainly want to manage them centrally. The most straightforward way of doing so is to use the Chrome Management tools in the Google Admin console. You may also want to consider third-party management tools that can manage Chrome OS, especially if your school already uses such a tool for other devices and operating systems.

Planning to Train Yourself and Your Colleagues

While evaluating the Chromebook for use in your school, you will likely develop your own Chromebook skills to the point where you need only minimal training, or only self-directed training, to use a Chromebook as a teaching tool yourself. But given how important it is for teachers to be not only proficient but also confident with the hardware they use in class, you should plan full training on Chromebook use for all your colleagues who will use Chromebooks for teaching. Some staff, especially those who have already used Chromebooks, will likely get up to speed with only short sessions of formal training, but others may need multiple sessions of individual training to develop the skill and confidence required.

Note   Chapter 3, "Essential Chromebook Skills for Administrators and Teachers," will provide in-depth coverage of the Chromebook skills you and your colleagues will need to know. Chapter 8 will cover running a class with the Google Classroom app.

To make your training as effective as possible, get feedback from the teachers you train, both at the end of each training session and after they have been teaching with Chromebooks for a few weeks or months. If you will be training many teachers, you will likely benefit from creating a feedback questionnaire and logging the responses you get. If you know you will be training only a few teachers, less formal feedback may be all you need to identify any areas of the training that need strengthening; other topics from which teachers will benefit; and any existing information that is confusing, incomplete, or unnecessary.

Tip   Aim to develop an ongoing process of review and improvement for your Chromebook deployment, training, and teaching. You will need to involve teachers, support staff, students, and in some cases students' parents in the process.

Checking Your School's Wireless Network Infrastructure and Bandwidth

Next, you need to make sure that your school's network infrastructure will be able to handle the additional load that the Chromebooks will impose on it. You also need to make sure that the network and the Internet connection have enough bandwidth for the traffic the Chromebooks will cause.

SHOULD YOU BOOST EXISTING NETWORK CAPACITY OR ADD A SEPARATE NETWORK FOR CHROMEBOOKS?

If you find that your school's Wi-Fi network will not be adequate to handle the extra traffic from the Chromebooks you are planning to add, you may need to decide between boosting the capacity of the existing network and adding a separate network to handle only the Chromebooks.

Which approach makes more sense for you will depend on the school's existing network and the amount of capacity you need to add to bring the network up to scratch. But if you find yourself evaluating this issue, don't dismiss out of hand the possibility of adding a separate Wi-Fi network for the Chromebooks. Rather, look into any benefits that a separate, Chromebook-only network can offer you, such as being able to give the Chromebooks different access rules to school resources and the Internet. If your existing network's management tools can identify the Chromebooks and implement filtering for them, that would be an argument in favor of beefing up the existing network rather than adding a network.

Determining Whether Your School's Wireless Network Infrastructure Is Adequate

You will need to determine whether your school's wireless network infrastructure is adequate to handle the additional load that the Chromebooks will generate. You will need to check four main things: the signal strength, coverage and dead spots, the network bandwidth, and the capacity for devices to connect. The following subsections will provide more detail on these topics.

Verifying the Signal Strength

Check that there is a strong Wi-Fi signal everywhere that students and teachers will use the Chromebooks in the school. For example, you may need to check the following areas:

- *Classrooms*: Make sure that each classroom has a strong Wi-Fi signal.

- *Other teaching areas*: Verify the signal strength in other teaching areas, such as labs, in which students and teachers will be using Chromebooks.

- *Teacher office and lounge*: Make sure that teachers will have an adequate Wi-Fi signal in the places where they prepare their lessons.

- *Common areas*: For a one-to-one deployment, check the signal in other areas where students will use their Chromebooks. For example, the student lounge and cafeteria will likely need good connectivity.

Like most wireless devices, Chromebooks *can* transfer data over weak connections, but data rates tend to drop, sapping performance. You will get better results if the signal is strong, especially when many Chromebooks are connecting to the same wireless access point. You may have to add wireless access points, repeaters, or antennae to boost the signal.

Tip   If your school's budget permits, *overspecify* the wireless network—make the network more powerful than you currently need—so that you can expand your deployment of Chromebooks and other devices easily in the future. Spending money on extra wireless access points and other infrastructure upfront will generally save you money in the long term by reducing performance problems that you need to troubleshoot.

Chromebooks are built to use Wi-Fi connections for mobility, but you may sometimes need to connect a Chromebook to a wired network via an Ethernet cable. You can do so by using a USB-to-Ethernet adapter. Various models are widely available, most costing between $15 and $25. Make sure the model you select is fully compatible with Chrome OS.

Checking for and Eliminating Wireless Dead Spots

While checking for signal strength, make sure that there are no dead spots—places where there is no wireless signal at all. Murphy's Law guarantees that if there any dead spots, students (or teachers) will find they need to use the Chromebooks there. You may need to add wireless access points to eliminate dead spots.

Tip   Add to your school's intranet site a page where students can report low signal or dead spots to the network administrators.

Checking the Network Bandwidth

Use a traffic analyzer to measure network bandwidth and see if you need to increase it to handle the number of Chromebooks you are expecting the school to use. To increase bandwidth, you may need to add access points or upgrade switches and cabling.

Checking the Capacity for Devices to Connect

Make sure that your wireless access points have enough capacity for all the Chromebooks and other devices that may connect at once. You may need to add wireless access points in order to get enough Chromebooks (and other devices) connected to the network at the speeds you require.

Caution   Take the advertised capacity of enterprise-grade wireless access points with a pinch of salt. In real-world use, you are likely to find that an access point with an advertised capacity of 100+ clients can handle only 50 or so clients effectively. Similarly, an access point that claims to be able to handle 200 or more clients may not perform well with more than, say, 75 active clients. Test the performance of your access points both when you install them and when your Chromebook deployment is up and running.

Determining Whether Your School's Internet Bandwidth Is Adequate

You will also need to determine whether your school's Internet bandwidth is adequate for the increased traffic that the Chromebooks will produce. As you'd expect, whether the bandwidth is adequate will depend partly on the speed of the Internet connection and how much of the bandwidth the school is using already—if the connection is already maxed out, you can be sure that adding the Chromebooks to the demand will make matters worse.

The effect of the Chromebooks will also depend on how the students and teachers are using them and what measures you can take to mitigate the amount of traffic the Chromebooks generate. For example, students may need to stream videos from YouTube to assist with their schoolwork. If each student in a class will need to watch the same video, having a caching server can greatly reduce the amount of Internet bandwidth needed. But if each student will need to watch their own choice of video, a caching server won't be able to help much because each video will need to be streamed across the Internet connection.

The nearby sidebar suggests some measures you can take to reduce the Internet bandwidth the Chromebooks require.

WAYS TO REDUCE THE INTERNET BANDWIDTH THE CHROMEBOOKS REQUIRE

Depending on your network, its configuration, and how your school will use its Chromebooks, you may be able to take some of the following measures to reduce the amount of Internet bandwidth the Chromebooks consume:

- *Spread the Chromebook lessons around the timetable*: If the timetable permits, schedule the Chromebook lessons likely to cause heavy Internet traffic so that they occur at different times rather than overlapping. This move works better in a class or classroom deployment than a one-to-one deployment.

- *Keep files on your intranet rather than on the Internet*: Where possible, have students and teachers store files on the school's intranet rather than on the Internet so that the files can be downloaded and shared quickly without burdening the Internet connection.

- *Restrict access to websites*: Chrome OS includes restrictions that enable you to limit the websites an Chromebook can access. You can choose between permitting only specific sites, blocking specific sites, and blocking sites that meet certain criteria (such as sites that identify themselves as having adult content). See Chapter 3 for details.

- *Use a caching server*: If multiple students will need to access the same content on the Internet, a caching server on your network can greatly reduce the amount of bandwidth required. Once one client has requested the content and the server has downloaded the content and saved it to its cache, the server can provide the content to other clients from the cache rather than having to download it again.

- *Control updates centrally*: Assuming you manage the Chromebooks centrally, you can schedule Chrome OS updates to occur at night, when your school's network is (or should be) less busy.

Summary

In this chapter, you have started planning your deployment of Chromebooks in the classroom. You know what the advantages and disadvantages of Chromebooks are, and you have examined how Chromebooks compare to laptops and tablets. You have chosen the deployment model for the Chromebooks, decided how to manage them, and determined whether your school's network and Internet connection have enough bandwidth to handle the additional traffic that the Chromebooks will generate.

In the next chapter, we will consider how to choose suitable Chromebooks and accessories for your school and its students.

CHAPTER 2

Choosing Chromebooks and Accessories

In this chapter, we will discuss the various types of Chromebooks available and consider how you can choose suitable Chromebooks for your school's planned deployment. You will also learn about accessories you may find helpful for school settings, such as hardcase shells to protect the Chromebooks and carts in which to store and charge them.

Choosing Chromebooks

As you will know if you have browsed Chromebooks online, a wide variety of Chromebooks is available from various manufacturers. This is good news in that it means there are likely to be Chromebook models that meet the needs of your school and its students and teachers—but it is bad news in that it means you will likely need to do a lot of research to identify those models.

As usual when you are choosing a computer, you need to consider many different features when choosing Chromebooks—especially if you will be ordering many units. This section will discuss the main features you should consider when evaluating Chromebooks.

© Guy Hart-Davis 2018
G. Hart-Davis, *Deploying Chromebooks in the Classroom*,
https://doi.org/10.1007/978-1-4842-3766-3_2

Which Hardware Features Do Chromebooks Have?

All Chromebooks should have the following standard features:

- *Processor*: Many Chromebooks use Intel processors, such as the i3 processor family or the Celeron family. Other Chromebooks use ARM processors, the kind of processors used in most smartphones and tablets.

- *Storage*: Most Chromebooks have solid-state devices (SSDs) for storage rather than a hard drive with rotating platters. Because Chrome OS is designed to store most data online, Chromebook models typically have much less local storage than regular laptops.

- *Screen*: Each Chromebook has a built-in screen on which to display output. Most Chromebooks can also connect to an external monitor, using it either instead of the built-in screen or to extend the display.

- *Keyboard*: Each Chromebook has a built-in keyboard.

- *Touchpad*: Each Chromebook has a built-in trackpad for navigating the user interface and giving commands. You can connect a mouse or another external pointing device via USB or Bluetooth if necessary.

- *Webcam*: Each Chromebook has a built-in webcam for video calling and self-portraits.

- *Battery and power supply*: Each Chromebook has a built-in battery to provide power, plus an external power supply to provide power from a socket and to charge the battery.

Some Chromebooks have extra features, such as the following:

- *Touchscreen*: The Chromebook's screen is a touchscreen that the user can manipulate using either a finger or a stylus.

- *Tablet mode*: The Chromebook folds so that the screen is on top and the keyboard is underneath, enabling the user to use the device like a tablet computer. Tablet mode normally accompanies a touchscreen.

- *Stylus support*: Some touchscreen Chromebooks support the use of a stylus, which enables the user to interact more precisely with the touchscreen. Styluses can be great for anything from handwriting practice to art, mathematics, and science. Some touchscreen Chromebook models include a stylus, but usually you will need to buy the stylus separately.

You will need to decide how much weight to give to each of these factors. The following sections will discuss the decisions that must be made, starting with the screen size, because this is likely to be the first decision for many people when choosing Chromebooks.

What Screen Size and Resolution Should You Get?

Chromebook screen sizes generally range from 10 inches to 15 inches. As you would likely expect, the sizes of the Chromebooks vary accordingly to accommodate the screens: a Chromebook with a 10-inch screen will likely be physically much smaller than a Chromebook with a 15-inch screen.

Caution   Some Chromebooks with 10-inch screens have keyboards that are smaller than full size. Such smaller keyboards can be good for young children but tend to be too small for comfortable use by older children and adults.

By contrast, screen resolutions for Chromebooks vary widely and are not necessarily closely related to screen size. You can get Chromebook models with small, high-resolution screens (for example, Samsung's 2-in-1 Convertible Chromebook Plus models have 2400x1600-pixel resolution on a 12.3-inch screen) as well as Chromebook models with small, low-resolution screens. While Chromebooks with large screens might seem more likely candidates for high-resolution screens, some models have screens with modest resolutions, such as 1366x768 pixels, usually to keep costs down.

When choosing a screen size for your school's Chromebooks, you will need to strike a balance between several competing factors, such as the following:

- *Getting screens that are large enough*: Will students and teachers need to look at multiple windows at once, or will they normally work in a single window? For multiple windows, larger screens and higher resolutions (which we will consider later in this section) are helpful.

- *Getting screens that have suitable resolution*: High-resolution screens can be great for those with perfect eyesight, especially as a higher resolution enables the screen to display more information at once. But to ensure all your school's students and teachers can comfortably view the Chromebooks, you will normally want to get screens with moderate resolution.

Note   As well as making sure the resolution is not too high for comfortable viewing, check that the screens of the Chromebook models you are evaluating are bright enough to be easy to see. Some Chromebook screens are dim and disappointing, especially at the budget end of the market.

- *Getting Chromebooks that will withstand student handling*: Generally speaking, the larger the screen on a tablet or portable computer, the more likely it is to get damaged. So, while Chromebooks with 14-inch or 15-inch screens might be great for the school's productivity, you may need to stick with a smaller screen size to make sure the Chromebooks are robust enough for survival.

Do Your Students or Teachers Need Touchscreens and Tablet Mode?

Some Chromebook models have touchscreens, enabling students to interact with the Chrome OS interface by tapping objects on the screen, much like using an iPad or a tablet. Most touchscreen models have a 360-degree hinge that enables the screen to fold back flat against the bottom of the Chromebook, turning it into a tablet-like device with the keyboard on the bottom. Switching to tablet mode turns off keyboard input so that you don't inadvertently type characters while holding the Chromebook; even so, pressing the keys while holding the Chromebook tends to feel odd.

Note . Touchscreen Chromebooks are usually not only more expensive than non-touchscreen models but also easier to damage.

The 360-degree hinge also enables you to fold the Chromebook into a tent shape so you can use it as a freestanding touchscreen device, as shown in Figure 2-1.

Figure 2-1. *Most touchscreen Chromebooks have a 360-degree hinge that enables you to prop the device up using the keyboard, as shown here, or to fold the Chromebook flat with the keyboard underneath it*

Note   If you get touchscreen Chromebooks, you may also want to get pens or styluses to use with them. See the section "Deciding Whether to Get Styluses for Touchscreen Chromebooks?" later in this chapter for suggestions on how to make this decision.

What Processors Should You Get?

As of this writing, Chromebooks are available with a wide range of processors—and the range is only getting wider. This plethora of options, and the rate at which Intel and other processor manufacturers are releasing new processors, makes it impossible to give you a definitive answer to the question of which processors you should get in your Chromebooks. Instead, this section will explain the processor types that Chromebooks typically use, outlining both their strong points and weak points.

Note   Given how many different processor types are available, you should aim to test each Chromebook model under consideration in order to check its performance and see how satisfactory the screen, keyboard, and touchpad are in use. If testing each Chromebook model is not possible, look online for up-to-date reviews and performance benchmarks to help you decide.

The following list explains the processor types that are most widely used in Chromebooks:

- *Intel Celeron*: Celeron is Intel's low-cost and relatively low-power chip. It provides adequate if unexciting performance.

- *Intel Pentium*: Pentium is one of Intel's older lines of processors, but some Chromebooks still use Pentium processors. Pentiums are inexpensive but fairly slow compared to more modern processors.

- *Intel Core i3*: Core i3 is Intel's low-end line of full-power dual-core processors. Generally speaking, Core i3 processors are a good choice for Chromebooks because they deliver enough power to run Chrome OS quickly, are fully compatible with Chrome OS, and are fairly affordable.

- *Intel Core i5*: Core i5 is Intel's mid-range line of full-power processors. Core i5 processors are either dual-core with hyper-threading or quad-core without hyper-threading. Core i5 processors are more expensive than similar-vintage Core i3 processors, so manufacturers tend to equip only high-end Chromebooks with Core i5 processors.

- *Intel Core i7*: Core i7 is Intel's line of high-end processors. Core i7 processors are either dual-core with hyperthreading or quad-core with hyperthreading. Core i7 processors deliver great performance, but because they are substantially more expensive than similar-vintage Core i5 processors, manufacturers tend to put them in only premium Chromebooks.

- *Intel Core M*: Core M is Intel's family of power-efficient mobile processors. The Core M lines deliver lower performance than the corresponding Core I lines—the Core m3 delivers lower performance than the Core i3, the Core m5 delivers lower performance than the Core i5, and so on—but give longer battery life.

- ARM: Various manufacturers, including Samsung and MediaTek, make processors using the ARM (Advanced RISC Machines) architecture. (In turn, RISC is the acronym for Reduced Instruction Set Computing.) ARM processors have been widely used in smartphones and tablets for many years, but now manufacturers are using them in some Windows laptops and in Chromebooks as well. ARM processors are thrifty on power, deliver good performance, and should be good at running Android apps.

When deciding which processors your school's Chromebooks should have, you will probably want to consider the following four factors:

- *Processing power needed*: Chrome OS is lightweight compared to full operating systems such as Windows and MacOS, so Chromebooks do not need as much computing power to run well. That said, it is a mistake to get underpowered Chromebooks, because laggy performance will color students'—and teachers'— experience of the lessons that use the computers. Be prepared to go to bat for processors that seem over specified today in order to get several years of productive use from the Chromebooks.

Caution   As when evaluating any computer, treat a Chromebook's initial performance as the best performance it is likely to deliver. Even though Chrome OS avoids many of the factors that cause computers running operating systems such as Windows and MacOS to run more slowly over time, Chromebook performance is likely to degrade as Chrome OS becomes more complex and adds more capabilities.

- *Cost*: The cost of the processor contributes substantially to the cost of the Chromebook, so inexpensive Chromebooks contain less-expensive processors. As of this writing, Intel Celeron processors and Intel Core i3 processors represent the best value for moderately-specified Chromebooks. Intel Core i5 processors and Core i7 processors tend to appear only in high-end Chromebooks, and most likely your school's students and teachers will not need this much processing power.

- *Power draw*: The more power the processor draws, the shorter the battery life will be, and the more heat the Chromebook will need to dissipate.

- *Compatibility*: Verify that the processor type you are evaluating is fully compatible with all Chrome OS features, such as the capability to run Android apps.

How Much RAM Do Your Chromebooks Need?

Many Chromebook models come with 2 GB of RAM, but this is more because it helps the manufacturers to keep prices competitive than because 2 GB is enough to run Chrome OS well. If the Chromebook is performing undemanding tasks, such as web browsing and email, 2 GB can give adequate performance but is not enough for normal or heavy usage.

For normal usage, look for Chromebooks with 4 GB of RAM. The improvement in performance is usually well worth the modest extra cost.

For power users, get Chromebooks with 8 GB of RAM. Consider getting models with 16 GB of RAM if they are affordable. However, relatively few Chromebook models are available with 16 GB.

MAX OUT THE RAM AT THE TIME OF PURCHASE

Some Chromebook models provide easy access to the RAM slots, enabling you to increase the amount of RAM. It is worth checking whether the models you are considering have accessible RAM. But even if they do, it is usually better to max out the RAM when buying than to pay extra to add memory later, especially as adding memory often involves removing the currently installed memory.

How Much Storage Do the Chromebooks Need?

Most Chromebook models come with 16 GB to 64 GB of storage. These amounts are substantially less than those on most laptops because Chrome OS is designed to store most of its data online rather than locally. But even so, each user account will need some storage space for cached data and for downloaded documents. The more user accounts you expect to set up on a Chromebook, the more storage space you should allow.

16 GB of storage works well enough for a consumer Chromebook that is used lightly by a single user or a handful of users, but it is typically not enough for the heavier use that a Chromebook is likely to see in a school. Getting Chromebooks with 32 GB of storage helps ensure that users do not run out of space and that you do not have to regularly clear space on the devices.

Note   Storage on Chromebooks is typically fixed rather than upgradable. It is worth checking whether you can increase the storage on the Chromebook models you are evaluating. However, even if you choose Chromebook models with upgradable storage, you will normally do better to buy the Chromebooks with the appropriate amount of storage than to upgrade the storage later.

How Much Battery Runtime Will the Chromebooks Need?

Most Chromebooks offer better battery runtime than standard laptops because Chromebooks typically use less powerful processors and have less power-hungry hardware. Whereas many laptops deliver three to five hours of runtime on the battery, most Chromebooks get around nine hours.

Unless your Chromebooks will need substantially longer than this, you should be able to treat battery runtime as a less important factor when evaluating Chromebook models. For example, if the Chromebooks will live in the classrooms and either be used when connected to power or be plugged in to power between lessons, battery runtime may not be a concern.

Note   Lengthy battery runtime will be more important if your school is going to issue Chromebooks to students as personal devices. In this case, there may be substantial benefit to choosing Chromebook models that can last the entire school day—and perhaps for students' journeys to and from school—without needing to be connected to power.

CHECKING THE EASE OF REPLACING THE BATTERY

When evaluating Chromebook models, see how difficult it is to replace the battery. Most Chromebook models have batteries that are built in rather than batteries that are accessible from the outside of the device, so replacing the battery typically involves opening the Chromebook's case. If you plan to replace the batteries yourself as they wear out, determine whether they are easily accessible once you have opened the Chromebook, and also verify that the battery's power supply involves a clip-together connector rather than being soldered in place.

What Resolution Should the Webcams Be?

Many Chromebooks have webcams with the 720p HD designation. 720p uses 1280x720-pixel resolution, which makes for 921,600-pixel frames. 720p HD is high-enough quality for communicating via video chat and shooting self-portraits to use as account photos, so it is normally a good choice.

Some Chromebooks have webcams with Full HD resolution— 1920x1080-pixel resolution, which gives 2,073,600-pixel frames. This higher resolution may be a boon as long as you do not have to pay substantially more for it.

Caution   If your students will use video calling extensively, evaluate the impact that Full HD or other high-resolution webcams will have on the school's network and Internet connection. Chromebook models with 720p webcams may be a better choice so as to avoid swamping the network and Internet connection.

Which Ports Will the Chromebooks Need?

When evaluating Chromebook models, you should make a list of the ports users will need the Chromebooks to have, such as USB ports for connectivity and video-output ports for connecting a monitor. Once you have created the list, make sure that the Chromebook models you are considering have all the ports required.

Common ports on Chromebooks include the following:

- *HDMI or micro HDMI*: The HDMI or micro HDMI port enables you to connect an external monitor to the Chromebook. Either port works fine; you just need the right kind of cable, such as a micro HDMI–to–HDMI cable. Because the micro HDMI port is so compact, it is widely used on smaller Chromebook models.

- *USB*: USB ports enable you to connect a wide range of devices to the Chromebook, such as an external keyboard or pointing device, a USB flash drive, or USB speakers. (Technically, these are USB-A ports—the kind with the flat rectangular connector.) When evaluating Chromebook models, make sure that the USB ports are USB 2.0 at a minimum, and preferably USB 3.0.

- *USB-C*: Some Chromebooks have USB-C ports, which combine charging and connectivity. USB-C ports enable manufacturers to reduce the total number of ports on a device, which can help make devices smaller and keep down costs (if not prices).

Caution   USB-C ports are a good addition to a Chromebook, but make sure that the Chromebook models you get have USB-A ports as well. Otherwise, users may need to carry a dongle (for example, from a USB-C port to a USB-C port and USB-A ports) to be able to connect devices to the Chromebook.

- *Micro SD card*: A micro SD card slot lets you add files from, or transfer files to, a micro SD card. For example, you might use a micro SD card to transfer files from a digital camera to the Chromebook and to your Google account.

- *Headphone port*: The headphone port enables you to listen to audio via either analog speakers or headphones.

- *Microphone port*: The microphone port enables you to connect an external microphone for recording audio.

Note   Some Chromebook models have a headphone/microphone combination port rather than a headphone port and a microphone port.

CHECKING THAT THE CHROMEBOOKS HAVE ADEQUATE WI-FI CAPABILITIES

All Chromebooks have built-in Wi-Fi for connectivity, so in theory any Chromebook should be able to connect to your school's Wi-Fi network without problems. But, in practice, some Chromebook models have much better Wi-Fi capabilities than others.

When evaluating Chromebooks, go online and look up professional reviews and user reviews of the models you are considering. Check to see if users consistently report problems establishing and maintaining Wi-Fi connections.

Do the Chromebooks Need to Be Able to Run Android Apps?

One of Google's recent additions to Chrome OS is the capability to run apps built for Android phones and tablets. This capability vastly expands the number of apps available for Chrome OS—but, as of this writing, only some Chromebooks are fully compatible with Android apps.

If your school's Chromebooks will need to run Android apps, verify that the Chromebook models you are evaluating are capable of this. You should be able to find this information listed for each Chromebook model, but you may find it quicker to consult a list such as the one at Android Central (`https://www.androidcentral.com/these-are-chromebooks-can-run-android-apps`).

Should You Get Ruggedized Models?

Various manufacturers make ruggedized models of Chromebooks—models armored up with rubber bumpers, extra padding, and (where possible) tougher components. Ruggedized Chromebooks can be a good fit for schools (or other physically challenging environments), especially if students will have the Chromebooks as personal devices (taking them home) or carry them from class to class during the school day.

Tip   If you are considering ruggedized Chromebooks, look for models that have "modular construction"—ones that are built so that the components are easier to replace when they break.

Ruggedized models have two main potential disadvantages compared with regular Chromebooks:

- *High cost*: Ruggedized models tend to be more expensive than similarly-specified regular Chromebooks.

- *Small screen size*: Ruggedized models normally have relatively small screens—11.6-inch screens are typical—because small screens are easier to protect than larger screens. However, if ruggedized Chromebooks suit your students, this limitation may be easy to ignore.

Figure 2-2 shows the Asus Chromebook Flip C213, a ruggedized model that features modular construction inside and rubber bumpers around the edges. You can see that the screen is protected by a thick bezel rather than running close to the edges of the device.

Figure 2-2. *The Asus Chromebook Flip C213 is a ruggedized Chromebook with rubber bumpers around the body and a thick bezel to protect the screen*

If you find the selection of ruggedized Chromebooks is too limited, look next at Chromebook models designed to meet Google's Chromebook for Work standard. These Chromebook models are also tougher than regular Chromebooks, but some of them come with larger screens; for example, the Acer Chromebook for Work line includes models with 14-inch screens.

Note   Instead of getting ruggedized Chromebooks, you may want to add hard shells to regular Chromebooks. See the section "Protecting a Chromebook with a Shell" later in this chapter for a discussion of the pros and cons of shells.

Do You Need Kensington Security Slots?

If you will need to be able to secure the Chromebooks physically with cables, make sure each model you're considering includes a Kensington Security Slot. The Kensington Security Slot, sometimes referred to as a K-Slot or a Kensington lock slot, is a reinforced hole in the device's frame to which you can connect a locking cable.

As of this writing, only some Chromebook models include a Kensington Security Slot; even some high-end models, such as Google's Pixelbook, lack this means of physically securing the device. You can find other security devices online, such as security docks, but most work for only some devices and are not portable enough for regular use.

Evaluating Chromebooks for Ease and Cost of Repair

When evaluating Chromebooks, you should factor in the ease and cost of repairs for the models you are considering buying. Sooner or later (likely sooner), some of the Chromebooks will suffer damage and will need repair. By planning from the start how you will deal with damaged Chromebooks, and preferably including funds for some spare parts in your budget, you can keep your Chromebook fleet operational with minimal downtime.

Tip   To learn how to repair a particular Chromebook model, search for instructions online. You can find teardown videos and repair videos for most Chromebook models, so search by the specific model to get the most relevant information. Sites such as iFixit (`www.ifixit.com`) include a Difficulty rating for each repair procedure, which helps you get an overview of how hard a particular Chromebook model is to repair.

You will likely find that students can break even the most improbable parts of Chromebooks, but the following components tend to suffer the most breakages:

- *Screen*: Usually the first victim of a device-open drop, the screen may also die from over-eager use of a pointing finger on a non-touchscreen Chromebook.

- *Keyboard and touchpad*: The keyboard and touchpad are vulnerable to spills as well as to blunt-force trauma.

- *Body*: The body may suffer damage if the Chromebook is dropped—whether open or closed—or if it is run into furniture, walls, doors, or other solid objects.

- *Ports*: The ports on a Chromebook can easily get damaged. For example, USB-A ports frequently die from having connectors mashed into them the wrong way or from correctly-connected devices being wrenched free.

Note   Components of typical Chromebooks are usually pretty affordable, so it is often best to buy new replacement parts and turn to used parts only when new ones are no longer available. If any of your school's Chromebooks gets damaged beyond repair, keep it as an organ donor for its siblings.

Standardizing on One Model or a Handful of Models

In a one-on-one deployment in which each student gets to choose a Chromebook for herself, you will likely find yourself needing to work with—and perhaps troubleshoot and support—a wide variety of Chromebook models. While having free choice is likely to make the students happy and vest them more deeply in their Chromebooks, it may well give you headaches.

But if you are planning a class-based or classroom-based deployment, you have the option of standardizing on a single Chromebook model or on a handful of models. For example, you might choose a ruggedized, small-screen Chromebook model for younger students; select a larger-screen model with a protective shell for older students doing more complex work in a lower-impact setting; and pick a powerful, high-resolution Chromebook for staff members who will need extra power and screen real estate for productivity.

Choosing Accessories for Chromebooks

In this section, we will quickly examine three types of accessories you may want to get to supplement your school's Chromebooks: styluses for touchscreen Chromebooks, hard shells to protect non-ruggedized Chromebooks from damage, and storage carts and cabinets for Chromebooks kept in the school.

Deciding Whether to Get Styluses for Touchscreen Chromebooks

If you do decide to get some Chromebooks that have touchscreens, consider also whether the students and teachers who use those Chromebooks would benefit from styluses. A stylus gives more precise interaction with the touchscreen, enabling the user to draw, handwrite, annotate, and so on. If users will perform such activities, the purchase may be a no-brainer. On the other hand, a stylus can be not only a distraction for a user not prepared to use it, but also easy to lose unless the Chromebook has a stylus holster or clip.

Protecting a Chromebook with a Shell

If you decide not to get ruggedized Chromebook models, you may want to get hard shells to armor up conventional Chromebook models. A hard shell is typically made of plastic or polycarbonate, usually comes in two pieces that clip onto the top and bottom of the Chromebook, and provides a layer of protection to the Chromebook's body.

Figure 2-3 shows a shell fitted to the bottom of a Chromebook. As you can see, the shell not only has air holes for ventilation and little rubber feet for grip, but also has flip-out legs to tilt the Chromebook to a better angle for typing on a flat surface.

Figure 2-3. *A hard shell can not only protect a Chromebook from the rigors of school life, but also improve the typing angle of the keyboard and increase airflow to the device's overheated parts*

Note   Apart from protection, shells give you a way to individualize the Chromebooks. For example, by getting shells with different colors or designs, you can make the Chromebooks easier to recognize. If the school issues Chromebooks to the students, the students can personalize the shells without affecting the Chromebooks themselves.

Deciding How to Store Your School's Chromebooks

If your Chromebooks will remain at school or in the classroom, you will need to choose a suitable storage location for them. Given how portable Chromebooks are, it is all too easy for someone to remove a Chromebook from the classroom undetected.

Here are suggestions for storing Chromebooks securely in the classroom or school:

- *Closet*: If the classroom has a lockable closet, placing the Chromebooks in it at the end of the lesson or the end of the school day may be adequate. If the closet contains power outlets, you can plug in power adapters to charge the Chromebooks so they are ready for their next assignment. If you need to charge many Chromebooks, you will probably want to have an electrician outfit the closet with extra power outlets that meet safety specifications rather than simply getting creative with extension sockets yourself.

- *Computer cart*: You can find a wide variety of carts designed to secure laptops or large tablets, charge them, and convey them safely from one classroom to another. Figure 2-4 shows the Core M cart from Bretford (`www.bretford.com`), which comes as either a 24-device model or a 36-device model (shown).

Figure 2-4. *Computer carts such as the Core M cart from Bretford are available*

- *Computer charging and syncing cabinet*: If the Chromebooks will remain in the same classroom, consider a charging and syncing cabinet rather than a cart. You can find various cabinets designed to hold laptops. For example, the Kensington AC12 Security Charging Cabinet shown in Figure 2-5 ($699.99, www.kensington.com) can hold up to 12 devices with 14-inch screens, charging each with up to 90W of power.

Figure 2-5.   *The Kensington AC12 Security Charging Cabinet holds up to a dozen 14-inch devices*

Summary

In this chapter, you have learned how to choose suitable Chromebooks for the classroom. We have discussed the hardware features of Chromebooks and explored how to make suitable choices from the wide range of options available for processors, memory, storage, screen size, screen resolution, and other features.

We have also looked at accessories you may want to consider adding to your Chromebook deployment. These accessories range from styluses for touchscreen Chromebooks to charging and security carts and cabinets for storing the Chromebooks safely in the school.

CHAPTER 3

Essential Chromebook Skills for Teachers and Administrators

This chapter will explain the essential skills you will need to master to use a Chromebook effectively as a teacher or an administrator. Most of these skills are ones that you will want your school's students to learn as well.

This is a long chapter. We will start by covering the actions you will need to take with a new Chromebook—performing basic setup, connecting the Chromebook to a Wi-Fi network, accepting the Chrome OS licensing terms, and signing in to the Chromebook. We will then move along to looking at how to control startup, sleep and wake, shutdown, and restart on a Chromebook; how to navigate the Chrome OS interface; and how to use and configure the keyboard, including in-depth coverage of the many keyboard shortcuts that Chrome OS offers.

From there, we will explore how to connect external devices—from a mouse to a monitor, from Bluetooth devices to external drives—to a Chromebook and use them with it. After that, you will learn how to work with apps and windows, how to make the most of the Chrome browser,

© Guy Hart-Davis 2018
G. Hart-Davis, *Deploying Chromebooks in the Classroom*,
https://doi.org/10.1007/978-1-4842-3766-3_3

and how to manage your files using the Files app. Finally, we will cover how to sign in to multiple user accounts on a Chromebook and switch quickly among them, and how to capture screenshots on Chromebooks for documentation or other purposes.

Note   In this chapter, we will look at some configuration changes you may need to make immediately, such as choosing essential accessibility settings and connecting the Chromebook to a Wi-Fi network. For in-depth coverage of other settings, turn to Chapter 4, which will cover configuring a Chromebook manually.

Setting Up a Chromebook

This section will show you how to get started with a new Chromebook—performing the initial startup steps, connecting the Chromebook to a Wi-Fi network, accepting the Chrome OS licensing terms, and signing in to the Chromebook.

Note   You can also use this procedure to set up a Chromebook that has been restored to its original settings using the Powerwash feature. See the section "Resolving Problems by Resetting and Powerwashing Chromebooks" in Chapter 9 for details on Powerwash.

First, start the Chromebook by pressing its power button. Most Chromebooks have a dedicated power button—you will need to find where the manufacturer has located it—but some use a key on the keyboard for power.

Navigating the Welcome! Dialog Box: Choosing Language and Accessibility Settings

Once you have started the Chromebook, the Welcome! dialog box will open (see Figure 3-1). This dialog box enables you to select the language and keyboard layout for the Chromebook and apply any needed accessibility settings before going through the rest of setup.

Figure 3-1. *From the Welcome! dialog box, you can configure the language, keyboard layout, and essential accessibility settings*

To select the language and keyboard layout, click the Language button—which shows the current language, such as *English (United States)* rather than the word *Language*—in the lower-left corner of the Welcome! dialog box. In the Choose your language & keyboard dialog box that opens (see Figure 3-2), select the language in the Language pop-up menu and the keyboard layout in the Keyboard pop-up menu, and then click the OK button to return to the Welcome! dialog box.

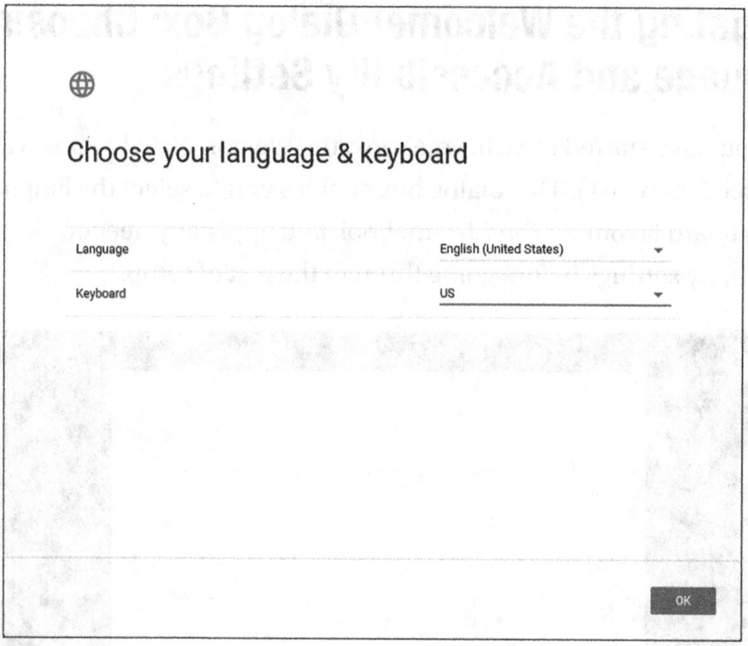

Figure 3-2. *In the Choose your language and keyboard dialog box, select the display language you want to use and then select the keyboard layout*

To apply Accessibility settings, click the Accessibility button and work in the Accessibility settings dialog box that opens (see Figure 3-3). You can configure these five settings:

- *ChromeVox*: Set this switch to On to enable ChromeVox spoken feedback during setup.

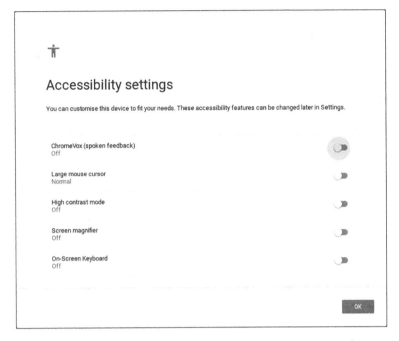

Figure 3-3. *In the Accessibility settings dialog box, you can enable five essential accessibility settings: ChromeVox spoken feedback, the large mouse cursor, high-contrast mode, the screen magnifier, and the on-screen keyboard*

- *Large mouse cursor*: Set this switch to On to pump up the pointer (the mouse cursor) to a huge size for easy visibility.

- *High-contrast mode*: Set this switch to On to apply a high-contrast mode that's similar to reverse video.

- *Screen magnifier*: Set this switch to On to magnify the screen. With the screen magnifier on, you will need to pan around the screen to see all of it.

- *On-screen keyboard*: Set this switch to On to display the on-screen keyboard, which enables you to type characters by clicking.

67

After making your choices in the Accessibility settings dialog box, click the OK button to return to the Welcome! dialog box.

Once you have finished with the Welcome! dialog box, click the Let's go button to start the main part of setup. The Connect to network dialog box then opens (see Figure 3-4).

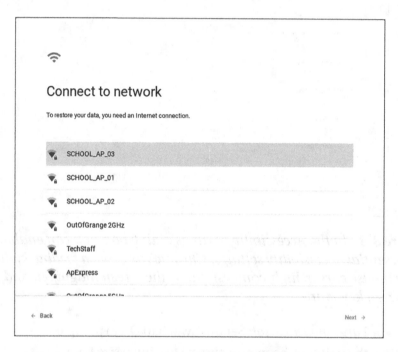

Figure 3-4.   *In the Connect to network dialog box, select the Wi-Fi network you want the Chromebook to use*

Working in the Connect to Network Dialog Box

The Connect to network dialog box shows a list of the available Wi-Fi networks that Chrome OS has detected. At the bottom of the dialog box is the Add other Wi-Fi network button, which enables you to connect the Chromebook to a network that does not appear in the list.

UNDERSTANDING SSIDS AND OPEN AND CLOSED WI-FI NETWORKS

Each Wi-Fi network has a name that identifies it. The name is formally known as a *service set identifier*, which is abbreviated as SSID. The name can be up to 32 characters or 32 bytes long. The characters can include upper- and lowercase letters (including spaces), numbers, and symbols (such as underscores or periods). An SSID is case sensitive, so School_AP1 is different from SCHOOL_AP1.

Most wireless access points come with default names that identify the device's manufacturer or the company that supplies it. If you are setting up the Wi-Fi network, you should give each wireless access point a name that makes sense for your school or institution so that staff and students can instantly tell whether a particular Wi-Fi network is part of the school or not. Unless your school's buildings are surrounded by open space, it is likely that some Wi-Fi networks from neighboring buildings will reach into your school's buildings. (Similarly, neighboring buildings will be able to see any of your school's wireless networks that reach beyond its grounds.)

A Wi-Fi network can be either open or closed. An *open* Wi-Fi network is one that broadcasts its SSID for all to see; any Wi-Fi–capable device within range will detect the network and can attempt to connect to it. By contrast, a *closed* Wi-Fi network does not broadcast its SSID, and anyone trying to connect a device to it must type in the correct SSID on the device.

At first glance, preventing a network from broadcasting its SSID appears to be a reasonable security measure. But because Wi-Fi scanning apps and devices can detect the SSID of even a closed network, closing a network works only to deter casual access. Anyone with a scanning app (which you can get for free) or a dedicated scanning device can learn the SSID in seconds and can then try to connect to the network. In most cases, it is better to create open Wi-Fi networks and implement effective security than to create closed networks.

If you get to choose the SSIDs for your network, you need to balance several conflicting factors:

- *Readability and clarity*: Normally, you will want to make the names readable (rather than gobbledygook) and their meanings clear. This way, you will be able to tell your colleagues and students clearly which networks they're supposed to be using.

- *Uniqueness in their context*: Each SSID should be unique so that users and devices can tell which network they're trying to connect to. Some devices assume that an SSID uniquely identifies a network. This assumption enables a malefactor to set up a malicious Wi-Fi hotspot that uses the same name and password as a genuine hotspot nearby, causing devices to connect to the malicious hotspot instead of the genuine one. (The malicious hotspot can capture information from the devices that connect to it.)

- *Security*: The Wi-Fi router uses the SSID, together with the security method you choose, to encrypt the information it transmits. So, technically it is better to choose a longer and more complex name than a short name.

Here is how to connect the Chromebook to a network that appears in the list in the Connect to network dialog box:

1. Click the button for the Wi-Fi network to which you want to connect the Chromebook. The Join Wi-Fi network dialog box for an open network opens (see Figure 3-5).

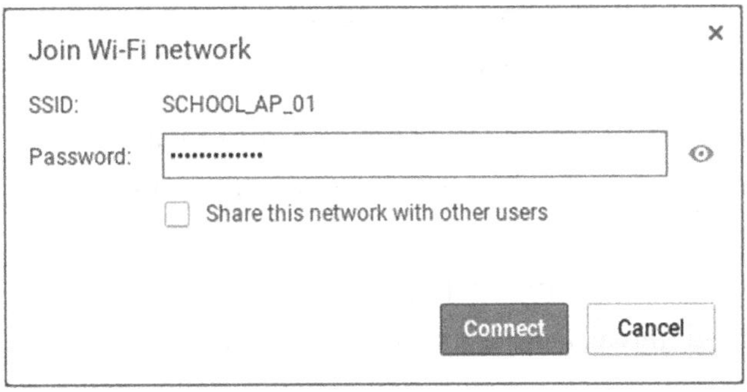

Figure 3-5. In the Join Wi-Fi network dialog box for an open network, enter the password or other security information for the network. Check the "Share this network with other users" check box if you want other users of this Chromebook to be able to use the network.

2. Click the Password box and type the password for the network. You can click the Show password icon (the eye icon) on the right of the Password box to reveal the characters you typed; this is especially handy for complex passwords.

3. Check the "Share this network with other users" check box if you want the network to be available to other users of this Chromebook. In a school situation, you will normally want to do this.

4. Click the Connect button. Chrome OS connects to the Wi-Fi network. Once the connection is established, the Wi-Fi icon on the shelf displays white bars to show the signal strength. The Join Wi-Fi network dialog box closes, and the Google Chrome OS terms dialog box opens.

Here is how to connect the Chromebook to a network that does not appear in the list in the Connect to network dialog box:

1.   Click the Add other Wi-Fi network button at the bottom of the list. If there are many networks, you may need to scroll down to reach this button. The Join Wi-Fi network dialog box for connecting to a closed network appears (see Figure 3-6).

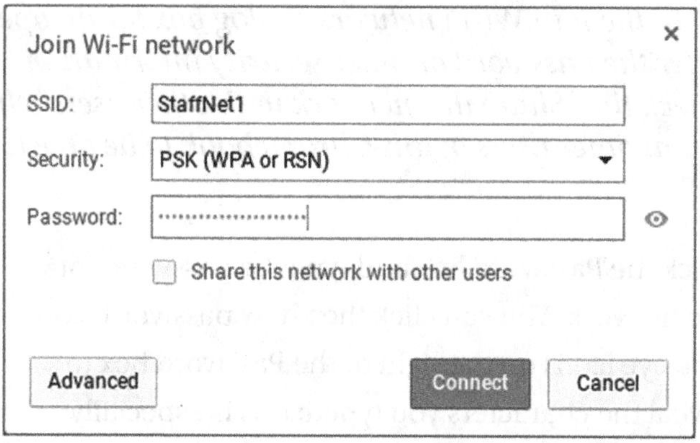

Figure 3-6. In the Join Wi-Fi network dialog box for other networks, type the network's SSID, choose the security type, and enter the password

---

Note   If you need to set up a Wi-Fi network connection that uses other types of authentication than a password, click the Advanced button at this point to expand the Join Wi-Fi network dialog box so that it shows extra fields. Then, skip to the section "Connecting to a Wi-Fi Network with Complex Authentication" later in this chapter for instructions.

---

2. Type the Wi-Fi network's name in the SSID box.

3. If the Wi-Fi network uses security (as most networks do), click the Security pop-up menu and then click the PSK (WPA or RSN) item or the WEP item. See the nearby sidebar titled "Wi-Fi Security: WEP, PSK, WPA, and RSN" for details on the acronyms. If the Wi-Fi network does not use security, leave the default setting, None, selected in the Security pop-up menu box.

WI-FI SECURITY: WEP, PSK, WPA, AND RSN

Wireless network security is a salad of acronyms. Here's what you need to know about WEP, PSK, WPA, and RSN:

- *WEP*: WEP is the acronym for Wired Equivalent Privacy. WEP is an older form of Wi-Fi security that is easy to crack, so few networks use it these days unless they need to provide backward compatibility for very old wireless hardware. Avoid using WEP unless there is no alternative.

- *PSK*: PSK is the acronym for Pre-Shared Key—in other words, a password or passphrase used for securing the network. PSK can use either RSN or WPA to negotiate the connection between the wireless access point and the wireless client.

- *RSN*: RSN is the acronym for Robust Security Network. RSN is a group of protocols that wireless access points and wireless clients can use to negotiate which authentication and encryption algorithms to use to secure the network connection.

- *WPA*: WPA is the acronym for Wi-Fi Protected Access, a security specification designed to be more secure than WEP.

4. Assuming the network uses security, click the Password box and type the password. You can click the Show password icon to the right of the Password box if you need to check what you are typing.

5. Check the "Share this network with other users" check box if you want the network to be available to other users of this Chromebook. In a school situation, you will normally want to do this.

6. Click the Connect button. Chrome OS connects to the closed Wi-Fi network. Once the connection is established, the Wi-Fi icon on the shelf shows the signal strength by the number of white bars. The Join Wi-Fi network dialog box closes, and the Google Chrome OS terms dialog box opens.

Note   If you are using this method to connect to a Wi-Fi network that's not within range of the Chromebook, Chrome OS attempts to connect to the network. When the attempt to connect times out, Chrome OS displays a Network Connection Error alert. Chrome OS also displays the Join Wi-Fi network dialog box for an open network so that you can re-enter the password, in case a wrong password caused the network connection error. Click the Cancel button to dismiss the Join Wi-Fi network dialog box. You can also click the Network Connection Error alert to display the Settings window for the Wi-Fi network; we'll examine this window in the section "Configuring the Settings for a Wi-Fi Network Connection" later in this chapter.

Navigating the Google Chrome OS Terms Dialog Box

In the Google Chrome OS terms dialog box (see Figure 3-7), first read the terms and conditions for using Chrome OS.

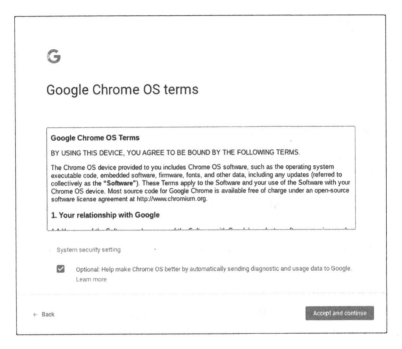

Figure 3-7. *In the Google Chrome OS terms dialog box, you can read the terms for Chrome OS, choose whether to automatically send diagnostic and usage data to Google, and access the System security setting*

If the System security setting link appears, you can click it to open the System security setting dialog box (see Figure 3-8). This dialog box shows a randomly generated secure module password assigned to the Chromebook. Note the password in your documentation and then click the OK button to return to the Google Chrome OS terms dialog box.

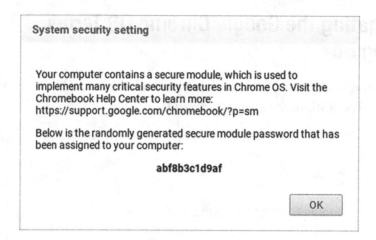

Figure 3-8.   *After opening the System security setting dialog box, note the randomly generated secure module password in your documentation*

Uncheck the "Optional: Help make Chrome OS better by automatically sending diagnostic and usage data to Google" check box if you don't want the Chromebook to report home about its usage and about errors that the operating system diagnoses. Then click the Accept and continue button to proceed with setup.

Next, the Checking for updates dialog box appears while Chrome OS checks for updates. If it finds updates, it installs them automatically and then restarts the Chromebook if necessary.

Once the updating (if any) is complete, the Sign in to your Chromebook dialog box opens.

Signing In to the Chromebook

The Sign in to your Chromebook dialog box (see Figure 3-9) is designed for the Chromebook's owner to sign in to the Chromebook using his or her existing Google account. However, it also enables you to create a new Google account, sign in using Guest mode, or set up the Chromebook for enterprise enrollment.

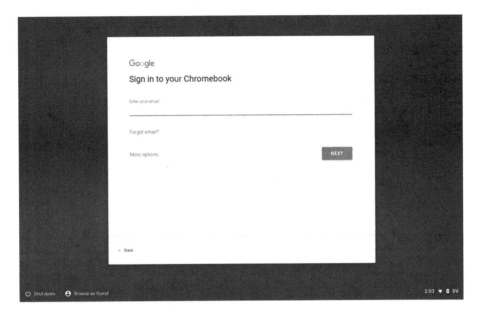

Figure 3-9. *From the Sign in to your Chromebook dialog box, you can sign in as an individual user, recover the details of your Google account, create a new Google account, launch Guest mode, or begin enterprise enrollment*

Setting Up the Chromebook as an Individual User

If you will use this Chromebook as an individual user, type the email address for your Google account in the "Enter your email" field and click the Next button. In the Hi dialog box that appears next (see Figure 3-10), type the password for your account; click the Show password button (the icon showing an eye with a line across it) if you want to view the characters you have typed. Then, click the Next button to sign in with that account.

77

Figure 3-10. *In the Hi dialog box, type your password and click the Next button. You can click the Forgot password? link to start the process of recovering a forgotten password.*

Note   If you have forgotten the password for your Google account, click the Forgot password? link to display the Find your email dialog box, type your phone number or recovery email address, click the Next button, and then follow the prompts to recover the details.

If you have enabled two-step verification for your Google account, you will now need to go through the second step of verification. For example, if you have set up two-step verification using your mobile phone, the 2-Step Verification dialog box will open on the Chromebook (see Figure 3-11), and Google will send a six-digit verification code to the mobile phone number you have associated with your Google account. Enter that code on the Chromebook and then click the Next button to proceed.

Figure 3-11. *In the 2-Step Verification dialog box, type the six-digit verification code that Google sends to your mobile phone*

The Chrome OS desktop then appears, with the Howdy dialog box open (see Figure 3-12). From here, you can click the Take a tour button to take a tour of Chrome OS or simply click the Close button (the X button in the upper-right corner) to close the dialog box so that you can start using the Chromebook.

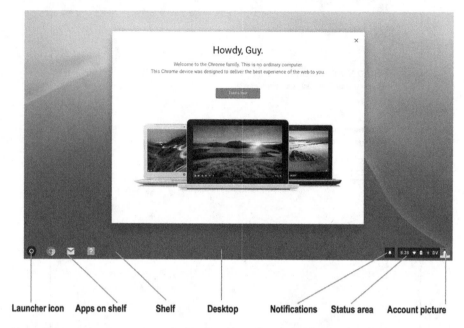

Launcher icon   Apps on shelf   Shelf   Desktop   Notifications   Status area   Account picture

Figure 3-12. *When the Howdy dialog box opens, either click the Take a tour button to learn about Chrome OS or click the Close (X) button in the upper-right corner to close the dialog box*

Using Guest Mode to Browse the Web

If you want to use the Chromebook in Guest mode, click the More options link in the Sign in to your Chromebook dialog box, then click the Guest mode item on the menu that opens. Chrome OS opens a browser window showing the message You are browsing as a guest, and you can start browsing.

Note   Chrome OS deletes files created during the Guest session when the guest logs out, so the Guest account takes up only a minimal amount of storage space between sessions. If you create any files you want to keep while using a Chromebook in Guest mode, you need to copy them to online storage—or perhaps email them to yourself—before you end the Guest session.

To end the Guest session, click the Guest button in the status area at the right of the shelf to display the status menu (see Figure 3-13), then click the Exit guest button.

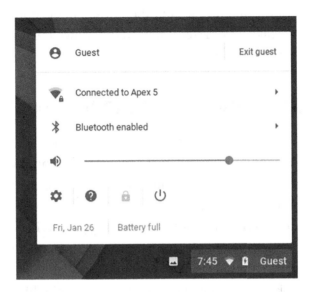

Figure 3-13. *When you are ready to exit the Guest session, click the Guest button in the lower-right corner of the screen and then click the Exit guest button on the status menu*

Setting Up the Chromebook to Use Enterprise Enrollment

If you are going to enroll the Chromebook in enterprise management, click the More options link on the Sign in to your Chromebook dialog box and then click the Enterprise enrollment item on the menu that opens. You can then follow the prompts to enroll the Chromebook.

Controlling Startup, Sleep and Wake, Shutdown, and Restart

This section will show you how to start the Chromebook; how to put it to sleep and how to wake it from sleep; how to shut down the Chromebook when you finish using it; and how to restart it.

Starting Up a Chromebook and Signing In

To start up a Chromebook, press the Power key on the keyboard or the Power button, depending on which power control the Chromebook has.

After Chrome OS starts, the sign-in screen appears. Depending on how the Chromebook is configured, the sign-in screen may display an entry—an icon and user name—for each existing user, as in Figure 3-14; if so, click your icon or user name, type your password, and press the Enter key to sign in. Otherwise, if the Chromebook displays the Sign in to your Chromebook screen (shown in Figure 3-9, earlier in this chapter), type your Google account email address and follow through the screens as explained in the section "Setting Up the Chromebook as an Individual User" earlier in this chapter.

Figure 3-14. *If the sign-in screen displays an icon and user name for each user, click your icon or user name, type your password, and press the Enter key or click the right-arrow button to the right of the "Password" field*

Locking a Chromebook

When you need to leave a Chromebook but intend to start using it again soon, you can lock it in either of these ways:

- *Keyboard*: Press Search+L.

- *Trackpad*: Click the status area to display the status menu and then click the Lock button.

83

Chrome OS displays the lock screen (see Figure 3-15), which displays your name and places the cursor in the "Password" field, ready for you to type your password and resume work. You can also take the following actions:

- *Display the status menu*: Click the status area as usual. Only some of the commands on the status menu are enabled. For example, you can change the keyboard layout and accessibility options, but you cannot connect to a different Wi-Fi network.

- *Sign out of the Chromebook*: Click the Sign out button in the lower-left corner of the lock screen. You can also sign out from the status menu.

- *Shut down the Chromebook*: Click the Shut down button in the lower-left corner of the lock screen. You can also click the Shut down button on the status menu, as usual.

Figure 3-15. *From the lock screen, you can unlock the Chromebook by typing your password and pressing the Enter key. You can also display the status menu, sign out of the Chromebook, or shut down the Chromebook.*

Note   If you will lock the Chromebook frequently, you may want to set up a PIN for unlocking it so that you do not have to type your password each time. See the section "Setting Up a Screen Lock" in Chapter 4 for instructions on setting up a PIN.

Putting a Chromebook to Sleep and Waking It Again

When you finish using a Chromebook for the time being but intend to return to it and resume work, you can put the Chromebook to sleep. When asleep, the Chromebook uses only a minimal amount of battery power.

Usually, the easiest way to put the Chromebook to sleep is to close its lid. By default, Chrome OS is configured to put a Chromebook to sleep when the lid closes.

Note   If closing the lid does not put the Chromebook to sleep, you need to set the "Sleep when lid is closed" switch on the Power screen in the Settings app to On. See the section "Configuring Power Settings" in Chapter 4 for more information about power settings.

To wake the Chromebook, open its lid (if the lid is closed) or press a key on the keyboard.

Signing Out of a Chromebook

When you finish using a Chromebook, you can sign out of it from either the status menu or the lock screen:

- *Status menu*: Click the status area to display the status menu and then click the Sign out button to the right of your user name.

- *Lock screen*: Click the Sign out button near the lower-left corner of the lock screen.

After you sign out, the sign-in screen appears. From here, another user can sign in, or you can sign in again.

Shutting Down a Chromebook

When you finish using a Chromebook and do not intend to use it for a while, you can shut it down. Normally, you do not need to shut down a Chromebook unless you want to make it reload the operating system (for example, to try to clear an intermittent error) or unless it has reached the end of its battery power.

You can shut down a Chromebook either from the status menu when you are logged in or from the sign-in screen:

- *Status menu*: Click the status area to display the status menu and then click the Shut down icon (see Figure 3-16).

- *Sign-in screen*: Click the Shut down icon in the lower-left corner.

Figure 3-16. *Click the Shut down icon on the status menu when you need to shut down the Chromebook*

Either way, the Chromebook shuts down and stops using power.

When you are ready to start using the Chromebook again, press the Power key or Power button. Chrome OS starts, the sign-in screen appears, and you can sign in.

Restarting a Chromebook

Unlike most other operating systems, Chrome OS does not provide a Restart command in the user interface. Instead of restarting, you normally shut down Chrome OS by using the Shut down command either from the status menu when you are signed in or from the sign-in screen when you are not signed in.

However, Chrome OS does have a keyboard shortcut for restarting. Press the Refresh key and the Power key or Power button together. If you are signed in, it is best to sign out before invoking this keyboard shortcut because Chrome OS restarts without giving you the chance to save any unsaved work.

Navigating the Chrome OS Interface

After you log in to a Chromebook, you see the Chrome OS interface. The following list explains the key elements of the interface, which you can see with labels in Figure 3-12, earlier in this chapter:

- *Desktop*: The desktop is the background area on which your apps appear. You can control the desktop's appearance by changing the wallpaper applied to it.

- *Shelf*: The shelf is a strip that appears at the bottom, the left side, or the right side of the Chrome OS desktop. The left shelf contains the Launcher icon and a row of app icons that are pinned in place. You can use these icons to launch apps that are not running and to switch to the apps when they are running. When you launch other apps, their icons appear on the shelf too, and you can use the icons to switch to the apps. You can either display the shelf all the time or make it hide itself automatically when you are not using it.

- *Launcher button*: The Launcher button appears at the left end of the shelf when the shelf is at the bottom of the desktop or at the top of the shelf when the shelf is on the left side or right side of the desktop.

- *Notifications:* The Notifications area displays icons for notifications that are awaiting your attention. See the section "Working with Notifications and Configuring Them" later in this chapter for details.

- *Status area*: The status area, which appears at the right end of the shelf, contains icons such as the time, the Wi-Fi network strength, the battery status, and the current keyboard layout (if the Chromebook is configured with multiple keyboard layouts). You can click any of the icons in the status area to display the status menu, which contains frequently used settings and also gives you access to the Settings app (which contains the full range of settings).

- *Account picture*: The account picture shows a thumbnail of the image associated with the Google account under which you are currently logged in. If you use only a single Google account, this reminder is largely superfluous, but if you log in using multiple accounts, you may find it helpful, especially as Chrome OS enables you to switch quickly among accounts. You can click your account picture to open the status menu.

Using the Touchpad

The touchpad on a Chromebook is straightforward to use. The following list explains the actions you can take:

- *Move the pointer*: Place a finger on the touchpad and move it in the direction you want the pointer to go.

- *Click*: Press with one finger on the side of the touchpad nearest to you (farthest from the keyboard).

Note   If the tap-to-click feature is enabled, you can click by tapping one finger anywhere on the touchpad. Similarly, you can right-click by tapping with two fingers anywhere on the touchpad and close a tab by pointing to the tab and tapping anywhere on the touchpad with three fingers. If the tap-dragging feature is enabled, you should be able to position the pointer over an object, such as a window title bar, tap and keep your finger on the screen to grab the object, and then slide your finger to drag the object; however, this feature seems to work only intermittently.

- *Right-click (secondary click)*: Hold down the Option key while you click. Alternatively, press with two fingers on the side of the touchpad nearest to you.

- *Drag and drop*: Point to the item you want to drag and drop. Click with one finger on the side of the touchpad nearer to you and keep holding the click while you drag the item to where you want it. Release the touchpad to drop the item.

- *Scroll up, down, left, or right*: Place two fingers on the touchpad and move them up, down, left, or right.

- *Go back and forward between pages*: Swipe left with two fingers on the touchpad to go back to the previous page you were on. After going back, you can swipe right with two fingers on the touchpad to go forward again to the page from which you went back.

- *Display all open windows*: Swipe down with three fingers on the touchpad.

Note   Chrome OS includes a feature called *Australian scrolling*—scrolling in which up is down. With Australian scrolling on, you swipe up with three fingers on the touchpad to display all open windows.

- *Close a tab*: Move the pointer over the tab and then click with three fingers on the side of the touchpad nearest to you.

- *Switch between browser tabs*: Swipe left or right with three fingers on the touchpad.

Using the Touchscreen

Some Chromebook models have a touchscreen rather than a regular screen. On a touchscreen Chromebook you can take the following actions:

- *Click*: Tap the item you want to click.

- *Drag*: Tap and hold for a moment, then drag. For example, to move a window, tap and hold its title bar and then drag the window to where you want it.

- *Right-click:* With two fingers, tap the item you want to right-click.

- *Display the shelf when it is hidden*: Swipe or drag up a short way from the bottom of the screen. You can swipe the shelf back down when you no longer need it displayed.

- *Display the Launcher screen*: Swipe up from the bottom of the screen. The Launcher screen disappears when you tap an icon on it, but you can also hide the Launcher screen by swiping down from the top of the screen.

- *Go forward or back in a Chrome tab's history*: Swipe right to go back to the previous page displayed in this tab. After going back, you can swipe left to go forward to the page from which you went back.

- *Zoom in or out on a web page*: Place two fingers (or a finger and a thumb) together on the screen and spread them apart to zoom in, or place them apart on the screen and move them together to zoom out. Zooming works only on web pages designed to use zoom.

Launching Apps with the Launcher

The standard way of launching an app on Chrome OS is to use the
Launcher. Start by clicking the Launcher icon at the left end of the shelf
(if the shelf is at the bottom of the screen) or the top end of the shelf (if
the shelf is positioned on the left or right of the screen). The Launcher bar
appears (see Figure 3-17).

Figure 3-17. *The Launcher first appears as a bar in the lower part of
the screen. Click the app's icon if it appears. Otherwise, click the up-
arrow button to expand the Launcher to full screen.*

If the app you want appears in the single line of apps, click its icon.
Otherwise, click the up-arrow button to expand the Launcher to full screen
(see Figure 3-18).

Figure 3-18. *When displayed full screen, the Launcher shows the full list of apps. If the apps stretch to multiple screens, white and gray dots appear on the right, with the white dot indicating the current screen. Click a gray dot to display that screen of apps.*

Locate the icon for the app. If there are more apps than will fit on the single screen, dots appear on the right side of the list. The white dot indicates the current screen of apps; the gray dots indicate other screens of apps. Click a gray dot to display another screen of apps.

You can also search for the app by starting to type its name. (Chrome OS puts the focus in the Search box when you open the Launcher, so you do not need to click the Search box.) Chrome OS returns a list of matches for apps and other items (see Figure 3-19).

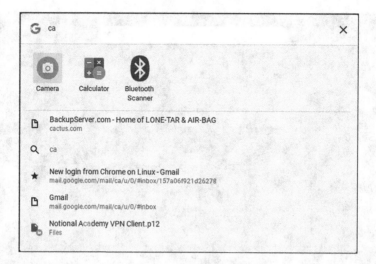

Figure 3-19. *After searching for an app, click the appropriate icon to launch the app*

When you find the app's icon, click it to launch the app. The Launcher screen disappears again, and the app opens.

Configuring the Shelf

The shelf is the strip that appears at the bottom of the screen by default. You can move the shelf to the left side or right side of the screen if you prefer; you can make the shelf hide itself automatically when you are not using it; and you can customize the icons that appear on the shelf.

Note The shelf provides some of the features of the taskbar and the notification area in Windows and the Dock and menu bar in MacOS.

Controlling the Shelf Position and Autohiding

By default, the shelf appears across the bottom of the screen, and you may well want to leave it there. If you want to move the shelf, right-click the Launcher icon, the shelf, or the desktop; click or highlight the Shelf position submenu; and then click the Left option button, the Bottom option button, or the Right option button, as needed.

By default, the shelf appears all the time unless you expand an app to full screen. But you can also set the shelf to hide itself automatically, which makes the shelf appear only when you move the pointer to the side of the screen on which the shelf is hiding. To turn autohiding on, right-click the Launcher icon, the shelf, or the desktop; then, click the "Autohide shelf" command, placing a check mark next to it. When you need to turn off autohiding, right-click the Launcher icon (or the shelf or the desktop) and click the "Autohide shelf" command again, removing the check mark.

Note   When you connect an external monitor to a Chromebook, you can choose a different "Autohide shelf" setting for each monitor if you want. This enables you to have the shelf appear on only one monitor consistently if you want.

Adding and Removing Shelf Items

By default, the Chrome icon and the Gmail icon are pinned to the shelf to make it easy for you to use these key Google features. You can customize the icons on the shelf by adding, removing, and rearranging them as needed.

You can add an app icon to the shelf in either of these ways:

- *Launcher*: Click the Launcher button to open the Launcher, and then click the up-arrow button to switch the Launcher to full screen. Right-click the icon for the app you want to add, then click the Pin to shelf item on the shortcut menu.

- *Running app*: If the app is already running, right-click its icon on the shelf and then click the Pin item on the shortcut menu.

You can also add an icon for a web page to the shelf. This is handy for any web page you (or your students) will need to access frequently. To add an icon for a web page, follow these steps:

1. In Chrome, navigate to the web page.

2. Click the More Actions button (the three vertical dots) to open the menu.

3. Click or highlight the More tools item to display the More tools menu.

4. Click the Add to shelf item. The Add to shelf dialog box opens (see Figure 3-20).

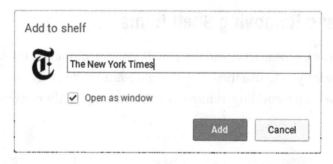

Figure 3-20. *In the Add to shelf dialog box, adjust the display name as needed. Uncheck the "Open as window" check box if you want the web page to open in a tab rather than in a new window. Then, click the Add button.*

5. Edit the default name in the text box as needed.

6. Uncheck the "Open as window" check box if you
    want Chrome to open the web page in a tab in the
    current window rather than in a new window.

7. Click the Add button. The icon for the website
    appears on the shelf.

Tip   After adding the icon for the web page to the shelf, you can
change whether the web page opens in a tab or in a new page by
right-clicking the icon and then clicking the Open as window item on
the shortcut menu.

To remove an icon from the shelf, right-click the icon on the shelf and
then click the Unpin item on the shortcut menu. Alternatively, open the
Launcher to full screen, right-click the icon, and then click the Unpin from
shelf item on the shortcut menu.

To rearrange the icons on the shelf, click an icon and drag it to where
you want it to appear.

Working with and Configuring Notifications

Chrome OS can display notifications for a wide range of events, such as a
new email or a reminder you previously set up. To avoid being distracted
unnecessarily, you will likely want to configure your Chromebook to make
it display only the notifications you will find useful.

Chrome OS also includes a Do not disturb feature that you can enable
when you want to suppress all interruptions.

Viewing Your Current Notifications

When an event occurs for which Chrome OS is configured to notify you, the notification pop-up panel appears briefly above the status area (see Figure 3-21). The pop-up panel shows the details of the notification and may offer actions, depending on the type of notification; for example, for the notification about a screenshot having been taken, you can click the notification to display the screenshot in its folder, or you can click the Copy to Clipboard button to copy the screenshot's image to the Clipboard.

If you take no action with the notification, it disappears after a few seconds.

Figure 3-21. *A notification appears as a pop-up panel above the status area and may contain buttons you can click to take actions. The notification disappears after a few seconds if you leave it alone.*

To see your current notifications, click the Notifications icon. The pop-up panel appears, showing a list of the notifications and a bar containing the Clear all button, the Do not disturb button, and the Settings button (see Figure 3-22). From here, you can take the following actions:

- *Expand a notification:* Click the down-arrow button to the right of the notification's time.

- *Take action on a notification*: Click one of the buttons in the notification, either when it is collapsed or after you expand it.

- *Clear the notification*: Move the pointer over the notification and then click the Close (X) button in its upper-right corner.

- *Clear all notifications*: Click the Clear all button.

- *Enable or disable Do not disturb mode*: Click the Do not disturb button.

- *Open the Settings panel*: Click the Settings icon.

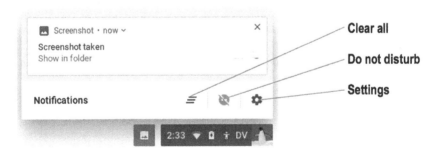

Figure 3-22. *Open the Notifications pop-up panel when you need to review your notifications, enable the Do not disturb feature, or change your settings for notifications*

Choosing Which Apps and Features Can Raise Notifications

To choose which apps and features can raise notifications, open
the Notifications pop-up panel and then click the Settings icon.
The Notifications panel shown in Figure 3-23 appears. In the Allow
notifications from the following list, check or uncheck each of the check
boxes to specify which notifications you want to see. You can also set the
Do not disturb switch to On or Off as needed.

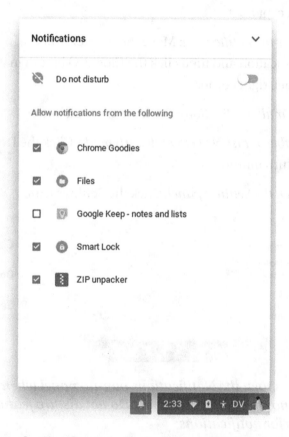

Figure 3-23. *In the Notifications panel, uncheck the check boxes in
the Allow notifications from the following list to specify which apps
and features can raise notifications. You can set the Do not disturb
switch to On to suppress all notifications.*

100

When you have finished choosing settings, you can click the down-arrow button to the right of the Notifications heading to return to the Notifications pop-up panel. Alternatively, simply click outside the Notifications panel to close the panel altogether.

Controlling Which Websites Can Send You Notifications

Chrome OS also enables you to control which websites can send you notifications. You can either block all websites from sending notifications or adopt a more nuanced approach, building a list of sites that are allowed to send you notifications and list of sites that are blocked from doing so. See the section "Choosing Content Settings" in Chapter 4 for details.

Setting Wallpaper

Like most operating systems, Chrome OS enables you to customize the wallpaper on the desktop. Chrome OS includes a selection of wallpaper pictures, but you can also use your own pictures. For example, you might want to apply a school-themed wallpaper picture.

Note   Chrome OS treats wallpaper as one of your account's settings. So, when you change the wallpaper on one Chromebook, the change carries across to any other Chromebook on which you sign in.

Follow these steps to set the wallpaper:

1. Right-click the Launcher icon, the shelf, or the desktop and then click the Set wallpaper item on the shortcut menu. The Set Wallpaper dialog box opens (shown in Figure 3-24 with a picture being chosen).

Figure 3-24. *In the Set Wallpaper dialog box, click the tab for the collection you want to view and then click the picture you want to apply*

2. At the top of the Set Wallpaper dialog box, click the tab for the picture collection you want to view: All (which lets you see all pictures, but with plenty of scrolling), Landscape, Urban, Colors, Nature, or Custom (which lets you use your own pictures).

3. Click the picture you want to use. Chrome OS downloads the picture (unless you have downloaded it already) and applies it to the desktop so you can see how it looks.

Note   You can check the "Surprise Me" check box to have Chrome OS automatically pick a picture, download it, and apply it as wallpaper.

4. If you want to use one of your own pictures as wallpaper, click the Custom tab and then follow these substeps:

    a. Click the Add (+) button to display the dialog box shown in Figure 3-25.

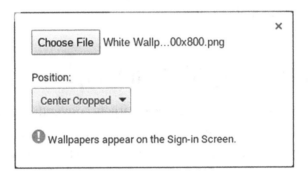

Figure 3-25.   *To use your own picture as wallpaper, click the Custom tab, click the Add (+) button, and then use this dialog box to select the file and specify how to position it on the screen.*

    b. Click the Choose File button to display the Select a File to Open dialog box.

    c. Navigate to the folder that contains the file you want to use and then click the file.

    d. Click the Open button. The file's name appears in the first dialog box.

e. Click the Position pop-up menu and then click the position you want to use: Center, Center Cropped, or Stretch. The Center Cropped setting is usually the best choice for realistic photos, but if you find the cropping removes vital parts from a photo, try using the Center setting instead. The Stretch setting distorts the photo as needed to fit the screen without cropping, so it is best used only for non-realistic photos.

5. When you have picked a wallpaper you like, click the Close (X) button in the upper-right corner of the Set Wallpaper dialog box.

Using and Configuring the Keyboard

A Chromebook has a keyboard that looks largely conventional at a quick glance but in fact contains plenty of built-in improvements and shortcuts. This section explains what you need to know to use the keyboard quickly and efficiently.

Understanding the Keys on a Chrome OS Keyboard

The Chrome OS keyboard layout differs from a standard PC keyboard in three main ways:

- *No Windows keys*: This should be no surprise, but it means there is more room for the Ctrl key, Alt key, and space bar.

- *Search key*: Where standard PC keyboards have a Caps Lock key, the Chromebook keyboard has a Search key. Pressing the Search key brings up a search window into which you can type search terms or a web address that you want to visit. The Search key also works as an extra modifier key for keyboard shortcuts.

- *Dedicated function keys*: Where standard PC keyboards have 12 (or sometimes more) function keys numbered F1 through F12 on the top row of the keyboard, above the number keys, the Chromebook keyboard has a row of dedicated function keys. Figure 3-26 shows the key names, and the following sublist explains what they do:

Figure 3-26. *The top row of the Chromebook keyboard contains dedicated function keys*

- *Escape key*: Press this key to cancel the current action—for example, to dismiss a dialog box.

- *Back key*: Press this key to go back to the previous page in a browser window.

- *Forward key*: Press this key to go forward again in a browser tab. You can only go forward after going back—otherwise, there is no page to go forward to.

- *Reload key*: Press this key to reload the current page.

- *Full Screen key*: Press this key to switch the current app to full screen. Press again to switch back from full screen to a window.

- *Switch Window key*: Press this key to display Overview Mode, which shows all your open windows. You can then close any unneeded windows or switch to another window.

- *Bright Down key*: Press this key to decrease the screen's brightness by one notch.

- *Bright Up key*: Press this key to increase the screen's brightness by one notch.

- *Mute key: Press this key to mute the sound. Press again to unmute the sound.*

- *Volume Down key*: Press this key to decrease the volume by one notch.

- *Volume Up key*: Press this key to increase the volume by one notch.

- *Lock/Power key*: Press this key to power on the Chromebook when it is off, to lock the Chromebook when it is unlocked, and to wake the Chromebook when it is sleeping. On some Chromebooks, this key is the Lock key only, and there is a separate Power button.

Note   You can use the dedicated function keys together with the modifier keys (the Ctrl, Alt, and Shift keys) to take other actions. We will get to these keyboard shortcuts soon.

Making the Most of Keyboard Shortcuts

Chrome OS supports many keyboard shortcuts that you can use to speed up your work by giving more commands from the keyboard. Chrome OS also gives you an easy way to view the available keyboard shortcuts. We will start with this feature.

Viewing the Available Keyboard Shortcuts

To view the available keyboard shortcuts, press Ctrl+Alt+? (you may need to press Shift as well in order to type the question mark). The screen displays a keyboard diagram with the key names, as shown in Figure 3-26.

Once you have displayed the keyboard diagram, you can press one or more of the modifier keys to see the available keyboard shortcuts. Figure 3-27 shows the keyboard shortcuts for the Ctrl key.

Figure 3-27. *Press one or modifier keys—this example uses the Ctrl key—to see the available keyboard shortcuts*

Table 3-1 explains the keyboard shortcuts for the Ctrl key.

Table 3-1. *Keyboard Shortcuts for the Ctrl Key*

Keyboard Shortcut	What It Does
Ctrl+Back	Displays the previous pane
Ctrl+Forward	Displays the next pane
Ctrl+Full Screen	Toggles an external monitor between mirroring the Chromebook's screen (for example, when you are giving a presentation) and extending the desktop (giving more space to work in)
Ctrl+Switch Window	Takes a screenshot
Ctrl+1–Ctrl+8	Displays Tabs 1 through 8 of the current window
Ctrl+9	Displays the last tab of the current window
Ctrl+0	Resets the zoom to 100 percent
Ctrl+Backspace	Deletes the previous word
Ctrl+Tab	Displays the next tab in the current window
Ctrl+P	Displays the Google Print dialog
Ctrl+F	Gives the Search command or Find command. Depending on the app or window, this command displays the "Search" field or the Find panel.
Ctrl+G	Gives the Find again command, finding the next instance of the item for which you previously searched
Ctrl+C	Copies the currently selected item to the Clipboard
Ctrl+X	Cuts the current selected item to the Clipboard
Ctrl+V	Pastes the Clipboard's contents at the current location

(*continued*)

Table 3-1. (*continued*)

Keyboard Shortcut	What It Does
Ctrl+R	Reloads the current page. (This is an alternative to the Reload button on the top row of keys.)
Ctrl+L	Selects the contents of the Address box so you can type another address
Ctrl+? or Ctrl+/	Opens the Chromebook Help window
Ctrl++ or Ctrl+=	Zooms in by one increment
Ctrl+-	Zooms out by one increment
Ctrl+A	Selects all the content of the current object or window
Ctrl+O	Gives the Open command, displaying a dialog box such as the Select a File to Open dialog box
Ctrl+E or Ctrl+K	Places the focus in the Address bar and activates the Search functionality
Ctrl+U	Displays the source code of the current web page
Ctrl+D	Adds a bookmark for the current web page
Ctrl+H	Displays the History screen, which shows a list of the web pages you have visited recently
Ctrl+T	Opens a new tab in the current window
Ctrl+N	Opens a new window
Ctrl+S	Saves the current document
Ctrl+Enter	Adds www. before and .com after the address you have typed and then opens the address
Ctrl+J	Opens the Downloads window in a new tab

(*continued*)

Table 3-1. (*continued*)

Keyboard Shortcut	What It Does
Ctrl+W	Closes the current tab
Ctrl+left arrow	Moves the insertion point to the beginning of the current word (if the insertion point is in a word) or to the beginning of the previous word (if the insertion point is not in a word)
Ctrl+right arrow	Moves the insertion point to the beginning of the next word

Table 3-2 shows the keyboard shortcuts you can invoke by pressing Ctrl+Alt.

Table 3-2. *Keyboard Shortcuts for the Ctrl+Alt Key Combination*

Keyboard Shortcut	What It Does
Ctrl+Alt+Switch Window	Takes a screenshot of the window that you click after pressing this shortcut
Ctrl+Alt+Bright Down	Reduces the magnification
Ctrl+Alt+Bright Up	Increases the magnification
Ctrl+Alt+,	Switches to the previous user when you have signed in multiple users
Ctrl+Alt+.	Switches to the next user when you have signed in multiple users
Ctrl+Alt+P	Toggles the display of touch points, circles that indicate where the touchscreen is detecting input
Ctrl+Alt+I	Toggles the Projection Touch HUD (heads-up display)
Ctrl+Alt+T	Opens a new crosh Terminal window
Ctrl+Alt+Z	Toggles ChromeVox spoken feedback on or off
Ctrl+Alt+up arrow	Gives the Home command
Ctrl+Alt+down arrow	Gives the End command

Table 3-3 explains the keyboard shortcuts you can invoke by pressing Alt+Shift.

Table 3-3. *Keyboard Shortcuts for the Alt+Shift Key Combination*

Keyboard Shortcut	What It Does
Alt+Shift+=	Centers the active window on the desktop
Alt+Shift+Tab	Displays the previous window
Alt+Shift+T	Puts the focus on the toolbar
Alt+Shift+I	Displays the Tell Us What's Happening dialog box for reporting an issue with Chrome OS
Alt+Shift+S	Displays the Status Menu pop-up panel
Alt+Shift+P	Displays the Stylus Tools pop-up panel
Alt+Shift+L	Puts the focus on the shelf, displaying it if it is hidden
Alt+Shift+B	Puts the focus on the Bookmarks bar
Alt+Shift+N	Displays the Message Center pop-up panel
Alt+Shift+M	Opens a Files window or activates an existing Files window

Table 3-4 explains the keyboard shortcuts you can invoke by pressing Ctrl+Shift.

Table 3-4. *Keyboard Shortcuts for the Ctrl+Shift Key Combination*

Keyboard Shortcut	What It Does
Ctrl+Shift+Reload	Rotates the display 90° clockwise
Ctrl+Shift+Switch Window	Takes a screenshot of the area over which you drag the crosshair pointer after pressing this shortcut
Ctrl+Shift+0 (zero)	Resets the screen zoom to 100 percent
Ctrl+Shift+− (hyphen)	Zooms the screen out by one increment
Ctrl+Shift++	Zooms the screen in by one increment
Ctrl+Shift+Backspace	Activates the Settings app and displays the Clear browsing data dialog box
Ctrl+Shift+Tab	Displays the previous tab in Chrome
Ctrl+Shift+Q	Signs you out
Ctrl+Shift+W	Closes the active window
Ctrl+Shift+R	Reloads the current page, bypassing the Chromebook's cache (to make sure the page is up to date)
Ctrl+Shift+T	Reopens the last tab you closed
Ctrl+Shift+U	Starts inputting a Unicode character. When you press this shortcut, an underlined *u* appears. Type the code for the Unicode character and then press Enter to make the Chromebook substitute the character.
Ctrl+Shift+I	Displays the Developer tools
Ctrl+Shift+O	Displays the Bookmark Manager when Chrome is the active app
Ctrl+Shift+D	Bookmarks all the tabs in the current window in Chrome
Ctrl+Shift+G	Gives the Find Previous command, finding the previous instance of the item for which you previously searched

(*continued*)

Table 3-4. (*continued*)

Keyboard Shortcut	What It Does
Ctrl+Shift+J	Opens a JavaScript console window
Ctrl+Shift+C	Displays the DOM Inspector window for the current element
Ctrl+Shift+V	Pastes the contents of the Clipboard as plain text
Ctrl+Shift+B	Toggles the display of the Bookmark in Chrome
Ctrl+Shift+N	Opens a new Incognito window in Chrome
Ctrl+Shift+?	Opens a Help window
Ctrl+Shift+spacebar	Switches the keyboard to the next input method
Ctrl+Shift+left arrow	Selects one word at a time to the left
Ctrl+Shift+right arrow	Selects one word at a time to the right

Table 3-5 explains the two keyboard shortcuts you can invoke by pressing Ctrl+Alt+Shift.

Table 3-5. *Keyboard Shortcuts for the Ctrl+Alt+Shift Key Combination*

Keyboard Shortcut	What It Does
Ctrl+Alt+Shift+?	Displays the keyboard overlay—the onscreen keyboard reference diagram
Ctrl+Alt+Shift+Reload	Rotates the active window 360°. This action is mostly for amusement.

Table 3-6 explains the keyboard shortcuts you can invoke by pressing the Search key.

Table 3-6. *Keyboard Shortcuts for the Search Key*

Keyboard Shortcut	What It Does
Search+Esc	Opens Task Manager
Search+Backspace	Deletes the character to the right of the cursor
Search+L	Locks the screen
Search+. (period)	Inserts the contents of the Clipboard
Search+Alt	Toggles Caps Lock on and off
Search+Left arrow	Issues the Home command
Search+Right arrow	Issues the End command
Search+Up arrow	Issues the Page Up command
Search+Down arrow	Issues the Page Down command

Connecting and Using External Devices

In this section, we will look at how to connect external devices to a Chromebook. We will start by covering how to connect and use Bluetooth devices, and then we will explore how to connect an external monitor, external drive, external pointing device, and external keyboard.

Connecting and Using Bluetooth Devices

You can connect Bluetooth devices to a Chromebook to extend its functionality. Many different types of Bluetooth devices are available, but the following types tend to be most useful for Chromebooks used in schools:

- *Mouse or other pointing device*: You may want to add a mouse or other external pointing device for students who find the built-in trackpad difficult to use. Or, if you use a Chromebook extensively yourself, you may prefer to use an external mouse for intensive work.

- *Keyboard*: Although each Chromebook has a built-in keyboard, you may sometimes want to connect an external keyboard for heavy-duty text input—especially on a Chromebook that has a smaller keyboard.

- *Headphones or headsets*: Bluetooth headphones and headsets are widely popular and can be helpful for study.

- *Speakers*: Bluetooth speakers can be a good way to supplement a Chromebook's built-in speakers, which tend to be small and not capable of loud output. In the classroom, you might use Bluetooth speakers to make a presentation audible to the whole class.

Note   Most Chromebooks have built-in Bluetooth, but some do not. To check whether a particular Chromebook has Bluetooth, click the status area to display the status menu and then see if a Bluetooth button appears on it. If so, you are in business. If not, you may be able to add Bluetooth capability by using a USB dongle.

Even in Chromebooks that have Bluetooth, as of this writing you cannot use Bluetooth for tethering a Chromebook to a phone or tablet's Internet connection. Use the Wi-Fi hotspot feature on the phone or tablet instead and connect the Chromebook to the device's hotspot as you would to any other hotspot.

Enabling and Disabling Bluetooth

You can quickly enable and disable Bluetooth from either the status menu or the Settings screen as follows:

- *Enable or disable Bluetooth from the status menu*: Click an icon in the status area to display the status menu. Click the Bluetooth button to open the Bluetooth status menu (see Figure 3-28). Then, set the switch at the top to On or Off as needed.

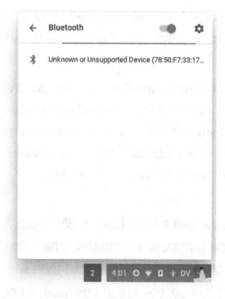

Figure 3-28. *You can quickly enable or disable Bluetooth by setting the switch at the top of the Bluetooth status menu to On or Off*

- *Enable or disable Bluetooth from the main Settings screen*: Set the Bluetooth switch in the Bluetooth section of the main Settings screen (see Figure 3-29) to On or Off as needed. You can also set the switch at the top of the Settings screen for Bluetooth to On or Off.

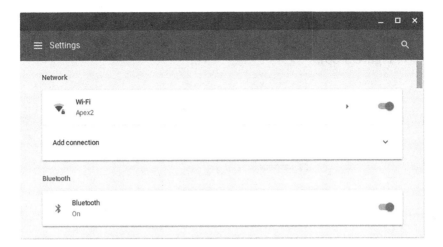

Figure 3-29. *You can enable or disable Bluetooth by setting the Bluetooth switch in the Bluetooth section of the main Settings window*

Pairing a Bluetooth Device with a Chromebook

As with most Bluetooth equipment, you need to pair a Bluetooth device with a Chromebook to make the two work together. Pairing works as a sort of formal introduction between the devices. After you have paired the device with the Chromebook, you can quickly connect and disconnect the device as needed.

Here is how to pair a Bluetooth device with a Chromebook:

1. Turn on the Bluetooth device and put it into pairing mode. How you do this depends on the device, so you will need to consult the instructions if you don't already know the details.

2. Click the status area to open the status menu.

3. Click the Bluetooth button to display the Bluetooth status menu.

117

4. If the switch at the top is set to Off, set it to On. The
    list of available Bluetooth devices will appear (see
    Figure 3-30).

Figure 3-30. *In the Bluetooth status menu, select the device you want
to pair with the Chromebook*

5. Select the device you want to pair with the
    Chromebook. The Add Bluetooth device dialog box
    opens (see Figure 3-31).

Figure 3-31. *The Add Bluetooth device dialog box appears while Chrome OS connects to the Bluetooth device*

6. Once Chrome OS has paired the device, an alert
    message will appear in the lower-right corner of the
    screen (see Figure 3-32). To dismiss the alert, move
    the pointer over the alert and then click the Close
    (X) button that appears.

Figure 3-32. *Chrome OS displaying an alert telling you that the Bluetooth device has been paired*

119

Connecting and Disconnecting Paired Bluetooth Devices

Once you have paired a Bluetooth device with a Chromebook, you can connect the device to and disconnect it from the Chromebook as needed.

You can connect a paired device from either the Bluetooth status menu or the Bluetooth screen in the Settings window:

- *Connect a paired device from the Bluetooth status menu*: Click an icon in the status area to display the status menu. Click the Bluetooth button to display the Bluetooth status menu (see Figure 3-33). Then, click the device's button in the Paired devices list. The Connected readout appears under the device's name once Chrome OS has established the connection.

Figure 3-33. *To connect a paired Bluetooth device, click the device's button in the Paired devices section of the Bluetooth status menu*

- *Connect a paired device from the Bluetooth screen*: Click an icon in the status area to display the status menu and then click the Settings icon to open the Settings window. Click the Bluetooth button to display the Bluetooth screen (see Figure 3-34). Click the device's button to connect the device.

Note   You can also connect a paired device by clicking the More Actions button (the three vertical dots) on the right of the device's button and then clicking the Connect item on the menu that appears. But usually simply clicking the device's button itself is faster and easier.

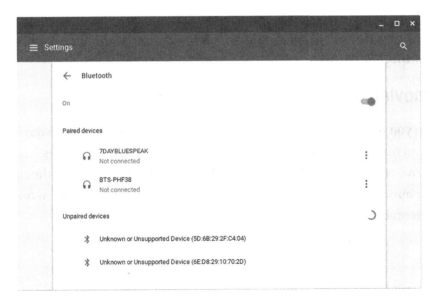

Figure 3-34. *You can also connect a paired Bluetooth device by clicking the device's button on the Bluetooth screen in the Settings window.*

To disconnect a paired device, you use the Bluetooth screen in the Settings window. Click the More Actions button (the three vertical dots) on the right of the button for the device, and then click the Disconnect item on the menu that appears (see Figure 3-35).

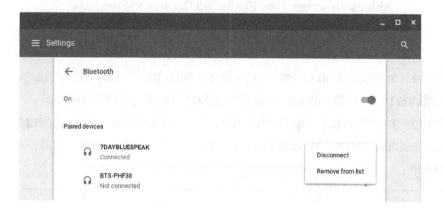

Figure 3-35. *To disconnect a paired device, click the More Actions button (the three vertical dots) to open the menu, and then click the Disconnect item on it*

Removing a Paired Bluetooth Device

When you no longer want a Chromebook to use a paired Bluetooth device, you can remove the pairing. On the Bluetooth screen in the Settings window, click the More Actions button (the three vertical dots) on the right of the button for the device, and then click the Remove from list item on the menu that opens.

Connecting an External Monitor

You can connect an external monitor to a Chromebook by using the HDMI port. Some Chromebook models have a standard, full-size HDMI port, but others use either a mini HDMI port or a micro HDMI port to save space. Each port type works fine, provided you have the right sort of cable—for example, a micro HDMI-to-HDMI cable.

After you connect the monitor to the Chromebook, Chrome OS will display a notification telling you it is extending the screen to the monitor (see Figure 3-36). You can click this notification to go straight to the Displays screen in the Settings app (see Figure 3-37). Otherwise, you can get to the Displays screen by clicking the status area to open the status menu, clicking the Settings icon to open the Settings window, and then clicking the Displays button in the Device section.

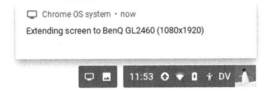

Figure 3-36. *Chrome OS displays a notification when you connect an external monitor to a Chromebook. You can click this notification to show the Displays screen in the Settings app.*

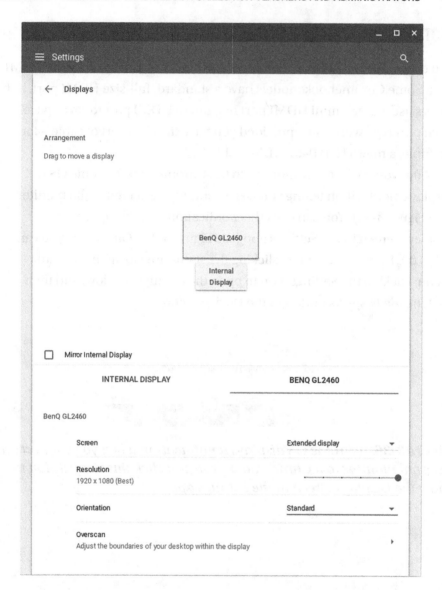

Figure 3-37. *On the Displays screen in the Settings app, you can specify where the external display is positioned relative to the Chromebook and choose whether to mirror the internal display. After selecting the tab for the external display, you can set its resolution, specify its orientation, and choose whether to use the display as the primary display or as an extended display.*

The Arrangement area shows how Chrome OS thinks the external display is positioned relative to the internal display. If the positioning is wrong, drag the icon for the external display to where it needs to be. Verify the positioning by moving the pointer from one display to the other and checking that the pointer appears at the correct point on each.

Next, if you want the external display to mirror the internal display, showing the same content at the same resolution, check the "Mirror Internal Display" check box. When you check this box, Chrome OS will remove the tab for the external display from the lower part of the Displays screen, leaving only the Internal Display tab.

Assuming you do not check the "Mirror Internal Display" check box, you can configure the external display manually using the controls on its tab, as follows:

- *Screen*: In this pop-up menu, choose the Extended display item if you want to use the external display as an extension of the Chromebook's internal display. The internal display remains the primary display. Choose the Primary display item if you want the Chromebook to treat the external display as the primary display.

Tip   Keyboard shortcuts can be especially handy for configuring displays quickly. You can press Ctrl+Full Screen to toggle the "Mirror Internal Display" feature on and off. You can press Alt+Full Screen to switch primary displays. You can press Ctrl+Shift+Reload to rotate the active screen 90° clockwise.

- *Resolution*: Drag this slider to set the resolution for the external display. Chrome OS displays "(Best)" next to the native resolution for an LCD screen.

- *Orientation*: If necessary, open this pop-up menu and click the orientation you need: Standard, 90, 180, or 270.

CONNECTING TWO EXTERNAL MONITORS TO A CHROMEBOOK

To get the most use out of a Chromebook, you may sometimes want to connect two external monitors to it. The Chromebook is not designed for this type of usage, but here are a couple of workarounds you can use:

- *USB-C hub or docking station with dual HDMI outputs:* If the Chromebook has a USB-C port, you can connect to that port a hub or docking station that has dual HDMI outputs. You can then connect a monitor to each of these HDMI outputs.

- *USB DisplayLink adapter:* Chrome OS supports the DisplayLink standard for connecting monitors, so you can connect a USB DisplayLink adapter to a USB port on the Chromebook and to a monitor. Various types of USB DisplayLink adapters are available; most use a standard USB port rather than a USB-C port.

For either of these multi-monitor solutions, read the hardware's specifications and user reviews to make sure that the item you plan to buy will work with Chrome OS.

If you need two external monitors on a Chrome OS device, consider getting a Chromebox (a Chrome desktop) instead of a Chromebook. Some Chromeboxes have two video outputs, enabling you to connect two external monitors with minimal effort.

Using an External Drive

You can connect an external drive to a Chromebook so that you can work with files on the drive or transfer files between the drive, the Chromebook, and your Google account. Depending on the Chromebook's configuration, you may have a choice of ways to connect a drive:

- *USB*: Connect the drive to one of the Chromebook's USB sockets. A USB flash drive tends to be the best solution for quick use, but you can also connect external hard drives—either drives with spinning platters or SSDs. An external hard drive may require its own power supply. If the external drive has a power button, power on the drive.

- *SD card or micro SD card*: If the Chromebook has an SD slot or micro SD slot, insert the card in the slot.

Note   You can also connect an SD card or micro SD card to a Chromebook by using a card reader that plugs into a USB socket.

WHICH FILE SYSTEMS CAN EXTERNAL DRIVES USE?

Chrome OS can read and write to external drives that use the following four file systems:

- *FAT16, FAT32, exFAT*: These file systems are widely used for removable drives. FAT16 has a recommended maximum file size of 2 GB and an absolute maximum file size of 4 GB. FAT32 has a maximum file size of 4 GB. exFAT has a maximum file size of 2 TB.

- *NTFS*: NTFS is the file system that Windows PCs use.

Chrome OS can also read from the HFS+ file system used by Macs, but it cannot write to it.

Most current USB flash drives, SD cards, and micro SD cards come formatted with FAT32 or exFAT, so you can normally use them with a Chromebook without having to reformat them.

Connecting an External Drive and Working with Files

When you connect the drive, the Chromebook will automatically detect the drive and mount it in the file system. Chrome OS may also display a notification, such as the one shown in Figure 3-38. You can click the notification to open the Files app to see the drive's contents. If no notification appears, you can open the Files app from the Launcher as usual.

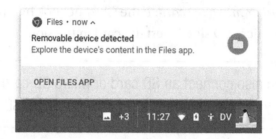

Figure 3-38. *If the "Removable device detected" notification appears when you connect an external drive, you can click the notification to display the drive's contents in the Files app*

Figure 3-39 shows an example of an external drive in the Files app. The drive appears under the name Lexar, has a USB symbol to the left of the name to indicate the means of connection, and has an Eject icon to the right of the name for ejecting the drive from the Chromebook's file system.

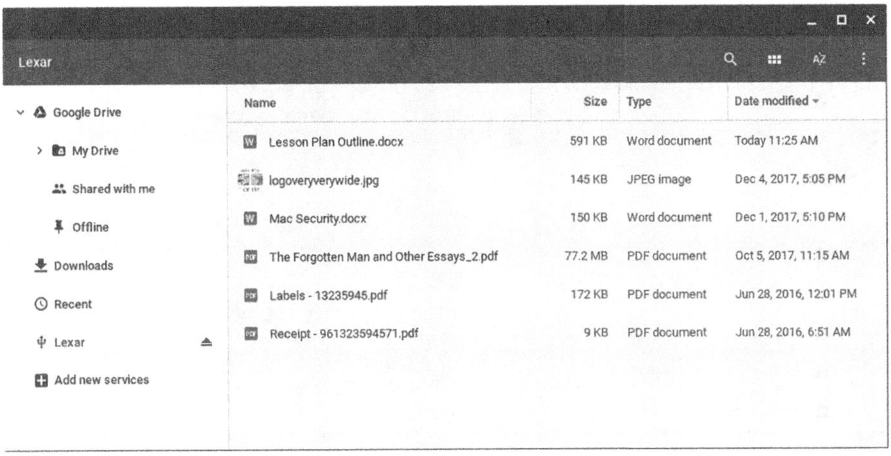

Figure 3-39. *The external drive appears as an entry in the Navigation pane in the Files app, with an Eject button for ejecting the drive from the file system*

Once you have displayed the files, you can perform regular file operations with them. For example, you can drag files to another folder to copy them there, or you can double-click a file to open it in the associated app (assuming the Chromebook has a suitable app).

Reformatting an External Drive

If you connect an external drive that has a file system Chrome OS cannot recognize, the Files app will display the message "This device cannot be opened because its filesystem was not recognized" (see Figure 3-40). To use the device, click the Format device button under this message to start the formatting process.

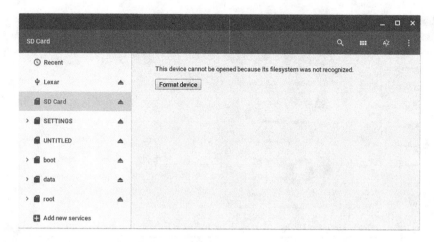

Figure 3-40. *If Chrome OS cannot recognize the file system on a device, click the Format device button to start formatting it*

You can also start formatting a device by right-clicking its entry in the Navigation pane and then clicking the Format device item on the shortcut menu.

Whichever way you start the formatting process, the dialog box shown in Figure 3-41 opens, warning you that formatting the device will erase all its data. Double-check that you have selected the right device and then click the OK button to proceed.

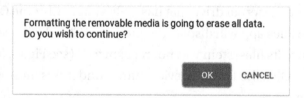

Figure 3-41. *When this dialog box opens, verify that you have selected the right device to format and then click the OK button*

The Files app then formats the device, displaying the "Formatting" notification (shown on the left in Figure 3-42) as it performs the format and then displaying the "Formatting finished" notification (shown on the right in Figure 3-42) when it has finished.

Figure 3-42. *The Files app displays the "Formatting" notification (left) while it formats the device and then displays the "Formatting finished" notification (right) when the formatting is complete.*

Ejecting and Disconnecting an External Drive

When you finish using an external drive, eject it from the Chromebook's file system before disconnecting it. Ejecting the device makes Chrome OS close any files that it has opened on the device.

To eject the device, either click the Eject icon to the right of its name in the Navigation pane, right-click the device's name and then click the Eject device item on the shortcut menu, or press Ctrl+Shift+E when the device is selected.

Note   Even if your school's Chromebooks normally live on desks in a classroom rather than get carried around the school, it is wise to avoid leaving an external drive connected to a Chromebook, because an external device increases the risk of damaging the Chromebook. USB sticks and SD cards also are at risk of being lost or pilfered.

If you do not eject an external drive before disconnecting it, Chrome OS will display a notification warning you that doing so may cause data loss (see Figure 3-43).

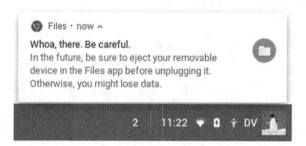

Figure 3-43. *Chrome OS displays the "Whoa, there. Be careful" message if you disconnect an external drive without ejecting it from the Chromebook's file system*

Connecting an External Mouse or Other Pointing Device

You can connect an external mouse or other pointing device to a Chromebook via either USB or Bluetooth. An external pointing device can be helpful for a student who finds the touchpad difficult to use, but you will likely want to minimize the number of additional devices in the classroom in order to keep the Chromebooks easy to handle and manage.

After connecting an external mouse, you can configure it in the Settings app. Click the Mouse and touchpad button in the Device section of the Settings window to display the Mouse and touchpad screen, and then choose the settings you need in the Mouse section.

REASONS TO PREFER USB OVER BLUETOOTH

While either USB or Bluetooth can work well for a keyboard or pointing device, USB is usually the better choice in the classroom for several reasons:

- You can see instantly which USB device is connected to which Chromebook. By contrast, a student playfully swapping several identical Bluetooth keyboards or pointing devices can disrupt a lesson.

- You do not have to pair a USB device.

- You do not have to keep a USB device charged.

Connecting an External Keyboard

As with an external pointing device, you can connect an external keyboard to a Chromebook via either USB or Bluetooth. USB is usually the better choice, especially for heavy-duty input, because USB keyboards typically respond faster than Bluetooth keyboards.

Once you have connected an external keyboard, you can use it instead of the built-in keyboard, or switch from one keyboard to the other, as needed.

Working with Apps and Windows

To get work done on a Chromebook, you run apps, much as on most other computers. The main difference is that, on Chrome OS, many of the apps are shortcuts that work in the Chrome browser rather than being full-fledged apps installed locally.

Launching Apps from the Shelf and the Launcher

As you saw earlier in this chapter, you can launch apps in two main ways:

- *Shelf*: If the app's icon is pinned to the shelf, click the icon to launch the app.

- *Launcher*: Click the Launcher icon to display the Launcher bar. If the app's icon appears on the Launcher bar, click it. Otherwise, click the up-arrow button to display the Launcher full screen and then click the app's icon.

Once the app is running, the app's icon appears on the shelf (assuming it was not already pinned there).

Organizing, Switching, and Managing Windows

Like most modern operating systems, Chrome OS includes features to make organizing, switching, and managing windows easy. This section will show you how to display two windows side by side and how to switch quickly among windows.

Displaying Two Windows Side by Side

When you need to position one window on the left half of the screen and another window on the right half of the screen, use Chrome OS's built-in feature for splitting the screen. Follow these steps:

1. Activate the window you want to place on the left half of the screen.

2. Click and hold the Maximize button in the upper-right corner of the window. A Left (<) button will appear to the left of the Maximize button, and a right (>) button will appear to the right of the Maximize button (see Figure 3-44).

Figure 3-44. *To position a window on the left half or right half of the screen, click and hold the Maximize button until the Left (<) button and Right (>) button appear, then drag the Maximize button to the appropriate button and release it.*

3. Drag the Maximize button to the Left (<) button and release it. The window will appear on the left half of the Chromebook's screen.

4. Activate the window you want to place on the right half of the screen.

5. Click and hold the Maximize button in the upper-right corner of this window. Again, the Left (<) and Right (>) buttons will appear.

6. Drag the Maximize button to the Right (>) button. The window will appear on the right half of the Chromebook's screen.

Switching Windows Using Alt+Tab

Chrome OS enables you to switch between windows quickly using the Alt+Tab keyboard shortcut. Press and hold the Alt key and then press the Tab key to display the window-switcher bar (see Figure 3-45). Press the Tab key to move the selection from one window thumbnail to another until the window you want is selected, and then release the Alt key. The window will then appear.

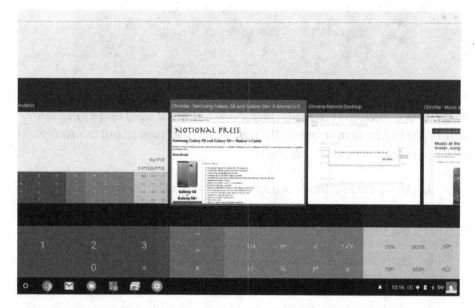

Figure 3-45. *Hold down the Alt key and press the Tab key to display the window-switcher bar. Press the Tab key to move the selection to the window you want to display, and then release the Alt key.*

Tip   While holding down the Alt key, you can press Shift+Tab to move the selection backward through the window thumbnails.

Displaying All Your Windows with the Window Switcher and Overview Mode

Overview Mode lets you see all your open windows so that you can switch among them or close any windows you no longer need. You can open Overview Mode in any of the following ways:

- *Trackpad*: Swipe down from the top of the touchpad with three fingers.

- *Touchscreen*: Swipe down from the top of the touchscreen with three fingers.

- *Keyboard*: Press the Switch Window button—the top-row button above the 6 key.

Once you have opened Overview Mode (see Figure 3-46), you can take the following actions:

- *Display a window*: Click the thumbnail for the window you want to display.

- *Close a window*: Click the X button in the upper-right corner of the window's thumbnail.

- *Search*: Press the spacebar to display a search field at the top of the Overview Mode screen and then start typing your search term. Chrome OS will highlight matching items, and you can click the window you want to display.

Figure 3-46. *Overview Mode lets you see all your open windows and select the window you want to display*

137

Note   With the keyboard, you can press the Tab key, the right-arrow key, or the down-arrow key to move the focus from one thumbnail to the next. Press Shift+Tab, the up-arrow key, or the left-arrow key to move the focus back to the previous thumbnail. Press the Enter key to display the window for the selected thumbnail. Press the Esc key to return to your previous window.

- *Return to your previous window*: Click open space anywhere.

Switching Windows Using the Shelf

You can also switch windows by using the shelf. If the shelf is set to hide itself, move the pointer to the appropriate edge of the screen to display the shelf. Then, click the shelf icon for the app you want to display. If the app has a single window open, Chrome OS will display that window. If the app has multiple windows, Chrome OS will display a pop-up menu listing the windows (see Figure 3-47), and you can click the window you want to display.

Figure 3-47. *Click the shelf icon for the app you want to display. If the pop-up menu opens, click the entry for the window you want.*

Closing a Crashed App with Task Manager

If an app crashes, you may be able to close it by using the Task Manager window (see Figure 3-48). You can open Task Manager in either of these ways:

- *Keyboard*: Press Search+Esc

- *More Actions menu*: In Chrome, click the More Actions button (the three vertical dots), click or highlight the More tools item to open the More tools submenu, and then click the Task Manager item.

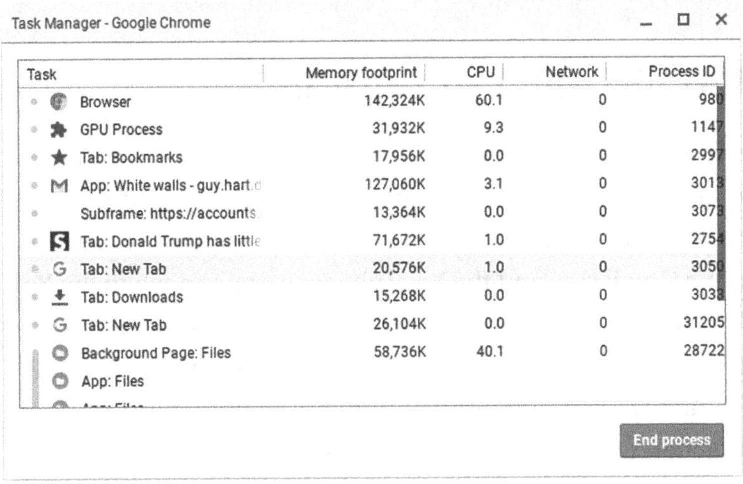

Task Manager - Google Chrome				
Task	**Memory footprint**	**CPU**	**Network**	**Process ID**
Browser	142,324K	60.1	0	98
GPU Process	31,932K	9.3	0	114
Tab: Bookmarks	17,956K	0.0	0	299
App: White walls - guy.hart.c	127,060K	3.1	0	301
Subframe: https://accounts	13,364K	0.0	0	307
Tab: Donald Trump has little	71,672K	1.0	0	275
Tab: New Tab	20,576K	1.0	0	305
Tab: Downloads	15,268K	0.0	0	303
Tab: New Tab	26,104K	0.0	0	31205
Background Page: Files	58,736K	40.1	0	28722
App: Files				

End process

Figure 3-48. *You can close a crashed app by clicking its process in Task Manager and then clicking the End process button*

You can sort the tasks by clicking the heading of the column by which you want to sort. An arrow will appear on the column heading, pointing down to indicate a descending sort or pointing up to indicate an ascending sort; click the column heading again if you need to reverse the sort order.

Tip Task Manager displays a handful of columns by default: Task, Memory footprint, CPU, Network, and Process ID. You can display various other columns by right-clicking in the Task Manager window and then clicking an item in the shortcut menu, placing a checkmark next to it. If you want to remove one of the displayed columns, click it on the shortcut menu to remove its checkmark.

When you identify the task you want to end, click its entry in Task Manager and then click the End process button. Task Manager will end the task without confirmation.

Making the Most of Chrome

The Chrome browser is the central app on a Chromebook, with many of the icons on the Launcher screen simply opening a Chrome tab to the appropriate website. For example, the Gmail icon opens a tab to your inbox on the Gmail site, and the YouTube icon opens a tab to the YouTube website. So, to get full use out of a Chromebook, you should become an expert in using Chrome and teach your students and your colleagues to become experts too.

This section will show you how to launch Chrome; how to navigate in it; how to work with windows and tabs and how to perform other essential browsing moves; and how to work with bookmarks and with your history.

Launching Chrome and Meeting Its Interface

You can launch Chrome either directly, by clicking the Chrome icon that appears on the shelf by default or on the Launcher screen, or indirectly, by clicking another icon for an "app" that relies on Chrome, such as Gmail or YouTube.

When you open a new Chrome window or tab, the tab will display the New Tab page, which contains thumbnails of frequently accessed sites. Figure 3-49 shows the New Tab page in a Chrome window, with the key features labeled. The following list explains the key features:

- *Tab*: Chrome enables you to open multiple tabs within the same window, with each tab containing a different page. You can then switch among the pages by clicking the tabs.

- *Close tab button*: Click this button to close the tab.

- *New tab button*: Click this button to open a new tab after the last current tab in the window.

- *Omnibox*: This box acts as a combined address box and search box. You can type a web address (a URL) to go to that address, or type the search terms for the search you want to perform.

- *Bookmark star*: This star appears in gray if the current web page is not bookmarked and in blue if the page is bookmarked. Click the gray star to create and start editing a bookmark for the current page. Click the blue star to remove the existing bookmark for the page.

- *More Actions button*: Click this button to display the menu, which contains further commands and submenus.

- *Reload button*: Click this button to reload the current page. You may find it easier to press the Reload key on the keyboard.

- *Back button*: Click this button to return to the previous page that was displayed in this tab. Click and hold this button to display a list of the previous pages.

141

- *Forward button*: Click this button to go forward again to a page from which you have gone back in this tab. Click and hold this button to display a list of the pages to which you can go forward.

- *Bookmarks bar*: This bar contains bookmarks you have added for quick access, plus the Other bookmarks button, which you can click to access other bookmarks. You can toggle the display of the Bookmarks bar by pressing Ctrl+Shift+B.

- *Bookmarks*: Click a bookmark on the Bookmarks bar to display the bookmarked web page.

- *Thumbnails*: Click a page thumbnail to display the associated web page. You can remove a thumbnail by moving the pointer over it and then clicking the Remove (X) button in the upper-right corner.

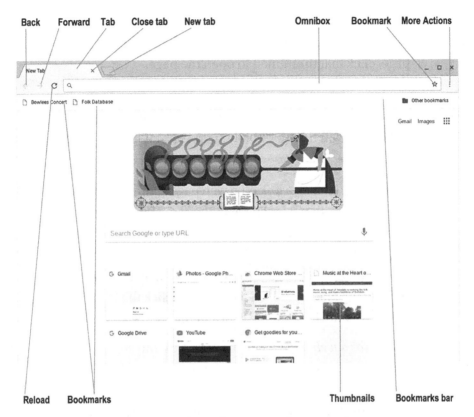

Figure 3-49. *Chrome displays the New Tab page when you open a new window or tab*

Going to a Web Page

In Chrome, you can go to a web page by using any of the following techniques:

- *Type or paste the web page's URL in the omnibox and press the Enter key*: Typing works well for short or simple addresses, whereas pasting is usually a better choice for long or complex addresses. However, if you have the address in another app on the Chromebook, you can usually open it in Chrome simply by clicking it; you do not need to copy the address in the other app and then paste it into Chrome.

143

- *Click a thumbnail on the New Tab page*: If the web page you want to open has a thumbnail on the New Tab page, click that thumbnail to open the page.

Note   As in most web browsers, the pointer in Chrome changes to a right-hand outline with a finger pointing up when it is over a link.

- *Follow a link*: Click a link on a web page. Doing so usually opens the linked page in the same tab, although some links are set up to open the linked page in a new tab, leaving the previous page still open. You can also choose to open a linked page in a new tab: instead of clicking the link, right-click it, and then click the Open link in new tab item on the shortcut menu.

- *Search for a web page*: Click the omnibox and start typing your search terms. As you type, Chrome will display a list of search suggestions and search results (see Figure 3-50). If a specific search result is what you want, click it. Otherwise, click the search suggestion that seems most suitable, such as one of the Google Search suggestions in the figure. Chrome will display the list of results that Google Search returns (see Figure 3-51), and you can click the result whose page you want to view.

Figure 3-50. *Chrome displays a list of search suggestions as you type your search terms*

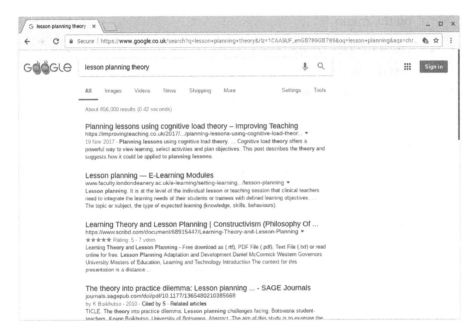

Figure 3-51. *Click the search result whose page you want to view*

Working with Windows and Tabs

Like most other browsers, Chrome enables you to open multiple windows, each of which can contain multiple tabs. Opening multiple windows is helpful both when you want to browse different topics, keeping each in its own window, and when you want to position two windows side by side to compare their contents.

The following list explains how to work with windows:

- *Open a new window*: Press Ctrl+N. Alternatively, click the More Actions button (the three vertical dots) and then click the New Window item on the menu. The new window will contain one tab.

- *Open a new incognito window*: Press Ctrl+Shift+N. Alternatively, click the More Actions button and then click the New incognito window item on the menu.

- *Open the Downloads window*: Press Ctrl+J. Alternatively, click the More Actions button and then click the Downloads item on the menu.

- *Close a window*: Click the Close (X) button in the upper-right corner of the window.

The following list explains how to work with tabs:

- *Open a new tab*: Click the New tab button to the right of the rightmost tab or press Ctrl+T. Alternatively, click the More Actions button (the three vertical dots) and then click the New Tab item on the shortcut menu.

- *Open a new tab showing the same page as a current tab*: Right-click the tab showing the page and then click the Duplicate item on the shortcut menu.

- *Close a tab*: Click the Close (X) button at the right side of the tab or press Ctrl+W. Alternatively, right-click the tab and then click the Close tab item on the shortcut menu.

- *Close all other tabs*: Right-click the tab and then click the Close other tabs item on the shortcut menu.

- *Close all other tabs to the right of this tab*: Right-click the tab and then click the Close tabs to the right item on the shortcut menu.

- *Pin the tab in place*: Right-click the tab and then click the Pin tab item on the shortcut menu. Chrome shrinks the tab's button and moves it to the left end of the tab bar, placing it to the right of any tabs you have already pinned there.

- *Unpin a pinned tab*: Right-click the pinned tab and then click the Unpin tab item on the shortcut menu.

- *Move the tab*: Drag the tab left or right along the tab bar to where you want it.

- *Mute a site*: Right-click the tab and then click the Mute site item on the shortcut menu.

- *Reload a tab's content*: Press the Reload button on the keyboard or press Ctrl+R. Alternatively, right-click the tab and then click the Reload tab item on the shortcut menu.

- *Reopen the last tab you closed in the active window*: Press Ctrl+Shift+T. Alternatively, right-click another tab in the window and then click the Reopen closed tab item on the shortcut menu.

- *Bookmark all the tabs in the current window*: Press Ctrl+Shift+D. Alternatively, right-click a tab in the window and then click the Bookmark all tabs item on the shortcut menu.

- *Activate another tab*: Click the tab. Alternatively, swipe left with three fingers on the touchpad to move to a previous tab, or swipe right to move to a subsequent tab. The further you swipe, the more tabs you move at once.

Performing Essential Browsing Moves

You can perform most of the essential browsing moves in Chrome using either the touchpad or the keyboard, as explained in the following list:

- *Zoom in or out*: Press Ctrl+Shift++ or Ctrl+Shift+= to zoom in by one increment; press Ctrl+Shift+- to zoom out by one increment. Alternatively, click the More Actions button to open the menu and then click the - button to zoom out or the + button to zoom in.

Note   On a touchscreen Chromebook, you can place two fingers together on the screen and spread them apart to zoom in or place two fingers apart on the screen and move them together to zoom out.

- *Go back one page in the current tab*: Click the Back button to the left of the omnibox or press Alt+Left arrow.

Tip   To go back or forward multiple pages, click and hold the Back button or the Forward button and then click the appropriate entry on the pop-up menu. The last item on each pop-up menu is the Show Full History item, which you can click to display your History screen.

- *Go forward one page in the current tab*: Click the Forward button to the left of the omnibox or press Alt+Right arrow.

- *Open a linked page*: Click the link.

- *Open a linked page in a new tab*: Right-click the link and then click the Open link in New Tab item on the shortcut menu.

- *Open a linked page in a new window*: Right-click the link and then click the Open link in new window item on the shortcut menu.

- *Open a linked page in a new incognito window*: Right-click the link and then click the Open link in incognito window item on the shortcut menu.

- *Save the linked page to your Downloads folder*: Right-click the link, click the Save link as item on the shortcut menu, enter the name in the Downloads dialog box that opens, and then click the Save button.

- *Copy the address of the linked page to the Clipboard*: Right-click the link and then click the Copy link address item on the shortcut menu.

Working with Bookmarks

Like most browsers, Chrome enables you to create bookmarks to mark web pages to which you want to be able to return easily. You can access your bookmarks from the Bookmarks bar below the toolbar in the Chrome window, from the More Actions ➤ Bookmarks submenu, or from the Bookmarks Manager screen.

Creating a Bookmark

Once you have displayed a web page you want to bookmark, follow these steps to create the bookmark:

1. Take one of the following actions to display the Bookmark added dialog box (see Figure 3-52):

   • Click the Bookmark icon (the star at the right side of the omnibox).

   • Press Ctrl+D.

   • Choose More Actions ➤ Bookmarks ➤ Bookmark this page.

Figure 3-52. *In the Bookmark added dialog box, edit the bookmark's name as needed, choose the folder in which to store it, and then click the Done button*

2. Edit the suggested name in the Name box as needed, or simply type a new name over it.

3. Open the Folder pop-up menu and click the folder in which to store the bookmark.

Tip   If you will access the bookmark frequently, select the Bookmarks bar folder in the Folder pop-up menu to put the bookmark on the Bookmarks bar.

4.   Click the Done button. Chrome will update the bookmark with the new information.

You can also take further action by clicking the Edit button in the Bookmark added dialog box and working in the Edit bookmark dialog box (see Figure 3-53). The following list explains what you can do in this dialog box:

- *Edit the bookmark's name*: Make the changes needed in the Name box.

- *Edit the URL*: Type or paste the new URL in the URL box.

- *Move the bookmark to a different folder*: Click the destination folder in the list.

- *Add a new folder*: Click the existing folder in which you want to place the new folder. Click the New folder button, type the name for the new folder, and then press the Enter key.

Figure 3-53. *In the Edit bookmark dialog box, you can edit the bookmark's name or URL, or move the bookmark to a different folder. Click the New folder button to start creating a new folder within the selected folder.*

Going to a Bookmark

The quickest way of going to a bookmark is to use the Bookmarks bar (see Figure 3-54). If the Bookmarks bar is not currently displayed, display it by pressing Ctrl+Shift+B or choosing More Actions ➤ Bookmarks ➤ Show bookmarks bar. Then, click the bookmark if it appears directly on the Bookmarks bar; if it does not, click the Other bookmarks button at the right end of the Bookmarks bar, navigate through the hierarchy of bookmarks folders to the bookmark, and click it.

Figure 3-54. You can go to a bookmark by clicking its button on the Bookmarks bar or by clicking the Other bookmarks button, navigating to the bookmark, and clicking it.

The second way of going to a bookmark is by clicking the More Actions button, clicking or highlighting the Bookmarks item to display the Bookmarks submenu, navigating to the bookmark, and clicking it. Figure 3-55 shows an example.

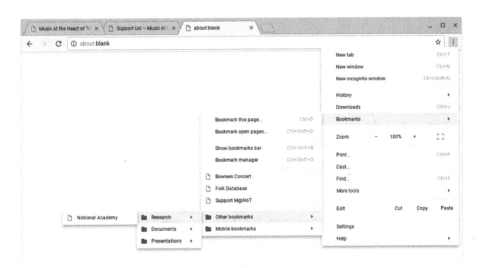

Figure 3-55. You can also use the More Actions ➤ Bookmarks submenu and its submenus to navigate to a bookmark

The third way of going to a bookmark is to use the Bookmark manager screen (see Figure 3-56), which you can display by pressing Ctrl+Shift+O or choosing More Actions ➤ Bookmarks ➤ Bookmark manager. Use the Navigation pane on the left to navigate the bookmark hierarchy to the appropriate folder. You can then double-click a bookmark to open it in a new tab in the same window, or click the More Actions button and then click the Open in new tab item, the Open in new window item, or the Open in incognito window item, as needed.

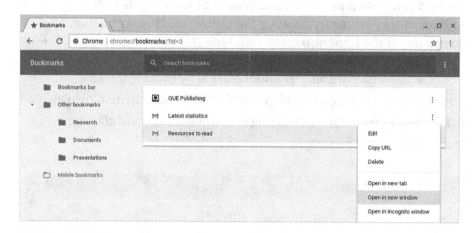

Figure 3-56. *From the Bookmark manager, you can manage your bookmarks or open a bookmark in a new tab, in a new window, or in an incognito window.*

Managing Your Bookmarks

As you saw in the previous section, you can use the Bookmark Manager screen to navigate to the bookmark for the web page you want to display. But, as its name suggests, the primary purpose of the Bookmark Manager screen is to enable you to manage your bookmarks.

To work with your bookmarks, press Ctrl+Shift+O or choose More Actions ➤ Bookmarks ➤ Bookmark manager to display the Bookmark Manager screen. You can then take the actions explained in the following list:

- *Display the bookmarks on the Bookmarks bar or in a folder*: Click the Bookmarks bar item or the folder in the Navigation pane.

- *Search for a bookmark*: Click the "Search bookmarks" field on the toolbar and then start typing your search term. A list of results will appear. You can then double-click a search result to open it in a new tab, or click the More Actions button and then choose a different action from the menu.

- *Rename a folder*: Right-click the folder, click the Rename item to display the Rename folder dialog box, type the new name, and then click the Save button.

- *Edit a bookmark*: Click the More Actions button on the right of the bookmark and then click the Edit item on the menu.

Note   You can also access the Edit command, the Copy URL command, the Delete command, the Open in new tab command, the Open in new window command, and the Open in incognito window command by right-clicking the bookmark to display its shortcut menu.

- *Copy a bookmark's URL*: Click the More Actions button on the right of the bookmark and then click the Copy URL item on the menu.

- *Move a bookmark to a different folder*: Drag the bookmark from its current folder to the destination folder.

- *Delete a bookmark*: Click the More Actions button on the right of the bookmark and then click the Delete item on the menu.

155

- *Open a bookmark*: Click the More Actions button on the right of the bookmark and then click the appropriate item on the menu: Open in new tab, Open in new window, or Open in incognito window.

- *Open all the bookmarks in a folder*: Right-click the folder in the Navigation pane and then click the appropriate item: Open all bookmarks, Open all in new window, or Open all in incognito window.

- *Import bookmarks from a file*: If you have a file containing bookmarks that you have exported from another browser, you can import them into Chrome. Click the More Actions button and then click the Import Bookmarks item on the menu. The Select a file to open dialog box appears. Navigate to the appropriate folder, click the file, and then click the Open button. Chrome OS will import the bookmarks, and you can then use them in Chrome.

- *Export your bookmarks*: Click the More Actions button and then click the Export Bookmarks item on the menu. The Save file as dialog box opens. In the Navigation pane, click the folder in which you want to save the file containing the exported bookmarks; if necessary, click the New Folder button and follow the prompts to create a new folder.

Navigating and Working with Your History

As you browse the Web, Chrome adds the URL of each web page you visit to a list called your History, which enables you to navigate backward and forward along the path of web pages you have browsed in each open tab in Chrome. History also lets you view, browse, and search the full list of web pages you have browsed. You can delete individual records from your History—for example, to remove potentially embarrassing sites you visited by accident—or clear your History entirely if you want to make a fresh start.

The Back pop-up menu and the Forward pop-up menu give you access not only to the list of pages you have browsed in the current tab but also to the History screen. Click and hold the Back button or the Forward button to display the pop-up menu (see Figure 3-57), and then click the Show Full History item.

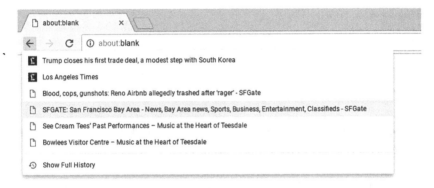

Figure 3-57. *The Back pop-up menu and Forward pop-up menu enable you to access the list of pages you have browsed in this tab. Click the Show Full History item to display the History screen.*

You can also access your History from the More Actions ➤ History submenu. As you can see in Figure 3-58, the History submenu displays the Recently closed category at the top, followed by categories for different devices you have used. You can click the History item at the top (choosing More Actions ➤ History ➤ History) to display the History screen.

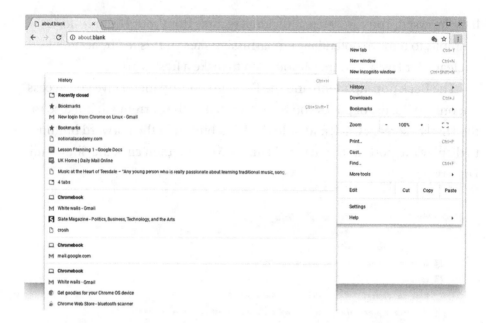

Figure 3-58. *The History submenu on the More Actions menu breaks down your History into categories such as Recently closed.*

You can also display the History screen by pressing the Ctrl+Shift+H keyboard shortcut or by typing `chrome://history` in the omnibox and pressing the Enter key. From the History screen (see Figure 3-59), you can take the actions explained in the following list:

- *View your Chrome history*: Make sure the Chrome history item is selected in the Navigation pane.

- *View your tabs from other devices*: Click the Tabs from other devices item in the Navigation pane.

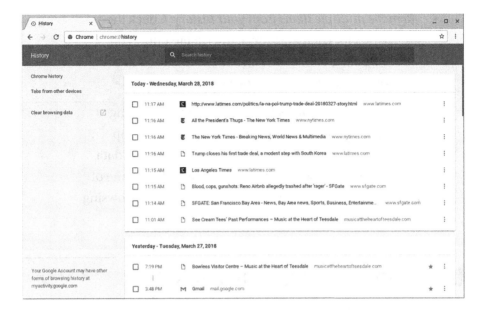

Figure 3-59.   *On the History screen, you can view your Chrome history, view your tabs from other devices, delete history items you no longer need, or clear some or all of your browsing data.*

- *Search your history*: Click the Search history box and then type your search terms. A list of results will appear.

- *Find more web pages from a site in your history*: Click the More Actions button to the right of the history item and then click the More from this site item on the menu. Chrome will search your history for the website identified by the history item and then display a list of results.

- *Go to a web page*: Click the history item for the page.

- *Remove an item from your history*: Click the More Actions button to the right of the history item and then click the Remove from history item on the menu.

- *Remove multiple items from your history*: Check the check box for each item, click the Delete button on the toolbar, and then click the Remove button in the Remove selected items dialog box.

- *Clear your browsing data*: Click the Clear browsing data item in the Navigation pane. The Settings app will become active, and then the Clear browsing data dialog box will open. You can then clear all or some of your browsing data. See the section "Clearing Browsing Data" in Chapter 4 for details.

Managing Files with the Files App

In this section, we will explore how to manage files on a Chromebook using the Files app. File management on a Chromebook is usually relatively simple because most files are stored online, so you can quickly get up to speed with the moves you need to know.

The Files app enables you to access not only files stored on the Chromebook itself but also files stored in Google Drive in your Google account and in other compatible online file services, such as a Box account. Your Google Drive files become available automatically when you sign in to the Chromebook. For other online file services, you must install the service's extension from the Chrome Web Store.

Caution   If your Chromebook's storage is running out of space, Chrome OS may automatically delete some of your older downloaded files to recover enough space to avoid problems.

Launching the Files App and Meeting Its Interface

You can launch the Files app in the same way as you do any other app:

1. Click the Launcher button to display the Launcher bar.

2. If the Files icon does not appear on the Launcher bar, click the up-arrow button to expand the Launcher to full screen.

3. Click the Files icon.

Figure 3-60 shows the Files app with its controls labeled. The following list explains the key features shown in the figure:

- *Navigation pane*: This pane, on the left side of the Files window, enables you to navigate among your different storage locations, such as Google Drive and the Downloads folder on the Chromebook. The Navigation pane also contains the Add new services item for adding other online file services.

- *Columns and column headings*: The Files app can display items either in list view (as in the figure) or in thumbnail view. List view shows four columns: Name, Size, Type, and Date modified. To control how the Files app sorts the items, click the heading of the column by which you want to sort. To reverse the sort order, click the column heading again.

Note   You can also change the sort order by clicking the Sort options button on the toolbar and then clicking the Name item, the Size item, the Type item, or the Date modified item on the pop-up menu. This is the only way to change the sort order in thumbnail view. In list view, it is usually easier to use the column headings.

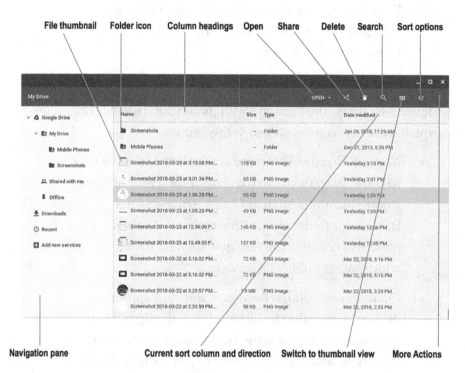

Figure 3-60.   *The Files app gives you access to files on the Chromebook and to files stored on Google Drive and other online file services*

- *Current sort column and direction*: An upward or downward triangle to the right of a column heading indicates the current sort column. An upward triangle indicates an ascending sort (A to Z, low numbers to high, earlier dates to later); a downward triangle indicates a descending sort (Z to A, high numbers to low, later dates to earlier).

- *Switch to thumbnail view*: Click this button to switch the view to thumbnail view, which displays a thumbnail picture for each folder and file. Thumbnail view is especially useful for working with images that you can identify by sight. In thumbnail view, the Switch to thumbnail view button is replaced by the Switch to list view button, which you can click to switch the window back to list view.

- *Open*: Click this button to display the Open pop-up menu, which shows the apps you can use to open the current item. This pop-up menu also contains the Change default item, which lets you choose which app to use as the default for this file type.

- *Share*: For items stored online, click this item to display the Share pop-up menu, and then click the Share with others item to open the Share with others dialog box (see Figure 3-61). In the "People" field, type the email address of the person with whom to share the file. Type any information needed in the "Add a note" field (for example, why you are sharing the file with this person), then click the Send button.

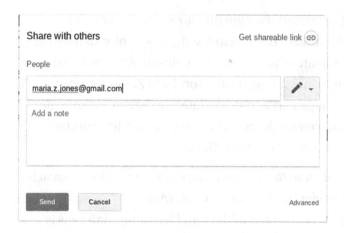

Figure 3-61. *In the Share with others dialog box, add the email address of the person with whom you want to share the file, add a note if necessary, and then click the Send button*

- *Delete*: To delete the selected file or files, click this button and then click the Delete button in the confirmation dialog box that opens.

- *Search*: Click this button to display the "Search" field and then type your search terms.

- *More Actions*: As usual, click this button to display a menu containing further actions you can take, either on the Files app as a whole or on the selected item or items.

The Navigation pane in the Files window contains the following items:

- *Google Drive*: This item represents your Google Drive in its entirety. If a right-arrow (>) appears to the left of this item, click the right-arrow or the Google Drive label to expand the item so that its contents appear: the My Drive, Shared with me, and Offline items. The right-arrow changes to a down-arrow, which you can click when you want to collapse the item again.

- *My Drive*: This item represents the files you have stored on Google Drive. You can expand or collapse the listing using the techniques explained in the previous bulleted paragraph.

- *Shared with me*: This item displays the files and folders that others have shared with you on Google Drive.

- *Offline*: This item displays the files and folders you have marked for offline usage. To mark a file for offline usage, right-click it and then click the Available offline item on the shortcut menu, placing a check mark next to this item. Repeat this move, removing the check mark, when you no longer want to have the file available offline.

Note   The Show hidden files item on the More Actions menu in the Files app enables you to toggle the display of files marked as hidden. Normally, you do not need to see these files, which is why Chrome OS hides them, but sometimes it is helpful to see which hidden files are there.

Performing Operations with Files and Folders

After opening a Files app window and navigating to the folder in which you want to work, you can perform the file-management operations explained in the following list:

- *Select a file or folder*: Click the file or use the arrow keys to move the highlight until the file or folder you want is selected.

- *Select a contiguous range of files or folders*: Using the
  touchpad, click the first file or folder, then hold down
  the Shift key and click the last file or folder in the range
  to select all the files or folders in between. Using the
  keyboard, press the arrow keys to move the highlight
  to the first file or folder, then hold down Shift while you
  press the arrow keys to extend the selection to the last
  file or folder. A blue circle containing a white check
  mark will appear to the left of each selected item.

- *Select a noncontiguous range of files or folders*: Click
  the first file or folder, then hold down the Ctrl key while
  you click each other file or folder you want to add to
  the selection. A blue circle containing a white check
  mark will appear to the left of each selected item (see
  Figure 3-62).

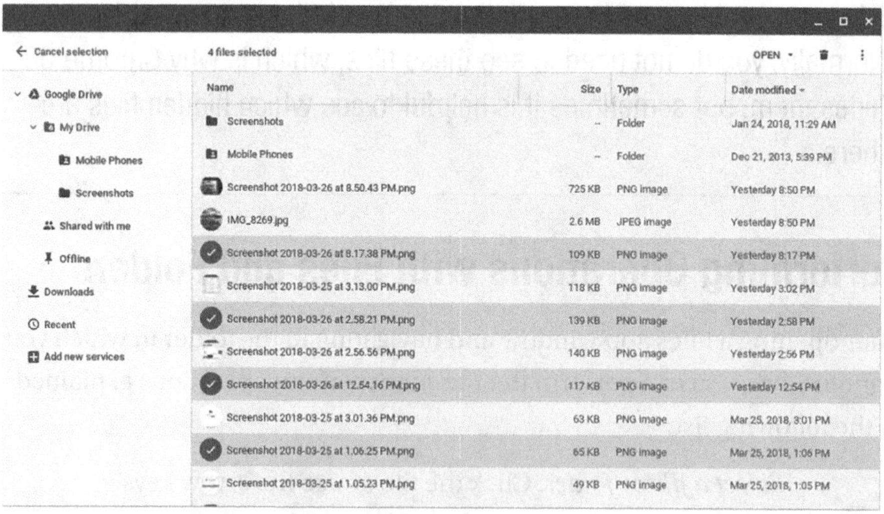

Figure 3-62. *You can select a noncontiguous range of files or folders
by clicking the first file or folder and then holding down Ctrl while you
click each other one. A blue circle containing a white check mark will
appear to the left of each selected item.*

166

- *View information on the selected file*: Press the spacebar. Alternatively, right-click the file and then click the Get info item on the shortcut menu. The Information window will appear (see Figure 3-63), showing a preview of the file (if one is available) and the Info pane. You can click the File info button to toggle the display of the Info pane on and off, the Open button to open the file in its default app, or the Back button to return to the Files window. You can also press the spacebar or the Esc key to return to the Files window.

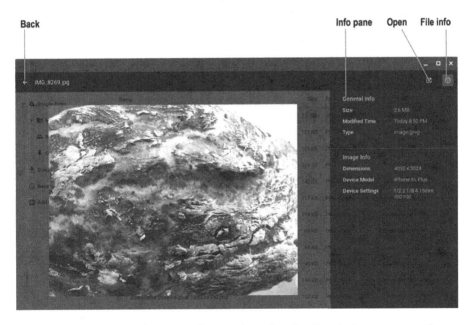

Figure 3-63. *Press the spacebar or invoke the Get info command on the shortcut menu to display the Info window for a file. You can click the File info button to toggle the display of the Info pane.*

Tip   After opening the Information window, you can press the Left arrow to display information about the previous file or the Right arrow to display information about the next file.

- *Delete one or more selected files or folders*: Press Alt+Backspace and then click the Delete button in the confirmation dialog box that opens.

- *Copy one or more selected files or folders*: Press Ctrl+C or right-click the selection and then click the Copy item on the shortcut menu. You can then right-click the destination folder and click the Paste into folder item on the shortcut menu. Alternatively, display the contents of the destination folder and either press Ctrl+V or right-click and then click the Paste item on the shortcut menu.

- *Move one or more selected files or folders*: Press Ctrl+X or right-click the selection and then click the Cut item on the shortcut menu. You can then right-click the destination folder and click the Paste into folder item on the shortcut menu. Alternatively, display the contents of the destination folder and either press Ctrl+V or right-click and then click the Paste item on the shortcut menu.

COPYING AND MOVING ITEMS USING DRAG AND DROP

You can use drag and drop to copy and move items in the Files app. If the destination folder is on the same device or service as the source folder, drag and drop moves the items. If the destination folder is on a different device or service, drag and drop copies the items.

Hold down Ctrl while you drag and drop if you want to copy items rather than move them.

- *Rename a file or folder*: Select the file or folder and then press Ctrl+Enter. The Files app will display an edit box around the file name and extension and select the file name (but not the extension). Type the new name and then press the Enter key.

- *Create a new folder*: Open the folder in which you want to create the new folder. Next, either press Ctrl+E or right-click and then click the New folder item on the shortcut menu. The Files app will display a folder icon with the default name New Folder, which will appear selected in an edit box. Type the name for the folder and then press the Enter key.

- *Compress the selection into a Zip file*: Right-click the selection and then click the Zip selection item on the shortcut menu. The Files app will create a Zip file containing the selection. If the selection is a single file, the Zip file will have the same file name as the item but with the .zip file extension. If the selection is multiple items, the Zip file will have the name Archive.zip or (if Archive.zip already exists in this folder) the next

169

available name, such as Archive (1).zip. If you need
to rename the Zip file, press Ctrl+Enter, type the new
name, and then press the Enter key.

Note   As of this writing, you cannot create Zip files on Google Drive
in the Files app.

- *Decompress a Zip file*: Double-click the Zip file. The
  Files app will mount the Zip file in the file system, add
  it to the Navigation pane with an Eject icon to the right
  of its name, and display its contents in the main part of
  the window. You can then drag the contents of the Zip
  file to the folder in which you want to store them. When
  you finish working with the contents, click the Eject
  icon to remove the Zip file from the Navigation pane.

Changing the Default App for Opening a File

Chrome OS comes with certain apps set as the defaults to use for certain
file types. For example, the Gallery app is the default app for the .png file
type, so when you double-click a .png file in a Files window, the file will
open in the Gallery app. When you install other apps, they may become
the default apps for some file types. You can also change the default app
manually, as explained here:

1. Open a Files window.

2. Navigate to a file of the appropriate type.

3. Click the Open pop-up button on the toolbar. The
   Open pop-up menu will open.

Note   If the Open button appears on the toolbar without the Open pop-up menu button, the selected file type is one for which you cannot change the default app.

---

4. Click the Change default item to display the Change default... pop-up panel (see Figure 3-64).

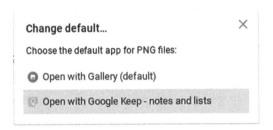

Figure 3-64. *In the Change default... pop-up panel, click the app you want to make the default app for the file type*

5. Click the Open with item for the app you want to make the default app for the file type. The pop-up panel will close, and Chrome OS will register your preference.

After making this change, try double-clicking a file of the same type and verify that it opens in the app you chose.

Connecting to Another Cloud File Service

If you store files on another cloud file service as well as on Google Drive, you may be able to connect your Chromebook to that file service. As of this writing, Chrome OS supports various cloud file services, including Box, Dropbox, and OneDrive.

Follow these steps to connect a Chromebook to another file service:

1. Launch the Files app if it is not already running. If the Files app is running, make one of its windows active.

2. In the left pane, click the Add new services item and then click the Install new from the webstore item on the pop-up menu. The Available services dialog box will open (see Figure 3-65).

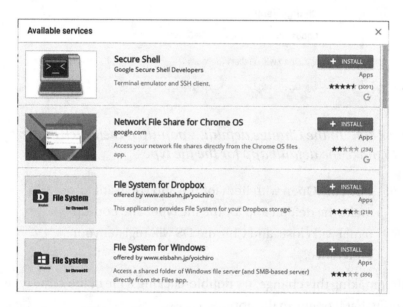

Figure 3-65. *In the Available services dialog box, click the Install button for the cloud file service to which you want to connect the Chromebook*

3. Click the Install button for the appropriate cloud file service. This example uses File System for Dropbox. The Add dialog box then opens (see Figure 3-66).

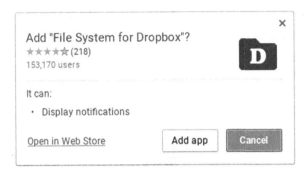

Figure 3-66. *In the Add dialog box for the service, verify what the service will be able to do and then click the Add app button if you want to proceed*

4. Look at the "It can:" list to see what the service will be able to do on the Chromebook. Make sure that the service will not have any capabilities you do not want to allow.

5. Click the Add app button. The Download manager window appears while Chrome OS downloads and installs the service. A window for setting up the service then opens, such as the Mount your Dropbox window shown in Figure 3-67.

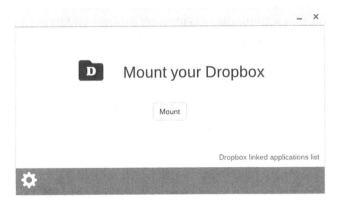

Figure 3-67. *To set up the Dropbox service, click the Mount button in the Mount your Dropbox dialog box*

6. Use the controls in the window and follow the subsequent prompts to set up the service. For example, for Dropbox, click the Mount button to open the Dropbox dialog box shown in Figure 3-68.

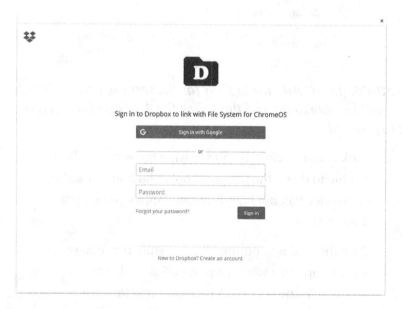

Figure 3-68. *For Dropbox, you can sign in using either your Google account or another account*

7. After you sign in, the service may prompt you to grant permission for File System for ChromeOS to access your files and folders stored on the service (see Figure 3-69, which is for Dropbox). Click the Allow button to grant permission, as the service will not be able to work without it.

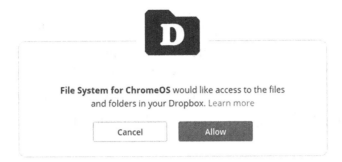

Figure 3-69. *Click the Allow button to allow File System for ChromeOS to access your files and folders stored on the service*

Once the connection is established, the online file service will appear in the left pane in the Files app, and you can then access your files and folders on the service using standard techniques. Figure 3-70 shows the Dropbox service added to a Chromebook.

Dropbox (Guy Hart-Davis) > Camera Uploads			
Name	**Size**	**Type**	**Date modified ▾**
2017-04-20 12.57.45.png	52 KB	PNG image	May 19, 2017, 7:18 PM
2017-04-20 12.58.17.png	46 KB	PNG image	May 19, 2017, 7:18 PM
2017-04-20 12.58.32.png	123 KB	PNG image	May 19, 2017, 7:18 PM
2017-04-20 12.58.38.png	45 KB	PNG image	May 19, 2017, 7:18 PM
2017-04-20 12.58.51.png	75 KB	PNG image	May 19, 2017, 7:18 PM
2017-04-20 12.59.16.png	82 KB	PNG image	May 19, 2017, 7:18 PM
2017-04-20 12.59.23.png	85 KB	PNG image	May 19, 2017, 7:18 PM
2017-04-20 12.59.36.png	74 KB	PNG image	May 19, 2017, 7:18 PM
2017-04-20 12.59.43.png	133 KB	PNG image	May 19, 2017, 7:18 PM
2017-04-20 12.59.49.png	134 KB	PNG image	May 19, 2017, 7:18 PM
2017-04-20 12.59.55.png	85 KB	PNG image	May 19, 2017, 7:18 PM
2017-04-20 13.00.01.png	83 KB	PNG image	May 19, 2017, 7:18 PM

Left pane: Google Drive, My Drive, Shared with me, Offline, Downloads, Recent, Dropbox (Guy Hart-Davis), APK, Apps, Backups, Camera Uploads, Code, Current

Figure 3-70. *The online file service will appear in the left pane in the Files app, and you can work with your files and folders on it*

Note   When you want to disconnect your Chromebook from an online file service, right-click the service's entry in the left pane in the Files app and then click the Close item on the shortcut menu. To reconnect, open the Launcher, click the service's icon, and then follow through the steps to mount the service again.

Signing In Multiple Users and Switching Among Them

Chrome OS includes a Multiple sign-in feature that enables you to sign in multiple users at once and switch quickly among them. This capability can be useful when you need to work with two different accounts at once.

To use the Multiple sign-in feature, follow these steps:

1.   Click the status area to display the status menu.

2.   Click your picture or user name at the top of the status menu. A pop-up menu will appear, showing only the Sign in another user item.

3.   Click the Sign in another user item. The Multiple sign-in dialog box will open (see Figure 3-71), explaining that this feature enables you to access any signed-in user without having to enter a password, and also warning you to use the feature only with accounts you trust.

Figure 3-71. *In the Multiple sign-in dialog box, uncheck the "Got it, don't show me this again." check box if you want to continue to receive the warning. Click the OK button to proceed.*

4. Uncheck the "Got it, don't show me this again." check box if you want to continue to receive this warning each time you use the Multiple sign-in feature.

5. Click the OK button. The sign-in screen will appear, prompting you to sign in another user.

6. Click the user you want to sign in.

7. Type the user's password and press the Enter key or click the right-arrow button. Chrome OS signs the user in, and the user's desktop appears.

Now that you have signed in, you can work in the other user account. When you want to use the other account, switch back in one of these ways:

- *Keyboard*: Press Ctrl+Alt+, (comma) to switch to the previous user, or Ctrl+Alt+. (period) to switch to the next user. (If you have only two users signed in, you can press either of these keyboard shortcuts to switch to the other account.)

- *Touchpad*: Click the status area to display the status menu, click your picture or user name, and then click the appropriate user account on the pop-up menu.

177

You can also switch to another user account as follows:

1. Click the status area to display the status menu.

2. Click your picture or user name at the top of the status menu. A pop-up menu will appear, showing the available user accounts. (If no other user accounts are available, the message "All available users have already been added to this session" will appear.)

3. Click the user account you want to add to the session.

Taking Screenshots on a Chromebook

Chromebooks make it easy to capture the full screen, a window, or just your chosen part of the screen. To capture a screenshot, you press the Switch Window key (the key on the top row above the 6 key) with the appropriate modifier keys. Here's what you need to know:

- *Capture the full screen*: Press Ctrl+Switch Window.

- *Capture a window*: Press Ctrl+Alt+Switch Window. The pointer will change to crosshairs. Click the window you want to capture.

- *Capture a part of the screen that you select*: Press Ctrl+Shift+Switch Window. The pointer will change to crosshairs. With the crosshairs, drag to select the area of the screen that you want to capture. When you release the drag, Chrome OS takes the screenshot.

Whichever method you use to take the screenshot, Chrome OS saves the screenshot automatically under a default name consisting of the word

Screenshot and the date and time, such as `Screenshot 2018-09-30` at `8:36.05` PM, in your Downloads folder.

A notification showing a thumbnail of the screenshot will appear briefly above the status area. You can click the notification to display the screenshot in the Files app—for example, if you want to check it immediately. To review the screenshots later, open the Files app from the Launcher and then click the Downloads item in the left column.

CAPTURING SIGN-IN SCREENS

You can capture sign-in screens, or even the Chrome OS setup screens, by using the three keyboard shortcuts explained in the main text. Chrome OS uses the same naming convention for these screenshots, but it stores them in the `/tmp` folder rather than within your user account. This is fine, but there are three complications:

- You cannot get to the `/tmp` folder using the Files app; instead, you must use a command shell.

- To use a command shell, you must enable Developer mode.

- Enabling Developer mode erases the Chromebook's contents— so you need to enable Developer mode before taking your screenshots of the sign-in or setup screens.

To enable Developer mode, follow these steps:

1. Shut down the Chromebook as usual by clicking the Shut down button on the status menu or on the sign-in screen.

2. Hold down the Esc key and the Refresh key and then press the Power key or Power button. The Chromebook will boot to the Recovery screen, which warns you that Chrome OS is missing or damaged.

3. Press Ctrl+D. Chrome OS will prompt you to press the Enter key to enable or disable Developer mode.

4. Press the Enter key to enable Developer mode.

5. Wait while the Chromebook restarts and erases itself.

6. When the Chromebook restarts, it boots to a Developer mode screen that tells you that OS verification is off and invites you to press the spacebar to reenable it. Wait for the Chromebook to launch Chrome OS. The Welcome dialog box then opens, and you can set up the Chromebook as explained in the section "Setting Up a Chromebook" at the start of this chapter.

You can take screenshots while setting up the Chromebook, when you reach the sign-in screen, or both. When you finish taking your screenshots, sign in to your account. You can then retrieve the screenshots by following these steps:

1. Press Ctrl+Alt+T to open a crosh (Chrome Shell) window or tab in the Chrome browser. The crosh prompt appears:

   `crosh>`

2. At the command prompt, type `shell` and press the Enter key to switch to a Linux shell. The Linux prompt appears:

   `chronos@localhost / $`

3. Type `cd /tmp` and press the Enter key to change directory to the `/tmp` folder.

4. Type `in *.png` and press the Enter key to display a list of all the PNG files in the folder.

5. Use the `cp` command to copy the appropriate screenshots to the Downloads folder in your account. For example, you could type `cp *.png ~/Downloads` and press the Enter key to copy all the PNG files to your Downloads folder. (The tilde, ~, represents your home folder.)

6. When you finish using the Linux shell, type `exit` and press the Enter key to exit to crosh.

7. Type `exit` and press the Enter key again to exit the crosh tab.

You can now open the Files app to the Downloads folder and view or use your screenshots.

After you have finished taking screenshots, you can disable Developer mode again. Doing so erases the Chromebook's contents, so make sure you have copied or moved any files you want to keep to your Google account or a removable drive.

To disable Developer mode, shut down the Chromebook and then restart it. When the Developer mode screen appears, telling you that OS verification is off, press the spacebar to reenable OS verification. Wait while the Chromebook erases its contents and restarts. The Welcome! dialog box then opens, and you can once more set up the Chromebook as explained in the section "Setting Up a Chromebook" at the start of this chapter.

Summary

In this chapter, you have learned a wide range of essential Chromebook skills that will serve you well as either a teacher or an administrator—most of which skills you will likely want to teach to your students. You know how to set up a new Chromebook, connect it to a Wi-Fi network, and sign in to it. You have learned how to control startup, sleep and wake, shutdown, and restart on a Chromebook; how to navigate the Chrome OS interface; and how to use and configure the keyboard. You have met Chrome OS's wide range of keyboard shortcuts and have (perhaps) learned those that will be most useful to you.

You are able to connect external devices, such as a keyboard and a monitor, to a Chromebook. You know how to work with apps and windows, how to work quickly and efficiently in the Chrome browser, and how to use the Files app to manage your files. You have also learned how to put a Chromebook into Developer mode, use the hidden Linux command shell to access areas of the file system that you cannot reach via the Files app, and disable Developer mode when you no longer need it.

CHAPTER 4

Configuring and Managing Chromebooks Manually

In this chapter, you will learn to configure and manage Chromebooks manually by working directly on a Chromebook, rather than by using administrative policy to configure and manage a Chromebook from another computer.

To configure and manage a Chromebook, you use the Settings app. This chapter will start by showing you how to open the Settings window and how to navigate in it. The chapter will then take you through each category of settings in turn, starting with the Network settings and moving through to the various subcategories of Advanced settings, such as the Privacy and security settings and the Accessibility settings.

© Guy Hart-Davis 2018
G. Hart-Davis, *Deploying Chromebooks in the Classroom*,
https://doi.org/10.1007/978-1-4842-3766-3_4

There are three major categories of settings this chapter will not cover. The first category is the Bluetooth settings, which the section "Connecting and Using Bluetooth Devices" in Chapter 3 covers. The second category is the Printing settings, which the section "Printing from Chromebooks" in Chapter 7 explains. The third category is the Reset settings, which the section "Resetting and Powerwashing a Chromebook" in Chapter 9 discusses.

Opening the Settings Window and Navigating in It

To get started configuring settings, open the Settings window. Click any icon in the status area at the right end of the shelf and then click the Settings icon (the gear icon) on the status menu.

The Settings window contains a large number of settings divided into different sections, such as the Network section, the Bluetooth section, the People section, and the Appearance section. These four sections appear at the top of the Settings window, as you can see in Figure 4-1.

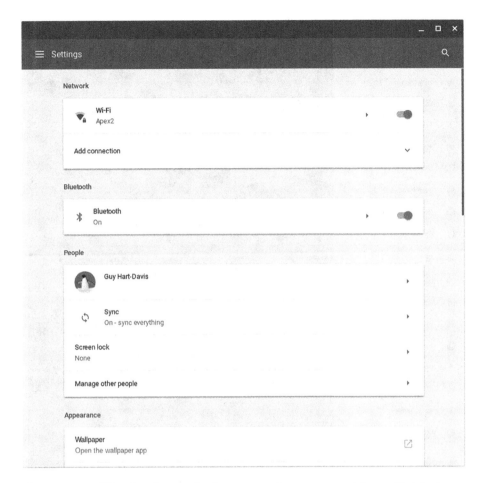

Figure 4-1. *The Settings window contains many settings divided into different sections, such as Network, Bluetooth, People, and Appearance*

You can navigate the Settings window by scrolling up and down, but when you need to navigate more quickly, click the Navigation button to the left of Settings in the upper-left corner to display the navigation panel (see Figure 4-2), which provides buttons you can click to move quickly to the categories. If the Advanced section of the navigation panel is collapsed, click the Advanced heading to display the buttons it contains and then click the button you need.

185

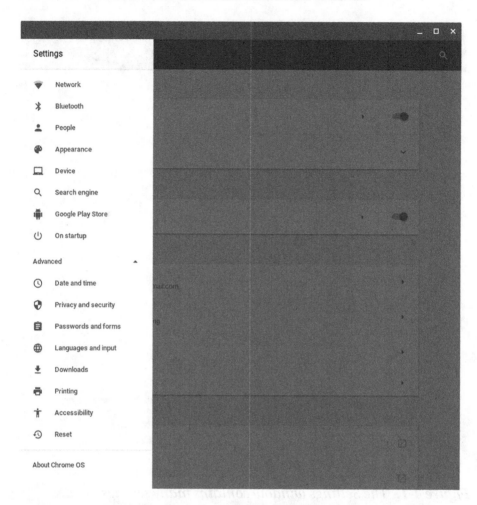

Figure 4-2. *The navigation panel gives you quick access to all the categories in the Settings window. If the Advanced section is collapsed, click the Advanced heading to expand its contents.*

Configuring Network Settings

Chromebooks are designed to be connected to the Internet pretty much the whole time, so you will need to give your school's Chromebooks Internet access by connecting them to the school's Wi-Fi network or networks. You may have already configured a Wi-Fi network connection while setting up the Chromebook, as discussed in Chapter 3. In this section, we will look at how to configure other Wi-Fi network connections and settings, as needed.

Note   Before we get started with the network settings, here is a quick reminder. Each Wi-Fi network has a name called a service set identifier, or SSID for short. The network may be open, broadcasting its SSID, or closed, not broadcasting it. See the sidebar titled "Understanding SSIDs and Open and Closed Wi-Fi Networks" in Chapter 3 for further details.

Connecting to an Open Wi-Fi Network

You can connect to an open Wi-Fi network starting either from the shelf or from the Settings window. Often, it is more convenient to work from the shelf, so we will start with that technique.

Connecting to an Open Wi-Fi Network from the Shelf

Here is how to connect a Chromebook to an open Wi-Fi network that's within range of the Chromebook, starting from the shelf rather than from the Settings window:

1. Click the Wi-Fi icon on the shelf to open the status menu.

2. Click the button for the current Wi-Fi network (if there is one) or the No network button. The Network status menu will open (see Figure 4-3).

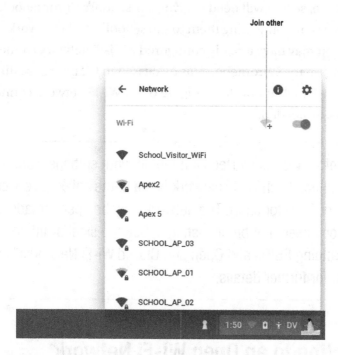

Figure 4-3. *On the Network status menu, click the button for the open Wi-Fi network to which you want to connect the Chromebook. The Join other button enables you to connect to a closed network.*

3. Make sure the Wi-Fi switch is set to On. If not, set the switch to On and then wait until the list of networks appears.

4. Click the button for the Wi-Fi network to which you want to connect the Chromebook. The Join Wi-Fi network dialog box for an open network opens (see Figure 4-4).

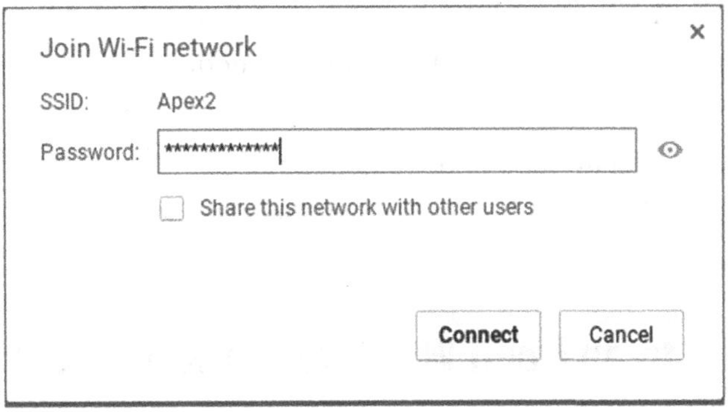

Figure 4-4. *In the Join Wi-Fi network dialog box for an open network, enter the password or other security information for the network. Check the "Share this network with other users" check box if you want other users of this Chromebook to be able to use the network.*

Note   If the Network status menu does not contain a button for the Wi-Fi network to which you want to connect the Chromebook, follow the instructions in the next section, "Connecting to a Closed Wi-Fi Network."

---

5. Click the Password box and type the password for the network. (If the network uses another means of security, enter the appropriate information instead.) You can click the Show password icon (the eye icon) to the right of the Password box to reveal the characters you typed; this is especially handy for complex passwords.

6. Check the "Share this network with other users" check box if you want the network to be available to other users of this Chromebook. In a school situation, you will normally want to do this.

189

7. Click the Connect button. Chrome OS will connect to the Wi-Fi network. Once the connection is established, you can look at the Wi-Fi icon on the shelf to get an idea of the signal strength—the more of the Wi-Fi icon that is white rather than gray, the stronger the signal is.

Connecting to an Open Wi-Fi Network from the Settings Window

Sometimes when connecting a Chromebook to an open Wi-Fi network that's within range of the Chromebook, you may want to start from the Settings window rather than from the shelf. In this case, click the right-arrow button on the right of the Wi-Fi button in the Network section at the top of the Settings window. (The Wi-Fi button's readout shows either Not connected or the name of the current Wi-Fi network.) The Wi-Fi screen will appear (see Figure 4-5), showing the networks the Chromebook has detected. From here, click the button for the Wi-Fi network to which you want to connect the Chromebook, displaying the Join Wi-Fi network dialog box, and then follow steps 5–7 in the previous section.

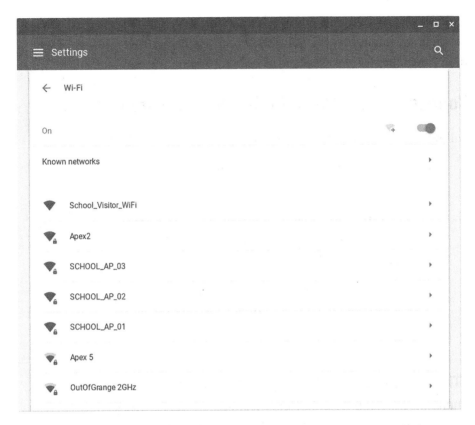

Figure 4-5. *On the Wi-Fi screen, click the button for the open network to which you want to connect the Chromebook*

Connecting to a Closed Wi-Fi Network

To connect to a closed Wi-Fi network that's within range of the Chromebook, you use a slightly different technique than that used for an open network. You can use the same technique to connect to a Wi-Fi network—either open or closed—that's currently out of range of the Chromebook. You will need to know the network's name, the security type, and the appropriate security information (such as the password).

As with an open Wi-Fi network, you can connect to a closed Wi-Fi network starting either from the shelf or from the Settings window. The shelf is usually the easiest place to start setting up the connection.

Connecting to a Closed Wi-Fi Network from the Shelf

Follow these steps to connect to a closed Wi-Fi network from the shelf:

1. Click the Wi-Fi icon on the shelf to open the status menu.

2. Click the button for the current Wi-Fi network (if there is one) or the No network button. The Network status menu will open.

3. Make sure the Wi-Fi switch is set to On. If not, set the switch to On and then wait until the list of networks appears.

Tip   You can also start setting up a connection to a closed Wi-Fi network from the main Settings window. In the Network section at the top, click the Add Connection button to expand the Add Connection section. Then click the Add Wi-Fi button to display the Join Wi-Fi network dialog box for other networks.

---

4. Click the Join other button, the button to the left of the Wi-Fi switch. The Join Wi-Fi network dialog box for other networks appears (see Figure 4-6).

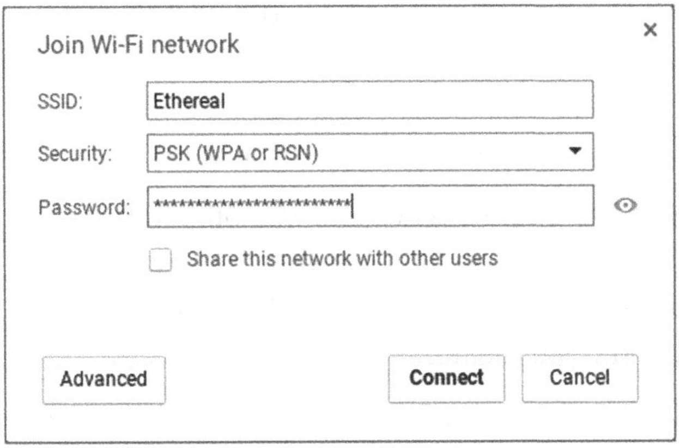

Figure 4-6. *In the Join Wi-Fi network dialog box for other networks, type the network's SSID, choose the security type, and enter the password*

Note   If you need to set up a Wi-Fi network connection that uses other types of authentication than a password, click the Advanced button at this point to expand the Join Wi-Fi network dialog box so that it shows extra fields. Then skip ahead to the section "Connecting to a Wi-Fi Network with Complex Authentication" later in this chapter for instructions.

5. Type the Wi-Fi network's name in the SSID box.

6. If the Wi-Fi network uses security (as most networks do), click the Security pop-up menu and then click the PSK (WPA or RSN) item or the WEP item. See the sidebar titled "Wi-Fi Security: WEP, PSK, WPA, and RSN" in Chapter 3 for details on the acronyms. If the Wi-Fi network does not use security, leave the default setting, None, selected in the Security pop-up menu box.

7. Assuming the network uses security, click the Security box and type the password. You can click the Show password icon to the right of the Password box if you need to check what you are typing.

8. Check the "Share this network with other users" check box if you want the network to be available to other users of this Chromebook. In a school situation, you will normally want to do this.

9. Click the Connect button. Chrome OS will connect to the closed Wi-Fi network. Once the connection is established, the Wi-Fi icon on the shelf will show the signal strength by the number of white bars.

Note   If you are using this method to connect to a Wi-Fi network that's not within range of the Chromebook, Chrome OS will attempt to connect to the network. When the attempt to connect times out, Chrome OS will display a Network Connection Error alert. Chrome OS will also display the Join Wi-Fi network dialog box for an open network so that you can re-enter the password, in case a wrong password caused the network connection error. Click the Cancel button to dismiss the Join Wi-Fi network dialog box. You can also click the Network Connection Error alert to display the Settings window for the Wi-Fi network; we'll examine this window in the section "Configuring the Settings for a Wi-Fi Network Connection" later in this chapter.

Connecting to a Closed Wi-Fi Network from the Settings Window

To start connecting to a closed Wi-Fi network from the Settings window rather than from the shelf, click the right-arrow button on the right of the Wi-Fi button in the Network section at the top of the Settings window. (The Wi-Fi button's readout shows either Not connected or the name of the current Wi-Fi network.)

On the Wi-Fi screen, click the Join other button, the icon to the left of the switch near the top of the screen. The Join Wi-Fi network dialog box will open, and you can set up the connection by following steps 5–9 in the previous section.

Connecting to a Wi-Fi Network with Complex Authentication

As you have seen in the sections on connecting to open and closed Wi-Fi networks, Chrome OS uses passwords as the default means of authentication on Wi-Fi networks. Generally, this works well, but for those school or organization networks that use stronger forms of authentication, such as digital certificates, you need to use the Advanced version of the Join Wi-Fi network dialog box.

Before setting up a Wi-Fi connection that uses complex authentication, make sure you have the information you need, together with any digital certificates required. Normally, you would consult your school's network administrator to get this information and the certificates.

Note If you need to install certificates, see the section "Managing Certificates" later in this chapter for instructions on how to do so.

Take the following steps to connect a Chromebook to a Wi-Fi network with complex authentication:

1. Begin connecting to the Wi-Fi network as usual, whether it is open, closed, or out of range.

2. Click the Advanced button in the Join Wi-Fi network dialog box to display a larger version of the dialog box (see Figure 4-7).

Note   The Advanced button appears in the Join Wi-Fi network dialog box for an open network only if Chrome OS determines that the network requires complex authentication. This button always appears in the Join Wi-Fi network dialog box for other networks because Chrome OS cannot determine what type of authentication the network requires.

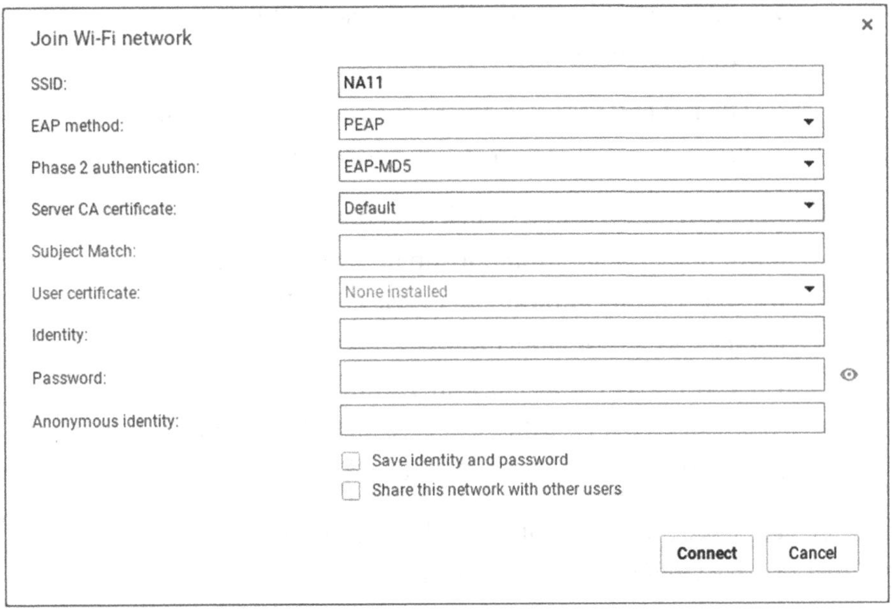

Figure 4-7. *Use the Advanced version of the Join Wi-Fi network dialog to set up a connection to a Wi-Fi network that uses stronger forms of authentication*

3. If you are connecting the Chromebook to a closed network or a network that is out of range, type the network's SSID in the SSID box. If you are connecting to an open network, Chrome OS already knows the network's name.

4. Click the EAP method pop-up menu and then click the appropriate Extensible Authentication Protocol (EAP) method:

    • **LEAP**: Choose this item to use Lightweight Extensible Authentication Protocol (LEAP). LEAP does not require digital certificates.

    • **PEAP**: Choose this item to use Protected Extensible Authentication Protocol (PEAP).

197

- **EAP-TLS**: Choose this item to use EAP Transport Level Security (EAP-TLS).

- **EAP-TTLS**: Choose this item to use EAP Tunneled Transport Level Security (EAP-TTLS).

5. For PEAP or EAP-TTLS, click the Phase 2 authentication method pop-up menu and then click the appropriate authentication type. For PEAP, the choices are Automatic, EAP-MD5, or MSCHAPv2. For EAP-TTLS, the choices are Automatic, EAP-MD5, MSCHAPv2, MSCHAP, PAP, or CHAP. LEAP and EAP-TTLS do not use this setting.

6. For PEAP, EAP-TLS, or EAP-TTLS, open the Server CA certificate pop-up menu and then click the server certificate. LEAP does not use this setting.

7. If the Subject match box is available, click it and then type the name of the server certificate. (The box is available if a cursor appears when you click the box.)

8. If the User certificate pop-up menu is available, click it and then then click the digital certificate for authenticating the user.

9. If the Identity box is available, click it and type the user identity.

10. If the Password box is available, click it and type the password for the identity.

11. If the Anonymous identity box is available, you can click it and type the identity to use for anonymous connections.

12. Check the "Save identity and password" check box if you want to save this identity and password for future usage. Normally, you would want to save the credentials unless you will use this Wi-Fi network only once.

13. Click the Connect button. The Join Wi-Fi network dialog box will close, and Chrome OS will attempt to establish the connection.

GIVING A CHROMEBOOK INTERNET ACCESS VIA A PHONE

Sometimes, you may need to use a smartphone to give one or more Chromebooks access to the Internet. For example, if you take a Chromebook home to get work done, and your Internet connection goes down, you could use the hotspot feature on your phone to get the Chromebook online.

In a pinch, you could use a phone hotspot to get several Chromebooks online at school; your phone's carrier controls how many devices can connect through the phone's hotspot, but most carriers allow between five and nine devices to customers who pay for the hotspot functionality. However, connecting a group of Chromebooks through your phone is probably one of the fastest ways of burning through your data plan.

To use your phone's hotspot, enable the hotspot functionality on the phone and then connect the Chromebook (or Chromebooks!) via Wi-Fi. Whereas Windows and MacOS support USB tethering, in which the smartphone provides Internet access to the PC or Mac at the other end of the USB cable, Chrome OS does not support tethering.

Configuring the Settings for a Wi-Fi Network Connection

After setting up a Wi-Fi network connection, you can configure it so that it behaves the way you want it to. The first subsection will show you how to open the settings for the Wi-Fi connection. The subsequent subsections will show you how to work with the following settings and groups of settings:

- Control whether the Chromebook prefers the network

- Control whether the Chromebook connects automatically to the network

- View the network connection details, such as the Chromebook's MAC address

---

Note   The MAC address is the hardware address of the Chromebook's Wi-Fi network interface. MAC stands for Media Access Control.

- Configure network settings manually

- Configure proxy settings for the connection

- View the list of networks to which the Chromebook has connected

Opening the Settings for a Wi-Fi Network Connection

To start configuring the settings for a Wi-Fi network connection, first open the settings for the connection. Follow these steps:

1. Click the Wi-Fi icon on the shelf to open the status menu.

2. Click the button for the current Wi-Fi network (if
    there is one) or the No network button. The Network
    status menu will open.

3. Click the Network Settings icon (the gear icon)
    in the upper-right corner of the Network status
    menu. The Settings screen will appear, showing the
    Network section at the top.

4. Click the Wi-Fi button (which shows the current
    network's name) to display the Wi-Fi screen (see
    Figure 4-8).

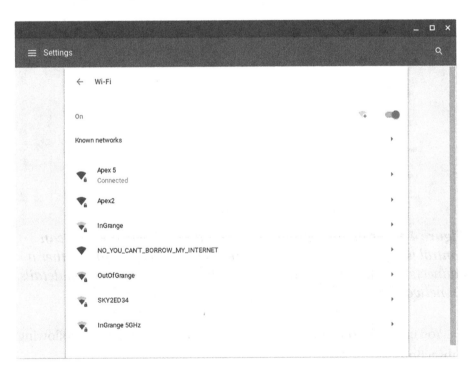

Figure 4-8. *On the Wi-Fi screen, click the Wi-Fi network you want to
configure*

5.   Click the right-pointing arrow on the button for the
     Wi-Fi network you want to configure. The Settings
     screen for that network will appear (see Figure 4-9,
     which shows the screen for the Wi-Fi network to
     which the Chromebook is currently connected).

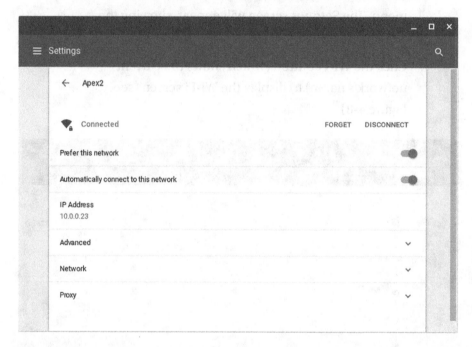

Figure 4-9. *From the Settings screen for a Wi-Fi network, you can
control whether the Chromebook prefers the network and whether it
connects to it automatically. You can also view the connection details,
set network information, and configure proxy settings.*

You can now configure the Wi-Fi network as explained in the following
subsections.

Note   If the Chromebook is currently connected to the Wi-Fi network whose Settings screen you are displaying, the Connected readout will appear below the network's name. You can click the Disconnect button to the right of the Connected readout to disconnect the Chromebook from the network.

Controlling Network Preference and Automatic Connection

Near the top of the Settings screen for a Wi-Fi network are two switches, as folllows:

- *Prefer this network*: Set this switch to On if you want the Chromebook to treat this network as a preferred network—a network to which the Chromebook will connect in preference to other networks that are not marked as preferred. You can set up multiple preferred networks on a Chromebook. We'll look at how to do this in the section "Working with the Chromebook's Known Networks" later in this chapter.

- *Automatically connect to this network*: Set this switch to On if you want the Chromebook to connect automatically to this network when it is within range of the network and is not connected to another Wi-Fi network.

Viewing Network Information

When the Chromebook is connected to the Wi-Fi network, the IP Address button shows the IP address, such as 192.168.1.155 or 10.0.0.55. The IP Address button does not appear for a Wi-Fi network to which the Chromebook is not connected.

To view other network information, click the Advanced button. The Advanced section will expand (see Figure 4-10), showing the following fields:

- *MAC address*: This readout shows the Media Access Control address (MAC address) for the Chromebook's wireless network adapter. The MAC address is an identifier burned into the device's hardware; the address is supposed to be unique, so that it identifies only a single device, but hackers can use software and hardware tools to make a device show a different MAC address. Changing the MAC address like this is called *spoofing*.

- *SSID*: This readout shows the SSID of the network—in lay terms, the network's name.

- *BSSID*: This readout shows the Basic SSID (BSSID) of the network. The BSSID is the MAC address of the wireless access point.

- *Security*: This readout shows the type of security used to secure the network, such as WPA-PSK.

- *Signal strength*: This readout shows the network's signal strength on a scale of 1 (weakest) to 100 (strongest).

- *Frequency*: This readout shows the frequency the network is using, such as 2412 or 5500. A frequency starting with 24 indicates that the network is using the 2.4 GHz band; a frequency starting with 5 indicates that the network is using the 5 GHz band.

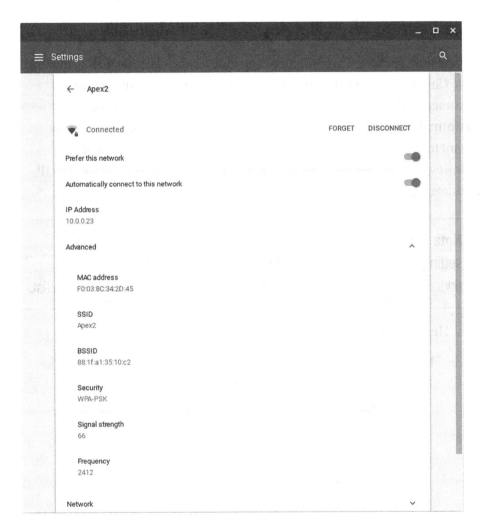

Figure 4-10. *The Advanced section of the Settings screen for a Wi-Fi network shows the MAC address, the network's SSID and BSSID, the security type, the signal strength, and the network's frequency*

Configuring Wi-Fi Network Settings Manually

By default, Chrome OS configures network settings automatically, making the Chromebook contact the network's Dynamic Host Configuration Protocol (DHCP) server to get an IP address and other network information. Assuming your school's network is using DHCP, you may want to stick with automatic configuration for most Chromebooks. However, if you need to ensure that some Chromebooks have specific IP addresses, you can assign them manually.

Note   If the only change you want to make to the Wi-Fi network settings is to use different name servers, leave the "Configure IP address" switch set to On and skip ahead to step 7 in the numbered list.

Here is how to configure Wi-Fi network settings manually:

1. After displaying the Settings screen for the appropriate Wi-Fi network, click the Network heading. The Network section will expand, showing several fields (see Figure 4-11).

Figure 4-11. *To configure network settings manually, expand the Network section of the Settings screen for the appropriate Wi-Fi network and then set the "Configure IP address automatically" switch to Off*

2. If the "Configure IP address automatically" switch is set to On, set it to Off. Further fields will appear (see Figure 4-12).

3. Click the "IP address" field and type the static IP address you want to assign to the Chromebook, such as 192.168.1.200 or 10.0.0.99.

4. Click the "Routing prefix" field and type the routing prefix (also called the *subnet mask*) for the network, such as 255.255.255.0.

5. Click the "Gateway" field and type the IP address at which the network gateway is located.

6. Click the "IPv6 address" field and type the IPv6 address, if the Chromebook needs one. Chrome OS automatically fills in this field with the IP address you set in the "IP address" field in step 3, and you do not need to change it unless the Chromebook needs an IPv6 address.

7. In the Name servers section, click the pop-up menu on the right and choose which name servers (DNS servers) the connection should use:

   • *Automatic name servers*: Select this item to use the name servers specified by the DHCP server.

   • *Google name servers*: Select this item to use Google's public name servers, 8.8.4.4 and 8.8.8.8.

   • *Custom name servers*: Select this item to specify the name servers yourself by typing their hostnames or IP addresses in the fields on the left. The upper field is for the primary name server, and the lower field is for the secondary name server.

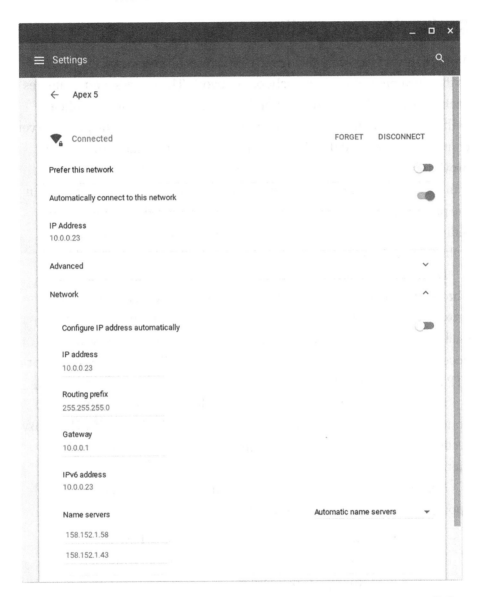

Figure 4-12. *After setting the "Configure IP address automatically" switch to Off, you can set the IP address, the routing prefix, the gateway, the IPv6 address, and the name servers*

Configuring Proxy Settings

A proxy server is a server that receives requests from network clients, such as the Chromebooks on your school's network. The proxy server evaluates each request and either fulfills it or denies it, depending on the policies with which it is configured. If the request is permitted, and the proxy server contains the required data in its cache, it returns the data from its cache, providing the client with data quickly and reducing the amount of data transferred across the Internet connection. If the request is permitted, but the proxy server's cache does not contain the required data, the server redirects the request to the appropriate destination (such as an Internet website) and then returns the resulting data to the client.

Depending on how your school's network is configured, the Chromebooks may automatically connect to the Internet through the proxy server. You can also configure proxy settings manually, which enables you to use different proxy servers for different protocols if necessary. For example, you might need to use a different proxy server for FTP than you use for HTTP.

If you need to configure proxy settings, click the Proxy heading at the bottom of the Settings screen for the appropriate Wi-Fi network. The Proxy section will expand, at first showing just the Connection Type pop-up menu.

Next, click the Connection Type pop-up menu and then click the appropriate item on it (see Figure 4-13):

- *Direct Internet connection*: Click this item to have the Chromebook connect directly to the Internet without going through a proxy server.

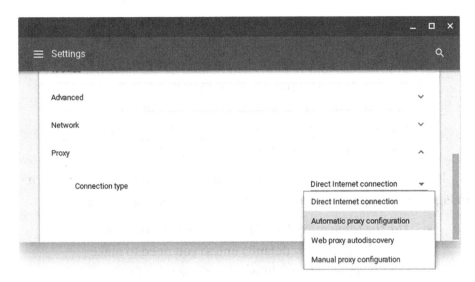

Figure 4-13. *In the Proxy section of the Settings screen for a Wi-Fi network connection, click the Connection type pop-up menu and then click the appropriate connection type*

- *Automatic proxy configuration*: Click this item to have the Chromebook automatically detect the network's proxy server and apply suitable proxy settings. In the "Autoconfiguration URL" field that appears, type or paste the URL at which the Chromebook should look for the proxy server.

- *Web proxy autodiscovery*: Click this item to have the Chromebook use the Web Proxy Auto-Discovery Protocol (WPAD for short) to detect and configure proxy settings. In the "Web Proxy Auto Discovery URL" field that appears, type or paste the URL at which the Chromebook will find the WPAD settings.

- *Manual proxy configuration*: Click this item if you want
  to enter the proxy settings manually, and then follow
  the instructions in the next bulleted item. Normally,
  you'd want to enter proxy settings manually only for
  Chromebooks that have special needs; for most of
  your school's Chromebooks, either automatic proxy
  configuration or Web Proxy Auto-Discovery is a better bet.

If you select the Manual proxy configuration item, the controls shown
in Figure 4-14 appear, and you can choose the following settings:

- *Use the same proxy for all protocols*: Leave this switch
  set to On (as it is by default) unless you need to make
  the Chromebook use different proxy servers for
  different protocols. To use different proxy servers, set
  this switch to Off and then enter the details of the proxy
  servers and ports on the HTTP Proxy row, the Secure
  HTTP Proxy row, the FTP Proxy row, and the SOCKS
  Host row (see Figure 4-15).

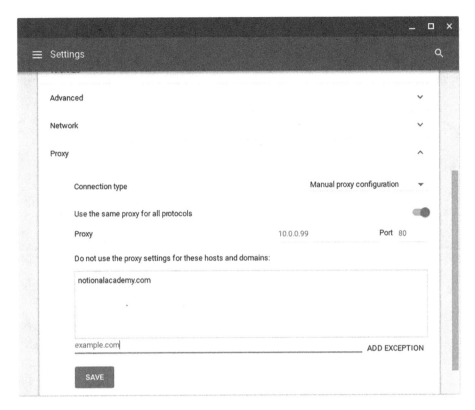

Figure 4-14. *After choosing the Manual proxy configuration item, you can set the proxy, specify the port, and add any proxy exceptions*

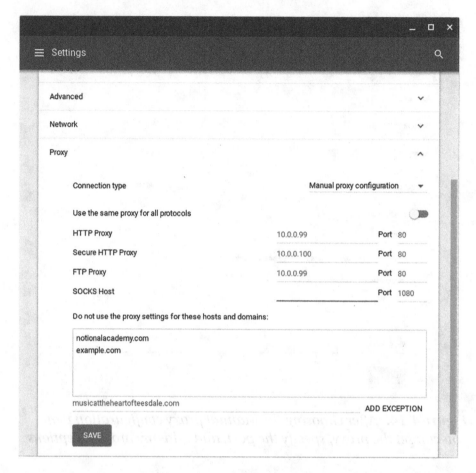

Figure 4-15. *To use different proxying for different protocols, set the "Use the same proxy for all protocols" switch to Off and then set the proxying details for the HTTP Proxy, Secure HTTP Proxy, FTP Proxy, and SOCKS Host rows*

- *Proxy*: Click this box and type the hostname or IP address of the proxy server.

- *Port*: Click this box and type the port for the proxy server.

- *Do not use the proxy settings for these hosts and domains*: In this box, create a list of any hosts or domains to which the Chromebook should connect directly rather than using the proxy service. Click the field to the left of the Add Exception button, type the hostname or domain name, and then click the Add Exception button to add it to the list.

When you finish specifying the details of the proxying, click the Save button to save the changes.

Working with the Chromebook's Known Networks

Chrome OS maintains a list of the Wi-Fi networks to which you have previously connected the Chromebook. These networks are called *known networks*; you can view them and work with them on the Known Networks screen.

To display the Known Networks screen, follow these steps:

1. Click the status area at the right end of the shelf to open the status menu.

2. Click the Settings icon to display the Settings window.

3. Click the right-arrow on the right side of the Wi-Fi button to display the Wi-Fi screen.

4. Click the Known networks button. The Known Networks screen will appear (see Figure 4-16).

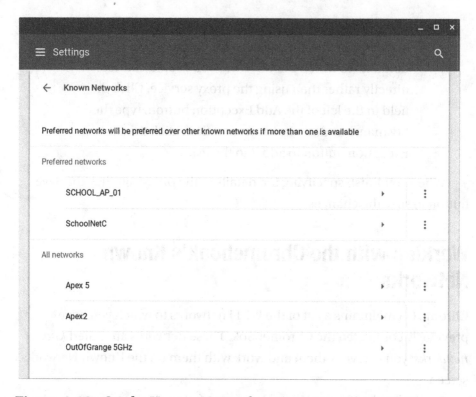

Figure 4-16. *On the Known Networks screen, you can set your preferred networks or forget networks you no longer want to use*

From the Known Networks screen, you can take the following actions:

- *Add a network to the Preferred networks list*: Click the network's More Actions button (the three vertical dots) in the All networks list and then click the Add to preferred item on the menu.

- *Remove a network from the Preferred networks list*: Click the network's More Actions button in the Preferred networks list and then click the Remove from preferred item on the menu.

- *Forget a network*: Click the network's More Actions button and then click the Forget item on the menu.

Note   As of this writing, you cannot set the order of the networks in the Preferred networks list.

Removing a Wi-Fi Network

When you no longer want a Chromebook to use a Wi-Fi network that's configured on it, you can remove the network by telling Chrome OS to forget the network.

To forget the network, go to the Wi-Fi screen in the Settings app. Next, go to the network's screen by clicking the right-arrow on the network's button. Then click the Forget button. Chrome OS will forget the network immediately with no confirmation.

Configuring People and Sync Settings

From the People section of the Settings window (see Figure 4-17), you can change the picture for the current user account. You can also configure sync for the current user account, set up a screen lock if one is needed, and start managing other people.

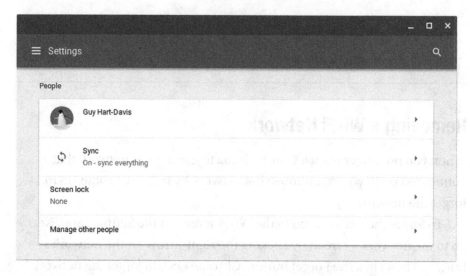

Figure 4-17. *From the People section of the Settings window, you can change the picture for the current account, configure sync settings, set up a screen lock, and start managing other people*

The following list explains the actions you can take:

- *Change the picture*: Click the current picture or username to display the Change picture screen; then click the picture you want to apply.

- *Configure sync settings*: Click the Sync button to display the Advanced sync settings screen (see Figure 4-18). You can then either set the "Sync everything" switch to On to sync all the items or set the individual switches for the following items to On or Off, as needed:

  - **Apps**: Set this switch to On to sync apps across devices running Chrome.

  - **Autofill**: Set this switch to On to sync Autofill data for forms.

- **Bookmarks**: Set this switch to On to sync bookmarks and bookmark folders.

- **Extensions**: Set this switch to On to sync Chrome extensions.

- **History**: Set this switch to On to sync the browsing history.

- **Passwords**: Set this switch to On to sync saved passwords for sites.

- **Settings**: Set this switch to On to sync Chrome settings.

- **Themes & Wallpapers**: Set this switch to On to sync the themes and wallpapers applied to the Chromebook.

- **Open Tabs**: Set this switch to On to sync the list of open tabs, enabling you to pick up browsing immediately on a different device running Chrome.

- **Credit cards and addresses using Google Payments**: Set this switch to On to sync credit card and address information you have saved.

- *Personalize Google services*: Click this button to open a Chrome window to the Activity Controls screen for your Google account. Here, you can set the "Web & App Activity" switch to On if you want to save your search activity or to Off if you do not. You can also check or uncheck the "Include Chrome browsing history and activity from websites and apps that use Google services" check box, as needed.

- *Manage synced data*: Click this button to open a
  Chrome window to the Data from Chrome sync screen
  for your Google account. Here, you can see how many
  of the synced items there are—how many apps, how
  many extensions, how many passwords, and so on. You
  can also click the Reset Sync button if you need to clear
  the data from the server; the data will remain on your
  devices, and you can sync it again if you so choose.

- *Encryption options*: In this area, select the "Encrypt
  synced passwords with your Google username and
  password" option if you want to encrypt just your
  passwords. Doing so provides a moderate level of
  security. For greater security, select the "Encrypt
  synced data with your own sync passphrase" option,
  type the passphrase in the "Password" field and the
  "Confirm Password" field, and then click the Save
  button.

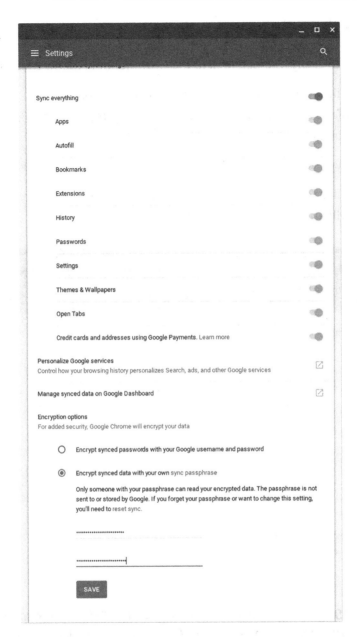

Figure 4-18. *On the Advanced sync settings screen, you can choose between syncing all items and syncing only specific items; visit pages for personalizing Google services and managing your synced data; and choose between different methods of encrypting your Chrome data*

Setting Up a Screen Lock

If you need to apply a screen lock to the Chromebook, follow these steps:

1. Click the Screen lock button in the People section of the Settings window. The Confirm your password dialog box will open.

2. Type your password in the "Password" field.

3. Click the Confirm button. The Screen lock screen will appear (see Figure 4-19).

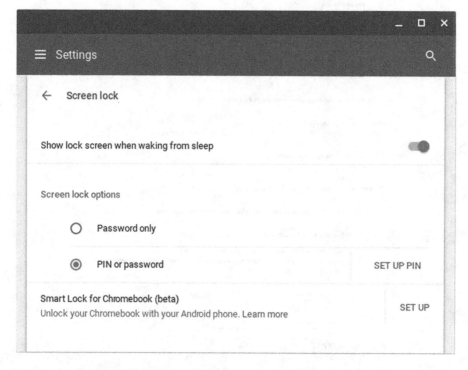

Figure 4-19. *On the Screen lock screen, set the "Show lock screen when waking from sleep" switch to On to protect the Chromebook during sleep and then choose between using only a password and using either a PIN or a password*

4. Set the "Show lock screen when waking from sleep"
    switch to On for greater security. When this switch is
    set to Off, anyone who wakes the Chromebook from
    sleep can start using it without having to provide the
    password or PIN.

5. In the Screen lock options area, select the "Password
    only" button or the "PIN or password" option. If
    you select the latter, click the Set Up PIN button,
    create the pin in the Enter your PIN dialog box that
    opens, and then click the Continue button. Re-enter
    the PIN in the Confirm your PIN dialog box, which
    opens next, and then click the Confirm button.

Note   Another option is to use your Android phone to unlock a
Chromebook. This feature looks promising but is in beta at this
writing. To explore this feature, click the Set Up button to the right of
the Smart Lock for Chromebook button on the Screen lock screen.

Managing Other People

To choose settings for other users and to control which of them can log in
to the Chromebook, click the Manage other people button in the People
section of the Settings window, and then work on the Manage other people
screen (see Figure 4-20).

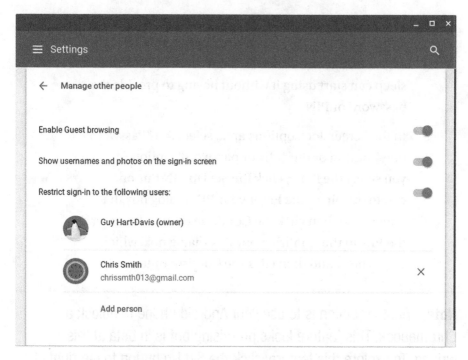

Figure 4-20. *On the Manage other people screen, you can enable or disable Guest browsing, control whether usernames and photos appear on the sign-in screen, and restrict sign-in to specific users*

Here, you can take the following actions:

- *Enable Guest browsing*: Set this switch to On to allow people to use the Guest account on the Chromebook. The Guest account enables the user to browse only, not to create files. Chrome OS wipes the Guest account clean when the guest user ends the session.

- *Enable supervised users*: If this switch appears, set it to On to enable supervised users. As the Chromebook's owner, you can monitor what supervised users do on the Chromebook.

- *Show usernames and photos on the sign-in screen*: Set this switch to On to have the sign-in screen show a list of usernames and photos, enabling users to start the sign-in process by clicking the appropriate username or photo. Set this switch to Off if you want the user to have to type in his or her username to log in. Setting this switch to Off is better for security, as it reduces the chance of an attacker's being able to guess a password from a username; you may also find it better for Chromebooks that are set up with more user accounts than fit easily on the sign-in screen.

- *Restrict sign-in to the following users*: If you need only some users to be able to sign in to the Chromebook, set this switch to On. You can then click the X (remove) button on the right of any existing user you want to remove from the list. To add a user, click the Add person button, type the user's email address in the Add person dialog, and then click the Add button.

Configuring Appearance Settings

From the Appearance section of the Settings window (see Figure 4-21), you can configure the following settings:

- *Wallpaper*: Click this button to launch the Wallpaper app (see Figure 4-22). You can then click the appropriate tab at the top—All, Landscape, Urban, Colors, Nature, or Custom—to display all the wallpapers or just a particular category. Once you find the wallpaper you want, click its thumbnail to apply it, and then click the Close (X) button to close the Wallpapers app.

225

Note   Here are three other things you should know about setting wallpaper. First, if you want to have Chrome OS select a wallpaper for you, check the "Surprise Me" check box in the lower-right corner of the Wallpapers window. Second, you can add your own photos to the Custom tab of the Wallpapers window by clicking the Add (+) button. And third, you can also set the wallpaper by right-clicking an image file in the Files app and then clicking the Set wallpaper item on the shortcut menu.

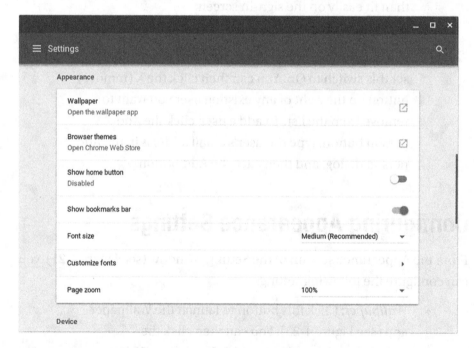

Figure 4-21. *From the Appearance section of the Settings window, you can change the wallpaper, apply browser themes, control the display of the home button and the bookmarks bar, customize the fonts, and set the page-zoom percentage*

Figure 4-22. *Use the Wallpapers app to apply one of the wallpapers built in to Chrome OS to the desktop. You can check the "Surprise Me" check box to have Chrome OS select a wallpaper. You can also add your own wallpapers using the controls on the Custom tab.*

- *Browser themes*: Click this button to open a Chrome tab to the Themes category in the Chrome Web Store, where you can browse the themes that are available. A *theme* is a coordinated look for the Chrome OS user interface.) Some themes are free, but others you must pay for.

- *Show home button*: Set this switch to On to make the Chrome browser display a Home button to the right of the Reload button on the toolbar. When you set this switch to On, two option buttons will appear below the "Show home button" line in the Appearance section. To make clicking the Home button display a new tab, select the "New Tab page" option. To make clicking the Home button display a specific web page, select the other option button (which has no name) and type the web page's URL in the text field.

- *Show bookmarks bar*: Set this switch to On if you want the Chrome browser to display the bookmarks bar. Set this switch to Off to hide the bookmarks bar.

- *Font size*: In this pop-up menu, select the font size for the Chrome browser to use: Very small, Small, Medium (Recommended), Large, or Very large.

- *Customize fonts*: Click this button to display the Customize fonts window (see Figure 4-23). Here, you can choose the following settings:

    - **Font size**: Drag the slider along the Tiny–Huge axis to set the standard font size.

    - **Minimum font size**: Drag the slider along the Tiny–Huge axis to set the minimum font size.

    - **Standard font**: In this pop-up menu, choose the standard display font.

    - **Serif font**: In this pop-up menu, choose the font for text marked to be displayed using a serif font. (*Serifs* are the little flick marks at the end of letters in fonts such as Times New Roman.)

- **Sans-serif font**: In this pop-up menu, choose the font for text marked to be displayed using a sans-serif font (one without serifs).

- **Fixed-width font**: In this pop-up menu, choose the font for text marked to be displayed in a fixed-width (monospace) font.

- **Advanced font settings**: If you need to be able to customize font settings for different scripts (for example, setting different fonts for Japanese or for Hebrew), click this button. Chrome OS will open a tab to the Advanced Font Settings extension in the Chrome Web Store. Click the Add to Chrome button to start adding the extension and then click the Add extension button in the Add "Advanced Font Settings"? dialog box that opens. After adding the extension, click the Advanced font settings button in the Customize fonts window. This will open a Chrome tab showing the controls for the Advanced Font Settings extension, which you can then use to customize the font settings on a per-script basis.

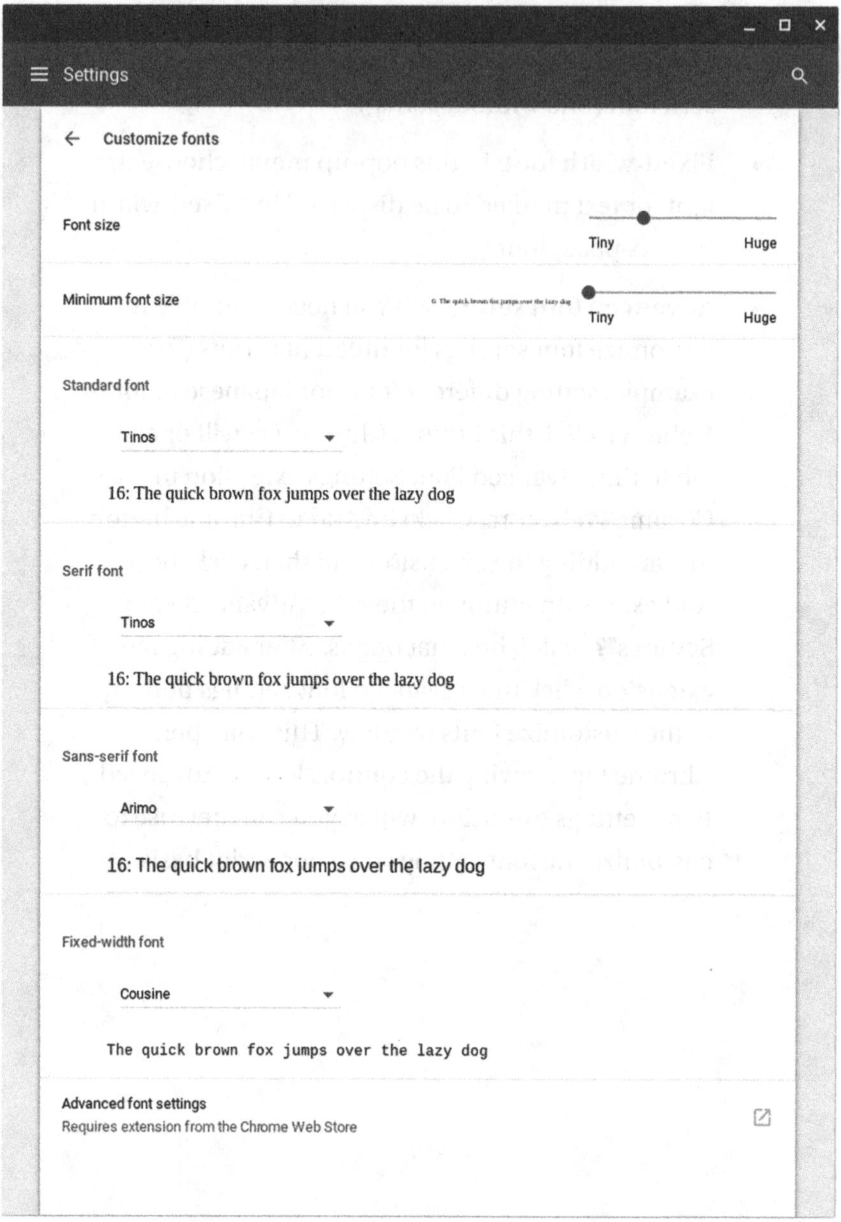

Figure 4-23. *The Customize fonts window enables you to set the default font size, the minimum font size, and the standard, serif, sans-serif, and fixed-width fonts*

- *Page zoom*: In this pop-up menu, choose the zoom percentage to apply to the screen. Your choices range from 25% to 500%; the default setting is 100%.

Note   Increasing the page zoom can be a big help in making text readable on small screens or high-resolution screens. The disadvantage, as you would expect, is that you can see less at once at a higher zoom percentage.

Configuring Device Settings

The Device section of the Settings window (see Figure 4-24) contains five buttons: Touchpad, Keyboard, Displays, Storage management, and Power. Clicking these buttons displays a screen for the corresponding category of settings: the Touchpad screen, the Keyboard screen, and so on.

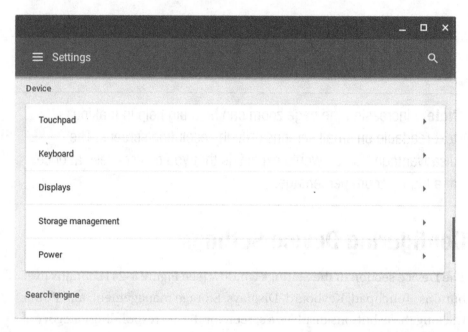

Figure 4-24. *Click the buttons in the Device section of the Settings window to display the corresponding screen of settings, such as the Touchpad screen*

Configuring Touchpad Settings

A Chromebook's touchpad enables you to take a wide variety of essential actions on a Chromebook, from selecting items to giving commands and switching among open windows. To get the best results from the touchpad, you may need to configure its settings.

To configure the touchpad, click the Touchpad button in the Device section of the Settings window. The Touchpad screen will appear (see Figure 4-25). You can then configure the following settings:

- *Enable tap-to-click*: Set this switch to On to let the user click by tapping the touchpad with one finger. Tap-to-click is usually useful, but some people find it makes the touchpad register clicks they don't intend. If the Chromebook's user has this problem, set the switch to Off.

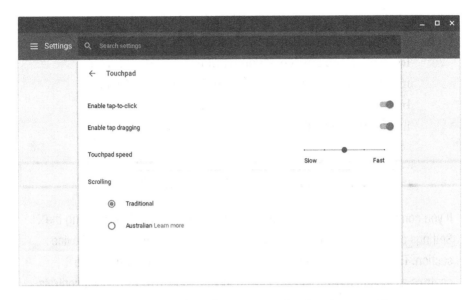

Figure 4-25. *On the Touchpad screen in the Settings app, you can enable the tap-to-click feature and the tap-dragging feature, set the touchpad speed, and choose between traditional scrolling and Australian scrolling*

- *Enable tap dragging*: Set this switch to On to let the user drag by tapping the touchpad and holding. If the Chromebook's user finds this feature unhelpful, set the switch to Off.

- *Touchpad speed*: Drag this slider left or right along the Slow–Fast scale to set the speed at which the pointer moves when a finger moves across the touchpad.

- *Scrolling*: In this area, select the "Traditional" option or the "Australian" option, as needed. With Traditional scrolling, you place two fingers on the touchpad and move them in the direction you want to scroll. For example, if you want to scroll down, you move your fingers downward. With Australian scrolling, you

233

place two fingers on the touchpad and move them in
the opposite direction from that in which you want
to scroll. For example, if you want to scroll down, you
move your fingers up. This sounds counterintuitive,
but because it is the way that many phones and tablets
implement scrolling, some users prefer it.

CHOOSING SETTINGS FOR A MOUSE

If you connect a mouse to a Chromebook, you can configure it by opening the
Settings app and then clicking the Mouse and touchpad button in the Device
section. The Mouse and touchpad screen will appear, showing the same
controls as in Figure 4-25, but also the Mouse section, which contains controls
for configuring the mouse.

For a standard mouse, the Mouse section contains these two controls:

- *Swap primary mouse button*: Set this switch to On to make
  the right mouse button the primary button instead of the left
  mouse button. Normally, you'd swap the primary mouse button
  for left-handed use.

- *Mouse speed*: Drag this slider along the Slow–Fast scale to set
  the speed at which the pointer moves when the user moves
  the mouse.

Depending on the type of mouse and the driver that Chrome OS has loaded for
it, the Mouse section may also contain other controls that you can configure.

Configuring Keyboard Settings

The keyboard's default settings work fine for many users, but other users will benefit from custom settings. Click the Keyboard button in the Device section of the Settings window to display the Keyboard screen (see Figure 4-26). You can then configure the following settings:

- *Search, Ctrl, Alt, Caps Lock, Escape, Backspace*: Use these six pop-up menus to set the functionality for the Search, Ctrl, Alt, Caps Lock, Escape, and Backspace keys. By default, each key is mapped to the command for its name, so the Search key invokes the Search function, the Ctrl key gives the Ctrl modification, and so on. You can map each key to any of the six commands—Search, Ctrl, Alt, Caps Lock, Escape, or Backspace—or to Disabled if you want the key to have no effect.

Note   The normal reason for remapping the keys is for users accustomed to a different keyboard layout. For example, because standard keyboards have a Caps Lock key where the Chrome OS keyboard has the Search key, you might want to map the Search key to give the Caps Lock command. If a user tends to press one of these keys unintentionally, you could set that key to Disabled to mitigate the problem.

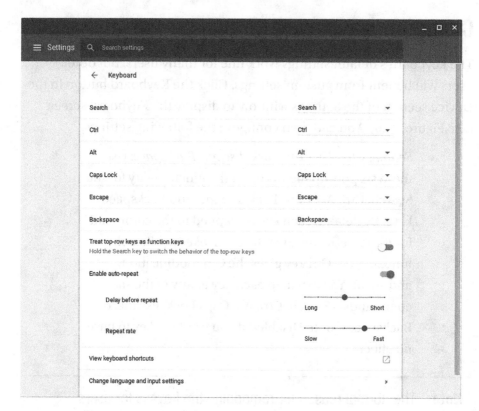

Figure 4-26. *The Keyboard screen in the Settings app enables you to configure individual keys, such as the Search key and the modifier keys, specify how to treat the top-row keys, and control automatic repetition*

- *Treat top-row keys as function keys*: Set this switch to On if you want to make the keys on the top row of the keyboard work as the function keys F1 through F12. This setting can be useful when you are using your Chromebook to access a remote system that uses function keys for commands. If you enable this feature, you can get the standard Chrome OS functionality back temporarily by holding down the Search key as you press the top-row keys.

- *Enable auto-repeat*: Set this switch to On if you want the keys on the keyboard to repeat when you hold them down. This feature is enabled by default and works well for many users, but if a user gets unintentional repetitions, you can either set the "Enable auto-repeat" switch to Off or adjust the Delay before repeat setting and the Repeat rate setting, as explained next.

Note   You can click the View Keyboard Shortcuts button on the Keyboard screen to display the on-screen map of keyboard shortcuts. The quick way to display this map is to press Ctrl+Alt+? (pressing Shift as needed to type the ? character).

- *Delay before repeat, Repeat rate*: Assuming the "Enable auto-repeat" switch is set to On, drag the Delay before repeat slider along the Long–Short scale to set the length of the delay before keys start repeating. Then drag the Repeat rate slider along the Slow–Fast scale to set how fast the keys repeat.

Note   If you want to configure language and input settings, you can click the Change language and input settings button on the Keyboard screen to go straight to them. We'll look at these settings in the section "Configuring Language and Input Settings" later in this chapter, which will also show you the more direct way to get to these settings.

Configuring Displays Settings

The Displays screen enables you to configure the Chromebook's built-in display or an external display you have connected. Click the Displays button in the Device section to show the Displays screen (see Figure 4-27). Here, you can configure the following settings:

- *Arrangement:* When you have connected an external display, drag the icons in this area to tell Chrome OS where the external display is positioned relative to the built-in display. When the icons are positioned correctly, the pointer should move logically from one screen to the other.

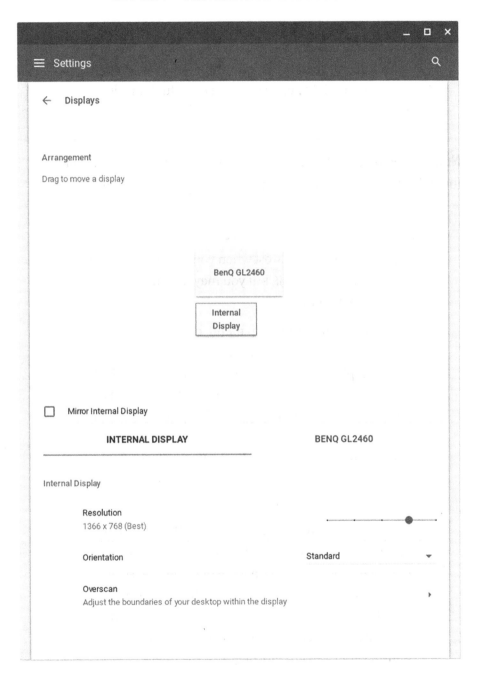

Figure 4-27. *The Displays screen lets you configure the Chromebook's internal display and any external display you have connected*

239

- *Mirror Internal Display:* When you have connected an external display, you can check this check box to make the external display show the same content as the internal display. Mirroring is useful for giving presentations.

Note   See the section "Connecting an External Display" in Chapter 3 for instructions on connecting and configuring an external display.

- *Resolution*: Drag this slider to set the resolution. The display should be clearest when you set the resolution that is marked "(Best)," but you may find another resolution easier to view.

- *Orientation*: In this pop-up menu, choose the orientation for the display: Standard, 90, 180, or 270. For example, if you have connected an external display in portrait orientation rather than landscape, apply the 90 setting or the 270 setting to make the content appear correctly. (Which setting you need depends on which way the monitor is rotated. Either 90 or 270 will be correct portrait orientation, whereas the other will be inverse portrait orientation.)

- *Overscan*: If the image does not reach the edges of the screen, leaving a black border, or if the image overlaps the edges, click this button to display the Overscan dialog box (see Figure 4-28). Press the arrow keys to shrink or expand the image, or hold down Shift and press the arrow keys to move the image. Click the OK button when you are satisfied with the image.

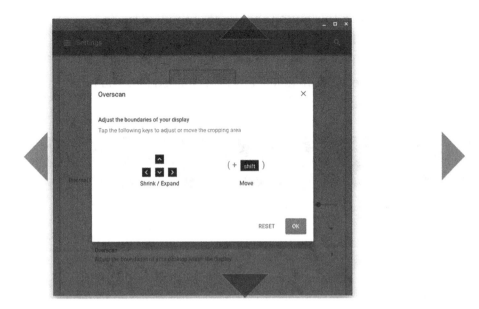

Figure 4-28. *Follow the instructions in the Overscan dialog box to enlarge, shrink, or reposition the image to fit the screen better*

Configuring Settings on the Storage Management Screen

The Storage management screen enables you to check how much of the Chromebook's storage is in use, how much is still available, and what categories of files are taking up space.

Click the Storage management button in the Device section of the Settings window to display the Storage management screen (see Figure 4-29), which contains the following controls:

- *Storage histogram*: The blue section shows how much space is in use; the gray section shows how much is still available.

241

- *Downloads*: This button shows the amount of space occupied by downloaded files. You can click this button to open a Files window showing the Downloads folder. From here, you can delete any downloaded files you no longer need.

Figure 4-29. *The Storage management screen shows how much of the Chromebook's storage is in use and how much is available. You can see how much space is taken up by different categories of files, such as offline files and other users' files.*

- *Offline files*: This button shows the amount of space being taken up by files you have selected for offline use. To delete all the offline files, click this button (or the Delete icon—the trash icon—at its right end) and then click the Delete Files button in the Delete offline files? dialog box that opens (see Figure 4-30).

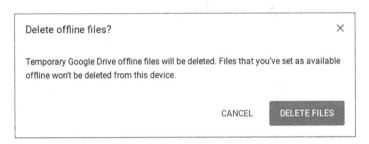

Figure 4-30. *Click the Delete Files button in the Delete offline files? dialog box to remove all your offline files from the Chromebook*

- *Browsing data*: This button shows the amount of space being occupied by data Chrome has gathered about your browsing. You can click this button to display the Clear browsing data dialog box, which enables you to clear some or all of this data. See the section "Clearing Browsing Data" later in this chapter for coverage of this topic.

- *Android storage*: This button, which appears only on Chromebooks that can run Android apps, shows how much storage space the Android subsystem is using for files. You can click this button to display the Internal shared storage screen in Android settings; see the section "Choosing Storage Preferences" later in this chapter for coverage of what this screen shows.

243

- *Other users*: This button shows how much space is being taken up by other users' files. You can click this button to display the Manage other people screen; see the section "Managing Other People" earlier in this chapter for coverage of this screen.

Configuring Power Settings

To view power status and configure power settings for a Chromebook, click the Power button in the Device section of the Settings window. The Power screen will appear (see Figure 4-31), providing the following controls:

- *Power source/Battery*: This readout shows "Power source: AC Adapter" when the Chromebook is getting power from its power supply. When the Chromebook is running on battery power, the readout shows "Battery" and the estimated runtime available, such as 12 hours and 52 minutes left.

- *When idle*: In this pop-up menu, choose what the Chromebook should do when it is left idle: Sleep, Turn off display, or Keep display on.

- *Sleep when lid is closed*: Set this switch to On if you want the Chromebook to go to sleep automatically when you close the lid. This is usually a good choice unless you are using an external keyboard, pointing device, and monitor, in which case you may want to run the Chromebook with the lid closed. (If you do this, make sure the Chromebook does not get too hot.)

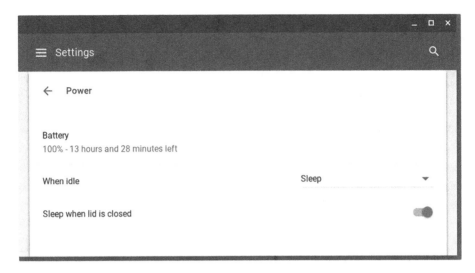

Figure 4-31. *The Power screen shows the power source—battery or AC power—and lets you choose what happens when the Chromebook is idle and when you close the lid*

Configuring Search Engine Settings

The Search engine section of the Settings window (see Figure 4-32) enables you to control which search engine Chrome OS uses. Click the "Search engine used in the address bar" pop-up menu and then click the search engine you want the address bar to use. Your choices vary depending on your location but may include Google, Yahoo!, Bing, Ask, and others.

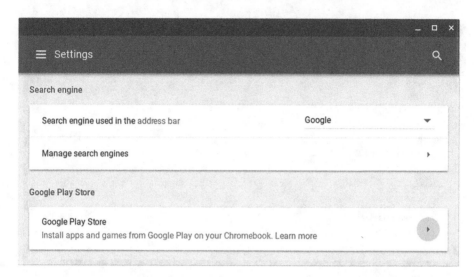

Figure 4-32. *In the Search engine section of the Settings window, you can configure the search engine used in the Chrome address bar*

If you want to edit the list of search engines that are available, click the Manage search engines button and then work on the Manage search engines screen (see Figure 4-33). Here, you can take the following actions:

- *Change the default search engine*: Click the More Actions button (the three vertical dots) on the right of the search engine's row and then click the Make default item on the menu.

- *Edit a search engine's URL*: Click the More Actions button on the right of the search engine's row, click the Edit item on the menu, make the changes in the Edit search engine dialog box, and then click the Save button.

- *Remove a search engine*: Click the More Actions button on the right of the search engine's row and then click the Remove from list item on the menu.

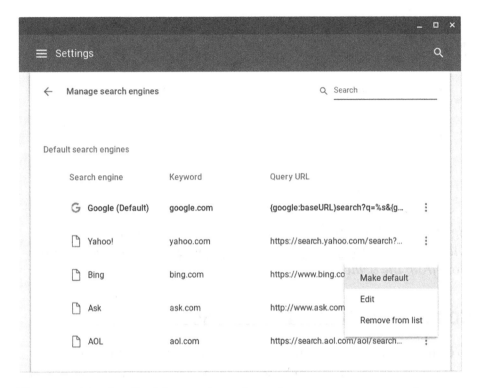

Figure 4-33. *On the Manage search engines screen, you can change your default search engine, edit a search engine entry, or remove a search engine entry from the list*

Configuring Google Play Store Settings

To control which apps and games the Chromebook can install from the Google Play Store, click the Google Play Store button in the Google Play Store section of the Settings window. The Google Play Store screen will appear (see Figure 4-34). From here, you can configure Android preferences or remove the Google Play Store from the Chromebook.

Note   The Google Play Store section of the Settings window appears only if the Chromebook supports Android apps.

247

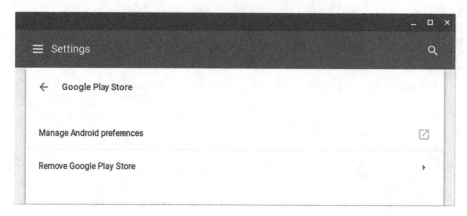

Figure 4-34. *From the Google Play Store screen, you can manage Android preferences for the Chromebook or remove the Google Play Store from the device*

Configuring Android Preferences

To configure settings for Android apps, click the Manage Android preferences button. The Settings screen for Android apps will then appear (see Figure 4-35). If you have used an Android phone or tablet in the last few years, you may feel at this point that you have fallen down the rabbit hole and ended up in an Android device—because what you will see is a selection of the settings categories found in the Settings app on a standard Android.

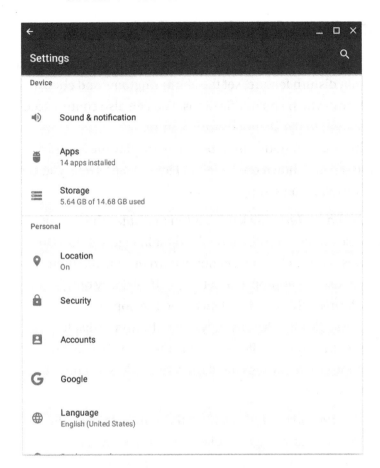

Figure 4-35. *The Settings screen for Android apps enables you to configure settings for any Android apps you install on the Chromebook*

Although this looks like a long list, it is only the settings that are relevant for running Android apps on a Chromebook.

The following subsections will explain the settings you can choose.

Choosing Sound & Notification Preferences

The sound and notification preferences enable you to configure settings for the Do not disturb feature, set the alarm ringtone, and choose when to receive which app notifications. You can also control access to notifications and to the Do not disturb feature.

Click the Sound & notification button to display the Sound & notification screen (shown on the left in Figure 4-36). Here, you can configure the following settings:

- *Do not disturb*: Click this button to display the Do not disturb screen (shown on the right in Figure 4-36). On this screen, click the Do not disturb button and then choose the appropriate setting—Off, Priority only, Alarms only, or Total silence—on the pop-up menu. Next, click the Priority only allows button to display the Priority only allows screen, and then choose the appropriate settings for alarms, reminders, events, and messages.

- *Default alarm ringtone*: Click this button to open the Default alarm ringtone dialog box. Click the "None" option or the option for the ringtone you want to use, and then click the OK button.

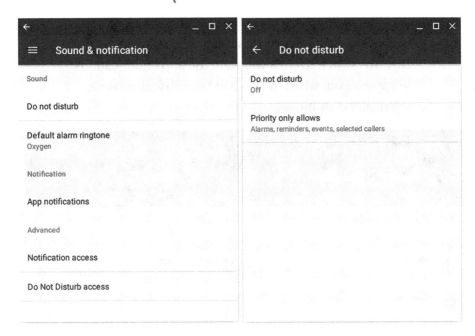

Figure 4-36. *The Sound & notification screen (left) lets you configure sounds, notifications, and access to notifications and the Do not disturb feature. The Do not disturb screen (right) allows you to control what notifications can disturb you and when.*

- *App notifications*: Click this button to display the App notifications screen (see the left screen in Figure 4-37). At first, this screen shows all the non-system apps installed on Android. You can display the system apps by clicking the More Actions button (the three vertical dots) and then clicking the Show system item on the menu. You can restrict the apps shown by clicking the Apps pop-up button (which shows All apps in the figure) and then clicking the Blocked item or Override Do Not Disturb item on the menu instead. Click an app's button to display the notifications screen for the app, such as the Notifications screen for the Clock app (see the right screen in Figure 4-37). You can then set

251

the "Block all" switch to On if you want to block all notifications for the app, or set the "Override Do Not Disturb" switch to On if you want the app's notifications to appear even when the Do Not Disturb feature is set to Priority Only mode.

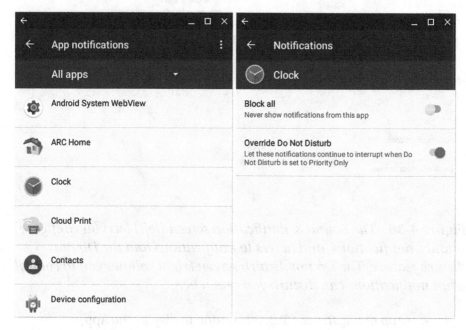

Figure 4-37. *Click an app on the App notifications screen (left) to display the Notifications screen for that app, such as the Notifications screen for the Clock app (right)*

- *Notification access*: Click this button to display the Notification access screen, which shows you the installed apps that have requested access to notifications.

- *Do Not Disturb access*: Click this button to display the Do Not Disturb access screen, which shows you the installed apps that have requested access to the Do Not Disturb feature.

Choosing App Preferences

The app preferences enable you to view the list of Android apps installed on the Chromebook. You can also force apps to stop, disable some apps, and configure settings for most apps.

Click the Apps button to display the Apps screen (shown on the left in Figure 4-38). At first, this screen lists only the non-system apps; if you want to see the system apps as well, click the More Actions button (the three vertical dots) and then click the Show system item on the menu.

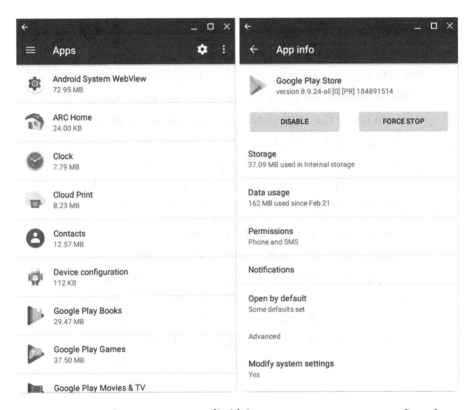

Figure 4-38. *The Apps screen (left) lists non-system apps at first, but you can add system apps by clicking More Actions and then Show system. Click an app to display its App info screen (right).*

You can click an app to display its App info screen (see the right screen in Figure 4-38). From this screen, you can take various actions, of which the following are normally the most useful:

- *Disable the app*: Click the Disable button. You would do this for an app that should not be running. For various system apps, the Disable button is itself disabled.

- *Force the app to stop*: Click the Force Stop button. You would do this for an app that you were not able to close normally.

- *View the app's use of storage*: Look at the Storage readout on the App info screen. For more detail, click the Storage button to display the Storage screen, which shows how much space the app itself occupies, how much space the app's data takes up, and how much cached data the app currently has. On the Storage screen, you can click the Manage Data button to display a Storage screen for managing the app's data, or click the Clear Cache button to clear the cached data.

- *View the app's data usage*: Look at the Data usage readout on the App info screen to see how much data the app has transferred. Data usage is a hot-button issue on Android phones and tablets that have cellular connections, but it is usually less important on a Chromebook unless it is a cellular model or is using metered Wi-Fi connections. If you want to dig into

the app's data usage, click this button to show the
App data usage screen for the app. Here, you can see
how much data the app transferred when it was in the
foreground (when it was the active window, in Chrome
OS terms) compared to when it was in the background
(when it was not the active window). You can set the
"Background data" switch to Off to prevent the app
from using cellular data when in the background,
and you can set the "Unrestricted data usage" switch
to On to allow the app unrestricted data usage when
Android's Data Saver feature is turned on; these
features, too, are usually not relevant to Chromebooks.

- *View and change the app's permissions*: Look at the
  Permissions readout on the App info screen to see what
  permissions the app has. To change the permissions,
  click the Permissions button and then set the switches
  on the App permissions screen (shown on the left in
  Figure 4-39). You can see that these permissions are
  designed for Android phones and tablets rather than
  Chromebooks, which typically lack body sensors,
  phone functionality, and SMS messaging.

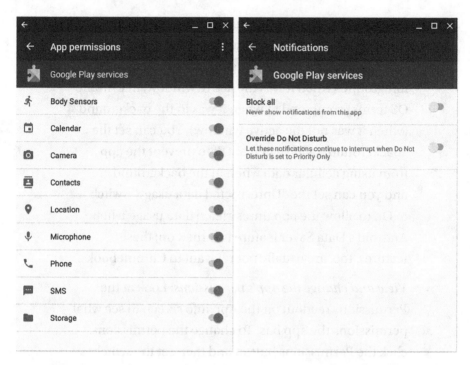

Figure 4-39. *On the App permissions screen (left), set the switches to Off or On to control which features the app can use. On the Notifications screen (right), you can block all notifications from the app or allow it to override Priority Only mode in Do Not Disturb.*

- *Configure notifications settings*: Click the Notifications button to display the Notifications screen for the app (shown on the right in Figure 4-39). Here, you can set the "Block all" switch to On if you want to block all notifications from the app. You can also set the "Override Do Not Disturb" switch to On if you want the app's notifications to appear even when the Do Not Disturb feature is set to Priority Only mode.

- *View and configure open-by-default settings*: Look at the Open by default button to see what items (if any) the app is set to open by default. To change the settings, click the Open by default button to display the Open by default screen, where you can click the Open supported links button and then click the appropriate item—Open in this app, Ask every time, or Don't open in this app—on the pop-up menu.

Choosing Storage Preferences

The storage preferences let you see how much space Android is occupying on the Chromebook. Click the Storage button in the Settings window to display the Internal shared storage screen (shown on the left in Figure 4-39), which shows the total amount of space occupied at the top and, below that, a breakdown of how much space each category of files occupies: Apps, Images, Videos, Audio, System, Other, and Cached data.

You can click one of the buttons to see more details. For example, click the Apps button to display the Apps storage screen (shown on the right in Figure 4-40), which displays details about each app.

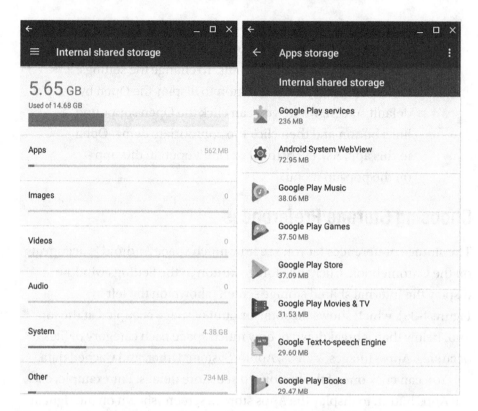

Figure 4-40. *The Internal shared storage screen (left) shows how much space Android is taking up on the Chromebook. Click a button to display a screen containing more information on a category, such as the Apps storage screen (right).*

Choosing Location Preferences

The location preferences enable you to control whether the Chromebook shares its location with Google. You can see which apps have recently requested location information, configure the location history, and check whether Google Location Sharing is on.

Click the Location button in the Settings window to display the Location screen (shown on the left in Figure 4-41). Here, you can set the master switch at the top to On if you want to let Android apps use location services or to Off to disallow their use.

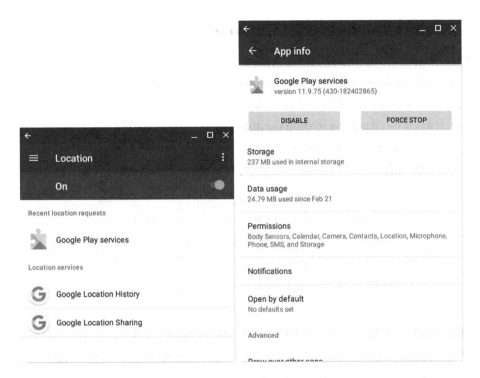

Figure 4-41. *On the Location screen (left), set the master switch at the top to On or Off to enable or disable use of location services. Click an app in the Recent location requests list to display the App info screen for the app (right).*

The Recent location requests list shows the apps that have requested location information recently. You can click an app here to display the App info screen for the app, such as the App info screen for Google Play services, shown on the right in Figure 4-41. From the App info screen, you can take various actions; see the section "Choosing App Preferences" earlier in this chapter for details.

Configuring Security Preferences

The security preferences enable you to permit the installation of Android apps from unknown sources, view information about the storage of digital credentials and install digital certificates to the Chromebook, and see which apps have access to data on app usage.

Click the Security button to display the Security screen (shown on the left in Figure 4-42). Here, you can take the following actions:

- *Allow the installation of apps from unknown sources*: First, enable Developer Mode in Chrome OS. You can then set the "Unknown sources" switch to On to allow the Android subsystem to install apps from sources other than the Google Play Store.

Caution   Installing apps from unknown sources is not safe unless the app is one that you or your school have developed and that you can be certain does not contain malevolent code.

- *View credential information*: The Storage type readout shows how the credentials are stored, such as "Hardware-backed"(secured by the device's security hardware). You can click the Trusted credentials button to display the Trusted credentials screen (shown on the right in Figure 4-42), whose two tabs—the System tab and the User tab—list the trusted certificates. You can set a certificate's switch to Off to stop using that certificate; you would do this if you learned that a certificate had been compromised. You can click the User credentials button to display the User credentials screen, which shows any user credentials installed (there may not be any).

260

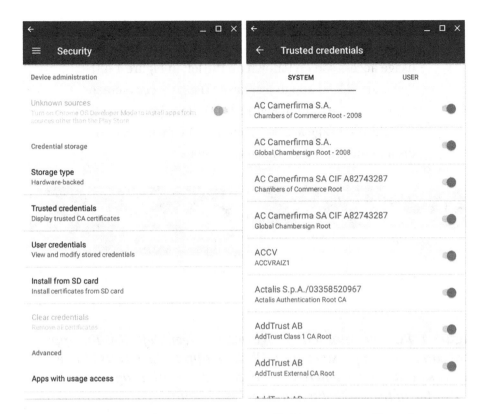

Figure 4-42. *From the Security screen (left), you can allow the installation of apps from unknown sources, view credential information, install digital certificates, and see which apps can access app-usage data. On the Trusted credentials screen (right), you can view system and user certificates and disable any compromised certificate.*

- *Install a digital certificate*: You can click the Install from SD card button to start installing a digital certificate from a file, either literally from an SD card or (more usually) from another location that you specify, such as the Downloads folder.

- *See which apps can view app-usage data*: Click the
  Apps with usage access button to display the Apps with
  usage access screen (shown on the left in Figure 4-43).
  You can click an app to display its Usage access screen
  (shown on the right in Figure 4-43). Here, you can set
  the "Permit usage access" switch to Off if you need to
  disable the app's access to usage data.

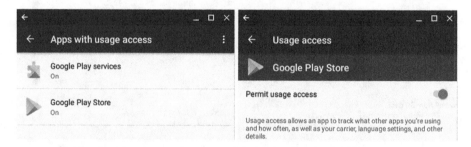

Figure 4-43. *The Apps with usage access screen (left) lists the apps
that can access app-usage data. Click an app to display its Usage
access screen (right), where you can set the "Permit usage access"
switch to Off to disable the app's access to app-usage data.*

Configuring Accounts Preferences

The Accounts screen (shown on the left in Figure 4-44) lists the accounts
that are set up for Android to use. At first, you may find that the only entry
is the Google account under which you are logged in to the Chromebook
and whose account data the Android subsystem picks up from Chrome
OS. To verify that the account is syncing data, click the More Actions
button (the three vertical dots) and make sure that the "Auto-sync data"
check box on the menu is checked.

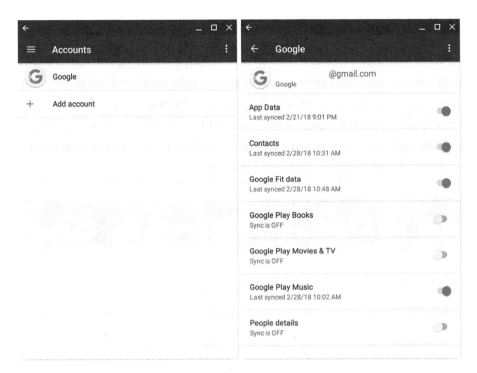

Figure 4-44. *The Accounts screen (left) shows the accounts set up for use by Android apps. Click an account to display the details screen (right), where you can choose which items to sync.*

To view an account's details or choose which items to sync, click the account's button. On the details screen that appears, such as the Google screen shown on the right in Figure 4-44, set the switches to On or Off to specify which items to sync.

Note   Any accounts you add on the Accounts screen in Android settings are for the Android subsystem to use, not for Chrome OS as a whole to use.

To add an account, click the Add account button and then follow the prompts.

Configuring Google Preferences

The Google screen (Figure 4-45 shows its upper part on the left and its lower part on the right) gives you access to a wide range of settings for your Google account. Some of these settings are Android specific, which may mean that the Android subsystem on the Chromebook is the best place to set them. Other settings are not related to Android, so there is no particular reason to set them via the Android subsystem.

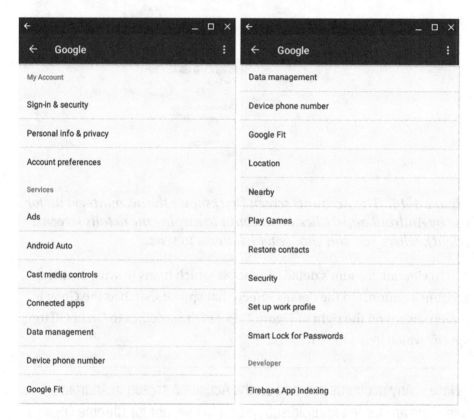

Figure 4-45. *From the Google screen (left and right), you can configure many settings for your Google account*

The My Account section of the Google screen contains these three buttons:

- *Sign-in & security*: Click this button to display the Sign-in & security screen, on which you can run a security checkup, change your password, configure two-step verification, set your recovery phone number and email address, and choose other security settings.

- *Personal info & privacy*: Click this button to display the Personal info & privacy screen, on which you can run a privacy checkup, edit your personal information, change your photo, and manage other related settings, such as settings for location sharing and search.

- *Account preferences*: Click this button to display the Account preferences screen, where you can review your purchase history, manage your purchase methods and subscriptions, set the language, and review your Google Drive storage. You can also delete individual Google services from your account or delete your Google account and all its data.

The Services section of the Google screen contains the following buttons:

- *Ads*: Click this button to display the Ads screen, on which you can learn your advertising ID, reset your advertising ID, and opt out of the Ads Personalization feature.

- *Android Auto*: Click this button to display the Android Auto screen, which lets you find out about the Android Auto app (which offers navigation help, media playback, messaging, and voice control) and download the app. As helpful as Android Auto can be, you probably will not want to install it on a Chromebook.

- *Cast media controls*: Click this button to display the Cast media controls screen, on which you can set the "Media controls for Cast devices" switch to On if you want the Android subsystem to display notifications that you can use to control playback to Chromecast devices and similar devices. These notifications are helpful on Android devices but less so on Chromebooks.

- *Connected apps*: Click this button to display the Connected apps screen, which shows a list of the apps and devices that are connected to your Google account. The list includes Chrome OS apps as well as Android apps.

- *Data management*: Click this button to display the Data management screen. Here, you can click the Update Drive-enabled app files button to choose how to update files: Over Wi-Fi or Cellular, or Over Wi-Fi only. Unless the Chromebook has a cellular connection, choose Over Wi-Fi only.

- *Device phone number*: Click this button to display the Device phone number screen. For Android phones, this screen displays the device's phone number. For Chromebooks, it does not.

- *Google Fit*: Click this button to display the Google Fit screen, which lets you view the apps and devices that are connected to Google Fit, manage your data sources, and delete your Google Fit history. While you *can* take these actions on a Chromebook, it is usually more helpful to take them on an Android phone that can provide Google Fit input.

- *Location*: Click this button to display the Location screen, on which you can configure Location settings. See the section "Choosing Location Preferences" earlier in this chapter for coverage of the Location screen.

- *Nearby*: Click this button to display the Nearby screen, on which you can set the "Notify you when links are available" switch to On if you want Android to show you information about apps and websites near your current location.

- *Play Games*: Click this button to display the Settings screen for Google Play Games. Here, you can configure settings for games, such as toggling your gamer profile between being hidden and being public, signing in automatically to games, and vibrating to announce notifications.

- *Restore contacts*: Click this button to display the Restore contacts screen, which provides controls for restoring contacts from your Google account to your device.

- *Security*: Click this button to display the Security screen. Here, you can click the Security code button to display your ten-digit security codes for signing in to your Google account when you have forgotten your password; click the Find My Device button to learn about ways to locate missing Android devices; and click the Google Play Protect button to control whether the Google Play Protect feature scans your device for security threats (usually a good idea).

- *Set up work profile*: Click this button to display the Set up work profile screen, which is your starting point for setting up a work profile on Android, installing the Android Device Policy app so that administrators can remotely manage your device. You would not normally want to set up a work profile on a Chromebook.

- *Smart Lock for Passwords*: Click this button to display the Smart Lock for Passwords screen. Here, you can set the "Smart Lock for Passwords" switch to On to have Android offer to save passwords to your Google account. You can also set the "Auto-sign in" switch to On to have Android apps automatically sign in to apps and websites that you have connected to your Google account. You can use the controls in the Saved passwords section and the Never save section to control which apps are allowed to save passwords.

The Developer section of the Google screen contains only the Firebase App Indexing button, which you can click to display the Applications screen. Here, you can set the "Capture Actions and Errors" switch to On to capture recent user actions and errors that have occurred. You would seldom need to use this setting on a Chromebook.

Configuring Language Preferences

The Language screen (shown on the left in Figure 4-46) gives you access to your personal dictionary, which contains your list of custom words and text shortcuts. A custom word is a word you add to prevent the Android spelling checker from querying an apparent misspelling. A text shortcut is a text sequence that Android automatically changes to the matching replacement string, which is usually longer or more complex; for example, you might create a text shortcut of vpr that expands to Vice Principal.

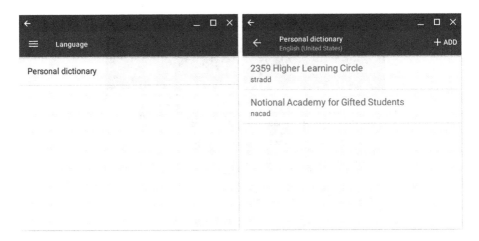

Figure 4-46. *On the Language screen (left), click the Personal dictionary button to display the Personal dictionary screen (right). Here, you can click the Add button to add a custom word or text shortcut.*

Click the Personal dictionary button on the Language screen to display the Personal dictionary screen (shown on the right in Figure 4-46). Here, you can click the Add button to display a screen on which you can create a new custom word or shortcut. To modify or delete an existing custom word or shortcut, click the button for that item.

Configuring Back Up My Data Preferences

Click the Back up my data button on the Settings screen to display the Back up my data screen (see Figure 4-47), which lets you enable or disable the automatic backup of your Google Play app data to Google Drive. Normally, you would want to set the "Back up my data" switch to On to make the Android subsystem back up data on each app you install from Google Play so that you can easily restore the app on another Chromebook if necessary.

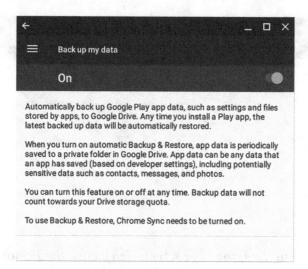

Figure 4-47. *Set the master switch on the Back up my data screen to On to have the Android subsystem back up your Google Play app data to Google Drive*

Note   Chrome Sync must be turned on for automatic backup to work.

Configuring Accessibility Preferences for Android

To configure accessibility preferences for Android, click the Accessibility button in the Settings window and then work on the Accessibility screen (shown on the left in Figure 4-48). This screen has two sections: Services and System. The Services section shows any accessibility services that have been installed; you may well find no services are listed. The System section enables you to configure the following four accessibility settings:

- *Captions*: Click this button to display the Captions screen (shown on the right in Figure 4-48). Set the master switch to On to enable captions. You can then click the Language button to open the Language dialog

box, in which you choose the caption language, and
click the Text size button to open the Text size dialog
box, in which you specify the text size (your options are
Very small, Small, Normal, Large, and Very large).

- *Display size*: Click this button to show the Display size
  screen, which enables you to change the size of items
  on the screen.

- *High contrast text*: Set this switch to On to increase the
  contrast of text.

- *Touch & hold delay*: Click this button to open the Touch
  & hold delay dialog box, in which you can set the delay
  for a touch-and-hold operation by tapping the "Short,"
  "Medium," or "Long" option buttons.

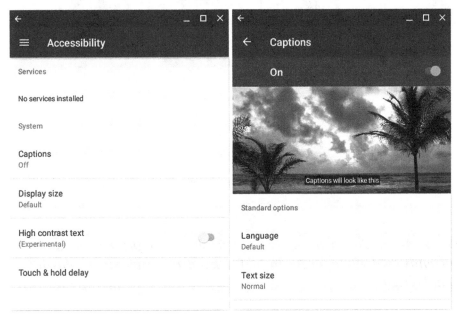

Figure 4-48. *The Accessibility screen (left) shows the accessibility
services and system settings available. Use the Captions screen (right)
to configure captions on Android apps.*

Configuring Printing Preferences

To configure printing preferences for Android, click the Printing button in the Settings window and then work on the Printing screen (shown on the left in Figure 4-49). Here, the Print services list shows the print services Android is set up to use. You can click a print service to display its details screen, such as the Cloud Print screen shown on the right in Figure 4-49, where you can enable or disable the service by moving its master switch to On or Off.

To add a print service to Android, click the Add service button. A window will open showing the print service plugins available on Google Play. You can then browse the print services and install the appropriate one for the printer you want to use.

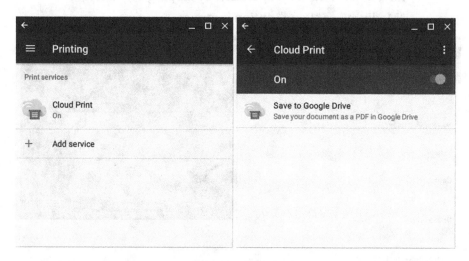

Figure 4-49. *The Printing screen (left) shows the print services currently configured for Android. Click a print service to display its details (right).*

Viewing About Device Preferences

To see the details about the Android subsystem, click the Device status button and then look at the four readouts on the Device status screen (shown on the left in Figure 4-50): Android version, Android security patch level, Kernel version, and Build number.

The Device status screen also contains the Legal information button, which you can click to display the Legal information screen (shown on the right in Figure 4-50). Here, you can click the Open source licenses button to display information about the open source licenses Android uses, or click the System WebView licenses button to display the credits for the System WebView components.

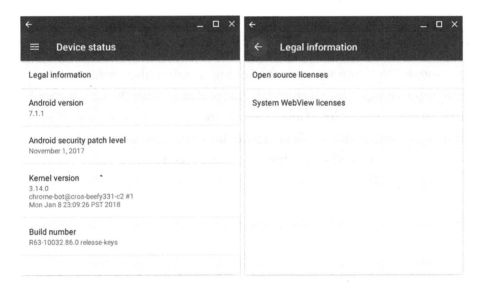

Figure 4-50. *The Device status screen (left) shows the Android version, Android security patch level, the kernel version, and the build number. Click the Legal information button to display the Legal information screen (right), from which you can examine the open source licenses and the System WebView licenses.*

DISPLAYING THE ANDROID DEVELOPER OPTIONS

The Settings app in Android includes a Developer Options section that is hidden by default because Google feels that most users are better off not using the settings intended for app developers. You can display the Developer Options section by clicking the Build number readout on the Device status screen six times. When the message "You are now a developer!" appears, click the Back button in the upper-left corner of the screen, and you will find the Developer options button has appeared above the About Device button in the Settings window.

Removing the Google Play Store

The Google Play Store screen in the Settings window also enables you to remove the Google Play Store and all Android apps from the Chromebook. To do so, click the Remove Google Play Store button on the Google Play Store screen and then click the Remove Android Apps button in the Remove Android apps? dialog box that opens (see Figure 4-51).

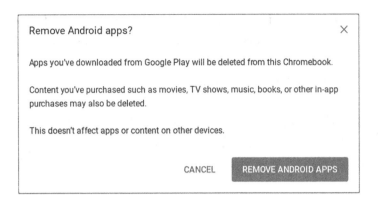

Figure 4-51. *Click the Remove Android Apps button in the Remove Android apps? dialog box if you want to remove the Google Play Store and all Android apps from the Chromebook.*

Configuring Startup Settings

In the On startup section of the Settings window for Chrome OS (see Figure 4-52), you can select one of the following three option buttons:

- *Open the New Tab page*: Select this option button to have Chrome display the New Tab page.

- *Continue where you left off*: Select this option button to have Chrome reload the pages you were using last. This can be a good way to resume what you were doing.

- *Open a specific page or set of pages*: Select this option button to have Chrome load the page or pages you specify. You can then click the Use current pages button to display a list of the pages you currently have open; you can remove a page from the list by clicking the More Actions button (the three vertical dots) and then clicking the Remove item on the menu that opens, or edit the address by clicking the More Actions button and then clicking the Edit item on the menu. To add a page, click the Add a new page button, type the URL in the "Site URL" field in the Add a new page dialog box, and then click the Add button.

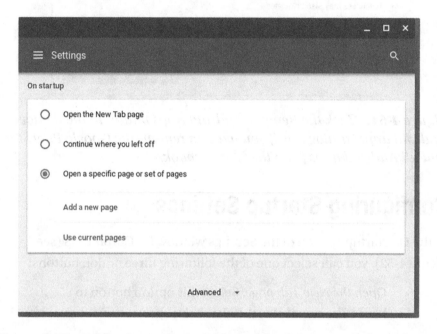

Figure 4-52. *In the On startup section of the Settings window, choose which pages you want the Chromebook to display when you log in.*

Configuring Date and Time Settings

Chrome OS can set the date and time automatically, but you can also set them manually if you prefer. You can also choose whether to set the time zone automatically and whether to use the 24-hour clock.

In the Date and time section of the Settings window (see Figure 4-53), you can configure the following settings:

- *Set time zone automatically using your location*: Set this switch to On to have Chrome OS detect your location and set the time zone accordingly. To set the time zone manually, set this switch to Off, click the pop-up menu, and then click the appropriate time zone.

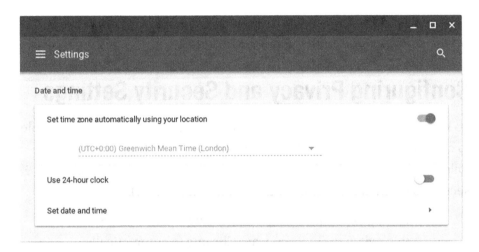

Figure 4-53. *In the Date and time section of the Settings window, you can choose between setting the time zone automatically and setting it manually. You can also use the 24-hour clock and set the date and time.*

- *Use 24-hour clock*: Set this switch to On to make Chrome display the time in 24-hour format, such as 13:18 instead of 1:18.

- *Set date and time*: To set the date and time, click this button, adjust the date and time as needed in the Check your system time dialog box (see Figure 4-54), and then click the Done button.

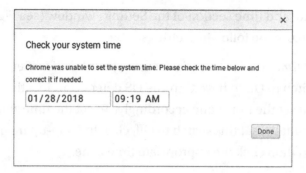

Figure 4-54. *The Check your system time dialog box enables you to set the Chromebook's date and time manually*

Configuring Privacy and Security Settings

To keep the Chromebook secure and to protect your privacy, it is advisable to configure the security and privacy settings that Chrome OS offers. The following list explains the settings you can configure in the Privacy and security section of the Settings window (see Figure 4-55):

- *Use a web service to help resolve navigation errors*: Set this switch to On if you want Chrome to automatically provide suggestions when the browser is unable to connect to a web page. Chrome sends the web address to Google, which returns the suggestions for correcting the address or accessing similar addresses. Set this switch to Off if sharing browsing data with Google like this is a privacy concern.

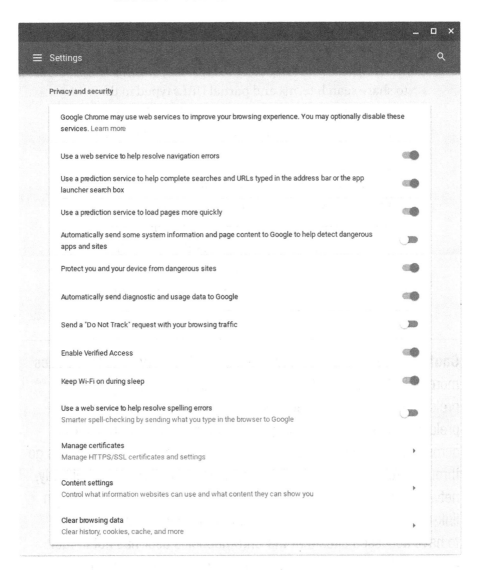

Figure 4-55. *The Privacy and security section of the Settings window includes settings for protecting the Chromebook and its user from dangerous websites, for managing certificates and customizing content settings, and for clearing browsing data*

- *Use a prediction service to help complete searches and URLs typed in the address bar or the app launcher search box*: Set this switch to On to allow Chrome OS to share search terms and partial URLs typed in the Chrome omnibox or in the app launcher with your search engine in order to provide search results or to complete the URLs.

- *Use a prediction service to load pages more quickly*: Set this switch to On to speed up browsing by preloading information on linked web pages. With this feature enabled, Chrome looks up the IP addresses of the web pages linked to the current page and preloads data from those pages so it can display a page more quickly when the page's link is clicked.

Caution   Be careful with the Use a prediction service to load pages more quickly setting. While this setting can speed up browsing, preloading data from linked web pages has two downsides. First, preloading linked pages increases the amount of data transferred across the Internet connection; even if your school's Chromebooks go through proxy servers rather than connecting to the Internet directly, network performance may take a hit from preloading, especially on link-heavy pages. Second, preloading may make Chrome appear to have accessed sites that the Chromebook's user has not in fact accessed. For example, preloading may cause Chrome to store cookies from sites whose pages are linked to a page that was actually visited.

- *Automatically send some system information and page content to Google to help detect dangerous apps and sites*: Set this switch to On to allow Chrome OS to share system information and web-page content with Google when the OS detects a dangerous app or a dangerous website.

- *Protect you and your device from dangerous sites*: Set this switch to On to have Chrome check the websites you visit against a list of known bad sites. Chrome displays a warning when you go to access a site that may be harmful.

- *Automatically send diagnostic and usage data to Google*: Set this switch to On to have Chrome OS automatically send data about the Chromebook's usage and about diagnosed errors to Google.

- *Send a "Do Not Track" request with your browsing traffic*: Set this switch to On to have the Chrome browser request that websites not track your browsing. Many websites do not honor Do Not Track requests.

- *Enable Verified Access*: Set this switch to On to enable the Verified Access security feature. Verified Access enables network devices, such as your school's Wi-Fi access points and servers on the Internet, to obtain a cryptographic guarantee of the identity of the Chromebook and its user.

- *Keep Wi-Fi on during sleep*: Set this switch to On to allow Chrome OS to use the Wi-Fi even when the Chromebook is asleep. Keeping Wi-Fi on during sleep uses some battery power, but it enables the Chromebook to update notifications and app data so that when you wake the Chromebook the content is

up to date and you can resume work more quickly.
Chrome OS can also connect to a different Wi-Fi
network if necessary while the Chromebook is
asleep—for example, because the Chromebook is
moved to a different location or because the previous
Wi-Fi network goes offline.

- *Use a web service to help resolve spelling errors*: Set this
  switch to On to make Chrome send the text you type to
  Google servers to resolve any spelling errors in search
  terms and other content you type online. Set this switch
  to Off if sharing this data with Google raises privacy
  concerns.

Managing Certificates

Chrome OS and its apps can use digital certificates–units of encrypted
code–to secure communications and verify identity. To display the Manage
certificates screen, click the Manage certificates button in the Privacy and
security section of the Settings window. As you can see in Figure 4-56, the
Manage certificates screen contains four tabs:

- *Your Certificates*: This tab lists the certificates that
  identify you. (You may find no certificates here.) You
  can add a certificate by clicking the Import button and
  then following the prompts. You can add a certificate
  and bind it to the Chromebook's Trusted Platform
  Module (TPM) encryption hardware by clicking
  the Import and Bind button and then following the
  prompts. You can view a certificate by clicking its
  More Actions button (the three vertical dots) and then
  clicking the View item on the menu. You can delete a
  certificate by clicking the More Actions button and then
  clicking the Delete item on the menu.

Figure 4-56. *The Manage certificates screen contains four tabs: Your Certificates, Servers, Authorities, and Others*

Note   A digital certificate bound to the Chromebook's TPM has "(hardware backed)" after its display name. For example, a digital certificate listed as `Maria Z. Jones (hardware backed)` is bound to the TPM, whereas a digital certificate listed as `Maria Z. Jones` is not bound.

- *Servers*: This tab lists the certificates that identify specific servers. You can add a certificate by clicking the Import button and then following the prompts. You can view a certificate's details by clicking the More Actions button and then clicking the View item on the menu. You can export a certificate by clicking the More Actions button and then clicking the Export item on the menu.

- *Authorities*: This tab lists the certificates that identify certificate authorities, the bodies that issue digital certificates. Here, too, you can add a certificate by clicking the Import button, view a certificate's details by clicking the More Actions button and then clicking the View item, and export a certificate by clicking the More Actions button and then clicking the Export item. You can also edit the trust settings for a certificate authority's certificate like this:

    a.   Click the More Actions button for the certificate and then click the Edit item on the menu. The Certificate authority dialog box will open (see Figure 4-57).

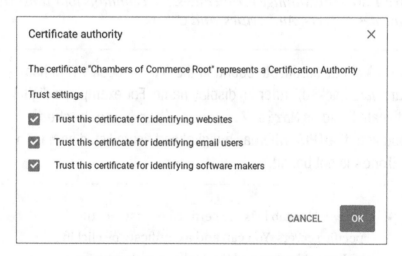

Figure 4-57.   You can edit the trust settings for a certificate authority by checking and unchecking the check boxes in the Certificate authority dialog box

    b.   Check or uncheck the "Trust this certificate for identifying websites" check box, as needed.

   c. Check or uncheck the "Trust this certificate for identifying email users" check box, as needed.

   d. Check or uncheck the "Trust this certificate for identifying software makers" check box, as needed.

   e. Click the OK button to close the Certificate authority dialog box.

- *Others*: This tab lists other certificates installed on the Chromebook. You may find no certificates here; if there are any, you can view their details and export them from the More Actions menu.

Choosing Content Settings

Chrome's content settings enable you to specify what content websites can display on the Chromebook, control which of the device's features websites can use, and control what information websites can use. For example, you can prevent websites from displaying pop-up messages and allow only specific websites to access the Chromebook's camera and microphone. You can also control whether websites are allowed to ask to become default handlers for specific protocols; for example, the site mail.google.com is the default handler for the mailto protocol, which is used for sending email messages.

You can configure content settings for all websites, for specific sites, or for a combination of the two.

To choose content settings, click the Content settings button at the bottom of the Privacy and security section of the Settings window. The Content settings screen will appear (see Figure 4-58), showing a long list of buttons, each of which gives access to the screen for a category of settings: the Cookies category, the Location category, the Camera category, and so on. Where a category of settings has a global setting, its current status appears on the button for quick reference. For example, in Figure 4-58, the Cookies category button shows the status "Allow sites to save and read cookie data," and the Location category button shows the status "Ask before accessing."

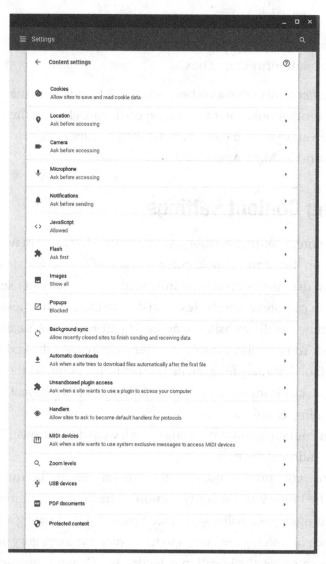

Figure 4-58. *The Content settings screen gives you tight control over the actions that websites are able to take on the Chromebook*

Most of these category screens have similar controls to each other and are based around a Block list and an Allow list. The Block list contains sites that are explicitly blocked from using that particular feature, and the Allow list contains sites that are explicitly allowed to use it. Some of the screens enable you to edit the Block list and the Allow list directly, whereas others let you edit the lists only indirectly, by clicking the Allow button or the Block button when Chrome prompts you for permission for a site. Some screens also have a master switch at the top that you can set to On or Off to control the default setting for the feature. Confusingly, the name displayed for this switch changes depending on the setting. For example, on various screens, the switch is labelled "Ask first (recommended)" when it is set to On and "Blocked" when it is set to Off.

For example, Figure 4-59 shows the Flash screen, which lets you configure settings for the Adobe Flash Player plugin. At the top is the master switch, which appears with the label "Ask first (recommended)" because it is set to On; if you set the switch to Off, its label changes to "Block sites from running Flash." Below that is the Adobe Flash Player Storage settings button, which you can click to display a browser window showing the Website Storage Settings panel on the Macromedia website. (Side note: The Website Storage Settings panel itself requires Flash Player.)

Figure 4-59. *The Flash screen in Settings includes the "Ask first (recommended)" switch, the Block list, and the Allow list. The starlike symbol to the right of Files, Smart Lock, and Gallery indicates that the blocking is enforced by a Chrome extension.*

Below these two settings is the Block list, which shows apps and sites blocked from using Flash Player. In the figure, you can see that the Files app, the Smart Lock app, and the Gallery app are blocked from using Flash. The starlike symbol that appears on the right side of the buttons for these apps denotes "This setting is enforced by an extension," which means that you cannot change it.

Below the Block list is the Allow list, which contains individual sites permitted to use Flash. You can customize either the Block list or the Allow list in the following ways:

- *Add a site*: Click the Add button at the right end of the Block or Allow headings to open the Add a site dialog box. Type or paste the site's URL in the Site box and then click the Add button.

- *Remove a site*: Click the More Actions button (the three vertical dots) to the right of an item to display the menu, and then click the Remove item.

- *Edit a site*: Click the More button (the three vertical dots) to the right of an item to display the menu, and then click the Edit button. In the Edit site dialog box that opens, edit the URL as needed and then click the Edit button.

- *Block an allowed site*: Click the More button (the three vertical dots) to the right of an allowed site to display the menu, and then click the Block item. Chrome OS will move the site to the Block list.

- *Allow a blocked site*: Click the More button (the three vertical dots) to the right of an item to display the menu, and then click the Allow item. Chrome OS will move the site to the Allow list.

When you finish choosing settings on the category screen, click the Back button (the arrow in the upper-left corner) to return to the Content settings screen.

The following list gives brief details on the categories that appear on the Content settings screen:

- *Cookies*: The Cookies screen enables you to specify which sites can save cookies on the Chromebook and how long the cookies persist. We'll look at the specific settings on this screen in the example in the next section.

- *Location*: The Location screen lets you control whether websites can learn the Chromebook's location. Set the switch at the top to On, setting its label to "Ask before accessing (recommended)," if you want Chrome to prompt the user to allow location access; otherwise, set the switch to Off, changing its label to "Blocked." The Block list shows sites that have been blocked from accessing the location, and the Allow list shows sites that have been permitted to access it.

- *Camera*: The Camera screen enables you to control which websites can use the Chromebook's camera or cameras. If the Chromebook has multiple cameras (either built-in or connected), choose the appropriate camera in the pop-up menu at the top and then set the switch at the top to On, setting its label to "Ask before accessing (recommended)," or to Off, setting its label to "Blocked."

- *Microphone*: The Microphone screen lets you control which websites can use the Chromebook's microphone or microphones. In the pop-up menu at the top, choose the Default item to configure the default microphone; otherwise, select the specific microphone you want to affect. Then set the switch to On, setting its label to

"Ask before accessing (recommended)," if you want the microphone to be available; set the switch to Off, setting its label to "Blocked," if you want to prevent websites from accessing it.

- *Notifications*: The Notifications screen allows you to specify which sites can send notifications. Set the switch at the top to On, setting its label to "Ask before sending (recommended)," if you want notifications to be available; otherwise, set the switch to Off, setting its label to "Blocked." Next, use the controls to adjust the Block list and the Allow list. The Allow list contains entries for Google Docs, Google Drive, and Google's mail servers that are enforced by extensions.

- *JavaScript*: The JavaScript screen enables you to allow or disallow JavaScript by setting the switch to the top to On, setting its label to "Allowed (recommend)," or to Off, setting its label to "Blocked." You can also customize the Block list and the Allow list.

- *Flash*: The Flash screen, as explained earlier in this section, contains the master switch and the Adobe Flash Player Storage settings button as well as the Block list and the Allow list.

- *Images*: The Images screen enables you to control whether specific websites can display images. Set the switch at the top to On, setting its label to "Show all (recommended)," if you want websites to be able to display images by default; if you want to block images, set the switch to Off, changing its label to "Do not show any images." You can then customize the Block list and the Allow list as needed.

- *Pop-ups*: The Pop-ups screen lets you control whether websites can display pop-up windows. When set to Off, the switch has the label "Blocked (recommended)"; when set to On, the switch has the label "Allowed." After setting the switch, customize the Block list and the Allow list as needed.

- *Background sync*: The Background sync screen allows you to control whether websites can sync data in the background. To permit background sync, set the switch at the top to On, which sets its label to "Allow recently closed sites to finish sending and receiving data (recommended)." To prevent background sync, set the switch to Off, which sets its label to "Do not allow recently closed sites to finish sending and receiving data." After setting the switch, customize the Block list and the Allow list as necessary.

- *Automatic downloads*: The Automatic downloads screen enables you to control whether a website can prompt the user to allow it to download further files after the user downloads one file manually. To allow this prompting, set the switch at the top to On, so its label appears as "Ask when a site tries to download files automatically after the first file (recommended)"; to prevent the prompting, set the switch to Off, so its label appears as "Do not allow any site to download multiple files automatically." You can then customize the Block list and the Allow list as needed.

- *Unsandboxed plugin access*: The Unsandboxed plugin access screen enables you to control whether sites can ask to use plugins to access the Chromebook without working in the sandbox, the protected area to which a plugin is normally restricted for safety. Set the switch to On, making its label "Ask when a site wants to use a plugin to access your computer (recommended)," to allow sites to prompt the user. Otherwise, set the switch to Off, making its label "Do not allow any site to use a plugin to access your computer." Next, customize the Block list and the Allow list as needed.

- *Handlers*: The Handlers screen enables you to control whether sites can ask to become the default handlers for specific networking protocols. To allow sites to ask permission, set the switch to On, making its label "Allow sites to ask to become default handlers for protocols (recommended)"; otherwise, set the switch to Off, making its label "Do not allow any site to handle protocols." You can then customize the settings in the mailto section and the webcal section. The mailto protocol is for sending email messages, and the webcal protocol is for calendaring.

- *MIDI devices:* The MIDI devices screen enables you to control whether sites can ask to get exclusive access to MIDI devices. To allow requests for exclusive access, set the switch to On, making its label "Ask when a site wants to use system exclusive messages to access MIDI devices (recommended)"; to prevent requests, set the switch to Off, making its label "Do not allow any sites to use system exclusive messages to access MIDI devices."

- *Zoom levels:* The Zoom levels screen lists sites for which a custom zoom level is set in Chrome. You cannot adjust any of the custom zoom levels here, but you can get rid of a custom zoom level by clicking the Remove zoom level (X) button to its right.

- *USB devices*: The USB devices screen shows USB devices connected to the computer.

- *PDF documents*: The PDF documents screen contains only the "Download PDF files instead of automatically opening them in Chrome" switch, which you can set to On to make Chrome download PDF files instead of displaying them. This setting is useful if you want to store PDF files on the Chromebook so you can read them offline.

- *Protected content*: The Protect content screen enables you to control whether sites can play protected content, such as movie files protected by licenses. Set the "Allow sites to play protected content (recommended)" switch to On or Off, as needed. Set the "Allow identifiers for protected content (computer restart may be required)" switch to On if you want to allow content services to store unique identifiers on the Chromebook for authorizing access to protected content. You can also customize the Block list and the Allow list as needed.

An Example of Content Settings: Configuring Cookies

As an example of configuring content settings, let us look at the Cookies category of content. Cookies, as you likely know, are small text files that websites set on a computer. A cookie enables a site to track the user's movement around the site and is needed for features such as keeping a list of items you have browsed on the site or maintaining the contents of a shopping cart.

Cookies set by the websites you visit are called *first-party cookies* and are usually beneficial, so you would normally not want to prevent websites from setting them. But advertisers on the websites you visit can also set cookies that track your movement from one site to another. These cookies are called *third-party cookies* and are not usually beneficial. Various browsers, including Chrome, block third-party cookies by default.

Click the Cookies button on the Content settings screen to display the Cookies screen (see Figure 4-60). Here, you can take the following actions:

- *Control whether sites in general can set cookies*: Set the switch at the top to On, making its label "Allow sites to save and read cookie data (recommended)," to allow cookies. Set the switch to Off, making its label "Blocked," to block cookies.

Figure 4-60. *The Cookies screen enables you to control which websites can save cookies on the Chromebook*

- *Set Chrome to delete cookies at the end of each session*: Set the "Keep local data only until you quit your browser" switch to On. With this switch set to Off, the cookies will persist from one browsing session to another, which is what you normally want.

- *Block third-party websites from setting cookies*: Set the "Block third-party cookies" switch to On. This is usually a good idea.

- *See all cookies and data*: Click this button to display the All cookies and site data screen, which shows a complete list of all the sites that have set cookies. You can dig into the details of the cookies, delete cookies for individual sites, or delete all the cookies.

- *See which sites you have blocked, set to be cleared at the end of the browsing session, or allowed*: Look at the Block list, the Clear on exit list, or the Allow list.

- *Add a site to the Block list, the Clear on exit list, or the Allow list*: Click the Add button, type or paste the URL in the Site box, and then click the Add button.

- *Allow a blocked site*: Click the More Actions button (the three vertical dots) on its line and then click the Allow item on the menu.

- *Set a site to be cleared at the end of your browsing session*: Click the More Actions button on the site's line and then click the Clear on exit item on the menu.

- *Edit a site's URL*: Click the More Actions button on the site's line, click the Edit item on the menu, edit the URL in the Edit site dialog box, and then click the Edit button.

- *Remove a site from its current list*: Click the More Actions button on the site's line and then click the Remove item on the menu.

- *Block an allowed site*: Click the More Actions button on the site's line in the Allow list and then click the Block item on the menu.

Clearing Browsing Data

Browsing the Web causes the Chrome browser to store a variety of different types of data—the list of web pages visited, the list of files downloaded, cookie files from sites that set them, and various other types of data. Chrome enables you to clear some or all of your browsing data as needed. You can choose to delete just some types of data, just a specific time range, or both.

To clear browsing data, click the Clear browsing data button at the bottom of the Privacy and security section of the Settings window. The Clear browsing data dialog box will open. This dialog box has two tabs: the Basic tab (shown on the left in Figure 4-61) and the Advanced tab (shown on the right in Figure 4-61).

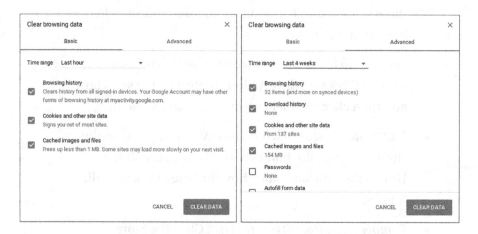

Figure 4-61. *In the Clear browsing data dialog box, click the Basic tab (left) or the Advanced tab (right) as needed. Choose the appropriate time range in the Time range pop-up menu, check or uncheck the check boxes to specify what data to clear, and then click the Clear Data button.*

The Basic tab contains the following three check boxes:

- *Browsing history*: The browsing history contains the list of websites visited in Chrome when it is not in incognito mode.

- *Cookies and other site data*: Cookies are small text files that websites use to track a visitor's movement around the site. Other site data comprises non-cookie files that websites store on your computer, such as data for plugin software required by the site.

- *Cached images and files*: Cached images and files are the items that Chrome stores so that it can display web pages again more quickly when you return to them. For example, if you frequently visit the same website, Chrome will cache images such as the site's logo so that it does not need to download them on each visit.

The Advanced tab also contains the "Browsing history" check box, the "Cookies and other side data" check box, and the "Cached images and files" check box. Beyond these, it also contains the following six check boxes:

- *Download history:* The download history contains the list of files downloaded. Clearing the download history does not remove the downloaded files themselves.

- *Passwords*: The Passwords list contains the passwords you have chosen to store in Chrome.

- *Autofill form data*: The Autofill form data contains data you have stored in Chrome for automatically populating the fields in forms—for example, name and address information.

- *Content settings*: The Content settings category contains sites for which you have configured special settings, as explained in the section "Choosing Content Settings" earlier in this chapter. For example, you might block a site from raising notifications.

- *Hosted app data*: The hosted app data is data stored by apps installed on the Chromebook from the Chrome Web Store.

- *Media licenses*: The media licenses are digital files that permit Chrome to play back protected content, such as movies or music files. When you acquire a media license the first time you play back a protected file, Chrome saves the license so you can play the file again later. You wouldn't normally want to delete media licenses unless you will no longer be using the Chromebook—for example, because you are passing it on to someone else.

To clear browsing data, follow these steps in the Clear browsing data dialog box:

1. Click the Basic tab or the Advanced tab, depending on which categories of browsing data you want to clear.

2. Click the Time Range pop-up menu and then click the time period for which you want to clear the data. Your choices are Last hour, Last 24 hours, Last 7 days, Last 4 weeks, or All time.

3. Check the check box for each category of data you want to clear.

4. Click the Clear Data button.

Configuring Passwords and Forms Settings

The Passwords and forms section of the Settings window (see Figure 4-62) enables you to configure settings for automatically filling out online forms and for specifying which of your passwords Chrome OS should offer to save for future use.

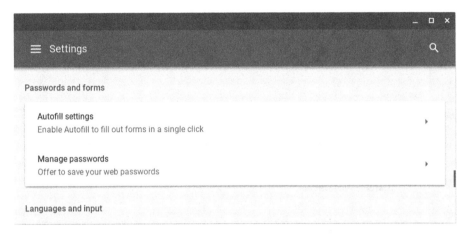

Figure 4-62. *From the Passwords and forms section of the Settings window you can configure autofill settings and settings for managing passwords.*

Configuring Autofill Settings

Chrome's Autofill feature can automatically fill out standard fields on online forms with information such as your name, address, and payment details. To configure Autofill settings, click the Autofill settings button in the Passwords and forms section of the Settings window and then work on the Autofill screen (see Figure 4-63). Here, you can take the following actions:

- *Enable or disable Autofill*: Set the master switch to On or Off as needed.

- *Add an address*: Click the Add button on the Addresses line, enter the details in the Add address dialog box that opens, and then click the Save button.

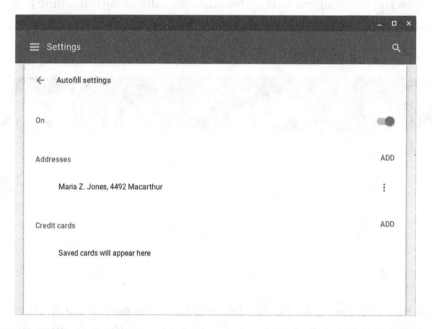

Figure 4-63. *The Autofill screen lets you enable and disable autofill, add and edit addresses, and add and edit credit card details*

- *Edit an existing address*: Click the More Actions button (the three vertical dots) to the right of the address and then click the Edit item on the menu. Make the changes needed in the Edit address dialog box (see Figure 4-64) and then click the Save button.

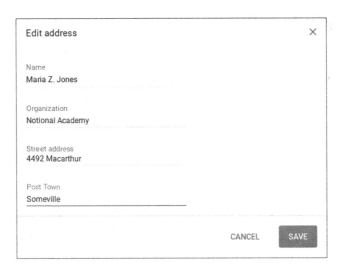

Figure 4-64. *Use the Edit address dialog box to edit an existing address for Autofill*

- *Remove an existing address*: Click the More Actions button to the right of the address and then click the Remove item on the menu.

- *Add a credit card*: Click the Add button on the Credit cards line, enter the details in the Add card dialog box, and then click the Save button.

- *Edit an existing card*: Click the More Actions button to the right of the card and then click the Edit item on the menu. Change the details as needed in the Edit card dialog box and then click the Save button.

- *Remove an existing card*: Click the More Actions button to the right of the card and then click the Remove item on the menu.

Managing Your Passwords

Chrome OS can save passwords for you so that it can automatically enter them on subsequent visits to those websites. Storing passwords like this is a major time saver, so you will likely want to use it for many sites.

To manage your passwords, click the Manage passwords button on the Passwords and forms screen, displaying the Manage passwords screen (see Figure 4-65). Here, you can take the following actions:

- *Search for a website's password*: Click the Search passwords box in the upper-right corner and then start typing the website's name. A list of matches will appear in the Saved Passwords area, and you can take other actions for the password—for example, viewing it or deleting it. Click the Clear (X) button at the right end of the Search passwords box when you finish searching.

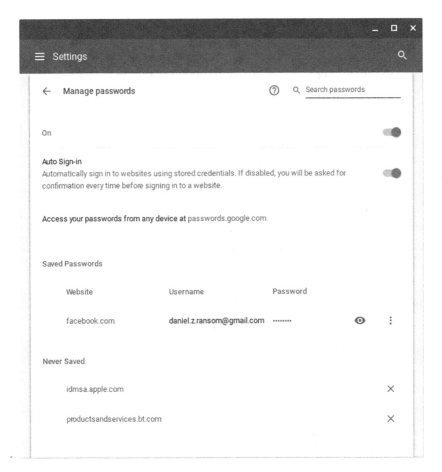

Figure 4-65. *On the Manage passwords screen, you can choose whether to store passwords and whether to sign in automatically to websites. You can also review your saved passwords and the sites for which you have chosen not to save passwords.*

- *Enable or disable storing passwords*: Set the master switch to On or Off as needed.

- *Enable or disable the Auto Sign-in feature*: Set the "Auto Sign-in" switch to On or Off as needed. If you disable Auto Sign-in, Chrome will prompt you to allow the use of each stored password.

- *Review the list of saved passwords*: Look at the Saved Passwords list.

- *View a saved password*: Click the Show password icon (the eye icon) on the site's row.

- *View the details for the saved password*: Click the More Actions button (the three vertical dots) on the site's row and then click the Details item on the menu. The Saved password details dialog box opens, showing the website address, the username, and the password (as dots; click the Show password icon to display the characters). Click the Done button when you are ready to close the Save password details dialog box.

- *Remove a saved password*: Click the More Actions button on the site's row and then click the Remove item on the menu.

- *Review the sites for which you have chosen not to save passwords:* Look at the Never Saved list.

- *Remove a site from the Never Saved list*: Click the X (Remove) button on the site's row.

Configuring Languages and Input Settings

The Languages and input section of the Settings window (see Figure 4-66) enables you to set the language or languages for the Chromebook to use, set up keyboard layouts, and configure spell checking.

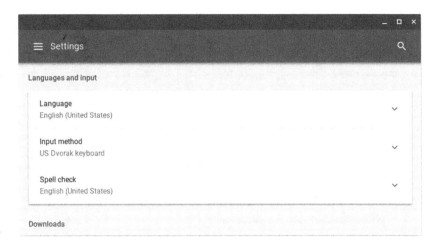

Figure 4-66. *From the Languages and input section of the Settings window you can configure the language, the input method, and the language for spell checking*

Note   You can also access the Languages and input section of the Settings window by clicking the Change language and input settings button on the Keyboard screen.

Setting Up the Languages for the Chromebook

Normally, the Chromebook will be set up to use a single language, such as English (United States). If the Language button in the Languages and input section of the Settings screen shows the right language, and you don't need to add any other languages, you are all set.

If you do need to make changes, click the Language button to expand the Language section. The controls shown in Figure 4-67 appear.

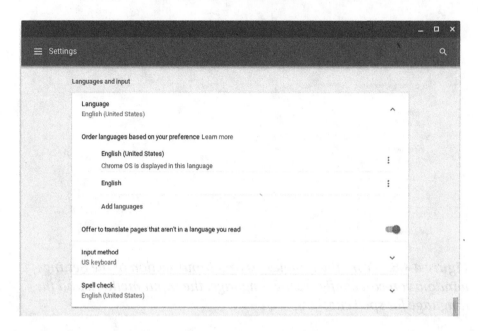

Figure 4-67. After you click the Language button at the top of the Languages and input section, the controls for adding and configuring languages appear

Adding or Removing a Language

To add a language, follow these steps:

1. Click the Add languages button to display the Add languages dialog box (see Figure 4-68).

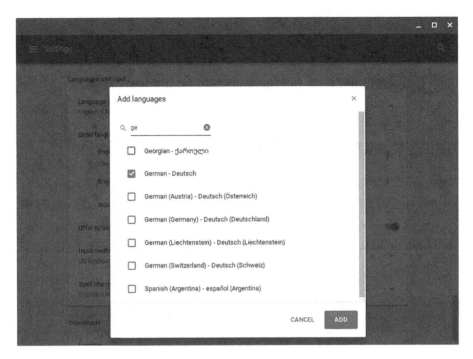

Figure 4-68. *In the Add languages dialog box, you can narrow the selection of languages by starting to type the name of the language you want. When you locate the language, check its check box and click the Add button.*

2. Either scroll down the list to find the language you want to add or start typing its name in the search box at the top of the Add languages dialog box.

3. Check the check box for the language or languages you want to add.

4. Click the Add button to close the Add languages dialog box and add the language. The language will appear in the "Order languages based on your preferences" list in the Settings window.

Note   If you want to remove a language, click its More Actions button (the three vertical dots at the right end of the button for the language) and then click the Remove item on the menu.

Putting the Languages into Your Preferred Order

After adding any languages you need, shuffle the languages into your preferred order. To do so, click the More Actions button (the three vertical dots) at the right end of the button for the language you want to affect; then click the Move to the top item, the Move up item, or the Move down item on the menu as desired (see Figure 4-69).

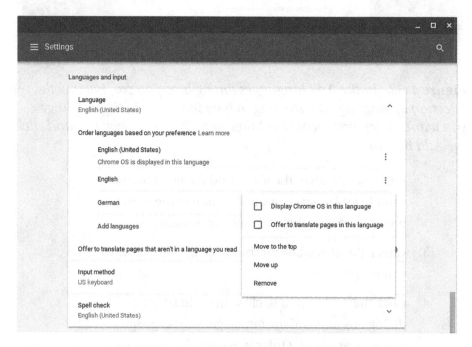

Figure 4-69. To change the order of the languages in the "Order languages based on your preference" list, click the More Actions button (the three vertical dots) on a language's button and then click the Move to the top item, the Move up item, or the Move down item on the menu

Note   If the "Display Chrome OS in this language" check box on the menu is available, you can check it and then click the Restart button (which appears when the menu closes) to restart the Chromebook and switch the display to that language. If the "Offer to translate pages in this language" check box on the menu is available, you can check it to make Chrome OS offer to translate pages that it detects are in that language. These two check boxes are available only for some languages; if the check boxes and the text are dimmed, they are not available for that language.

Configuring the Chromebook's Input Methods

Each Chromebook has a built-in keyboard that serves as the prime input method—as usual, you press the keys on the keyboard to enter characters in a document or to give commands (often including modifier keys). Normally, a Chromebook's input method is configured so that pressing a key enters the character shown on the key—for example, when you press the s key on the keyboard, you get an *s* in the document. But you can change the logical keyboard layout that Chrome OS uses to interpret the keyboard. For example, you might apply the Dvorak keyboard layout, which some people use because it is considered more efficient than the standard QWERTY layout.

To configure the Chromebook's input methods, follow these steps in the Settings window:

1. In the Languages and input section, click the Input method button to display the Input method controls (see Figure 4-70).

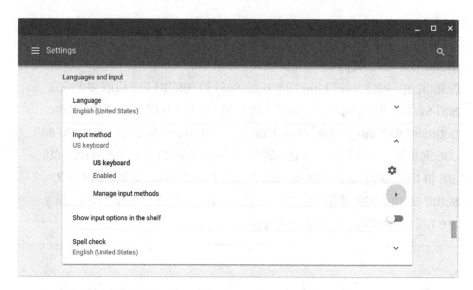

Figure 4-70. *In the Languages and input section of the Settings window, click the Input method button to display the Input method controls. You can then click the Manage input methods button to add or remove input methods.*

2.   Click the Manage input methods button to display
     the Manage input methods screen (see Figure 4-71).

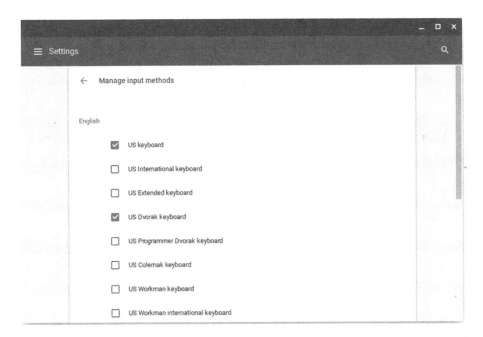

Figure 4-71. *On the Manage input methods screen, check the check box for each input method you want to add*

3.   Check the check box for each input method you want to add. For example, you might check the "US Dvorak keyboard" check box to add the standard Dvorak layout, or check the "US Programmer Dvorak" keyboard check box to add the Programmer Dvorak layout.

4.   Uncheck the check box for any input method you want to remove.

Note   The Chromebook needs an input method at all times, so if only one input method's check box is checked on the Manage input methods screen, you cannot uncheck that input method's check box until you have checked the check box for another input method.

5. Click the Back button (the left-arrow button) in the upper-left corner of the Manage input methods screen, or press the Back key on the keyboard, to return to the Languages and input screen. The input method you added will appear in the list.

After you have set up the input methods for the Chromebook, you can switch among them like this:

1. Click the status area to display the status menu.

2. Click the button for the current input method to display the Input methods status menu (see Figure 4-72).

Figure 4-72. *Use the Input methods status menu to switch from one input method to another*

3. Click the input method you want to use.

Configuring Downloads Settings

The Downloads section in the Settings window (see Figure 4-73) enables you to configure these three settings for downloading files:

- *Location*: This button shows the folder in which Chrome OS stores files you download—usually the Downloads folder. To use a different folder, click the Change button, click the folder in the Select a folder to open dialog box, and then click the Open button.

- *Ask where to save each file before downloading*: Set this switch to On if you want Chrome OS to prompt you as to where to save each file you go to download. Set this switch to Off if you want Chrome OS to put all the files in the folder specified on the Location button.

- *Disconnect Google Drive account*: Set this switch to On if you want to disconnect your Google Drive account from the Chromebook.

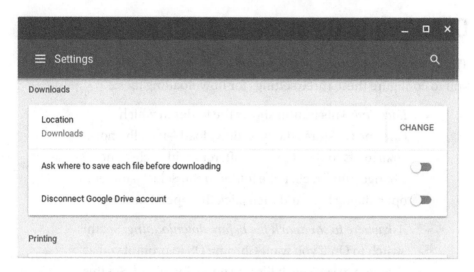

Figure 4-73. *In the Downloads section of the Settings screen, you can change the default folder for downloads, control whether Chrome OS prompts you to decide where to save each file you download, and disconnect your Google Drive account*

Configuring Accessibility Settings

To configure accessibility settings for the Chromebook, navigate to the Accessibility section near the bottom of the Settings window.

First, set the "Always show accessibility options in the system menu" switch to On if you want the Accessibility button to always appear in the status menu. This is helpful if the user needs quick access to accessibility features.

Next, click the Manage accessibility features button to display the Manage accessibility features screen. This is a long screen, and Figure 4-74 shows the upper half of it.

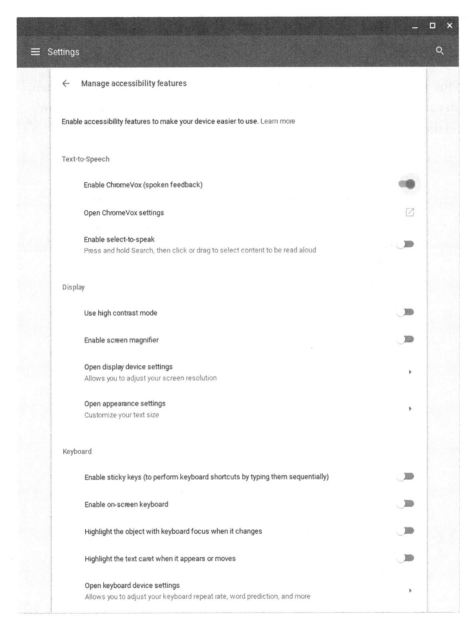

Figure 4-74. *The upper half of the Manage accessibility features screen includes the Text-to-Speech features, the Display features, and the Keyboard features*

Configuring Text-to-Speech Accessibility Features

In the Text-to-Speech section of the Manage accessibility features screen, you can configure settings for the ChromeVox spoken-feedback feature and the Select-to-Speak feature. Here are the details:

- *Enable ChromeVox (spoken feedback)*: Set this switch to On to enable the ChromeVox feature, which gives spoken feedback about what is shown on screen. When you set this switch to On, the Open ChromeVox settings button will appear. Click this button to open a browser window showing the ChromeVox Options screen (see Figure 4-75), in which you can configure the following settings:

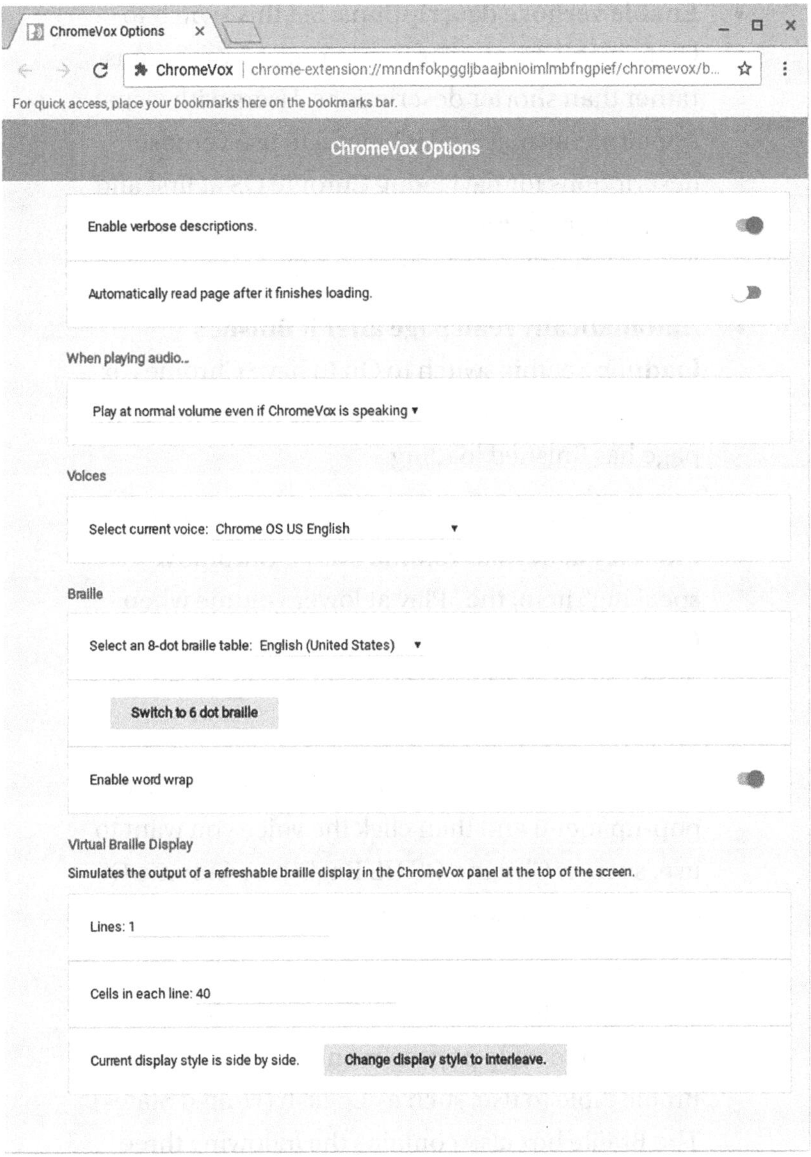

Figure 4-75. *After enabling ChromeVox, you can configure its settings on the ChromeVox Options screen*

- **Enable verbose descriptions**: Set this switch to On to have ChromeVox give verbose descriptions rather than shorter descriptions. Users with visual impairments may find it helpful to use verbose descriptions for navigating Chrome OS at first and then switch to shorter descriptions once they have become familiar with Chrome OS.

- **Automatically read page after it finishes loading**: Set this switch to On to have ChromeVox automatically read the active page aloud when the page has finished loading.

- **When playing audio**: In this pop-up menu, select the "Play at normal volume even if ChromeVox is speaking" item, the "Play at lower volume when ChromeVox is speaking" item, or the "Pause playback when ChromeVox is speaking" item, as needed.

- **Voices**: In this box, click the Select current voice pop-up menu and then click the voice you want to use, such as Chrome OS US English or Chrome OS español de Estados Unidos.

- **Braille**: In this box, configure settings for the ChromeVox Braille feature. Open the Select an 8-dot Braille table pop-up menu and then click the Braille table to use, such as English (United States). The Braille box also contains the following three settings:

- **Switch to 6-dot braille**: Click this button to switch from 8-dot Braille to 6-dot Braille. The Switch to 8-dot Braille button replaces the Switch to 6-dot Braille button, and you can click it to switch back to 8-dot Braille.

- **Enable word wrap**: Set this switch to On to enable the Word Wrap feature for ChromeVox.

- **Virtual Braille Display**: Use the controls in this box to configure the virtual Braille display, which simulates a refreshable Braille display in the ChromeVox panel. In the Lines box, type the number of lines to include in the display; the default setting is 1 line. In the "Cells in each line" field, type the number of cells to include in each line; the default setting is 40 cells. The virtual Braille display can use either a side-by-side style or an interleave style. Click the Change display style to interleave button or the Change display style to side by side button to switch between side-by-side style and interleave style.

- *Enable select-to-speak*: Set this switch to On to enable the Select-to-Speak feature. With Select-to-Speak enabled, you can hold down the Search key and drag the pointer over on-screen content to have ChromeVox read it aloud.

Configuring Display Accessibility Features

In the Display section of the Manage accessibility features screen, you can configure the following settings:

- *Use high contrast mode*: Set this switch to On to apply a high-contrast mode that's similar to reverse video.

- *Enable screen magnifier*: Set this switch to On to magnify the screen. With the screen magnifier on, you will need to pan around the screen to see all of it.

- *Open display device settings*: Click this button to go to the Displays screen, in which you can configure the display resolution, orientation, and other settings. See the section "Configuring Display Settings" earlier in this chapter for coverage of these settings.

- *Open appearance settings*: Click this button to display the Appearance screen, in which you can configure fonts, wallpaper, themes, and other appearance settings. See the section "Configuring Appearance Settings" earlier in this chapter for coverage of these settings.

Configuring Keyboard Accessibility Settings

In the Keyboard section of the Manage accessibility features screen, you can configure the following settings:

- *Enable sticky keys (to perform keyboard shortcuts by typing them sequentially)*: Set this switch to On to enable the Sticky Keys feature. Sticky Keys lets you press the modifier keys for keyboard shortcuts in sequence rather than having to press the keys together. For example, instead of pressing Ctrl+P to give the Print command, you can press Ctrl and then press P.

- *Enable on-screen keyboard*: Set this switch to On to display the on-screen keyboard, which enables you to type characters by clicking.

- *Highlight the object with keyboard focus when it changes*: Set this switch to On to have Chrome OS apply a highlight to the screen object that has the keyboard focus when the focus changes. For example, when you press Tab to move the keyboard focus to the next object in a window, Chrome OS will apply a highlight to that object. The highlight is a gray circle for objects such as switches and expansion buttons (the triangular buttons) and a blue outline for text items.

- *Highlight the text caret when it appears or moves*: Set this switch to On to have Chrome OS display a highlight circle around the text caret when it appears on screen and when it moves. This setting is useful if the user finds it difficult to locate the text caret.

- *Open keyboard device settings*: You can click this button to display the Keyboard screen, where you can configure the settings discussed in "Configuring Keyboard Settings" earlier in this chapter.

Configuring Mouse and Touchpad Accessibility Settings

In the Mouse and touchpad section of the Accessibility screen (see Figure 4-76), you can configure the following settings:

- *Automatically click when the mouse cursor stops*: Set this switch to On to have Chrome OS generate a mouse click shortly after the mouse cursor stops moving. Then

open the Delay before click pop-up menu and choose
the delay: extremely short (0.6s), very short (0.8s), short
(1s), long (2s), or very long (4s). This automatic click
can be helpful for users who have trouble clicking, but
you will typically need to experiment to find which
delay works best for a particular user.

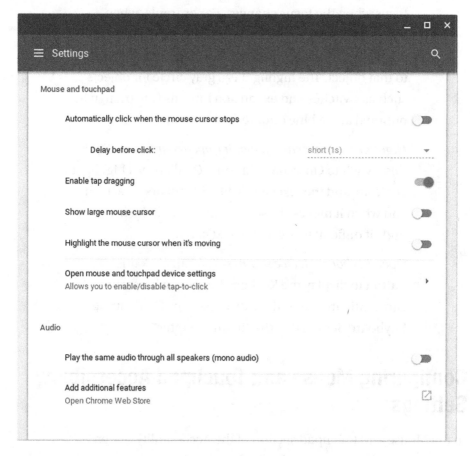

Figure 4-76. *The Mouse and touchpad section of the Accessibility
screen enables you to configure automatic clicks and tap dragging,
enlarge the pointer, and hide the pointer when it is moving*

- *Enable tap dragging*: Set this switch to On to enable the Tap Dragging feature, which lets you tap and hold (without clicking) an object, such as the title bar of a window, and then drag it to a different position. This feature appears not to work consistently across all Chromebooks.

- *Show large mouse cursor*: Set this switch to On to display the mouse cursor (the pointer) at a larger size. Drag the Adjust cursor size slider to set the exact size. This setting is especially useful for small, high-resolution screens on which the pointer goes missing.

- *Highlight the mouse cursor when it's moving*: Set this switch to On to display a red circle around the mouse cursor when it is moving. This circle, too, is helpful for making the mouse cursor easier to see.

- *Open mouse and touchpad settings*: Click this button to display the Touchpad screen (if no mouse is connected) or the Mouse and touchpad screen (if one or more mice are connected). See the section "Configuring Touchpad Settings" and the sidebar "Choosing Settings for a Mouse," both earlier in this chapter, for coverage of these settings.

Configuring Audio Accessibility Settings

The Audio section of the Settings screen contains one switch and one button:

- *Play the same audio through all speakers (mono audio)*: Set this switch to On if you want the Chromebook to play back audio in mono rather than stereo.

- *Add additional features*: Click this button to display
  the Chrome Accessibility page in the Chrome Web
  Store. This page displays various types of accessibility
  features, not just audio features.

Summary

In this chapter, you have learned how to configure a Chromebook
manually by working directly on the Chromebook rather than managing it
via administrative policy. You know how to open the Settings app, navigate
to the appropriate category of settings, and configure the settings to
achieve the results you want.

In the next chapter, we will consider how to configure and manage
Chromebooks with Google Management Console.

CHAPTER 5

Configuring and Managing Chromebooks via Policy

In this chapter, you will learn how to configure and manage Chromebooks via policy. To do so, you sign in to your school's Google Admin console and use the tools it provides to manage Chromebooks centrally. The primary tool is the Chrome Management console, which is fully integrated into the Google Admin console.

In the first section, we will cover how to get Chrome subscription licenses for your school's Chromebooks. If someone else has already taken care of the licenses, you can probably skip this section and go straight to the second section, "Getting Started with Your Google Admin Console," instead.

Once you are up to speed with your Google Admin console, we will go through the process of enrolling your school's Chromebooks, controlling forced re-enrollment, and disabling and deprovisioning Chromebooks. We will then dig into the many user settings you can configure to customize the user experience before exploring the equally plentiful device settings you can configure to customize the Chromebooks themselves.

© Guy Hart-Davis 2018
G. Hart-Davis, *Deploying Chromebooks in the Classroom,*
https://doi.org/10.1007/978-1-4842-3766-3_5

Getting Chrome Subscription Licenses

To manage your school's Chromebooks centrally, you will need to sign up for Google's Chrome Education service and get a subscription license for each Chromebook. This section will explain how to accomplish these tasks. Along the way, this section will also briefly cover Google's three other Chrome services and their licenses because the license types overlap somewhat but vary enough to be confusing.

Note   Apart from Chrome Education, Google offers three other Chrome services: Chrome Enterprise, Chrome Nonprofit, and Chrome Kiosk. As the names suggest, Chrome Enterprise is for business administration of Chrome OS devices; Chrome Nonprofit is for use by nonprofit organizations, such as charities; and Chrome Kiosk is for deploying Chrome OS devices in single-app kiosk-style situations, such as using a Chromebook as a point-of-sale device or as a digital sign.

Signing Up for the Chrome Education Service

To sign your school up for the Chrome Education service and to buy licenses for managing the school's Chromebooks, you must work with a Google Cloud partner. To view a list of partners for Chrome OS, open the address `https://cloud.withgoogle.com/partners/?products=CHROME&sort-type=RELEVANCE#` in a web browser.

The Google Cloud partner handles the signup process for your school. The partner also provides and manages the subscription licenses; you do not manage them directly yourself.

Note   Google's licensing models, including Chrome Enterprise and Chrome Education, are based on domains. Your school may use its existing domain name (such as `notionalacademy.com`) or set up a new domain name to use for Chrome Education. Each domain can be divided into multiple subunits called *organizational units* for more granular administration.

Getting Subscription Licenses for Your School's Chromebooks

For the Chrome Education service, Google offers only one type of license, which is called a *perpetual license* and costs $30.00 per device as of this writing. "Perpetual" sounds great, but Google's use of the word has a meaning closer to "lifetime" than the conventional meaning of "never-ending":

- A perpetual license is tied to a particular Chrome OS device.

- If a Chrome OS device fails, you can transfer its license to another Chrome OS device from the same manufacturer. Normally, the device needs to be the same model, but you can get a dispensation to transfer the license to a different model from that manufacturer.

- Apart from in the case of the Chrome OS device failing (as explained in the previous bulleted paragraph), you cannot transfer a perpetual license to another device in the same domain. You also cannot transfer a perpetual license to a device in another domain.

Note   Google also offers perpetual licenses for the Chrome
Enterprise service and the Chrome Nonprofit service, but not for
the Chrome Kiosk service. For the Chrome Enterprise service and
the Chrome Kiosk service, Google also offers annual subscription
licenses. As the name suggests, this is a license for which the
business or organization pays a yearly fee. Google allows the
business or organization to unenroll a Chrome OS device and transfer
its license to another device in the same domain, but not to another
device in a different domain.

Getting Started with Your Google Admin Console

In this section, we will look at how to get started with your Google
Admin console. The Google Admin console is Google's overarching
tool for administering and managing G Suite and devices, including
Chromebooks. The Google Admin console gives you seamless access to
various other tools, including the Chrome Management console, which is
designed for managing Chrome devices.

Note   If you are already familiar with your Google Admin console,
you may want to skip this section.

Signing In to Your Google Admin Console

To get started, sign in to your Google Admin console using the administrator account arranged by your school's Google Cloud partner. Follow these steps:

1. Open the Chrome app or another web browser.

2. Go to the Google Admin home page,
    `https://admin.google.com`.

3. Click the Add account button. The Sign in dialog box
    will open (see Figure 5-1).

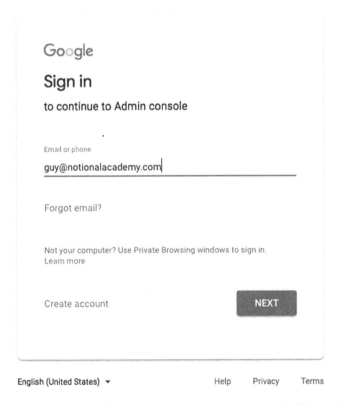

Figure 5-1. *Type your administrator username in the "Email or phone" field in the Sign in dialog box on the Google Admin home screen and then click the Next button*

4. In the "Email or phone" field, type the email address for your administrator account.

5. Click the Next button. The Password dialog box will open.

6. Type your administrator password.

7. Click the Next button. For a new account, follow through any further verification checks that Google throws at you. For example, you may need to enter a six-digit code sent via text message to your mobile phone or telephoned via an automated system.

8. If the Welcome to your new account screen appears (see Figure 5-2), read the information, following as many links as necessary to make sure you know what you are agreeing to. Then, click the Accept button.

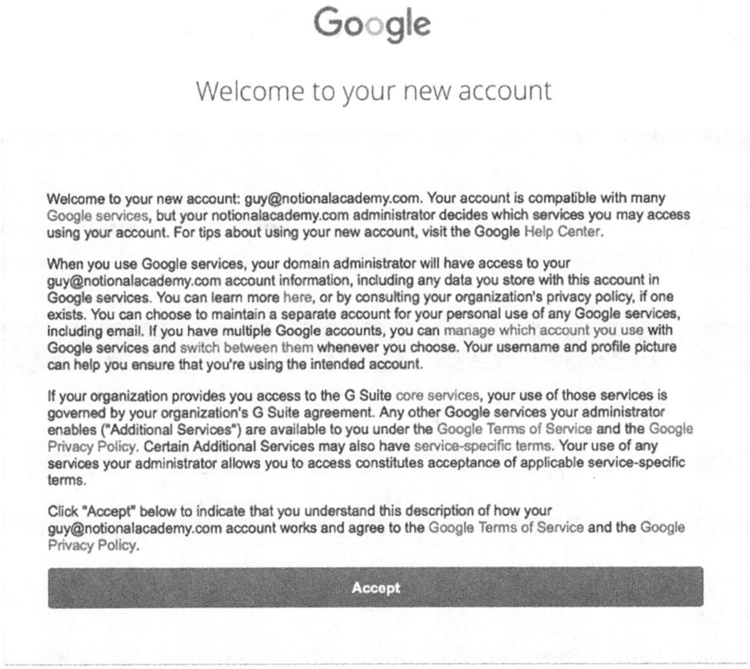

Google

Welcome to your new account

Welcome to your new account: guy@notionalacademy.com. Your account is compatible with many Google services, but your notionalacademy.com administrator decides which services you may access using your account. For tips about using your new account, visit the Google Help Center.

When you use Google services, your domain administrator will have access to your guy@notionalacademy.com account information, including any data you store with this account in Google services. You can learn more here, or by consulting your organization's privacy policy, if one exists. You can choose to maintain a separate account for your personal use of any Google services, including email. If you have multiple Google accounts, you can manage which account you use with Google services and switch between them whenever you choose. Your username and profile picture can help you ensure that you're using the intended account.

If your organization provides you access to the G Suite core services, your use of those services is governed by your organization's G Suite agreement. Any other Google services your administrator enables ("Additional Services") are available to you under the Google Terms of Service and the Google Privacy Policy. Certain Additional Services may also have service-specific terms. Your use of any services your administrator allows you to access constitutes acceptance of applicable service-specific terms.

Click "Accept" below to indicate that you understand this description of how your guy@notionalacademy.com account works and agree to the Google Terms of Service and the Google Privacy Policy.

Accept

Figure 5-2. *The Welcome to your new account screen includes links to various information resources, including the Google Terms of Service and the Google Privacy Policy. Click the Accept button if you want to proceed.*

At this point, Google Admin may prompt you to perform some setup actions. Once you have completed these actions, you will see the Google Admin Home screen.

Navigating the Google Admin Home Page

Your home base in the Google Admin console is the Home page
(see Figure 5-3).

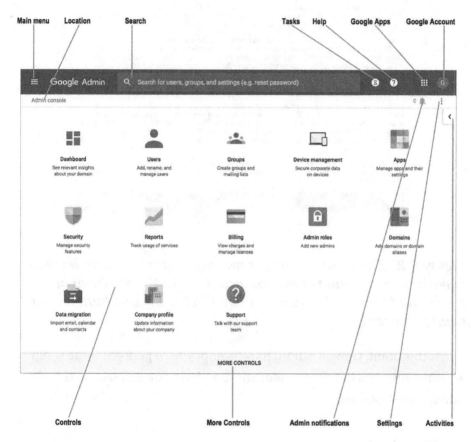

Figure 5-3.   *The Home page in the Google Admin console*

The following list explains the main features of the Home page:

- *Main menu*: Click this button to display the Main menu on the left side of the screen (see Figure 5-4).

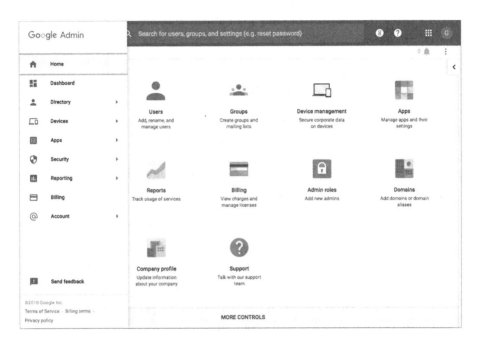

Figure 5-4. *The Main menu provides quick access to the key areas of Google Admin*

- *Location*: This bar shows the location of the current page—in this case, Admin console. As you move from one page to another, the Location bar will change to show your current location, including a "breadcrumb bar" that enables you to navigate back. For example, when you click the Device management icon on the Home page, the Location bar will show Device management to indicate you are viewing the Device management page. If you then click the Chrome

335

devices button on the Device management page, and then click the User Settings icon, the Location bar will show `Device management ➤ Chrome ➤ User Settings`. You can click the Chrome item to return to the Chrome page or click the Device management item to return to the Device management page.

- *Search*: Click this box to search for users, groups, or settings by using keywords.

- *Tasks*: Click this button to display a pop-up pane showing your ongoing tasks—or none, if you are lucky.

- *Help*: Click this button to display a Help pane, in which you can browse help topics or search using keywords.

- *Google apps*: Click this button to display a pop-up pane showing the leading Google apps, such as Mail, Drive, and Docs. Click the button for the app you want to launch. If the app you want does not appear at first, click the More button at the bottom of the pop-up pane to extend the pane, revealing other apps.

- *Google Account*: Click this button to display the Account pop-up pane. Here, you can click the My Account button to manage your account, click another account to switch to it, click the Add account button to add another Google account, or click the Sign out button to sign out of your Google Admin console.

- *Admin notifications*: Click this button to display a pop-up pane showing administrative notifications.

- *Activities*: Click this button to display the Activities pane (see Figure 5-5), which shows your recent activities, gives you access to reports, and provides a Tools list of links and a Common tasks list of links.

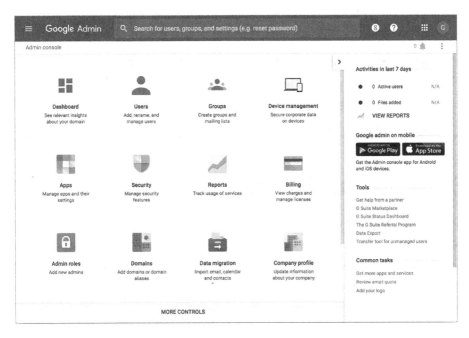

Figure 5-5. *The Activities pane shows your recent activities, gives you access to reports, and provides links to tools and common tasks*

- *Controls pane*: This pane shows icons for the main controls in Google Admin, such as the Dashboard icon, the Users icon, the Groups icon, and the Device management icon.

- *More Controls*: Click this bar to display any controls that are not currently displayed in the main pane.

CUSTOMIZING THE CONTROLS PANE

You can customize the Controls pane by dragging the icons into your preferred order. If you find you seldom or never use certain icons, you may be able to remove them by dragging them to the More Controls bar, which changes to a Delete bar (with a Trash icon) when you drag an icon you are allowed to delete.

However, Google Admin does not allow you to delete some icons, such as the Billing icon. If you try to drag one of these icons to the More Controls bar, the bar will show the message "This icon cannot be removed from Dashboard" instead of the Trash icon.

Enrolling Your School's Chromebooks

Now that you are up and running with your Google Admin console, you need to enroll your school's Chromebooks in the school's domain. You can enroll Chromebooks manually either yourself or by having users enroll them. You can also force re-enrollment for Chromebooks that have been wiped or recovered.

Making Sure a Chromebook Is Ready for Enrollment

For enrollment, each Chromebook must be in a clean, unused state, with no user—not even an administrator—having signed in on the Chromebook. If anyone has signed in on the Chromebook, you must wipe the Chromebook clean before you can enroll it.

To wipe the Chromebook clean, you switch it into Developer mode and then switch it back to Normal mode. Follow these steps:

1. Shut down the Chromebook as usual by clicking the Shut down button on the status menu or on the sign-in screen.

2. Hold down the Esc key and the Refresh key and then press the Power key or Power button. The Chromebook will boot to the Recovery screen, which warns you that Chrome OS is missing or damaged.

3. Press Ctrl+D. Chrome OS will prompt you to press the Enter key to enable or disable Developer mode.

4. Press the Enter key to enable Developer mode.

5. Wait while the Chromebook restarts and erases itself. This takes several minutes.

6. When the Chromebook restarts, it will boot to a Developer mode screen that tells you that OS verification is off and invites you to press the spacebar to re-enable it. Press the spacebar to re-enable OS verification.

7. Press the Enter key to confirm you want to turn OS verification on. The Chromebook will restart into Normal mode.

The Chromebook is now clean, and you can enroll it.

Note   Wiping some Chromebook models requires extra steps, such as removing the battery for a few seconds and then reinserting it. It is a good idea to consult the documentation for the particular Chromebook model to see if extra steps are needed.

Enrolling a Chromebook Manually

Follow these steps to enroll a Chromebook manually:

1. Make sure the Chromebook is clean, as explained in the previous section.

2. Power on the Chromebook. Chrome OS will start, and the Welcome! dialog box will open.

3. Choose language and accessibility settings as needed. See the section "Navigating the Welcome Dialog Box! Choosing Language and Accessibility Settings" in Chapter 3 for details.

4. Connect the Chromebook to a network. See the section "Working in the Connect to Network Dialog Box," also in Chapter 3, for details.

5. Accept the terms and conditions in the Google Chrome OS terms dialog box. (If necessary, see the section "Navigating the Google Chrome OS Terms Dialog Box" in Chapter 3 for more information.)

6. When the sign-in screen appears, press Ctrl+Alt+E. The enrollment screen will appear.

7. Type your Google admin username and password.

Note   At this point, if the person enrolling the Chromebook is a user rather than an administrator, the user enters his G Suite username and password. You need to have made this G Suite user eligible to enroll the Chromebook.

---

8. Click the Enroll device button. Chrome OS will enroll the Chromebook, and you will see a confirmation message saying that the device has been enrolled.

DEALING WITH ENROLLMENT ERRORS

During enrollment, you or the Chromebook users may encounter these two common errors:

- *You do not have enough software licenses to enroll this device*: This error is straightforward—you have run out of licenses, so none are available for this Chromebook. Get in touch with your Chrome Education partner to get more licenses.

- *This user account is not eligible for the service*: This error occurs when a user whose user account does not have the Enrollment Permissions policy is trying to enroll the Chromebook. The solution is for an administrator to add the Enrollment Permissions policy via the Admin console.

Apart from these two common errors, there is an esoteric one: The Samsung Chromebook 303 model may give an *Invalid parameters* error. The solution is to restart the Chromebook and wait for 90 seconds or more at the Terms of Service screen before proceeding with enrollment.

Controlling Forced Re-Enrollment for Wiped or Recovered Chromebooks

Enrolling a Chromebook automatically applies the Forced Re-Enrollment device policy to it. This policy is designed to make sure that a Chromebook cannot be removed from the management system by being wiped.

CONSIDERATIONS FOR FORCED RE-ENROLLMENT

Normally, you will want to keep Forced Re-enrollment enabled for most of your school's Chromebooks to avoid the possibility that someone could wipe a Chromebook and thus remove it from your management system. However, you may need to exempt some Chromebooks from Forced Re-enrollment so as to use features such as Developer mode, which is not compatible with Forced Re-enrollment.

You can configure Forced Re-enrollment at the domain level or at the organizational-unit level. What is usually best is to turn on Forced Re-enrollment at the domain level so every Chromebook is protected by default. You can then turn off Forced Re-enrollment for a particular organizational unit, such as the organizational unit to which you and your IT colleagues belong.

Another way to exempt a Chromebook from Forced Re-enrollment is to deprovision it. Normally, you would want to deprovision a Chromebook only when getting rid of a Chromebook or sending it in for repair.

You can turn Forced Re-Enrollment on or off by following these steps:

1. In the Google Admin console, click the Device
    management icon. The Device management page
    will appear (see Figure 5-6).

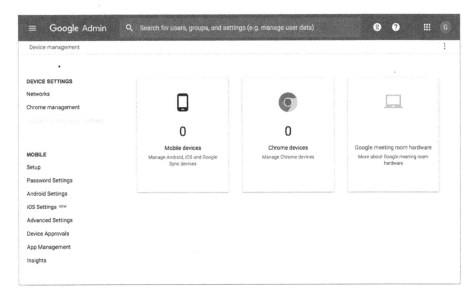

Figure 5-6. *On the Device management page, click the Chrome*
management item in the Device Settings list in the left pane

2. In the Device Settings list in the left pane, click
    the Chrome management item. The Chrome
    Management page will appear (see Figure 5-7).

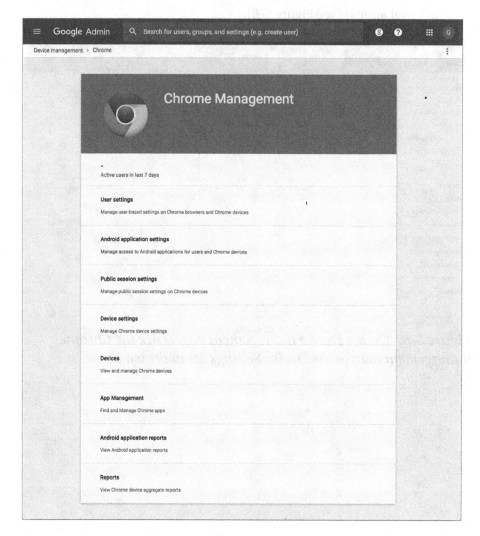

Figure 5-7. *On the Chrome Management page, click the Device settings button*

3. Click the Device settings button to display the Device Settings page.

Note   If your domain contains multiple organizational units, go to the organizational tree and click the domain or organizational unit for which you want to control Forced Re-enrollment.

---

4. In the Enrollment & Access section at the top of the Device Settings page, select the appropriate setting for Forced Re-enrollment:

    - *Force device to re-enroll into this domain after wiping*: Select this setting to turn on Forced Re-enrollment.

    - *Device is not forced to re-enroll after wiping*: Select this setting to turn off Forced Re-enrollment.

5. Click the Save button.

Note   It may take an hour or so for the Forced Re-enrollment setting to take effect on all your school's Chromebooks.

Disabling and Re-Enabling a Missing Chromebook

If a Chromebook goes missing, you can disable it to prevent whoever has it from using it. When you disable a Chromebook, you can display a message on the locked screen telling the reader how and where to return the Chromebook. When (or if) the Chromebook does return, you can re-enable it.

Note   The Forced Re-enrollment device policy needs to be enabled for you to be sure you can disable a Chromebook. (If this device policy is not enabled, whoever has taken the Chromebook can wipe it, thus freeing it from your management.)

Disabling a Chromebook

To disable a Chromebook after it goes missing, follow these steps:

1. In the Google Admin console, click the Device management icon.

2. Click the Chrome devices icon.

3. Make sure the Filters pane is open on the left. If it is not, click the Filter button to open the Filters pane.

4. Go to the By Status section on the left and click the Provisioned status.

5. In the left pane, click the organization that contains the Chromebook. A list of the devices in the organization will appear.

6. Check the check box for the Chromebook you want to disable.

7. Click the More Actions button at the top of the screen and then click the Disable item. The Disable dialog box will open.

8. In the text field, type the message to display on the locked screen of the Chromebook. Normally, you would want to include contact details, such as the school's email address and phone number.

9. Click the Disable button. The Disable dialog box will close, and Chrome OS will disable the Chromebook.

Re-Enabling a Chromebook

To re-enable the Chromebook after it has returned to the fold, follow the same steps as in the list in the previous section, but select the Disabled status in the By Status list. In the list of disabled Chromebooks, check the check box for the Chromebook you want to re-enable, then click the More Actions button and click the Re-enable item. In the confirmation dialog box that opens, click the Re-enable button.

Deprovisioning a Chromebook

When you need to remove management features from a Chromebook, you can *deprovision* it. Normally, you would deprovision a Chromebook before sending it in for repair or before disposing of it—for example, selling the Chromebook or donating it.

To deprovision a Chromebook, follow these steps:

1. In the Google Admin console, click the Device management icon.

2. Click the Chrome devices icon.

3. Make sure the Filters pane is open on the left. If it is not, click the Filter button to open the Filters pane.

4. Go to the By Status section on the left and click the Provisioned status.

Note   If the Chromebook has been disabled, click the Disabled
status in the By Status section instead.

---

5. In the left pane, click the organization that contains
    the Chromebook. A list of the devices in the
    organization will appear.

6. Check the check box for the Chromebook you want
    to deprovision.

7. Click the More Actions button at the top of the
    screen and then click the Deprovision item. The
    Deprovision dialog box will open to confirm
    the action and to prompt you for the reason for
    deprovisioning.

8. Check the confirmation check box.

9. Click the reason for deprovisioning the
    Chromebook:

    -   *Same Model Replacement*: Select this reason if
        you are replacing a defective Chromebook with
        another Chromebook of the same model, or if
        you are replacing a defective Chromebook under
        warranty with a new Chromebook from the same
        manufacturer.

    -   *Different Model Replacement*: Select this reason
        if you are replacing a Chromebook with a newer
        model.

- *Retiring from Fleet*: Select this reason if you are removing the Chromebook from use, selling it, or donating it.

10. Click the Deprovision button. The Deprovision dialog box will close.

After deprovisioning a Chromebook, you can wipe it to remove all device management from it. See the section "Making Sure a Chromebook Is Ready for Enrollment" earlier in this chapter for instructions on wiping a Chromebook.

Configuring User Settings

The Chrome Management console enables you to configure a wide range of settings to control the user experience on your school's Chromebooks. In this section, we will first navigate to the User Settings page, which contains those settings, and then explore the various sections and many settings on that page.

Displaying the User Settings Page

To display the User Settings page, follow these steps in your Google Admin console:

1. On the Home page, click the Device management icon to display the Device management page.

2. In the Device Settings list in the left pane, click the Chrome management item to display the Chrome Management page.

3. Click the User settings button to display the User Settings page. Figure 5-8 shows the top part of this long page.

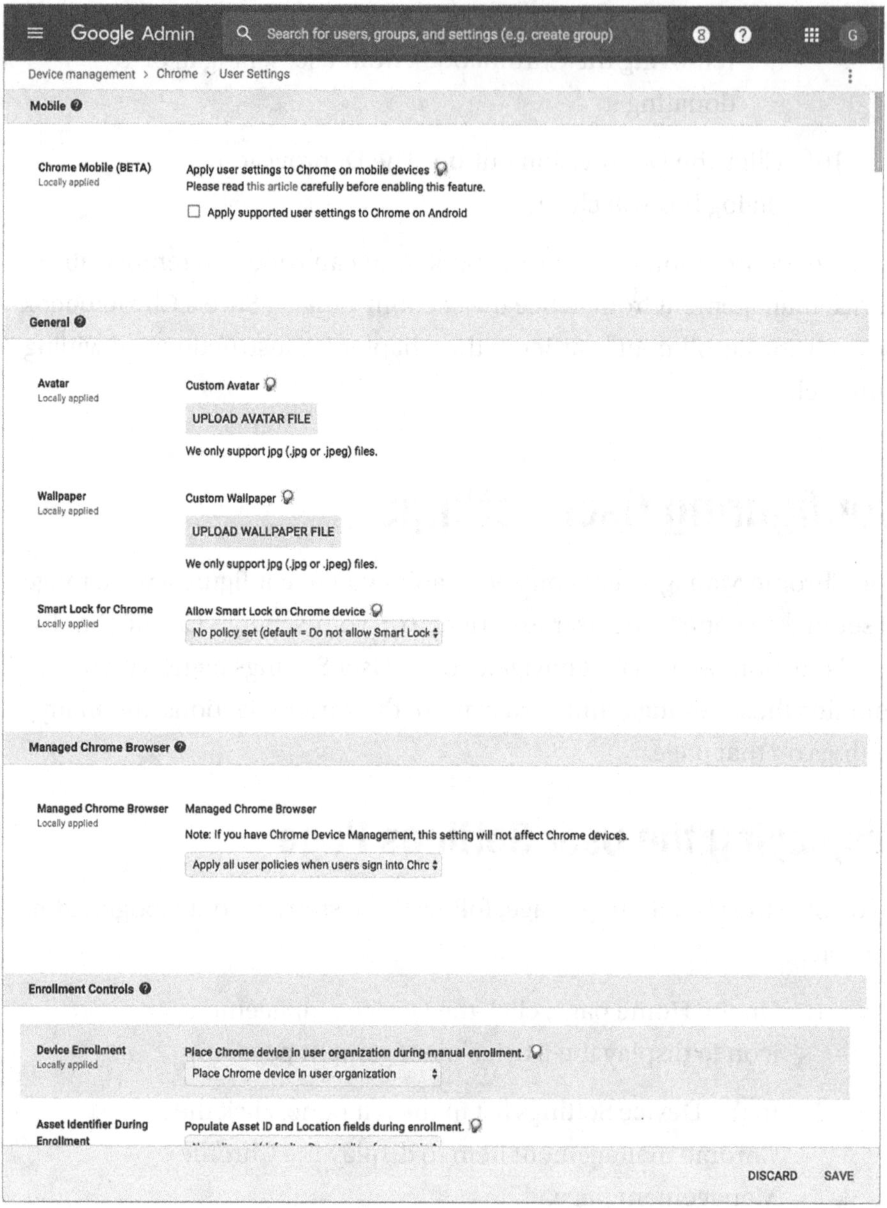

Figure 5-8.   *The top part of the User Settings page includes the Mobile section, the General section, the Managed Chrome Browser section, and the Enrollment Controls section*

Configuring Mobile Options

In the Mobile section of the User Settings page, you can check the "Apply supported user settings to Chrome on Android" check box if you want to use the Chrome Mobile feature to apply user settings to Chrome on Android devices. As of this writing, the Chrome Mobile feature is still in beta, so it may not work consistently.

If you are mostly concerned with managing Chromebooks, you likely need not use this feature.

Configuring General Settings

In the General section of the User Settings page, you can configure the settings explained in the following list:

- *Avatar*: Click the Upload Avatar File to start uploading a JPEG image file to replace the default avatar. This file has a maximum size of 512 KB.

- *Wallpaper*: Click the Upload Wallpaper File button to start uploading a JPEG file to use as wallpaper. For example, you might upload your school's preferred wallpaper file. This file has a maximum size of 16 MB, but it is usually better to keep wallpaper files considerably smaller than this.

- *Smart Lock for Chrome*: If you want to allow users to use their Android phones to unlock their Chromebooks, open the Allow Smart Lock on Chrome device pop-up menu and select the Allow Smart Lock for Chrome item. If you prefer to prevent the use of this feature, select the Do not allow Smart Lock for Chrome item. If you do not want to control this setting via policy, select the "No policy set (default = Do not allow Smart Lock for Chrome)" item.

351

Configuring Managed Chrome Browser Settings

The Managed Chrome Browser pop-up menu in the Managed Chrome Browser section of the User Settings page is relevant only if you do not have Chrome Device Management. If this is the case, you can open the Managed Chrome Browser pop-up menu and select the appropriate item on it:

- Apply all user policies when users sign in to Chrome, and provide a managed Chrome experience

- Do not apply any policies when users sign in to Chrome. Allow users access to use Chrome as an unmanaged user.

Configuring Enrollment Controls Settings

In the Enrollment Controls section of the User Settings page, you can configure the settings explained in the following list:

- *Device Enrollment*: Open the Place Chrome device in user organization during manual enrollment pop-up menu and select the Place Chrome device in user organization item if you want to move the Chrome device to a user organization. If you want to leave the Chrome device where it is, select the Keep Chrome device in current location item.

- *Asset Identifier During Enrollment*: Open the Populate Asset ID and Location fields during enrollment pop-up menu and select the Users in this organization can provide asset ID and location during enrollment item if you want each user to be able to enter an asset ID and a location when enrolling a Chromebook. When you do this, Chrome will display the Device Information screen with suggested data in the fields; the user can accept the suggestions or change them. To prevent users from adding this information, select the Do not allow for users in this organization item. If you do not want to control this setting via policy, select the "No policy set (default = Do not allow for users in this organization)" item.

- *Enrollment Permission*: Open the Enrollment Permission pop-up menu and select the appropriate item on it:

  - **Allow users in this organization to enroll new or re-enroll existing devices**: Select this item to let users both enroll new devices and re-enroll existing devices.

  - **Only allow users in this organization to re-enroll existing devices (cannot enroll new or deprovisioned devices)**: Select this item to allow re-enrollment but prevent new enrollment.

  - **Do not allow users in this organization to enroll new or re-enroll existing devices**: Select this item to prevent both enrollment and re-enrollment.

  - **No policy set (default = Allow users in this organization to enroll new or re-enroll existing devices)**: Select this item if you do not want to control enrollment permission via policy.

Configuring Apps and Extensions Settings

In the Apps and Extensions section of the User Settings page (see Figure 5-9), you can configure the settings explained in the following list:

- *Allowed Types of Apps and Extensions*: In the Allowed Types of Apps and Extensions list, check or uncheck the following check boxes to specify which types of apps and extensions Chrome OS should allow:

  - **Extension**: An extension is a small program that adds functionality to the Chrome browser.

  - **Theme**: A theme is a custom look for Chrome OS.

  - **Google Apps Script**: A Google Apps Script is an automated series of actions in a Google Apps app (such as Docs or Sheets).

  - **Hosted App**: A hosted app is an app that runs on a web host rather than running locally on Chrome OS.

  - **Legacy Packaged App**: A Legacy Packaged app is a full app for installation on Chrome OS, but in an older format than a Chrome Packaged app.

  - **Chrome Packaged App**: A Chrome Packaged app is a full app for installation on Chrome OS—for example, an app that you download from the Chrome Web Store.

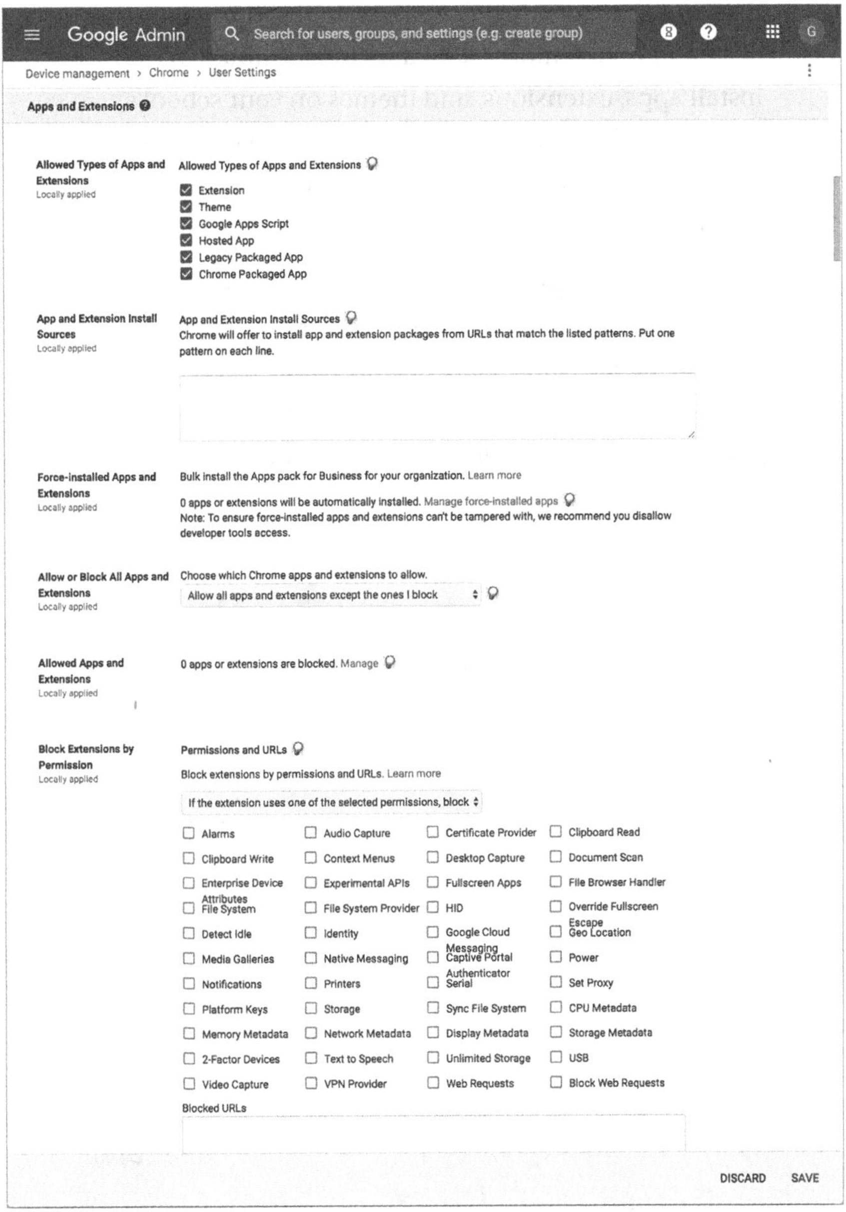

Figure 5-9. *In the Apps and Extensions section of the User Settings page, you can set up apps and extensions to be installed automatically. You can also block unwanted items.*

- *App and Extension Install Sources*: In this box, you can enter one or more URLs that are permitted to install apps, extensions, and themes on your school's Chromebooks. When a Chromebook navigates to one of these URLs, Chrome OS will prompt the user to install the app, extension, or theme.

- *Force-installed Apps and Extensions*: In this area, click the Manage force-installed apps link to display the Force-installed Apps and Extensions dialog box (see Figure 5-10). Select the apps and extensions you want to force-install, and then click the Save button.

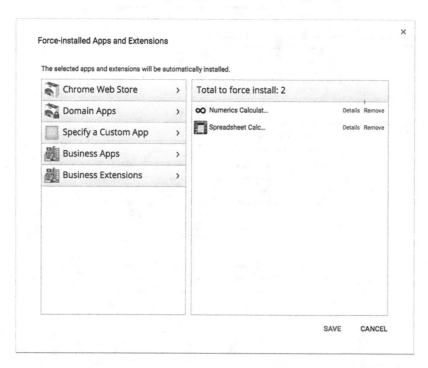

Figure 5-10. *In the Force-installed Apps and Extensions dialog box, select the apps and extensions you want to install automatically, and then click the Save button*

- *Allow or Block All Apps and Extensions*: Open the Choose which Chrome apps and extensions to allow pop-up menu and select the Allow all apps and extensions except the ones I block item or the Block all apps and extensions except the ones I allow item.

- *Allowed Apps and Extensions*: In this area, click the Manage link to display the Allowed apps and extensions dialog box or the Blocked apps and extensions dialog box, depending on which Allow or Block All Apps and Extensions setting you chose. Both these dialog boxes look and work like the Force-installed Apps and Extensions dialog box shown in Figure 5-10. Select the apps and extensions you want to allow or block and then click the Save button.

- *Block Extensions by Permission*: In this area, specify which extensions to block by the types of permissions they need. First, choose whether you will specify blocked permissions or allowed permissions; to do so, open the Block extensions by permissions and URLs pop-up menu and select the "If the extension uses one of the selected permissions, block users from installing or using it" item if you want to specify blocked permissions; select the "If the extension uses a permission that is not selected, block users from installing or using it" item if you want to specify allowed permissions. Then, go to the list of permissions and check the appropriate check boxes to specify which permissions to block or allow. In the Blocked URLs box, enter any URLs you want to block. Then, in the Allowed URLs box, enter any URLs you want to allow.

- *Task Manager*: Open the Task Manager pop-up menu and select the "Allow users to end processes with the Chrome task manager" item if you want users to be able to use Task Manager. Select the "Block users from ending processes with the Chrome task manager" if you want to prevent users from using Task Manager. If you do not want to apply policy to Task Manager, select the "No policy set (default = Allow users to end processes with the Chrome task manager)" item.

Choosing Site Isolation Settings

The Site Isolation section of the User Settings page (see Figure 5-11) contains only the Manage Site Isolation controls. *Site isolation* is Chrome's feature for separating web pages from different websites programmatically to make it harder for malevolent sites to bypass security measures.

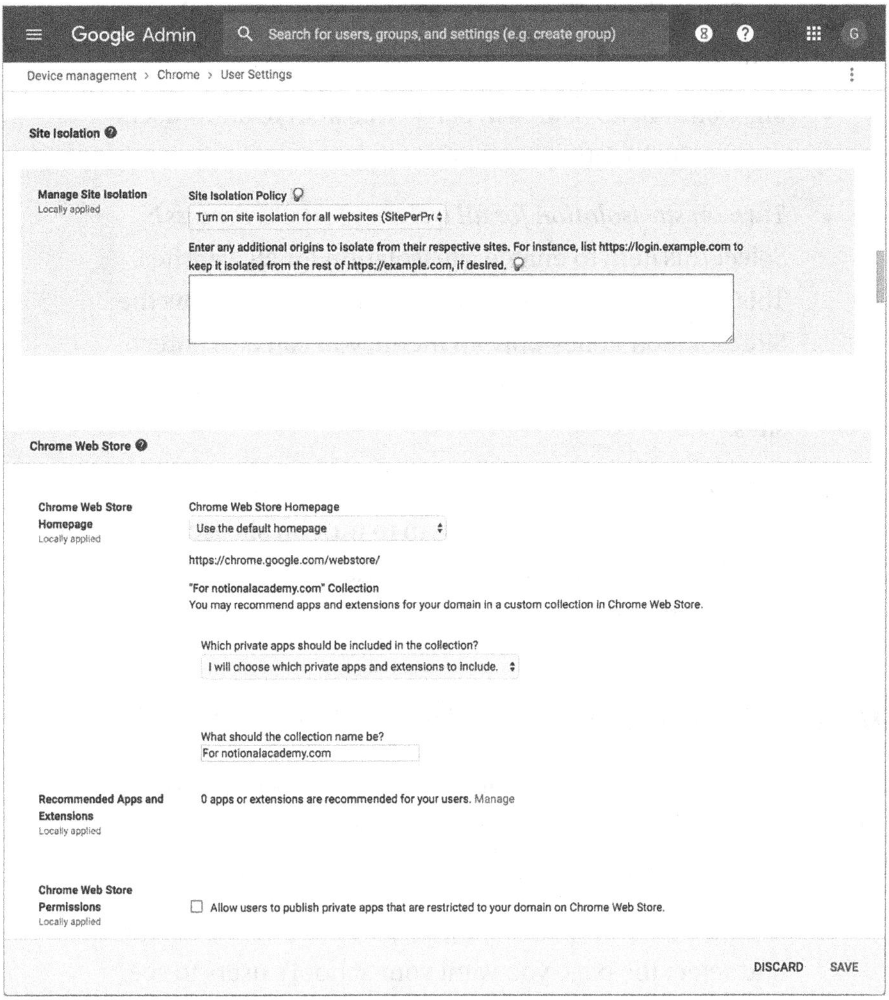

Figure 5-11. *The Site Isolation section of the User Settings page lets you specify which websites to isolate. The Chrome Web Store section enables you to add private apps to the users' view of the Chrome Web Store.*

Open the Site Isolation Policy pop-up menu and select the appropriate item:

- *Site isolation not enabled*: Select this item to allow users to turn site isolation on or off.

- *Turn on site isolation for all websites (SitePerProcess)*: Select this item to enable site isolation for all websites. This is the most secure setting. In the text box below the Site Isolation Policy pop-up menu, you can also enter specific web pages you want to isolate from their own sites.

- *Turn on site isolation for specific websites, set below (IsolateOrigins)*: Select this item to turn on site isolation only for the websites you enter in the text box below the Site Isolation Policy pop-up menu.

Configuring the Chrome Web Store Settings

In the Chrome Web Store section of the User Settings page, you can customize how the Chrome Web Store appears to users of your school's Chromebooks. The following list explains the settings you can configure:

- *Chrome Web Store Homepage*: Open this pop-up menu and select the page you want your school's users to see as the home page of the Chrome Web Store:

  - **Use the default homepage**: Select this item to use the Chrome Web Store's default home page.

  - **Use the "For [your school's domain]" collection**: Select this item to use the collection of apps, extensions, and themes that the Chrome Web Store provides for your school. You can customize this collection.

- **Use a custom page, set below**: To use a custom page, select this item and type the URL of the page within the Chrome Web Store that you want to use.

- *Which private apps should be included in the collection?*: In this pop-up menu, choose the I will choose which private apps and extensions to include item or the Include all private apps and extensions from my domain item, as needed.

- *What should the collection name be?*: In this text field, type the description you want the Chrome Web Store to show for your school's collection.

- *Recommended Apps and Extensions*: In this area, click the Manage button. The Recommended apps and extensions dialog box will open. This dialog box is similar to the Force-installed Apps and Extensions dialog box (see Figure 5-10, earlier in this chapter) and works in a similar way. Select the apps you want to include and then click the Save button.

- *Chrome Web Store Permissions*: In this area, check the "Allow users to publish private apps that are restricted to your domain on Chrome Web Store" check box if you want users to be able to publish apps. Normally, you would allow only your school's developers to publish apps. If you check this check box, the "Allow users to skip verification for websites not owned" check box appears. You can check this check box to enable users to publish apps without having to prove that they own your school's domain.

Choosing Settings in the Android Applications Section

In the Android applications section of the User Settings page, you can configure settings for Android apps running on Chrome devices. This feature is currently in beta, and we will not explore it here.

Configuring Security Settings

In the Security section of the User Settings page (see Figure 5-12), you can configure the settings explained in the following list:

- *Password Manager*: In this pop-up menu, select the Allow user to configure item, the Always allow use of password manager item, or the Never allow use of password manager item, as needed.

- *Lock Screen*: In this pop-up menu, select the Allow locking screen item if you want the Chromebooks to display the locking screen; if not, select the Do not allow locking screen item. If you do not want to configure this setting via policy, select the "No policy set (default = Allow locking screen)" item.

Figure 5-12. *The Security section of the User Settings page gives you access to a wide range of important settings*

- *Idle Settings*: In this area, specify settings for idle time, lid closing, and sleep:

  - **Idle time in minutes (leave empty for system default)**: In this box, type the number of minutes a Chromebook should remain idle before going to sleep or signing the user out. Leave this box empty to use the system default setting.

  - **Action on idle**: In this pop-up menu, select the Sleep (default) item or the Logout item to specify what the Chromebook should do at the end of the idle period.

  - **Action on lid close**: In this pop-up menu, select the Sleep (default) item or the Logout item to specify what the Chromebook should do when someone closes its lid.

  - **Lock screen on sleep**: In this pop-up menu, select the Lock screen item if you want the Chromebook to lock the screen when it goes to sleep. Select the Don't lock screen item to leave the screen unlocked. Select the Allow user to configure item to let the user configure which action occurs.

- *Incognito Mode*: In this pop-up menu, select the Allow incognito mode item if you want to allow users to use Incognito mode in the Chrome browser. Otherwise, select the Disallow incognito mode item.

- *Browser History*: In this pop-up menu, select the Always save browser history item or the Never save browser history item, as needed.

- *Clear Browser History*: In this pop-up menu, select the Allow clearing history in settings menu item if you want to allow the user to clear the browsing history, or the Do not allow clearing history in settings menu item if you do not. If you do not want to configure this setting via policy, select the "No policy set (default = Allow clearing history in settings menu)" item.

- *Force Ephemeral Mode*: In the Erase local data when the browser is closed pop-up menu, select the Do not erase local user data item or the Erase all local user data item, as needed.

- *Online Revocation Checks*: In the Online OCSP/CRL Checks pop-up menu, select the Perform online OCSP/CRL checks item if you want Chrome OS to check that websites' digital certificates are valid. If not, select the Do not perform online OCSP/CRL checks item.

Note   OCSP is the abbreviation for Online Certificate Status Protocol, a protocol for verifying the validity of digital certificates. CRL is the abbreviation for Certificate Revocation Lists, which are lists of certificates that have been revoked.

- *Safe Browsing*: In this pop-up menu, select the Always use Safe Browsing item if you want to enforce the use of Safe Browsing, a Chrome feature that provides some protection from websites that contain malware. Select the Always disable Safe Browsing item if you want to turn off Safe Browsing. Select the Allow user to decide whether to use Safe Browsing item if you want to let the user make the choice.

- *Malicious Sites*: In this pop-up menu, choose the Allow user to proceed anyway to malicious sites item if you want to allow users to disregard warnings about potentially dangerous sites and go to them anyway. Select the Prevent user from proceeding anyway to malicious sites item if you want to prevent the user from going to such sites.

- *Geolocation*: In this pop-up menu, select the appropriate item to control the use of geolocation services:

  - **Allow sites to detect users' geolocation**: Select this item to allow sites to detect geolocation.

  - **Do not allow sites to detect users' geolocation**: Select this item to block sites' attempts to detect geolocation.

  - **Always ask the user if a site wants to detect their geolocation**: Select this item to have Chrome OS prompt the user when a site asks for geolocation information.

  - **Allow user to configure**: Select this item to enable the user to configure geolocation settings.

- *Single Sign-On Online Login Frequency*: In the Force online login flow for SAML-based Single Sign-On accounts pop-up menu, select the frequency with which to force login. For example, you might select the Every two weeks item.

- *Single Sign-On*: In the SAML-based Single Sign-On for Chrome Devices pop-up menu, select the Enable SAML-based Single Sign-On for Chrome item or the Disable SAML-based Single Sign-On for Chrome item, as needed.

- *Remote access clients*: In the "Remote Access Host Client Domain" field, enter the domain name that remote access clients should enter.

- *Local Trust Anchors Certificates*: In the Local Anchors Sha1 pop-up menu, select the appropriate item to control how the Chromebooks treat SHA-1 signed certificates issued by local trust anchors:

  - **Allow SHA-1 for local trust anchors**: Select this item to allow SHA-1.

  - **Follow the publicly announced SHA-1 deprecation schedule**: Select this item to make the Chromebooks follow the publicly announced schedule for discontinuing use of SHA-1 certificates (which have certain security problems).

  - **No policy set (default = Follow the publicly announced SHA-1 deprecation schedule)**: Select this item if you do not want to configure this feature via policy.

- *Local Anchors Common Name Fallback*: In this pop-up menu, select the Allow item to allow certificates issued by local trust anchors that are missing the subjectAlternativeName extension; select the Block item to block such certificates; or select the "No policy set (default = Block)" item to avoid configuring this feature via policy.

- *Symantec Corporation's Legacy PKI Infrastructure*: In
  this pop-up menu, select the Allow item if you want
  to trust certificates issued by Symantec Corporation's
  Legacy PKI operations; select the Block item if you
  want to block such certificates: or select the "No policy
  set (default = Block)" item to avoid configuring this
  feature via policy.

Configuring Session Settings

In the Session Settings section of the User Settings page (see Figure 5-13),
you can configure the Show Logout Button in Tray setting, which controls
whether the Sign out button appears in the Chrome OS tray. Open the
Show Logout Button in Tray pop-up menu and select the Show logout
button in tray item, the Does not show logout button in tray item, or the
"No policy set (default = Does not show logout button in tray)" item, as
needed.

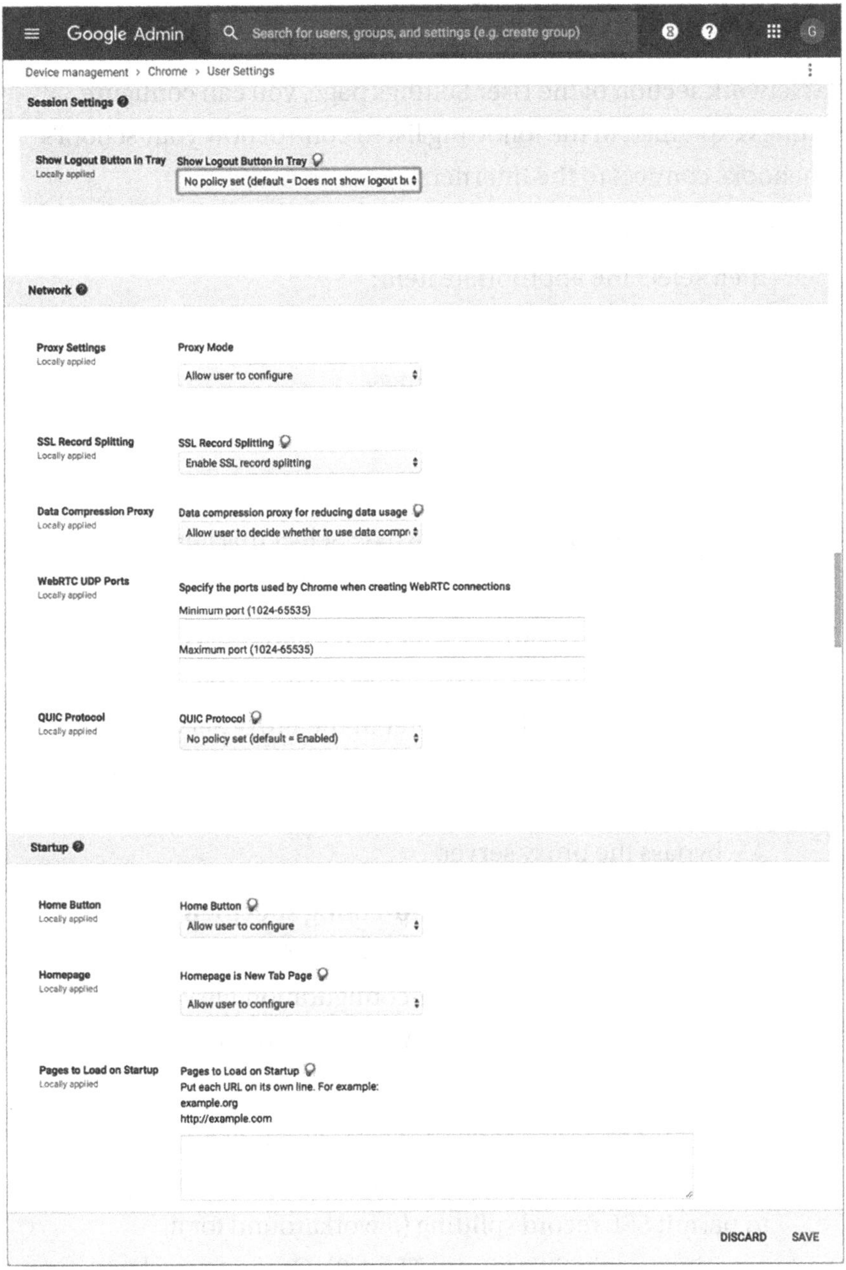

Figure 5-13. *The Session Settings section, Network section, and Startup section of the User Settings page*

Configuring Network Settings

In the Network section of the User Settings page, you can configure the settings explained in the following list to control how your school's Chromebooks connect to the Internet:

- *Proxy Settings*: Open the Proxy Mode pop-up menu and then select the appropriate item:

  - **Allow user to configure**: Select this item to let the user configure proxy settings.

  - **Never use a proxy**: Select this item to turn off proxying.

  - **Always auto detect the proxy**: Select this item to use auto-detection of the proxy server.

  - **Always use the proxy specified below**: Select this item to make the Chromebooks use the proxy server whose URL you enter in the Proxy Server URL box. If necessary, you can then go to the Proxy Bypass List box and enter a list of URLs that should bypass the proxy server.

  - **Always use the proxy auto-config specified below**: Select this item to make the Chromebooks use the proxy server auto-configuration file you enter in the Proxy Server Auto Configuration File URL box.

- *SSL Record Splitting*: Open this pop-up menu and select the Enable SSL record splitting item if you want to permit SSL record splitting (a workaround for a security issue in SSL 3.0 and TLS 1.0). Otherwise, select the Disable SSL record splitting item.

- *Data Compression Proxy*: Open this pop-up menu and select the Always enable data compression proxy item if you want your school's Chromebooks to use Google's data compression proxy service, which is intended to reduce cellular data usage and speed up mobile browsing. Select the Always disable data compression proxy item if you want to turn off the use of the data compression proxy service. To leave the choice up to the user, select the Allow user to decide whether to use data compression proxy.

- *WebRTC UDP Ports*: In the Specify the ports used by Chrome when creating WebRTC connections area, specify the port range that Chrome OS should use for real-time connections over the Web. Enter the minimum port in the Minimum port (1024–65535) box and the maximum port in the Maximum port (1024–65535) box.

- *QUIC Protocol*: Open this pop-up menu and select the Enabled item if you want to allow Chrome OS to use the Quick UDP Internet Connections (QUIC) protocol. Select the Disabled item if you do not want Chrome OS to use QUIC. If you do not want to configure this feature via policy, select the "No policy set (default = Enabled)" item.

Choosing Startup Settings

In the Startup section of the User Settings page, you can configure the settings explained in the following list:

- *Home Button*: Open this pop-up menu and select the Always show "Home" button item if you want the Chrome browser to display the Home button. If you prefer to suppress the Home button, select the Never show "Home" button item. To let the user decide, select the Allow user to configure item.

- *Homepage*: Open the Homepage is New Tab Page pop-up menu and select the appropriate item:

  - **Allow user to configure**: Select this item to let the user configure the home page.

  - **Homepage is always the new tab page**: Select this item to set the home page to the new tab page.

  - **Homepage is always the Homepage URL, set below**: Select this item to make the home page the page at the URL you enter in the Homepage URL box.

- *Pages to Load on Startup*: In this box, enter a list of the web pages you want the Chrome browser to load on startup. Place each URL on a separate line.

Choosing Content Settings

In the Content section of the User Settings page (see Figure 5-14), you can configure the settings explained in the following list:

- *Safe Search and Restricted Mode*: In this area, you can configure the Google Safe Search feature and the Restricted Mode for YouTube feature:

  - **Google Safe Search for Google Web Search queries**: Open this pop-up menu and select the Always use Safe Search for Google Web Search item if you want to ensure the Chromebooks always use the Safe Search feature. Select the Do not enforce Safe Search for Google Web Search item if you do not require Safe Search. If you do not want to configure this feature via policy, select the "No policy set (default = Do not enforce Safe Search for Google Web Search)" item.

  - **Restricted Mode for YouTube**: Open this pop-up menu and select the Enforce Strict Restricted Mode on YouTube item, the Enforce at least Moderate Restricted Mode on YouTube item, or the Do not enforce Restricted Mode on YouTube item, as needed. If you do not want to configure this feature via policy, select the "No policy set (default = Do not enforce Restricted Mode on YouTube)" item.

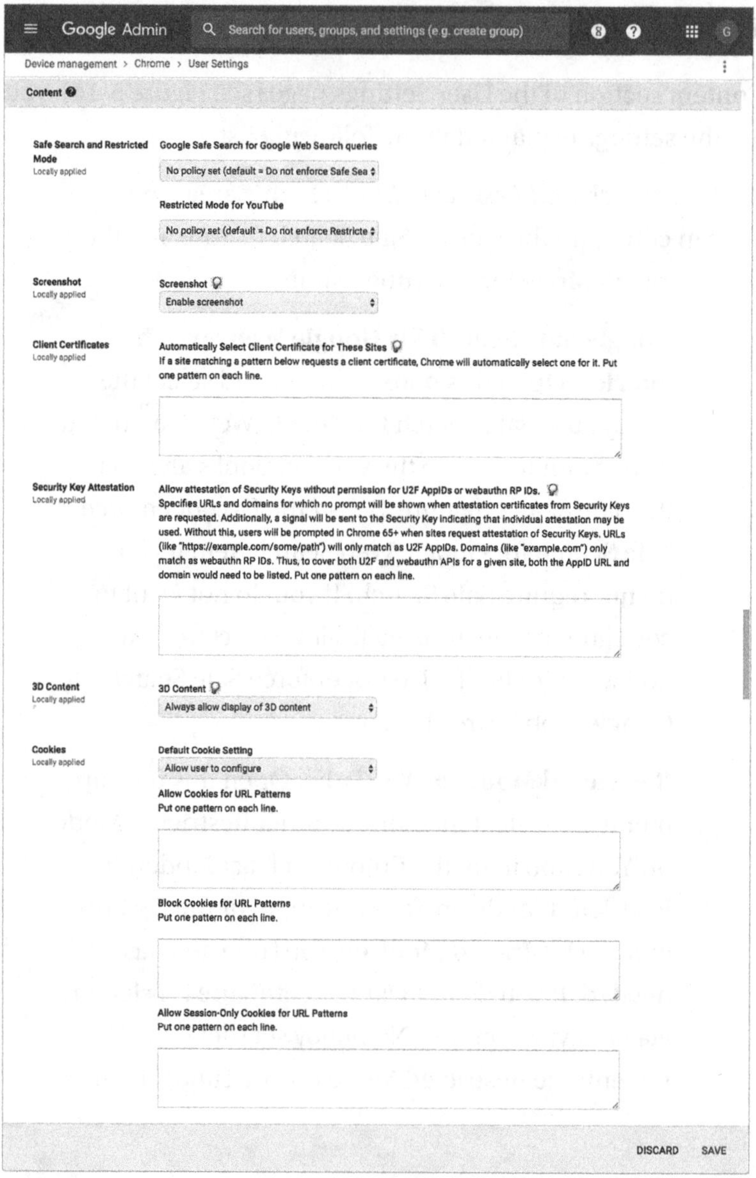

Figure 5-14. *The Content section of the User Settings page enables you to control Safe Search, Restricted Mode for YouTube, screenshots, cookies, and more*

- *Screenshot*: In this pop-up menu, select the Enable screenshot item if you want to let users take screenshots, or select the Disable screenshot item if you do not.

- *Client certificates*: In the Automatically Select Client Certificate for These Sites box, enter a JSON string containing a list of patterns specifying the websites for which Chrome OS should automatically select client certificates.

- *Security Key Attestation*: In this box, you can enter a JSON string containing a list of URLs and domains for which you want to suppress prompts when attestation certificates from security keys are requested.

- *3D Content*: Open the 3D Content pop-up menu and select the Always allow display of 3D content item or the Never allow display of 3D content item, as needed.

- *Cookies*: Use the controls in this area to specify how to handle cookies:

    - **Default Cookie Setting**: Open this pop-up menu and select the Allow sites to set cookies item, the Never allow sites to set cookies item, the Keep cookies for the duration of the session item, or the Allow user to configure item, as needed.

    - **Allow Cookies for URL Patterns**: In this box, enter a list of URL patterns specifying sites for which to allow cookies.

375

- **Block Cookies for URL Patterns**: In this box, enter a list of URL patterns specifying sites for which to block cookies.

- **Allow Session-Only Cookies for URL Patterns**: In this box, enter a list of URL patterns specifying sites that are permitted to set session-only cookies.

- *Third-Party Cookie Blocking*: Open this pop-up menu and select the Allow third-party cookies item, the Disallow third-party cookies item, or the Allow user to decide whether to allow third-party cookies item, as needed.

- *Images*: Open this pop-up menu and select the Show images item, the Do not show images item, or the Allow user to configure item, as needed. In the Show Images on These Sites box, enter a list of URL patterns specifying sites that are allowed to show images. In the Block Images on These Sites box, enter a list of URL patterns specifying sites to block from showing images.

- *JavaScript*: Open this pop-up menu and select the Allow sites to run JavaScript item, the Do not allow sites to run JavaScript item, or the Allow user to configure item, as needed. In the Allow These Sites to Run JavaScript box, enter a list of URL patterns specifying sites allowed to run JavaScript. In the Block JavaScript on These Sites box, enter a list of URL patterns specifying sites to block from running JavaScript.

- *Notifications*: Open this pop-up menu and select the Allow sites to show desktop notifications item, the Do not allow sites to show desktop notifications item, the Always ask the user if a site can show desktop notifications item, or the Allow user to configure item, as needed. In the Allow These Sites to Show Desktop Notifications box, enter a list of URL patterns specifying sites allowed to show desktop notifications. In the Block Desktop Notifications on These Sites box, enter a list of URL patterns specifying sites to block from displaying desktop notifications.

- *Plug-ins*: Open this pop-up menu and select the Run plug-ins automatically item, the Block all plug-ins item, or the Allow user to configure item, as needed. In the Allow Plug-ins on These Sites box, enter a list of URL patterns specifying sites allowed to run plugins. In the Block Plug-ins on These Sites box, enter a list of URL patterns specifying sites to block from running plugins.

- *Enabled and Disabled Plug-ins*: In the Enabled Plug-ins box, enter a list containing the names of plugins to always enable. These names are case sensitive. You can use wildcards (such as *). In the Disabled Plug-ins box, enter a list containing the names of plugins to always disable. In the Exceptions to Disabled Plug-ins box, enter a list of plugins that users can enable or disable even if those plugins appear in the Disabled Plug-ins box.

- *Plug-in Finder*: Open this pop-up menu and select the Enable automatic search and installation of missing plug-ins item or the Disable automatic search and installation of missing plug-ins item, as needed.

- *Plug-in Authorization*: Open this pop-up menu and select the Ask for user permission before running plug-ins that require authorization item or the Always run plug-ins that require authorization item, as needed.

- *Outdated plug-ins*: Open this pop-up menu and select the Allow outdated plug-ins to be used as normal plug-ins item, the Ask user for permission to run outdated plug-ins item, or the Disallow outdated plug-ins item, as needed.

- *Pop-ups*: Open this pop-up menu and select the Allow all pop-ups item, the Block all pop-ups item, or the Allow user to configure item, as needed. In the Allow Pop-ups on These Sites box, enter a list of URL patterns specifying sites allowed to display pop-ups. In the Block Pop-ups on These Sites box, enter a list of URL patterns specifying sites to block from displaying pop-ups.

- *URL Blocking*: In the URL Blacklist box, enter a list of URLs to block. In the URL Blacklist Exception list, enter a list of URLs to allow even if they appear in the URL blacklist.

- *Google Drive Syncing*: Open the Syncing Data with Google Drive pop-up menu and select the Enable Google Drive syncing item, the Disable Google Drive syncing item, or the Allow user to decide whether to use Google Drive syncing item, as needed.

- *Google Drive Syncing over Cellular*: Open the Syncing
  Data with Google Drive over Cellular Connections
  pop-up menu and select the Enable Google Drive
  syncing over cellular connections item or the Disable
  Google Drive syncing over cellular connections item, as
  appropriate.

- *Cast*: Open the Allow users to Cast from Chrome pop-
  up menu and select the Allow users to Cast item, the
  Do not allow users to Cast item, or the "No policy set
  (default = Allow users to Cast)" item, as needed. Open
  the Show Cast Icon in the toolbar pop-up menu and
  select the Always show the Cast icon in the toolbar
  item, the Do not show the Cast icon in the toolbar item,
  or the "No policy set (default = Do not show the Cast
  icon in the toolbar)" item, as required.

Configuring Printing Options

In the Printing section of the User Settings page (see Figure 5-15), you can
configure the settings explained in the following list:

- *Printing*: Open this pop-up menu and select the
  Enable printing item or the Disable printing item, as
  appropriate.

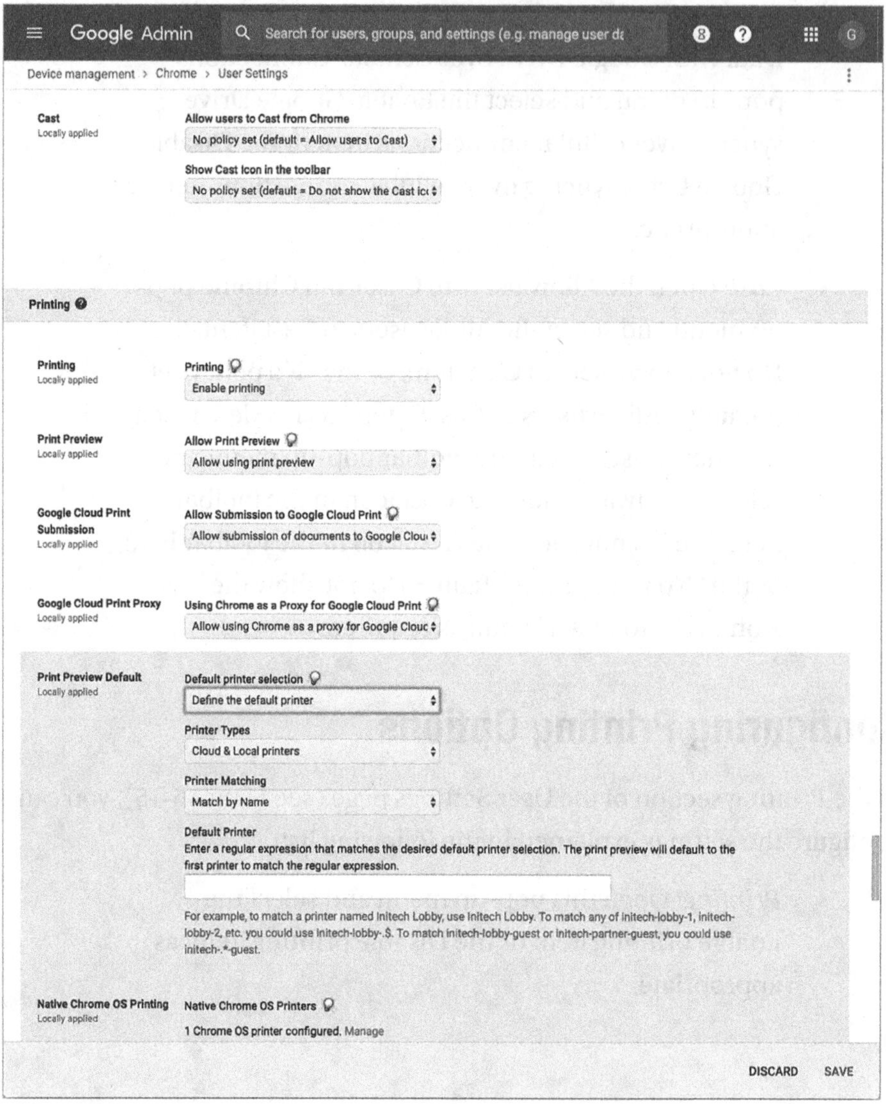

Figure 5-15. *In the Printing section of the User Settings page, you can enable and disable printing and print preview, configure Google Cloud Print, and configure native Chrome OS printing*

- *Print Preview*: Open the Allow Print Preview pop-up menu and select the Allow using print preview item or the Always use the system print dialog instead of print preview item, as needed.

- *Google Cloud Print Submission*: Open the Allow Submission to Google Cloud Print pop-up menu and select the Allow submission of documents to Google Cloud Print item or the Disallow submission of documents to Google Cloud Print item, as needed.

- *Google Cloud Print Proxy*: Open the Using Chrome as a Proxy for Google Cloud Print pop-up menu and select the Allow using Chrome as a proxy for Google Cloud Print item or the Disallow using Chrome as a proxy for Google Cloud Print item, as appropriate.

- *Print Preview Default*: Open the Default printer selection pop-up menu and select the Use default print behavior item or the Define the default printer item. If you select the Define the default printer item, open the Printer Types pop-up menu and select the appropriate printer type: Cloud & Local printers, Cloud only, or Local only. Open the Printer Matching pop-up menu and select the Match by Name item or the Match by ID item, as needed. Then, click in the Default Printer box and type a regular expression that identifies the printer you want to use as the default.

- *Native Chrome OS Printing*: In this area, click the
  Manage link to display the Native Chrome OS Printers
  dialog box (shown on the left in Figure 5-16). Click the
  Add a Printer button to display the Add a native printer
  dialog box (shown on the right in Figure 5-16), enter
  the printer's details, and then click the Save button.
  The printer will then appear in the Native Chrome
  OS Printers dialog box. When you have added all the
  printers, click the Save button to close the dialog box.

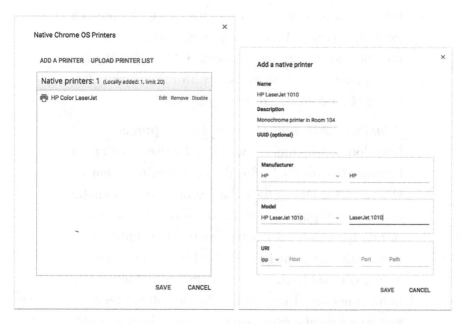

Figure 5-16. *In the Native Chrome OS Printers dialog box (left), click the Add a Printer button to display the Add a native printer dialog box (right). Specify the printer's details and then click the Save button.*

Configuring User Experience Settings

In the User Experience section of the User Settings page (see Figure 5-17), you can configure the settings explained in the following list:

- *Managed Bookmarks*: In the "Managed Bookmarks Folder Name" field, type the name that the Chromebooks should display for the managed bookmarks you provide. For example, you might call the folder School Links. Add each managed bookmark by typing its name in the URL column, typing a descriptive name in the Name column, and then clicking the Add (+) button.

- *Bookmark Bar*: Open this pop-up menu and select the Enable bookmark bar item, the Disable bookmark bar item, or the Allow user to decide whether to enable bookmark bar item, as needed.

- *Bookmark Editing*: Open this pop-up menu and select the Enable bookmark editing item or the Disable bookmark editing item, as needed.

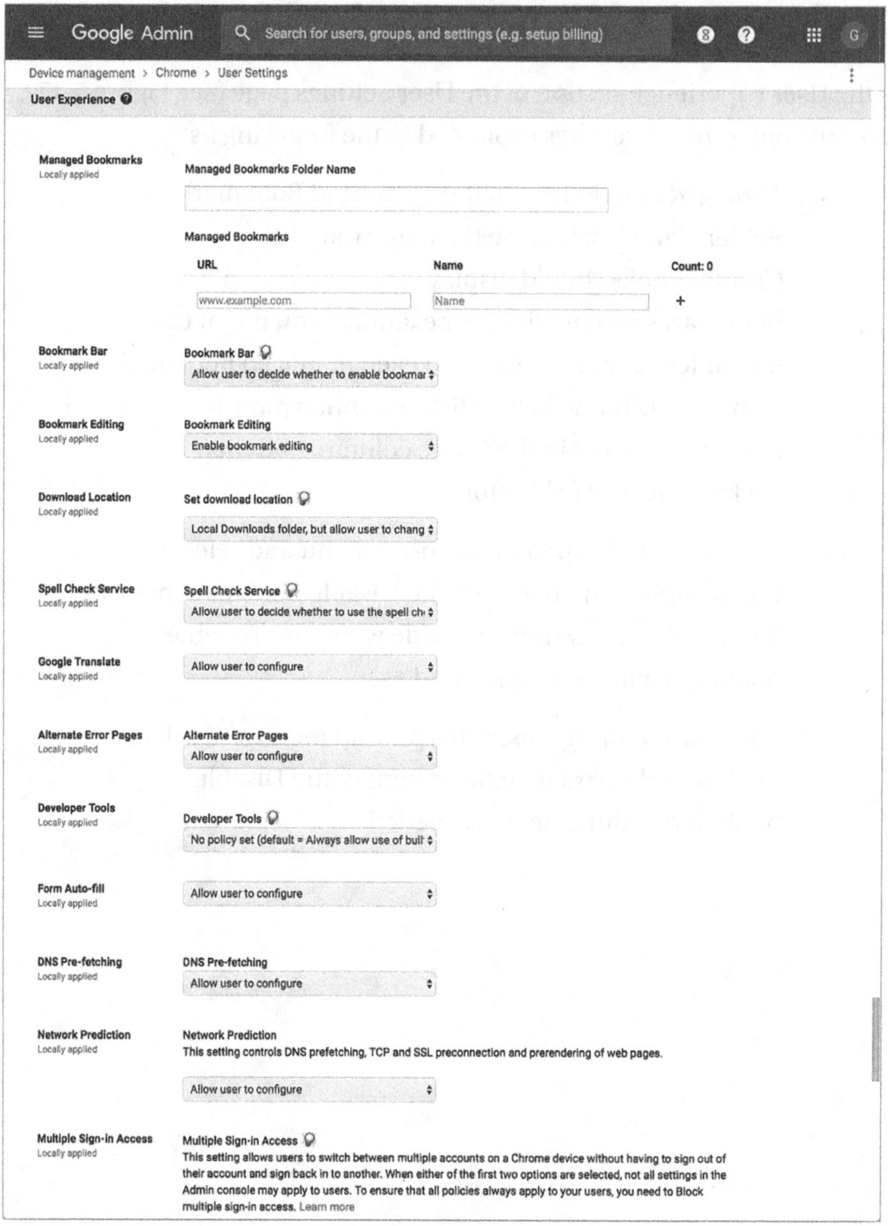

Figure 5-17. *The User Experience section of the User Settings page enables you to control a wide range of aspects of the user experience, from bookmarks to network prediction*

- *Download Location*: Open this pop-up menu and select the appropriate location:

  - **Set Google Drive as default, but allow user to change**: Select this setting when it is better to have users store files on Google Drive but it is okay to store files locally as well.

  - **Local Downloads folder, but allow user to change**: Select this setting when users use the same Chromebooks regularly—for example, when each student has been issued a Chromebook.

  - **Force Google Drive**: Select this setting when you need to make sure that users keep files on Google Drive rather than locally—for example, when the users use shared Chromebooks.

- *Spell Check Service*: Open this pop-up menu and select the Enable the spell checking web service item, the Disable the spell checking web service item, or the Allow user to decide whether to use the spell checking web service item, as needed.

- *Google Translate*: Open this pop-up menu and select the Always offer translation item, the Never offer translation item, or the Allow user to configure item, as needed.

- *Alternate Error Pages*: Open this pop-up menu and select the Always use alternate error pages item, the Never use alternate error pages item, or the Allow user to configure item, as needed. Alternate error pages contain the suggestions that the Chrome browser shows when it is unable to connect to a particular web address.

385

- *Developer Tools*: Open this pop-up menu and select the Always allow use of built-in developer tools item, the Never allow use of built-in developer tools item, or the "No policy set (default = Always allow use of built-in developer tools)" item. Normally, you would restrict developer tools to developers and those learning programming.

- *Form Auto-fill*: Open this pop-up menu and select the Never auto-fill forms item or the Allow user to configure item, as appropriate.

- *DNS Pre-fetching*: Open this pop-up menu and select the Always pre-fetch DNS item, the Never pre-fetch DNS item, or the Allow user to configure item, as needed.

UNDERSTANDING DNS PRE-FETCHING AND NETWORK PREDICTION

DNS pre-fetching is the Chrome feature that automatically looks up the IP address of each link on a web page that is displayed in the Chrome browser. DNS pre-fetching can speed up browsing, but it increases use of your school's Internet connection somewhat. In Chrome Settings, the "Predict network actions to improve page performance" check box controls DNS pre-fetching.

Network prediction is a wider-ranging feature that not only pre-fetches DNS data but also connects to web pages linked to the current page (this is called *TCP and SSL preconnection*) and downloads their contents (this is called *pre-rendering*) so as to be able to display any page quickly when the user clicks its link. Network prediction can greatly increase the usage of the Internet connection because it involves downloading much more data.

- *Network Prediction*: Open this pop-up menu and select the Predict network actions item, the Do not predict network actions item, or the Allow user to configure item, as needed. See the nearby sidebar "Understanding DNS Pre-Fetching and Network Prediction."

- *Multiple Sign-in Access*: Open this pop-up menu and select the appropriate item:

  - **Block multiple sign-in access for users in this organization**: Select this item to disable multiple sign-in access.

  - **Managed user must be the primary user (secondary users are allowed)**: Select this item to allow multiple sign-in access as long as the primary user is a managed user.

  - **Unrestricted user access (allow any user to be added to any other user's session)**: Select this item to allow multiple sign-in access to all users.

  - **No policy set (default = Managed user must be the primary user (secondary users are allowed))**: Select this item if you do not want to configure multiple sign-in access via policy.

- *Unified Desktop*: To use the Unified Desktop feature, which enables an app to span multiple displays and is in beta as of this writing, open the Unified Desktop pop-up menu and select the Make Unified Desktop mode available to user item. To prevent the use of Unified Desktop, select the Do not make Unified Desktop mode available to user item. If you do not want to manage this feature via policy, select the "No policy set (default = Do not make Unified Desktop mode available to user)" item.

Configuring Omnibox Search Provider Settings

In the Omnibox Search Provider section of the User Settings page, you can configure the settings explained in the following list:

- *Search Suggest*: To control whether the Chrome browser uses a prediction service to suggest completions for web addresses or search terms, open the Search Suggest pop-up menu and select the Always allow users to use Search Suggest item, the Never allow users to use Search Suggest item, or the Allow user to configure item.

- *Omnibox Search Provider*: Open the Omnibox Search Provider pop-up menu and choose the Allow user to select the Omnibox Search Provider item if you want to allow the user to choose the search provider. The alternative is to select the Lock the Omnibox Search Provider settings to the values below item and then enter the details in the boxes that appear.

Configuring Hardware Settings

In the Hardware section of the User Settings page, you can configure the settings explained in the following list:

- *External Storage Devices*: Open the Secure Digital (SD) Cards, USB Flash Drive Devices, and MTP devices pop-up menu and select the Allow external storage devices item, the Allow external storage devices (read only) item, or the Disallow external storage devices item.

- *Audio Input*: Open the Microphone and Audio Input pop-up menu and select the Disable audio input item or the Prompt user to allow each time item, as needed.

- *Audio Output*: Open the Speakers and Audio Output pop-up menu and select the Enable audio output item or the Disable audio output item, as needed.

- *Video Input*: Open the Video Input pop-up menu and select the Enable video input item or the Disable video input item, as needed.

- *Keyboard*: Open the Set default top-row key behavior pop-up menu and select the appropriate item:

  - **Treat top-row keys as media keys, but allow user to change**: Select this item to have the top row of keys provide the functionality displayed on them, such as navigation and volume controls, but also allow the user to switch the keys to work as function keys.

- **Treat top-row keys as function keys, but allow user to change**: Select this item to have the top row of keys work as function keys but also allow the user to switch them to media keys.

- **No policy set (default = Treat top-row keys as media keys, but allow user to change)**: Select this item if you do not want to control the top-row functionality via policy.

Choosing Verified Access and User Verification Settings

In the Verified Access section of the User Settings page, open the Verified Access pop-up menu and select the Enable for Enterprise extensions item if you want to allow Chrome extensions in the user session to interact with the Trusted Platform Module (TPM). Otherwise, select the Disable for Enterprise extensions item.

The User Verification section of the User Settings page contains only the Verified Mode area. Open the Verified Mode Boot Check pop-up menu and then select the Require verified mode boot for Verified Access item if you want the Chromebooks to boot with verified boot mode in order to use the Verified Access feature. This is normally a good idea. If you need to allow some Chromebooks to boot into Developer mode (which is not verified) but still use Verified Access, select the Skip boot mode check for Verified Access item instead.

Note   If you will use the Skip boot mode check for Verified Access setting, use it only for an organizational unit to which you assign those teachers or users who require Developer mode.

- *Service accounts which are allowed to receive device ID*:
  In this box, you can list the email addresses of service
  accounts that you want to give full access to the Google
  Verified Access application programming interface
  (API).

Note   A *service account* is a developer account created in the
Google Developers Console.

- *Service accounts which can verify devices but do not
  receive device ID*: In this box, you can list the email
  addresses of service accounts that you want to give
  limited access to the Google Verified Access API.

Choosing Chrome Management—Partner Access Settings

In the Chrome Management—Partner Access section of the User Settings
page, you can check the "Enable Chrome Management—Partner Access"
check box to enable your school's Google Cloud partner to access
your school's Chromebooks programmatically to manage policies, get
information about the Chromebooks, and control them remotely. If you
check this check box, follow through the confirmation screens to confirm
the action.

Saving Your Changes to the Settings

When you have finished making changes on the User Settings page,
click the Save button in the lower-right corner of the screen to save your
changes.

Configuring Device Settings for Chromebooks

In this section, we will cover the settings that you can configure on the Device Settings page in the Chromebook Management console. We will start by displaying the Device Settings pane and then dig into the many sections and settings it contains.

Displaying the Device Settings Page

To display the Device Settings page, follow these steps in your Google Admin console:

1. On the Home page, click the Device management icon to display the Device management page.

2. In the Device Settings list in the left pane, click the Chrome management item to display the Chrome Management page.

3. Click the Device settings button to display the Device Settings page. Figure 5-18 shows the topmost section of the Device Settings pane.

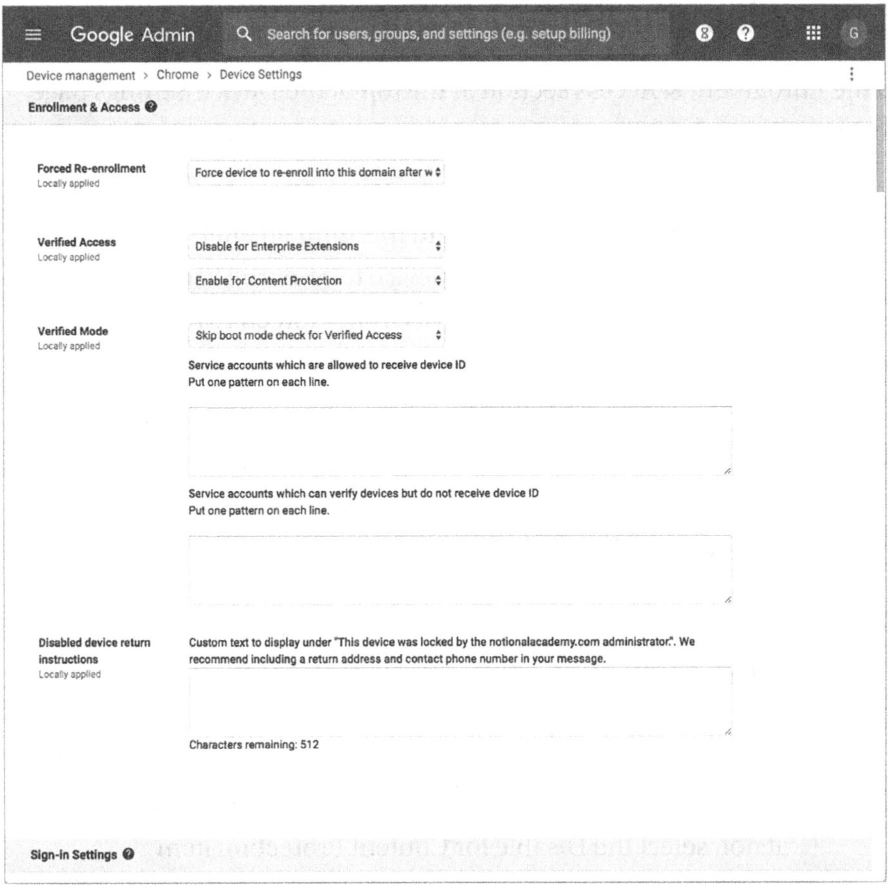

Figure 5-18. *The topmost part of the Device Settings screen contains the Enrollment & Access section of settings*

Controlling Enrollment & Access

In the Enrollment & Access section at the top of the Device Settings page, you can choose the following settings to control enrollment and access:

- *Forced Re-enrollment*: In this pop-up menu, choose the Force device to re-enroll in this domain after wiping item if you want the device to re-enroll itself automatically. Select the Device is not forced to re-enroll after wiping item if you want to free the device from Forced Re-enrollment.

- *Verified Access*: In the upper pop-up menu, select the Enable for Enterprise Extensions item if you want to enable the Verified Access feature, which allows Chrome extensions to interact with the Trusted Platform Module (TPM) on the Chromebook; if not, select the Disable for Enterprise Extensions item. In the lower pop-up menu, select the Enable for Content Protection item if you want to have the Chromebooks verify their identity to content providers using the TPM; if not, select the Disable for Content Protection item instead.

- *Verified Mode*: In this pop-up menu, select the Require verified boot mode for Verified Access if you want the Chromebooks to boot with verified boot mode in order to use the Verified Access feature. This is normally a good idea. If you need to allow some Chromebooks to boot into Developer mode (which is not verified) but still use Verified Access, select the Skip boot mode check for Verified Access item instead.

Note   If you will use the Skip boot mode check for Verified Access setting, use it only for an organizational unit to which you assign those teachers or users who require Developer mode.

- *Service accounts which are allowed to receive device ID*: In this box, you can list the email addresses of service accounts that you want to give full access to the Google Verified Access application programming interface (API).

Note   A *service account* is a developer account created in the Google Developers Console.

- *Service accounts which can verify devices but do not receive device ID*: In this box, you can list the email addresses of service accounts that you want to give limited access to the Google Verified Access API.

- *Disabled device return instructions*: In this box, you can type the information you want to display on disabled Chromebooks to encourage whoever has them to return them to the school. The screen receives the automatic heading "This device was locked by the [your school's domain name] administrator." Normally, you would include contact information, such as the school's email address, phone number, and address.

In the Google Admin console, click the Device management icon. The Device management page will appear.

Choosing Sign-In Settings to Control Sign-In to Chromebooks

To control who can sign in on your school's Chromebooks and how those people sign in, you can configure settings in the Sign-in Settings section of the Device Settings page. Figure 5-19 shows the top part of the Sign-in Settings section.

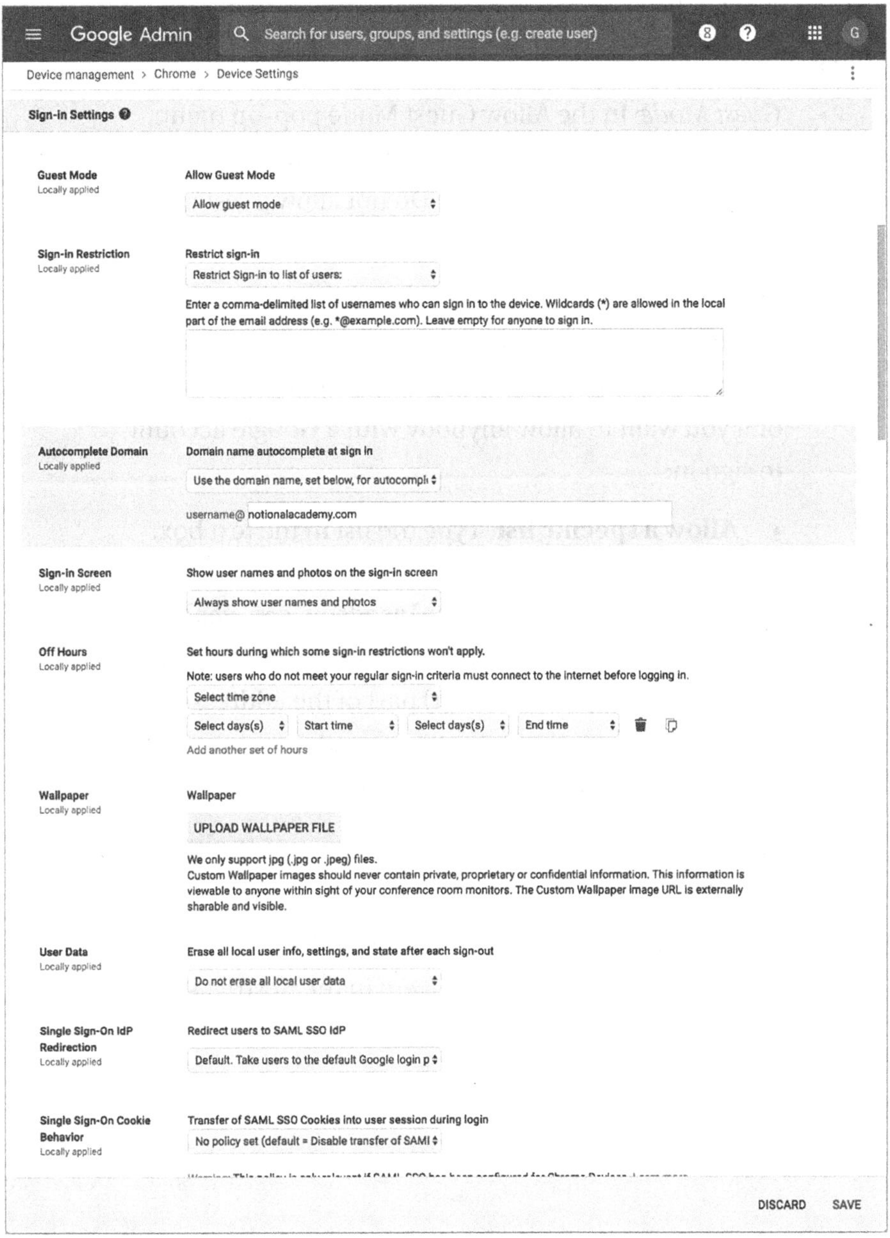

Figure 5-19. *In the Sign-in Settings section of the Device Settings page, you can configure many sign-in options for your school's Chromebooks*

The following list explains the settings you can configure in the Sign-in Settings section:

- *Guest Mode*: In the Allow Guest Mode pop-up menu, select the Allow guest mode item if you want to allow guest usage. If not, select the Do not allow guest mode item.

- *Sign-in Restriction*: In the Restrict sign-in pop-up menu, select the Restrict Sign-in to list of users item if you want to either allow a specific list of users to sign in or if you want to allow anybody with a Google account to sign in:

  - **Allow a specific list**: Type the list in the text box, using commas to separate the addresses—for example, llaigh@notionalacademy.com, vhaller@notionalacademy.com. You can use the * wildcard in the local (non-domain) part of the address—for example, entering *@notionalacademy.com allows any user from that domain to sign in.

  - **Allow anybody with a Google account to sign in**: Leave the text box empty.

  - **Prevent anyone from signing in**: Select the Do not allow any user to Sign-in item in the Restrict sign-in pop-up menu.

- *Autocomplete Domain*: In the Domain name autocomplete at sign in pop-up menu, choose the appropriate setting:

    - **Use the domain name, set below, for autocomplete at sign in**: Choose this setting to have the Sign-in screen suggest the domain you enter in the text box. This setting is usually helpful.

    - **Do not display an autocomplete domain on the sign in page**: Choose this setting if you do not want the Sign-in screen to suggest a domain.

    - **No policy set (default = Do not display an autocomplete domain on the sign in page)**: Choose this setting if you do not want to control the Autocomplete Domain setting via policy.

- *Sign-in Screen*: In the Show user names and photos on the sign-in screen pop-up menu, select the Always show user names and photos item or the Never show user names and photos item, as needed.

- *Off Hours*: If you need to apply sign-in restrictions only during some hours, use the five pop-up menus to specify the time zone, the starting day, the starting time, the ending day, and the ending time. After specifying the first set of hours in the first row, you can click the Copy icon at the end of that row to copy the settings to a second row of controls; you can then make minor adjustments to that row as needed. You can also click the Add another set of hours link to add another row of boxes without copying existing data into them.

- *Wallpaper*: To upload a JPEG graphic for use as wallpaper, click the Upload Wallpaper File button, select the file in the unnamed dialog box that opens, and then click the Open button. For example, you might upload a wallpaper graphic that identifies your school, provides inspiring quotes, or both.

- *User Data*: In the Erase all local user info, settings, and state after each sign-out pop-up menu, choose the Do not erase all local user data item or the Erase all local user data item, as needed. On a shared Chromebook, erasing local user data can help avoid the storage getting filled with user files, but it means that when a user signs in again on a Chromebook she has used before, the Chromebook will need to sync all her user data from the cloud instead of only those parts that have changed since her last use.

- *Single Sign-On IdP Redirection*: In this pop-up menu, choose the "Default. Take users to the default Google login page" item if you want users to log in at the regular Google login page. Choose the Allow users to go directly to SAML SSO IdP page item if you have configured Security Assertion Markup Language (SAML) Single Sign-On (SSO) for your school's domain and want users to go straight to your SAML Identity Provider (IdP) page instead.

- *Single Sign-On Cookie Behavior*: If you have configured SAML SSO, you can open the Transfer of SAML SSO Cookies into user session during login pop-up menu and choose the Enable transfer of SAML SSO Cookies into user session during login item to enable Single Sign-On users to log in to your school's internal websites by using the SAML SSO cookies. If you have configured SAML SSO but do not want to use this feature, choose the Disable transfer of SAML SSO Cookies into user session during login item instead. If you have not configured SAML SSO, make sure the "No policy set (default = Disable transfer of SAML SSO Cookies into user session during login)" item is selected in this pop-up menu.

- *Single Sign-On Camera Permissions*: If you have configured SAML SSO, you can click in the Whitelist of single sign-on camera permissions box (see Figure 5-20) and enter a whitelist of third-party apps or services that can directly access the camera on the user's Chromebook. Enter the URL for each app or service on a separate line in the box.

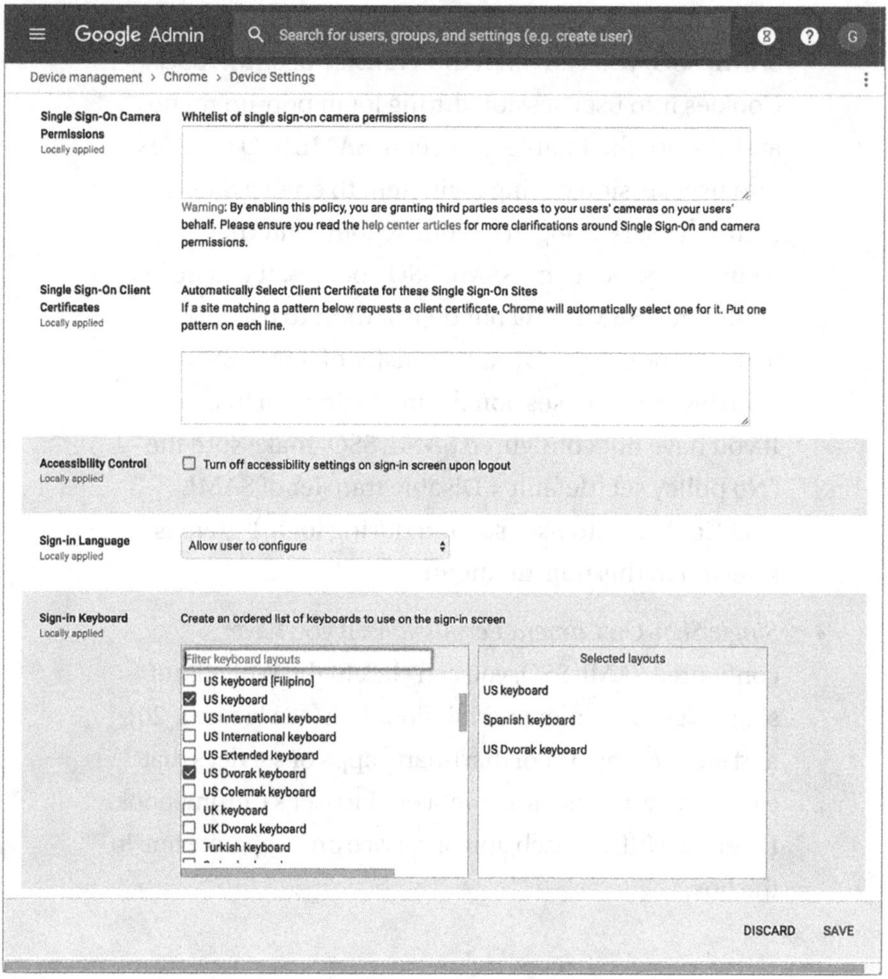

Figure 5-20. *The controls in the lower part of the Sign-in Settings section of the Device Settings screen enable you to configure Single Sign-On camera permissions, Single Sign-On client certificates, accessibility control, the sign-in language, and the sign-in keyboard*

- *Single Sign-On Client Certificates*: If you have configured SAML SSO, you can go to the Automatically Select Client Certificate for these Single Sign-On Sites box and enter a JSON string that contains a list of URL patterns identifying those certificates to use automatically when accessing particular sites that require credentials.

- *Accessibility Control*: Check the "Turn off accessibility settings on sign-in screen upon logout" check box if you want to disable the accessibility settings on the sign-in screen when a user logs out of the Chromebook. You might use this setting on shared Chromebooks if your school prefers to have teachers manually enable accessibility options only for those students who actually need them. For Chromebooks issued to individual students, make sure this check box is unchecked so that the Chromebooks will automatically use the accessibility settings from one session to the next.

- *Sign-in Language*: In this pop-up menu, either choose the specific language—such as English (United States)—you want the Sign-in screen to use or select the Allow user to configure item if you want the Chromebook's user to be able to select the language.

- *Sign-in Keyboard*: In the Create an ordered list of keyboards to use on the sign-in screen box, go to the left box and check the check box for each keyboard needed on the Sign-in screen. You can filter the keyboards shown by clicking in the Filter keyboard layouts box and starting to type a keyword (for example, French). Those keyboards you check will appear in the right box, the Selected layouts box, where you can drag them into the order you need.

Configuring Device Update Settings

The Device Update Settings section of the Device Settings screen (see Figure 5-21) enables you to control the updating of your school's Chromebooks. The following list explains the settings you can configure:

- *Auto Update Settings*: This category contains the following four pop-up menus:

    - **Auto Update**: In this pop-up menu, select the Allow auto-updates item if you want to use automatic updating; select the Stop auto-updates item if you do not.

    - **Restrict Google Chrome version to at most**: In this pop-up menu, choose the No restriction item if you want to allow Chrome OS to update to the newest versions when they become available. If your school is using tools that you know have problems with the newest versions of Chrome OS, you can choose a specific version number (such as 65.* as of this writing) to specify the most recent version you want to use.

    - **Randomly scatter auto-updates over**: In this pop-up menu, choose the None item to allow auto-updates to occur when Chrome discovers them. To stagger auto-updates to reduce the impact on your school's network and Internet connection, choose one of the other items in the pop-up menu. The items range from 1 day to 14 days.

    - **Auto reboot after updates**: In this pop-up menu, select the Allow auto-reboots item or the Disallow auto-reboots item, as needed.

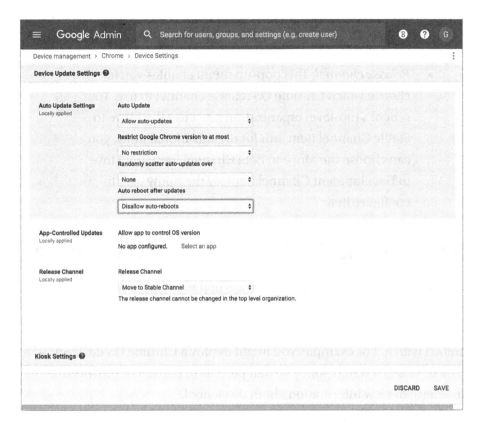

Figure 5-21. *In the Device Update Settings section of the Device Settings screen, you can specify how to update your school's Chromebooks*

Note   As of this writing, the Allow auto-reboots setting works only for Chrome devices configured as public-session kiosks. For Chrome devices configured any other way, such as your school's Chromebooks, you will need to reboot the Chromebooks manually.

- *App-controlled updates*: This setting applies only to kiosk apps.

- *Release channel*: This pop-up menu enables you to choose which Chrome OS release channel to use. Your school's top-level organization must use the Move to Stable Channel item, but for organizational units, you can choose the Move to Beta Channel item, the Move to Development Channel item, or the Allow user to configure item.

Understanding the Purpose of the Kiosk Settings

The settings in the Kiosk Settings section of the Device Settings screen enable you to configure a Chrome OS device to act as a kiosk device—a device that you leave running in a public setting so that passers-by can interact with it. For example, you might deploy a Chrome OS device as a kiosk device in a school lobby so that parents of current or prospective students can view information about the school.

Deploying a Chrome OS device as a kiosk device is outside the scope of this book, so I will leave you to explore the Kiosk Settings section of the Device Settings screen on your own.

Configuring the User & Device Reporting Settings

In the User & Device Reporting section of the Device Settings screen (see Figure 5-22), you can configure the following settings:

- *Device Reporting*: This section contains the Device State Reporting pop-up menu and the Device User Tracking pop-up menu:

    - **Device State Reporting**: Open this pop-up menu and select the Enable device state reporting item if you want to monitor the state of Chrome devices enrolled in your domain; select the Disable device state reporting item if you do not. With device reporting enabled, each device reports information including its firmware version, its Chrome version, its platform version, and its boot mode.

    - **Device User Tracking**: Open this pop-up menu and select the Enable tracking recent device users item if you want to be able to track recent users of your Chromebooks; otherwise, select the Disable tracking recent device users item.

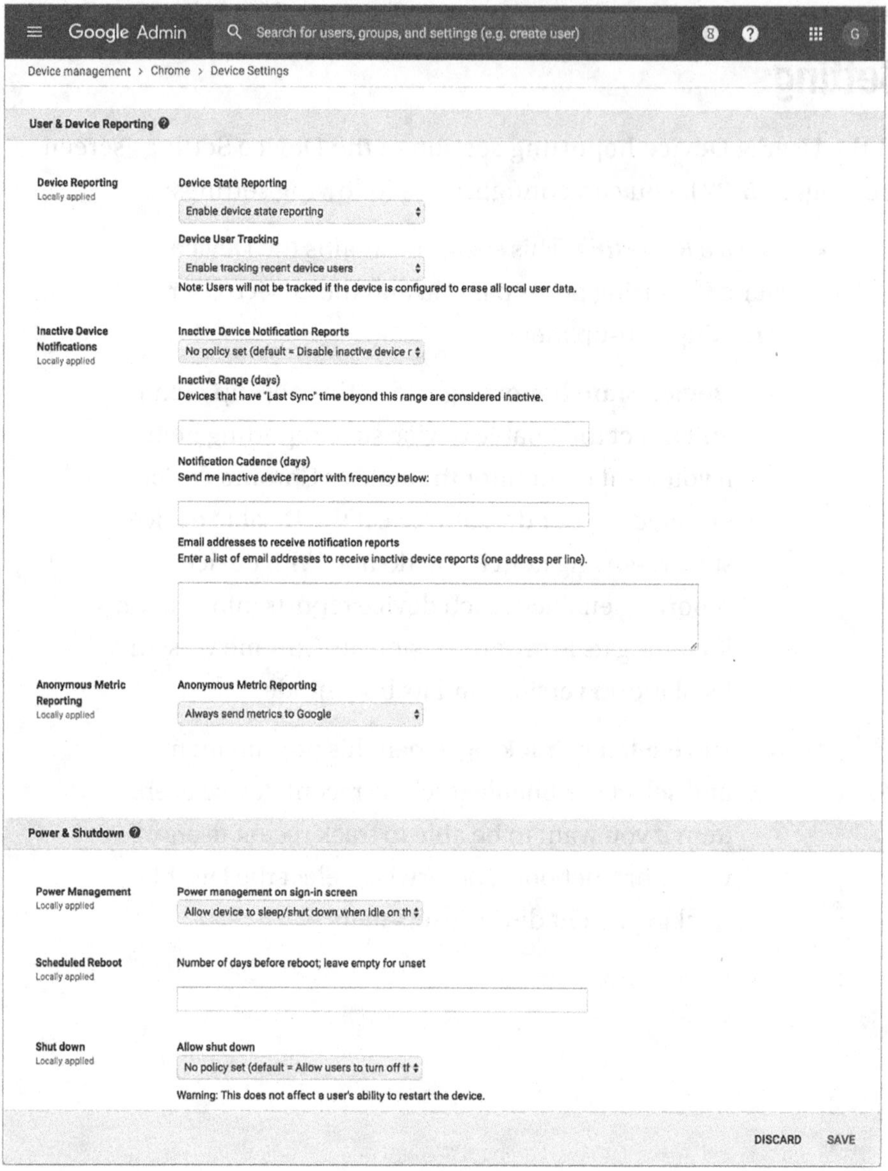

Figure 5-22. *The User & Device Reporting section of the Device Settings gives you control over device reporting and inactive device notifications. The Power & Shutdown section lets you control power management, schedule reboots, and control shutdown.*

Note   If you have selected the Erase all local user data item in the Erase all local user info, settings, and state after each sign-out pop-up menu in the Single Sign-In section, the Device User Tracking feature does not work.

- *Inactive Device Notifications*: Use the controls in this area to configure reporting about inactive devices:

  - **Inactive Device Notification Reports**: Open this pop-up menu and select the Enable inactive device reporting item if you want to receive information about Chromebooks that haven't synced in the number of days you specify in the Inactive Range (days) box. If you do not want to receive reports, select the Disable inactive device reporting item. If you do not want to control inactive device notifications via policy, select the "No policy set (default = Disable inactive device reporting)" item.

  - **Inactive Range (days)**: In this box, type the number of days Chrome OS should wait before deeming a Chromebook to be inactive.

  - **Notification Cadence (days)**: In this box, type the number of days to wait between successive reports of inactivity.

  - **Email addresses to receive notification reports**: In this box, enter the email addresses to which the notification reports should be sent. Put each email address on a separate line.

- *Anonymous Metric Reporting*: Open this pop-up menu and select the Always send metrics to Google item or the Never send metrics to Google item, as needed.

Choosing Power & Shutdown Settings

In the Power & Shutdown section of the Device Settings screen, you can configure the settings explained in the following list:

- *Power Management*: Open the Power management on sign-in screen pop-up menu and select the Allow device to sleep/shut down when idle on the sign-in screen item or the Do not allow device to sleep/shut down when idle on the sign-in screen item, as needed. Normally, you would want to allow Chromebooks to go to sleep on the sign-in screen; keeping a Chrome device awake is more useful in a kiosk setting.

- *Scheduled reboot*: In the "Number of days before reboot; leave empty for unset" box, you can in theory type the number of days to wait before automatically rebooting a Chrome OS device. As of this writing, this setting works only for devices configured as Public Session kiosks.

- *Shut down*: Open the Allow shut down pop-up menu and select the "Allow users to turn off the device via the Shut down icon on the screen, or the physical power button" item if you want to allow users to shut down the Chromebooks via the keyboard, trackpad, screen, or power button. If you prefer to let users shut down Chromebooks only using the power button, select the "Only allow users to turn off the device using the physical power button" item instead. If you do not want to control shutdown via policy, select the "No policy set (default = Allow users to turn off the device via the Shut down icon on the screen, or the physical power button)" item.

Choosing Other Settings on the Device Settings Screen

In the Other section of the Device Settings screen, you can configure the settings explained in the following list:

- *Cloud Print*: In this area, click the Manage link to start the process of enabling Cloud printers.

- *Time Zone*: Open the System timezone pop-up menu and then click either the Keep timezone as it is on device currently item or the item for the specific timezone you want the Chromebook to use, such as the GMT-07:00 Pacific Time (Los Angeles Time) item. Open the System timezone automatic detection pop-up menu and select the appropriate option:

  - **No policy set (default = Let users decide)**: Select this item to set no policy for determining the timezone.

  - **Let users decide**: Select this item to enable the user to set the Chromebook's timezone.

  - **Never auto-detect timezone**: Select this item to disable Chrome OS's automatic detection of timezones.

411

- **Always use coarse timezone detection**: Select this item to have Chrome OS use the Chromebook's IP address to determine the timezone the device is in.

- **Always send WiFi access-points to server while resolving timezone**: Select this item to use the Wi-Fi access point to which the Chromebook is connected as the basis for determining the timezone. This is the most accurate way of determining the timezone.

- *Mobile Data Roaming*: In this pop-up menu, select the Allow mobile data roaming item if you want to allow cellular Chromebooks to use mobile data roaming. Otherwise, select the Do not allow mobile data roaming item. If your school's Chromebooks are Wi-Fi–only, this setting does not apply.

- *USB Detachable Whitelist*: In this box, you can enter a list of USB devices that are directly accessible to apps. You enter each USB device on a separate line, putting the USB vector identifier (VID) first, a colon next, and then the product identifier (PID)—for example, if a device's VID is 541E and the PID is 8114, you would enter 541E:8114 to add the device to the whitelist. Both the VID and PID are hexadecimal values.

- *Bluetooth*: Open the Disable Bluetooth on device pop-up menu and select the appropriate item:

  - **No policy set (default = Do not disable Bluetooth)**: Choose this item if you do not want to control Bluetooth via policy. Choosing this item leaves Bluetooth enabled.

  - **Do not disable Bluetooth**: Choose this item to leave Bluetooth enabled.

  - **Disable Bluetooth**: Choose this item to disable Bluetooth.

- *Throttle Device Bandwidth*: Open the Throttle network bandwidth consumption at the device level pop-up menu and then select the Enable network throttling item or the Disable network throttling item, as needed. If you select the Enable network throttling item, enter the maximum download speed in the Download speed in Kbps box and the maximum upload speed in the Upload speed in Kbps box.

- *TPM Firmware Update*: Open this pop-up menu and then select the appropriate setting for updating the Trusted Platform Module (TPM) firmware on your school's Chromebooks:

  - **No policy set (default = Block users from performing TPM firmware updates)**: Select this item if you do not want to control TPM firmware updates via policy.

413

- **Block users from performing TPM firmware updates**: Select this item if you want to prevent users from updating the TPM firmware on Chromebooks. This is normally the best choice for Chromebooks deployed to students.

- **Allow users to perform TPM firmware updates**: Select this item to allow users to update the TPM firmware on Chromebooks.

Choosing Settings in the Chrome Management—Partner Access Section

In the Chrome Management—Partner Access section of the Device Settings screen, you can check the "Enable Chrome Management—Partner Access" check box to enable your school's Google Cloud partner to access your school's Chromebooks programmatically to manage policies, get information about the Chromebooks, and control them remotely. If you check this check box, follow through the confirmation screens to confirm the action.

Summary

In this chapter, you have learned how to configure and manage Chromebooks using your Google Admin console and its Chrome Management console component. You know how to get Chrome subscription licenses for your school's Chromebooks; how to sign in to your Google Admin console; and how to perform essential maneuvers, such as enrolling the Chromebooks in your school's domain, controlling forced re-enrollment, and disabling and deprovisioning Chromebooks. You have also learned how to work with the many user settings and device settings to customize the user experience and the Chromebooks themselves.

In the next chapter, we will examine how to manage Chrome apps and extensions.

CHAPTER 6

Managing Chrome Apps and Extensions

In this chapter, we will look at how to manage Chrome apps and extensions manually on Chromebooks. We will start by examining the differences between Chrome apps and extensions and exploring the two different types of apps that Chrome OS devices can run. We will then go through how to install apps and extensions from the Chrome Web Store and how to manage them. Finally, we will discuss how to troubleshoot problems with apps and extensions.

Understanding What Chrome Apps and Extensions Are

A Chromebook comes with various apps and extensions that offer a wide range of functionality. You can install further apps and extensions to add other functionality to the Chromebook. The main source of apps and extensions for Chrome OS is the Chrome Web Store, which you can access via the Web Store app.

© Guy Hart-Davis 2018
G. Hart-Davis, *Deploying Chromebooks in the Classroom*,
https://doi.org/10.1007/978-1-4842-3766-3_6

Understanding What Apps Are in Chrome OS

Chrome OS supports two types of items that are considered apps:

- *Chrome Web app*: A Chrome Web app is essentially a website that runs within the Chrome browser rather than being a separate app. The functionality for a web app is implemented through HTML, JavaScript, and other programming languages. Many of the apps that come with Chrome OS devices are Web apps. For example, the Gmail app, the Web Store app, and the Google Drive app are all Web apps; so is any other app that opens as a tab in Chrome rather than in a window of its own.

- *Chrome app*: A Chrome app is a full-fledged app that runs outside the Chrome browser, like apps on operating systems such as Windows or MacOS. Examples of Chrome apps that come with Chrome OS include the Files app, the Calculator app, and the Camera app.

You can browse the two types of apps either together or separately on the Chrome Web Store. The Web Store identifies Chrome web apps as "websites."

Understanding What Chrome Extensions Are

As well as apps, Chrome OS supports extensions. An *extension* is an add-on that extends the features of the Chrome browser. For example, the Google Docs Offline extension adds the capability for the Chromebook to work on Google Docs documents even when it is offline by caching copies of the documents on the Chromebook and syncing them when the Chromebook is online.

You can find many extensions on the Web Store. Some extensions are created by Google, such as the Share to Classroom extension, which provides an easy way to share a page with students via the Classroom app. Other extensions are created by third-party developers.

Installing and Managing Apps and Extensions

In this section, we will examine how to manage apps and extensions on Chrome OS. We will start by opening the Web Store app and navigating the Chrome Web Store site. We will then move on to installing an app or an extension, viewing your apps and extensions, and managing extensions and configuring their settings.

Note   This section explains how to install and manage apps and extensions manually. See the section "Configuring Apps and Extensions Settings" in Chapter 5 for coverage of how to install and manage apps and extensions via policy.

Opening the Web Store App

To get started finding and installing apps and extensions, first open the Web Store app. If a Web Store icon appears on the shelf, click that icon. If not, click the Launcher button and then click the Web Store icon, either on the Launcher bar or on the full Launcher screen.

The Web Store app is a Chrome Web app, so a Chrome tab will open showing the Chrome Web Store home screen. Figure 6-1 shows an example of the home screen.

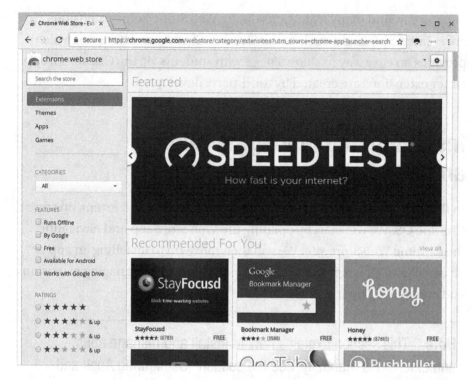

Figure 6-1. *On the Chrome Web Store home screen, you can start by choosing the type of items you want to find: Extensions, Themes, Apps, or Games.*

Navigating the Web Store

As usual, you can navigate the Chrome Web Store by browsing or by searching. Browsing is typically the best way to get an idea of what is available, but if you want to get a specific type of app or functionality, searching is the better bet.

Before you search, specify the type of item by clicking the appropriate entry in the list under the Search the store box in the navigation panel on the left:

- *Extensions*: As mentioned earlier, an extension adds functionality to the Chrome browser.

- *Themes*: A theme is a suite of settings that changes the look of the Chrome browser.

- *Apps*: This type includes both Chrome apps—the separate apps—and websites that run in Chrome.

- *Games*: Like the Apps type, the Games type includes both Chrome apps and websites that run in Chrome.

When you choose the type, the lower part of the navigation pane will display options for that type. For example, for the Apps type (see Figure 6-2), the navigation pane contains the options explained in the following list:

- *Types*: In this section, you can click the "Chrome Apps" option or the "Websites" option to restrict the types of apps displayed.

- *Categories*: In this pop-up menu, you can click the category—such as Education, Productivity, Social & Communication, or Utilities—and then the subcategory if there is one and if you want to be more specific.

- *Features*: In this section, check the check box for any specific features you need the item to have:

  - **Runs Offline**: Check this check box to ensure the item works when the Chromebook is offline.

  - **By Google**: Check this check box to restrict the items to ones developed by Google.

  - **Free**: Check this check box to display only free items.

  - **Available for Android**: Check this check box to display only items that work on Android as well as on Chrome OS.

  - **Works with Google Drive**: Check this check box to display only items that work with Google Drive.

419

- *Ratings*: In this section, you can click an option button
  to make the Chrome Web Store display only items that
  users have awarded that rating: Five Stars, Four Stars &
  up, Three Stars & up, or Two Stars & up.

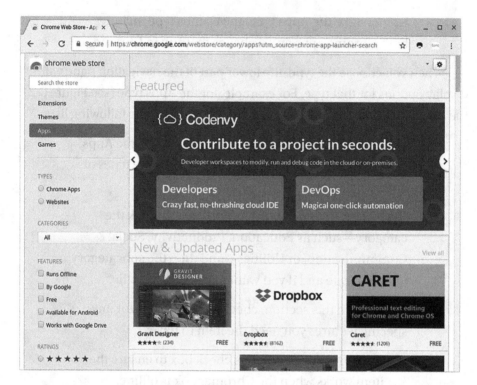

Figure 6-2. *After choosing the type of items, use the controls in the
lower part of the navigation pane to specify further details*

As you choose settings, the Web Store app will change the list of items
displayed to match your specifications. After choosing settings, you can
browse the displayed items by scrolling up and down or by clicking items,
or you can search by starting to type your search terms in the Search
the store box and then clicking the best match on the pop-up menu that
appears.

Figure 6-3 shows the results of a search for `scientific calculator` with the Runs Offline filter set. From the page of search results, you can take the following actions:

- *Add the item to Chrome*: Click the Add to Chrome button and then follow the prompts that appear. The following subsections show examples of adding items to Chrome.

- *Display an item's page*: Click the search result to display the page of information about the item. Figure 6-4 shows an example of an item's page. The page has four tabs:

  - **Overview tab**: This tab contains screenshots, a description, technical details (such as Runs Offline), and additional information (such as the version, the last update, the size, and the language).

  - **Reviews**: This tab contains user reviews of the item, with star ratings. You can click the Helpful subtab or the Recent subtab to change the selection of reviews displayed.

  - **Support**: This tab contains questions, suggestions, and problems submitted by users. You can click the All subtab, the Questions subtab, the Suggestions subtab, or the Problems subtab to change the items displayed. The Tell the Developer section enables you to submit your own questions, suggestions, or problems.

  - **Related**: This tab displays items related to the item you are viewing.

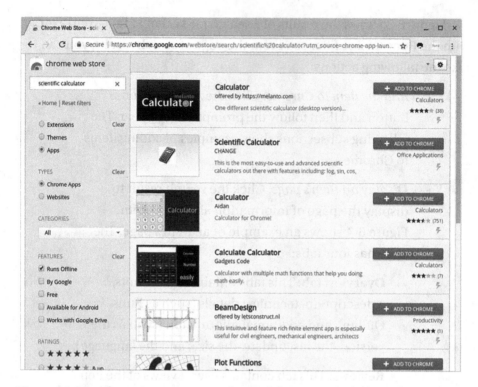

Figure 6-3. *After returning search results, you can click a result to display the page, set other filters to refine the results further, or click the Reset filters button to remove the filters. Alternatively, click the Home button to return to the Chrome Web Store's home page.*

- *Refine the search results*: You can set other filters to refine the search results further. For example, if a search returns a large number of results, you might check other check boxes in the Features section to narrow down the selection.

- *Remove the filters*: Click the Reset filters button under the search box.

- *Return to the home page*: Click the Home button under the search box.

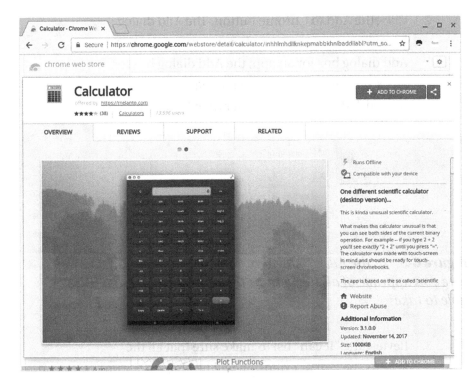

Figure 6-4. *From the page for an item, you can get an overview, read reviews, learn about support, or browse related products*

When you find an item you want to add to the Chromebook, you can install it as discussed next.

Installing an App or an Extension

To install an app or an extension, follow these steps:

1. In the Web Store app, navigate either to a listing page showing the item with an Add to Chrome button or to the item's page.

423

2. Click the Add to Chrome button. The Add dialog box will open. Figure 6-5 shows an example of the Add dialog box for an app; the Add dialog box for an extension is the same except that the button is named "Add extension" rather than "Add app."

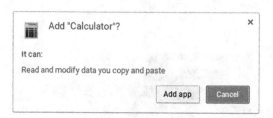

Figure 6-5. *In the Add dialog box, look at the "It can" list to make sure you approve of all the actions the app or extension will be able to take*

3. Review the "It can" list to make sure that all the actions the app or extension will be able to take on the Chromebook are acceptable to you.

Note   What actions you should accept will depend on what the app or extension is and what it does, but you should be able to identify anything obviously wrong. For example, a social-networking app may need to access contact data, but a calculator app or screenshot utility definitely should not need to.

4. Click the Add app button for an app or the Add extension button for an extension. If the shelf is displayed, a Download Manager notification will appear showing Chrome OS's progress in downloading and installing the app or extension.

Note   Once the app or extension has been installed, a web page may open in a new Chrome tab showing information about the app or extension and how to use it.

Removing an App

If you no longer need an app on a Chromebook, you can remove it quickly by following these steps:

1. Click the Launcher button to display the Launcher bar.

2. Unless the app you want to remove appears on the Launcher bar, click the up-arrow button to display the Launcher screen.

3. Right-click the app you want to remove. The shortcut menu will open (see Figure 6-6).

Figure 6-6. *On the Launcher bar or Launcher screen, right-click the app you want to uninstall and then click the Uninstall item on the shortcut menu*

425

4.   Click the Uninstall item. The Remove dialog box will
     open (see Figure 6-7).

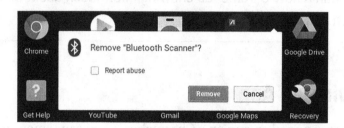

Figure 6-7. *Click the Remove button in the Remove dialog box to*
remove the app

5.   Click the Remove button. The Remove dialog box
     will close, and Chrome OS will remove the app.

6.   Press the Esc key to hide the Launcher screen.

Viewing Your Extensions and Apps

The Web Store app's My Extensions & Apps feature enables you to view
a list of the extensions and apps that you have installed on Chrome
OS devices. You can display a list of the items installed on the current
Chromebook or a list of the items in your "library," which means items
that you have used in the past (for example, on other devices) but have not
installed on the current Chromebook.

To use the My Extensions & Apps feature, click the Settings button
(the gear icon) to the right of the current Google account name in the
upper-right corner of the Web Store window, and then click the My
Extensions & Apps item on the menu that opens. The Installed tab
(see Figure 6-8) shows the items on the current Chromebook. Each app's
entry contains a Launch App button that you can click to launch the app.
Each extension's entry contains an Added to Chrome button that you can
click to display the extension's page in the Chrome Web Store.

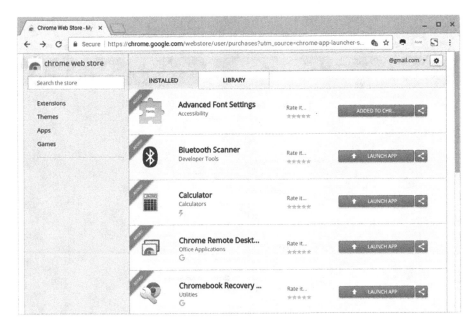

Figure 6-8. *The My Extensions & Apps feature enables you to see all the apps and extensions installed on the current Chromebook or those not installed but in your "library"*

Click the Library tab to display the list of items that are in your "library" but not installed on the current Chromebook. Here, you can click the Add to Chrome button for an item to install it on the current Chromebook.

Managing, Configuring, and Removing Extensions

Chrome's Extensions screen (see Figure 6-9) provides you with tools for managing extensions, configuring their settings, and removing them. You can display the Extensions screen in either of the following ways:

- *Menu*: In Chrome, choose More Actions ➤ More tools ➤ Extensions.

- *Keyboard*: Type `chrome://extensions` in the omnibox and then press the Enter key.

427

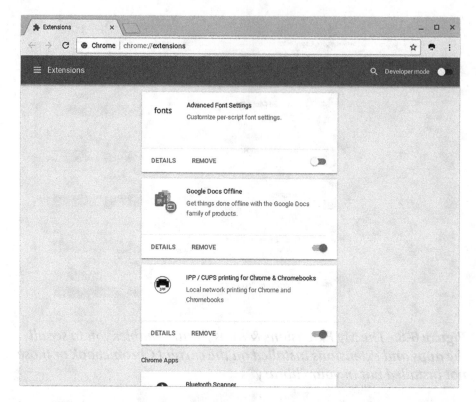

Figure 6-9. *From the Extensions screen, you can view the details for an extension, enable or disable the extension, or remove the extension*

From the Extensions screen, you can take the following actions:

- *View the details for an extension and change its setting:* Click the Details button to display the details screen for the extension (see Figure 6-10). Here, you can set the master switch at the top to Off if you want to disable the extension; usually, however, it is easier to simply use the switch on the Extensions screen itself. You can view the description, version, size, and permissions of the extension; set the "Allow in incognito" switch to On if you want to permit the extension to run in incognito windows; and click the Remove extension button to

428

start the process of removing the extension. Some
extensions have options that you can configure by
clicking the Extension options button.

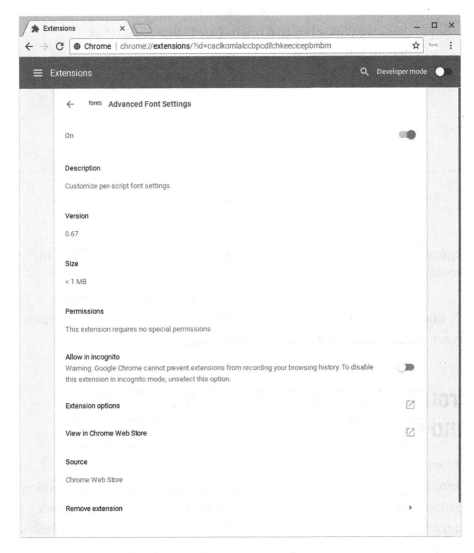

Figure 6-10. *The details screen for an extension enables you to view
the description, version, size, and permissions. You can also choose
whether to allow the extension's use in incognito mode.*

- *Enable or disable an extension*: Set the switch in the lower-right corner of the extension's box to On or Off as needed.

- *Remove an extension*: Click the Remove button. In the Remove dialog box that opens (see Figure 6-11), click the Remove button.

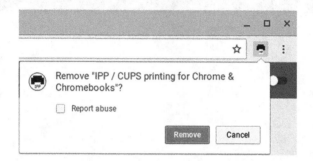

Figure 6-11. *Click the Remove button in the Remove dialog box to remove an extension*

Click the Back button (the left-arrow button) to return from the details screen for the extension to the Extensions screen.

Troubleshooting Problems with Apps and Extensions

Chrome OS is a mature operating system and normally runs stably on Chromebooks, staying responsive even when, behind the scenes, it is working to suppress problems that have occurred. But if you load up a Chromebook with many apps and extensions, you may find that error messages, slowdowns, or freezes occur. These problems may occur for two reasons:

- *Most software contains bugs*: Despite the best efforts of developers, most software contains at least some bugs.

- *Extensions may conflict with each other*: Two (or more) extensions may cause conflicts when run at the same time, even if each extension works fine on its own.

To reduce the risk of problems occurring, it is a good idea to test apps and extensions comprehensively before deploying them across your school's Chromebooks. Even so, you may sometimes need to troubleshoot problems with apps and extensions. This section will explain the moves you can use to resolve problems.

THREE REASONS FOR MINIMIZING APPS AND EXTENSIONS

Both apps and extensions can add necessary functionality to Chromebooks, so you will likely want to install at least some on your school's Chromebooks to enable your students and colleagues to perform all their tasks. But you should also look to keep the number of apps and extensions to the minimum necessary, for the following three reasons:

- *Simplicity*: Students may benefit from a streamlined configuration with fewer apps to distract them.

- *Load*: Apps and extensions increase the load on the Chromebooks. Even if the Chromebooks are well-specified models rather than barebones models, they may slow down.

- *Compatibility*: Some extensions may not run successfully on all Chromebooks. Normally, Chrome OS flags any conflicts when you go to install an incompatible extension

Striking the balance between functionality and simplicity can be difficult. You should monitor feedback from your school's students and teachers both about any functionality the Chromebooks are lacking and about any apps they do not use. You can then add or remove apps and extensions as needed, testing carefully before making any additions.

Troubleshooting Problems with Apps

If a Chromebook is exhibiting problems, and those problems seem to be tied to a specific app, restart the Chromebook and see if it runs normally before you launch the suspect app. If so, launch the app and see if the problems recur.

Assuming the problems do recur, remove the app by right-clicking its icon on the Launcher screen and then clicking the Uninstall item on the shortcut menu, as discussed in the section "Removing an App" earlier in this chapter.

If the problem app provided essential functionality, explore the Chrome Web Store for a similar app. An easy way to start locating a similar app is to look at the entries on the Related tab on the app's page.

Troubleshooting Problems with Extensions

If you suspect that an extension is making a Chromebook unstable, first try disabling the extension. As explained in the section "Managing, Configuring, and Removing Extensions" (earlier in this chapter), you can disable an extension by displaying the Extensions screen (`chrome://extensions`) and setting the switch on the extension's box to Off.

If the Chromebook recovers its stability once you have disabled the extension, you will probably want to remove the extension. To do so, click the Remove button in the extension's box on the Extensions screen and then click the Remove button in the Remove dialog box that opens.

Note   If a Chromebook remains unstable even after you have removed any apparently problematic extensions, you may need to reset the Chromebook to get it working normally again. See the section "Resolving Problems by Resetting and Powerwashing Chromebooks" in Chapter 9 for instructions on resetting a Chromebook.

Summary

In this chapter, you have learned how to manage apps and extensions on your school's Chromebooks. You know how an extension differs from an app and what the difference is between a Chrome app and a Chrome Web app. You have learned how to use the Web Store app to install apps and extensions and how you can manage those apps and extensions. You also know the key moves for troubleshooting problems with apps and extensions.

In the next chapter, we will examine how to connect the Chromebooks to resources and how to print from them.

CHAPTER 7

Connecting to Resources and Printing

In this chapter, we will first look at how to connect your school's Chromebooks to the school's network shares so they can access files locally. Next, we will examine how printing from Chromebooks works and how you can set up your Chromebooks to print to the school's printers. Finally, we will explore the ways in which you can display content from a Chromebook on a TV or monitor connected to a Chromecast device—for example, to share a document or a video with a class via a large screen.

Using Network Shares

As you well know by now, Chromebooks are designed to spend most of their lives working across Internet connections, storing data online and accessing it from there. But you can also connect your Chromebooks to your school's network shares so that they can access files on the shares. Accessing files locally can reduce the impact that the Chromebooks have on the school's Internet connection, so you will probably want to at least experiment with this method of sharing files.

© Guy Hart-Davis 2018
G. Hart-Davis, *Deploying Chromebooks in the Classroom*,
https://doi.org/10.1007/978-1-4842-3766-3_7

Connecting a Chromebook to a Network Share

To enable a Chromebook to connect to a network share, you need to install the File System for Windows service. Although the service's name includes "for Windows," the service also works for any computer sharing files via the Server Message Block protocol (SMB), so you can use it on MacOS by turning on SMB sharing or on Linux by running the Samba suite.

To install the File System for Windows service, follow these steps:

1. Launch the Files app if it is not already running. If the Files app is running, make one of its windows active.

2. In the left pane, click the Add new services item, and then click the Install new from the webstore item on the pop-up menu. The Available services dialog box will open (see Figure 7-1).

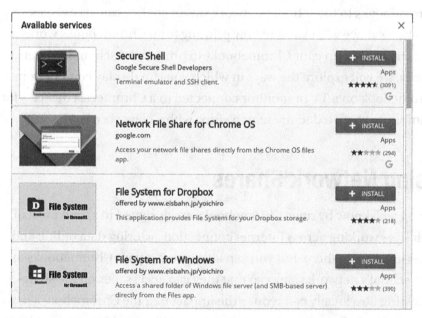

Figure 7-1. *In the Available services dialog box, click the Install button for the cloud file service to which you want to connect the Chromebook*

3. Click the Install button for the File System for Windows service. The Add "File System for Windows" dialog box will open (see Figure 7-2).

Figure 7-2. *In the Add "File System for Windows" dialog box, verify the actions the app will be able to take and then click the Add app button*

4. Read through the "It can:" list to make sure all the actions are ones you want the service to be able to take, such as "Exchange data with any device on the local network or internet."

5. Click the Add app button. A Download manager notification will appear while Chrome OS downloads the service and installs it. The Mount a new Windows file server screen will then appear (shown in Figure 7-3 with settings chosen).

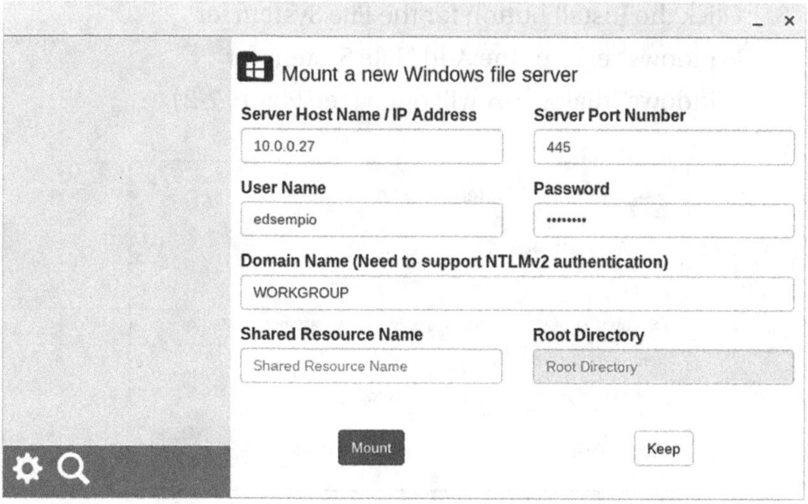

Figure 7-3. *In the Mount a new Windows file server dialog box, specify the details of the network share and then click the Mount button*

6. Enter the hostname (such as `winserver07`) or IP address (such as `10.0.0.101`) for the server in the Server Host Name/IP Address box.

7. Enter the port number in the Server Port Number box. For Windows, you can usually accept the default setting, port 445, which is the port that Windows uses for SMB sharing over TCP/IP.

8. Enter the username in the User Name box.

9. Enter the password in the Password box.

10. If the server is part of a Windows domain, enter the domain name in the Domain Name box. If the share is hosted on a machine that is part of a workgroup rather than a Windows domain, enter the workgroup name in the Domain Name box.

11. Optionally, enter the name of the shared folder in the Shared Resource Name box. You can also leave this box blank and then choose the shared folder from a dialog box.

12. Optionally, enter the root directory to use for the share in the Root Directory box. This is the directory (the folder) within the share that you want the user to see as the root directory. For example, if the share is named Spreads, and you want to use the folder Spreads/Development as the root directory, you would enter Development in the Root Directory box.

13. Click the Mount button if you want to mount the shared folder on the Chromebook now. If the shared folder is not available now and you are setting up the details so that the user can connect later, click the Keep button instead.

14. If you left the Shared Resource Name box blank, an unnamed dialog box will open showing the name of shared folders (see Figure 7-4). Click the option button for the folder to which you want to connect the Chromebook and then click the Connect button.

Figure 7-4. *In this dialog box, click the option button for the shared folder to which you want to connect the Chromebook*

Once you have connected the Chromebook to the network share, an item for the share will appear in the left pane in the Files app (see Figure 7-5). Click this item to display the contents of the network share. You can then work with the files and folders on the network share—for example, copying files to the Chromebook or to your Google account.

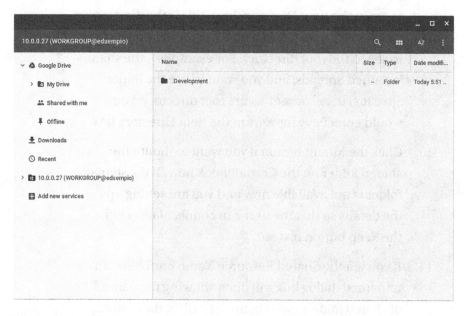

Figure 7-5. *The network share appears in the left pane of the Files app, and you can access its contents*

Disconnecting from a Network Share

When you have finished using the share, you can eject it from the Chromebook's file system by pressing Ctrl+Shift+E with the share active in the Files app. Alternatively, right-click the share in the Navigation pane in the Files app and then click the Close item on the shortcut menu.

Printing from Chromebooks

In this section, we will explore how to print from Chromebooks to your school's printers. We will start with an overview of how printing works on Chromebooks and Chrome OS, move on to making printers available on Google Cloud Print and managing them there, and then look at how to set up printers on Chromebooks and how to actually print on them.

Understanding How Printing from Chromebooks Works

If you are used to printing from Windows PCs, Macs, or even Linux boxes, you will find substantial differences in Chrome OS's approach to printing. This section will outline how printing from Chrome OS devices works. The following sections will walk you through the specifics.

There are different ways to print from Chrome OS, but the standard way has been—and remains, as of this writing—to use the Google Cloud Print service. As its name suggests, Google Cloud Print uses the "cloud"—the Internet—to handle printing. Instead of the client computer sending the print job to the printer across the network, the client sends the print job across the Internet connection to Google Cloud Print, which then sends the print job to the printer, again across the Internet connection.

As you will grasp immediately, sending the print jobs via Google Cloud Print has several implications:

- *Printer registration*: You need to set up your printers with Google Cloud Print so that it knows what the printers are and where to find them.

- *Remote printing*: You can print from anywhere the client computer has an Internet connection; it does not need to be connected to the same network as the printer.

441

- *Increased Internet traffic*: Sending the print jobs to the Google Cloud Print servers and receiving the print jobs back from them increases the amount of data being transmitted across the Internet connection or connections.

- *Data-protection issues*: Sending the print jobs via Google Cloud Print may raise data-protection issues. You may need to make sure that your school's privacy policies and computer-usage policies cover sharing data with Google Cloud Print in this way.

UNDERSTANDING ALTERNATIVES TO GOOGLE CLOUD PRINT

Google Cloud Print is the main way of printing from Chromebooks, but there are alternatives you may want to explore.

First, Google is gradually adding the capability to print to local printers via the CUPS printing system and the Internet Printing Protocol (IPP). This capability is currently patchy; it works for only some printers and works better with some Chromebooks than with others. Later in the chapter, we will examine how to connect to CUPS printers. In case you are wondering about the name, CUPS is a modular printing system for UNIX and similar operating systems; the name used to be an acronym for Common UNIX Printing System, but is now a name in its own right.

Second, some printer manufacturers provide apps or extensions for printing from Chrome OS to printers either connected directly via USB to a Chrome OS device or connected to the same local network. For example, HP provides the HP Print for Chrome app. Try searching the Chrome Web Store for an app or extension your printer manufacturer provides.

Third, some third-party developers provide apps or extensions for printing from Chrome to printers on the local network without going across the Internet. Try searching the Chrome Web Store for terms such as print local and see what you find.

Printing from a Chromebook via USB can be useful in some situations—for example, if you need to print from a Chromebook to your home printer. However, in a school situation, you will normally want to have the printers connected to the network so that more clients can print to them.

Making a Printer Available on Google Cloud Print

To make a printer available on Google Cloud Print, you go through a routine to add the printer to the service. How you do this varies depending on whether the printer is Google Cloud Print Ready or not. The first of the following sections will explain how to add a printer that is Google Cloud Print Ready; the second section will explain how to add a printer that is not Google Cloud Print Ready.

Note   To find out if a printer supports Google Cloud Print, look for the Google Cloud Print Ready logo on the box, on the printer itself, or on the manufacturer's web pages for the printer.

Setting Up a Google Cloud Print Ready Printer

If the printer is Google Cloud Print Ready, you can set it up by taking the following steps on a Chromebook, PC, or Mac:

1. Connect the printer to your network.

2. Power the printer on.

3. Open the Chrome browser.

4. Type www.google.com/cloudprint in the omnibox and press the Enter key. The Cloud Print page will appear, showing any print jobs you have (see Figure 7-6).

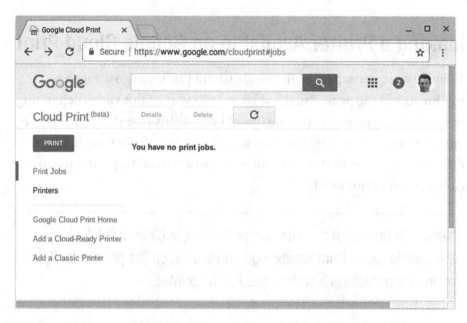

Figure 7-6. *On the Cloud Print screen, click the Add a Cloud-Ready Printer link to start adding a Cloud Print Ready printer*

5. Click the Add a Cloud-Ready Printer link on the left. The Cloud-ready printers screen will appear (see Figure 7-7).

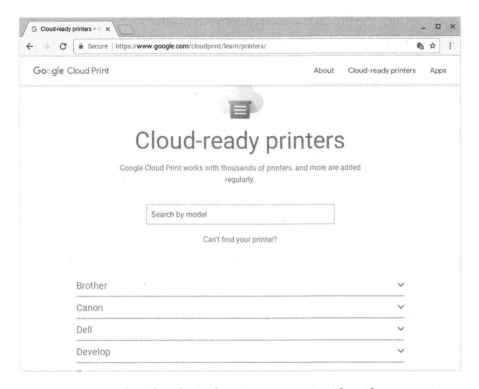

Figure 7-7. *On the Cloud-ready printers screen, identify your printer by searching or by browsing*

6.   Identify your printer in one of these ways:

   - *Search by model*: Click the Search by model box and then type enough of the name to distinguish the printer.

   - *Browse*: Click one of the headings (such as Canon or Dell) to display the list of printers from that manufacturer, and then browse to locate the printer.

445

7. Click the link in the section for your printer's manufacturer to display instructions for adding the printer to Google Cloud Print. Follow these instructions to add the printer.

8. After adding the printer, return to the Cloud Print page, either by using the Back button (or Back pop-up menu) in Chrome or by clicking the omnibox, typing the address (`www.google.com/cloudprint`), and pressing the Enter key. The printer will now appear in the left column.

Setting Up a Classic Printer on Google Cloud Print

If your printer is not Google Cloud Print Ready, Google considers it a "classic" printer. You can set up the printer to work with Google Cloud Print by connecting it to a PC or Mac and going through a routine for adding the printer. Follow these steps:

1. Connect the printer to a PC or a Mac.

2. Power the printer on.

3. On the PC or Mac, open the Chrome browser.

4. Type `chrome://devices` in the omnibox and press the Enter key. The Devices screen will appear (see Figure 7-8).

Note You can also display the Devices screen by choosing More Actions ➤ Settings, clicking the Advanced button on the Settings screen, clicking the Google Cloud Print button in the Printing section, and then clicking the Manage Cloud Print devices button.

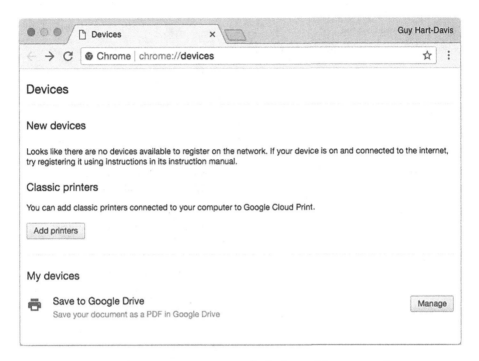

Figure 7-8. *On the Devices screen, click the Add printers button under the Classic printers heading to start adding a non–Cloud Print Ready printer to Google Cloud Print.*

5. Under the Classic printers heading, click the Add printers button. A Google Cloud Print screen will appear, showing the list of printers detected on the PC or Mac you are using (see Figure 7-9).

447

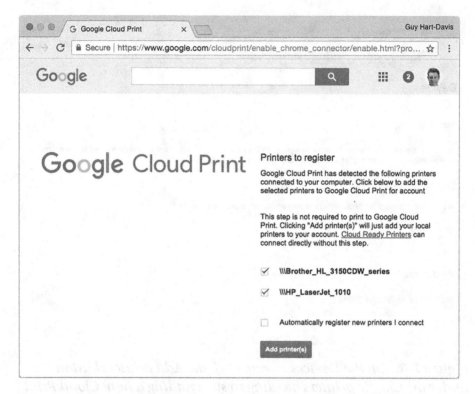

Figure 7-9. *In the Google Cloud Print window, uncheck the check box for any printer you do not want to register; uncheck the "Automatically register new printers I connect" check box, as needed; and then click the Add printer(s) button.*

6. In the list of printers, uncheck the check box for any printer you do not want to register on Google Cloud Print.

7. Uncheck the "Automatically register new printers I connect" check box if you prefer to add printers manually rather than have them added automatically.

8. Click the Add printer(s) button. Google Cloud Print will register the printers and then display the message "Thanks, you're ready to go!" (see Figure 7-10).

Figure 7-10. *Google Cloud Print displays the "Thanks, you're ready to go!" message once your printers have been registered. You can click the Manage your printers link to display the screen for managing your printers.*

You can click the Manage your printers link if you want to go to the screen for managing your printers. Otherwise, close the Chrome tab or window, or quit Chrome.

Managing Your School's Printers on Google Cloud Print

After you have added your printers to Google Cloud Print, you can manage them from the Printers page in Google Cloud Print for the Google account to which you have added them. To display the Printers page, open a browser tab to Google Cloud Print (`www.google.com/cloudprint`) and then click the Printers item in the navigation panel on the left.

From the Printers page (see Figure 7-11), you can take the following actions:

- *Select a printer*: Click the printer in the list.

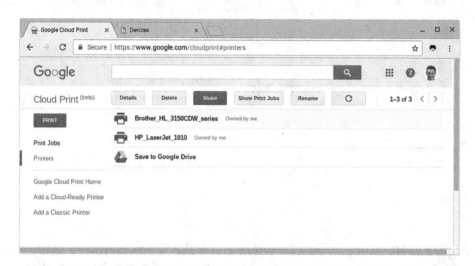

Figure 7-11. *Click the Printers item in the navigation panel to display the list of printers. You can then click the printer you want to manage*

- *View details for the selected printer*: Click the Details button to display the Details page (see Figure 7-12). At first, this page displays only brief details: the printer's ownership, when it was added, its location (if that information is available), and whether the printer is online and ready to print. You can click the Advanced Details button to display a wealth—or perhaps a surfeit—of further details. These details include whether the printer is a Google Cloud Print Ready model or a classic model, when it was last updated, and what its printer ID is. Click the Back button (an arrow pointing up and left) that replaces the Details button when you want to return to the Printers page.

Figure 7-12. *At first, the Details screen displays brief details about the printer, including its current status. You can click the Advanced Details button to display further information, including whether the printer is Google Cloud Print Ready or classic.*

- *Delete the selected printer*: Click the Delete button and then click the OK button in the Delete dialog box that opens.

Note   When you delete a classic printer, the Delete dialog box will prompt you to disable the Google Cloud Print connector on the computer to which your printer is connected so as to avoid Google Cloud Print registering the printer again. You need do this only if you checked the "Automatically register new printers I connect" check box when setting up Google Cloud Print on the computer.

451

- *Configure sharing for the selected printer*: Click the Share button to display the main sharing settings dialog box for the printer (see Figure 7-13). You can then either allow access to the printer to anyone who has the link for it or invite specific people to share the printer. To allow access to anyone with the link, click the Change button on the Private line, click the "Anyone with the link has access to the printer" option in the smaller sharing settings dialog box that opens (see Figure 7-14), and then click the Save button. To invite one or more people to use the printer, type their names or email addresses in the Invite people box; alternatively, type a group name to add a group. Next, choose the Can print item in the pop-up menu and then click the Share button. The names will appear in the Who has access list (see Figure 7-15); if you need to remove a person, click the Delete (X) button on the right of that person's row. Click the Close button to close the main sharing settings dialog box.

Note   If you want a person to be able to manage the printer, select the Can manage item in the pop-up menu in the main sharing settings dialog box and then click the Share button.

Brother_HL_3150CDW_series sharing settings

Who has access:

🔒   Private   Change...

👤   Guy Hart-Davis   Owner

Invite people:

maria.z.jones@gmail.com, | Can print ⇕ |
daniel.z.ransom@gmail.com

[Share]   [Close]

Figure 7-13.   *In the main sharing settings dialog box for a printer,*
you can click the Change button to open the smaller sharing settings
dialog box. You can also invite specific people to share the printer.

Brother_HL_3150CDW_series sharing settings

○ 👥   Anyone with the link has access to the printer
           Anyone with the link has access to this printer and can submit print jobs

● 🔒   Private
           Only people explicitly granted permission can add printer

[Save]   [Cancel]   Learn more about printing access

Figure 7-14.   *In this smaller sharing settings dialog box for a printer,*
you can select the "Anyone with the link has access to the printer"
option to make the printer more widely available

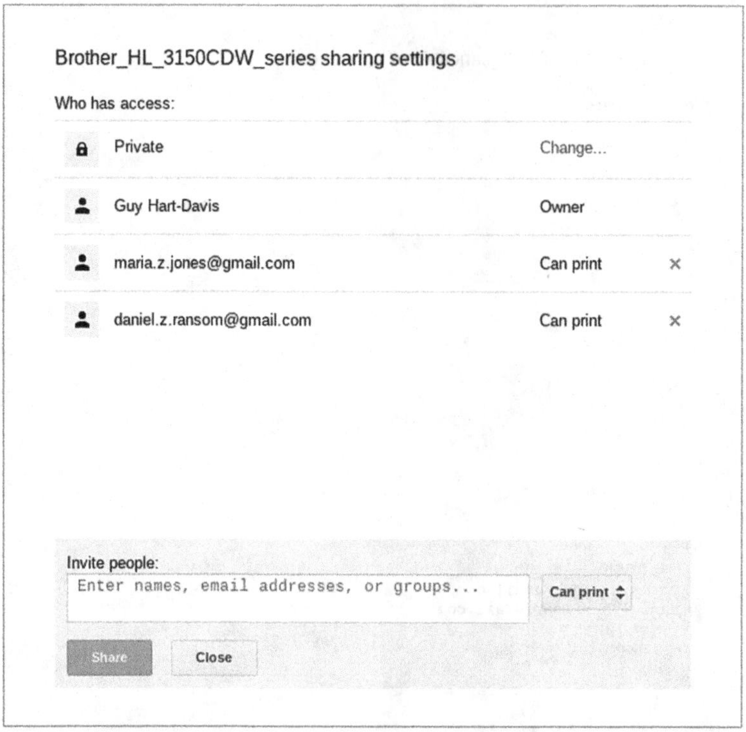

Figure 7-15. *The people you added appear in the Who has access list in the main sharing settings dialog box. You can remove a person by clicking the Delete (X) button on the right of that person's row.*

- *Manage the print jobs for the selected printer*: Click the Show Print Jobs button to display a list of the print jobs (see Figure 7-16). You can then click a print job and click the Details button to view its details, or click the Delete button to delete the print job.

Figure 7-16. *After displaying the list of print jobs for a printer, you can view the details of the selected print job or simply delete the print job*

- *Rename the selected printer*: Click the Rename button, type the new name in the edit box that appears around the current name, and then click the Rename button to the right of the edit box.

Note Click the Refresh button (the circular arrow to the right of the Rename button) to refresh the list of printers.

Setting Up Printers on a Chromebook

After adding your school's printers to Google Cloud Print, you can set up the printers on the Chromebooks. You may also be able to set up printers on your school's local network, depending on whether they are models that Chrome supports.

Whichever way you will add a printer, you begin by opening a Settings window and displaying the Printing section of it.

Displaying the Printing Section of the Settings Window

To set up a printer, first open the Settings window to the Printing section. Follow these steps:

1. Click the status area to display the status menu.

2. Click the Settings icon to open the Settings window.

3. Click the Navigation button to display the Settings pane on the left.

4. If the Advanced category is collapsed, click it to display its contents.

5. Click the Printing item to display the Printing section of the Settings window (see Figure 7-17).

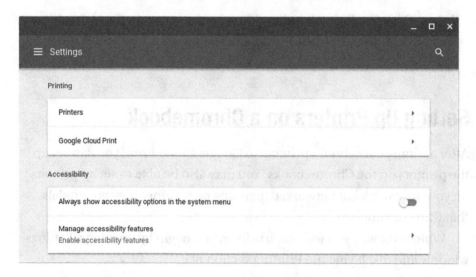

Figure 7-17. *From the Printing section of the Settings window, you can start to configure printers or configure Google Cloud Print*

Adding a Printer on the Network

Chrome OS enables you to add printers that it can detect on the same network as the Chromebook. As of this writing, this feature works with only some printers that comply with the CUPS standard.

To add a network printer, follow these steps from the Printing section of the Settings window:

1. Click the Printers button to display the Printers screen (see Figure 7-18).

Figure 7-18. *On the Printers screen in the Settings window, click the Add Printer button to start adding a printer*

2. Click the Add Printer button to open the Add a nearby printer dialog box (see Figure 7-19) or the Add a printer manually dialog box (shown in Figure 7-22, later in this chapter). These two dialog boxes work as a pair, and you can switch from one to the other by clicking the Add Manually button in the Add a nearby printer dialog box or the Add Nearby Printers button in the Add a printer manually dialog box.

3. If the Add a printer manually dialog box opens, click
    the Add Nearby Printers button to switch to the Add a
    nearby printer dialog box. The main part of this dialog
    box shows any printers that Chrome OS has detected
    on the network.

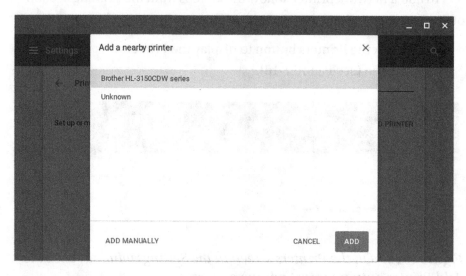

Figure 7-19. In the Add a nearby printer dialog box, click the printer
you want to add and then click the Add button

4. Click the printer you want to add.

5. Click the Add button. The Select a printer
    manufacturer and model screen appears
    (see Figure 7-20).

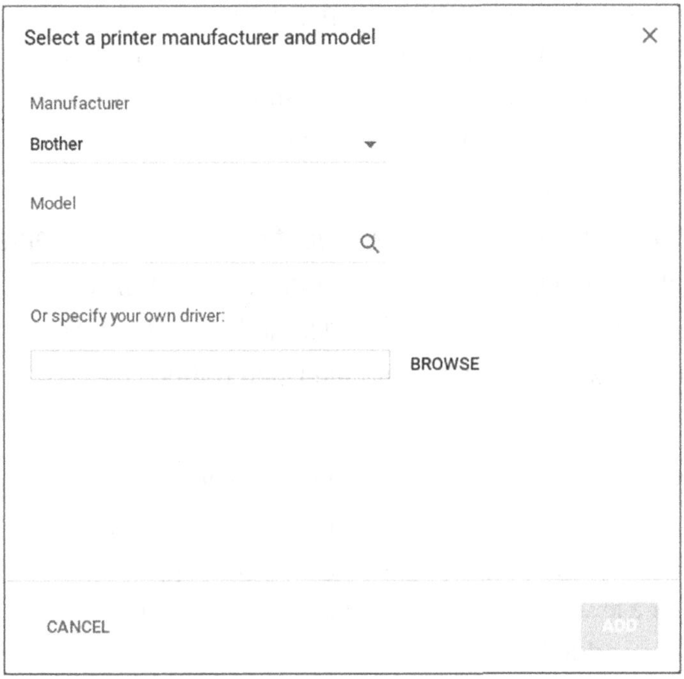

Figure 7-20. *In the Select a printer manufacturer and model dialog box, identify the printer you want to add. You can either choose which of Chrome OS's built-in drivers to use or provide a driver you have obtained elsewhere.*

6. Click the Manufacturer pop-up menu and then click the printer's manufacturer.

7. Use the controls in the Model area to specify the model in one of these ways:

    •   *Search*: You can click in the search box, type a distinguishing part of the printer's name or number, and then press the Enter key. In the list of matches that Chrome OS returns, click the best match.

- *Scroll*: You can open the pop-up menu and simply scroll to locate the most suitable printer. However, depending on the printer manufacturer you selected, the list may be long.

Note   If you have downloaded a driver file for this printer, enter its name and location in the Or specify your own driver box by clicking the Browse button, clicking the location and file in the Select a file to open dialog box, and then clicking the Open button.

---

8. Click the Add button. The dialog box will close, and the Printer will appear on the Printers screen (see Figure 7-21). A pop-up message will appear for a few seconds, announcing that the printer has been added.

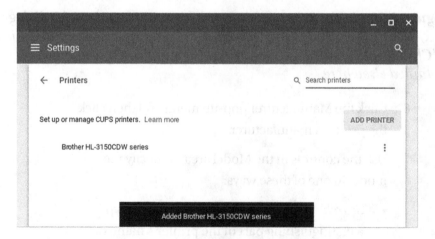

Figure 7-21. *The printer appears on the Printers screen. A pop-up message appears for a few seconds, announcing that the printer has been added.*

Adding a Printer Manually

You can also add a printer to a Chromebook manually—for example, when the network (or the printer) is not available or when Chrome OS cannot detect the printer on the network.

Caution   As of this writing, this method of adding a printer is not always successful—the Chromebook does gain an entry for the printer, but it may not be able to print to the printer even when the printer is there.

To set up a printer manually, you will need to know the following information:

- *Printer name*: This is the descriptive name you will assign to the printer.

- *Printer address*: This is the network address, such as `BRN30055C504EFA.local:631`.

- *Printing protocol*: This is the protocol used for printing to the printer, such as Internet Printing Protocol (IPP).

- *Print queue*: This is the queue type for the printer, such as `ipp/printer`.

To add a printer manually, follow these steps from the Printing section of the Settings window:

1. Click the Printers button to display the Printers screen.

2. Click the Add Printer button to open the Add a nearby printer dialog box (shown in Figure 7-19, earlier in this chapter) or the Add a printer manually

dialog box (see Figure 7-22). As mentioned earlier, these two dialog boxes work as a pair, and you can switch from one to the other by clicking the Add Manually button in the Add a nearby printer dialog box or the Add Nearby Printers button in the Add a printer manually dialog box.

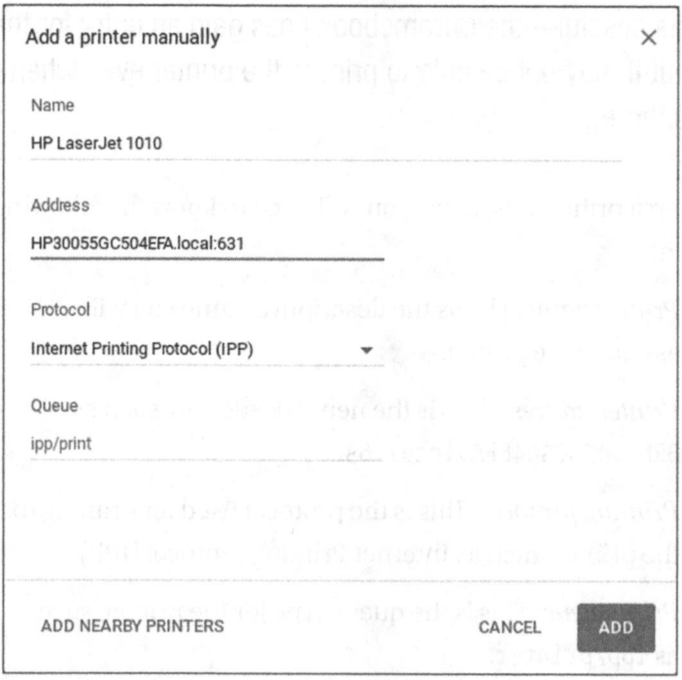

Figure 7-22. *In the Add a printer manually dialog box, enter the details for the printer and then click the Add button*

3. If the Add a nearby printer dialog box opens, click the Add Manually button to switch to the Add a printer manually dialog box.

4. Type the display name for the printer in the Name
    box. This is the name you want the user to see; it does
    not have to be what the printer is actually called. For
    example, you might give the printer a name such as
    `Color Printer in Room 142`.

5. In the Address box, type or paste the address for the
    printer.

6. Click the Protocol pop-up menu and then click
    the appropriate printing protocol. The choices are
    Internet Printing Protocol (IPP), Internet Printing
    Protocol (IPPS), Internet Printing Protocol (HTTP),
    Internet Printing Protocol (HTTPS), AppSocket
    (TCP/IP), and Line Printer Daemon (LPD).

7. In the Queue box, enter the print queue, such as
    `ipp/print` for Internet Printing Protocol (IPP).

8. Click the Add button. The Select a printer
    manufacturer and model dialog box opens
    (see Figure 7-20, earlier in this chapter).

9. Click the Manufacturer pop-up menu and then click
    the printer's manufacturer.

10. Use the controls in the Model area to specify the
    model in one of these ways:

    •   *Search*: You can click in the search box, type
        a distinguishing part of the printer's name or
        number, and then press the Enter key. In the list
        of matches that Chrome OS returns, click the best
        match.

- *Scroll*: You can open the pop-up menu and simply scroll to locate the most suitable printer. However, depending on the printer manufacturer you selected, the list may be long.

Note   If you have downloaded a driver file for this printer, enter its name and location in the Or specify your own driver box by clicking the Browse button, clicking the location and file in the Select a file to open dialog box, and then clicking the Open button.

---

11.   Click the Add button. The dialog box will close, and the Printer will appear on the Printers screen. A pop-up message will appear for a few seconds, announcing that the printer has been added.

Editing and Removing Network Printers

After adding a network printer, you may need to edit its details—for example, to change the printer's name. You may also need to remove the printer if you are no longer using it.

To edit a printer, click the More Actions button (the three vertical dots) on the right of its row on the Printers screen and then click the Edit button. The Edit Printer dialog box will open (see Figure 7-23).

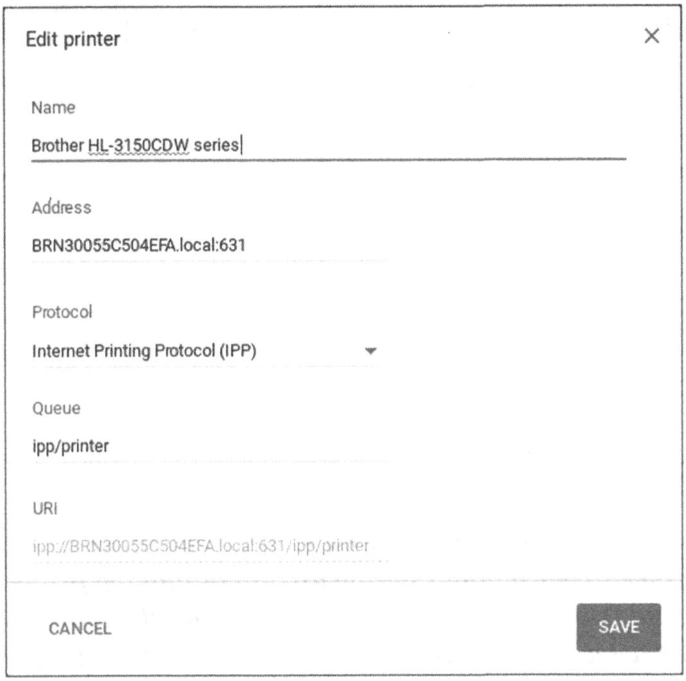

Figure 7-23. *The Edit Printer dialog box enables you to change a printer's name or configuration*

To remove a printer, click the More Actions button and then click the Remove button. Chrome OS will remove the printer from the list without confirmation.

Configuring Google Cloud Print and Your Devices

To configure Google Cloud Print, you work on the Google Cloud Print screen (see Figure 7-24). To display this screen, click the Google Cloud Print button in the Printing section of the Settings window.

465

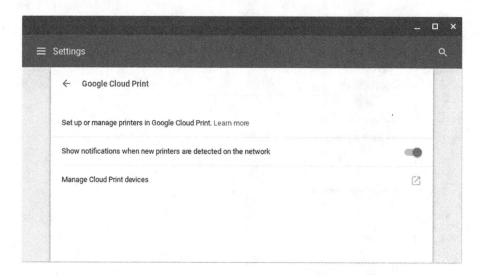

Figure 7-24. *From the Google Cloud Print screen in the Settings window, you can learn about setting up and managing printers in Google Cloud Print, choose whether to display notifications when new printers are detected, and open a Chrome tab for managing Cloud Print devices*

As of this writing, the Google Cloud Print screen contains three controls:

- *Set up or manage printers in Google Cloud Print*: Click the Learn more link next to this item to open a Chrome tab to the "Print from Chrome" topic in Google Chrome Help.

- *Show notifications when new printers are detected on the network*: Set this switch to On if you want the Chromebook to display notifications about new printers that Chrome OS detects on the network; set this switch to Off if you do not want the notifications. In a school deployment, you would normally want to set this switch to Off.

- *Manage Cloud Print devices*: Click this button to open a tab to the Devices page for Chrome. You can also go directly to the Devices page by typing chrome://devices in the omnibox and pressing the Enter key.

Managing Devices on the Devices Page

When you need to manage your Google Cloud Print devices, display the Devices page by either clicking the Manage Cloud Print devices button on the Google Cloud Print screen or by typing chrome://devices in the omnibox and pressing the Enter key.

As you can see in Figure 7-25, the Devices page provides the My devices list, which contains entries for the printing devices set up on the Chromebook. You can click the Manage button for a device to open a new tab to the Cloud Print page for managing that device.

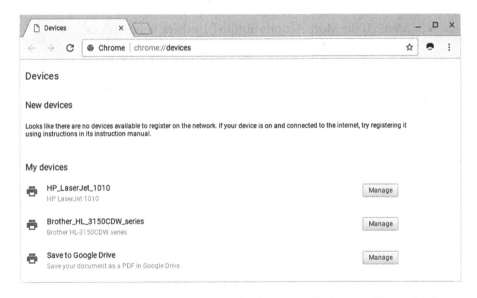

Figure 7-25. *The Devices page includes the My devices list, which shows the printing devices set up on the Chromebook. You can click the Manage button on a device's row to open a new tab showing the Cloud Print page for managing that device.*

467

Printing from a Chromebook

Once you have set up a Chromebook's printers, printing from the Chromebook is straightforward. This section will explain what you need to know, starting with giving the Print command, going through choosing settings for printing, and ending with coverage of managing your print jobs.

Giving the Print Command

Once you have displayed the content you want to print, give the Print command. How you do so depends on the app you are using:

- *Keyboard shortcut*: In most apps that support printing, press Ctrl+P to give the Print command. (Some apps, such as Camera and Calculator, do not support printing.)

- *Print icon*: If a Print icon appears, click it.

- *Menu*: If the More Actions button (the three vertical dots) appears, click it to open the menu, and then click the Print item.

Whichever way you give the Print command, the app displays the Print panel, which you use to choose printing options. Figure 7-26 shows the Print panel for a Google Docs document.

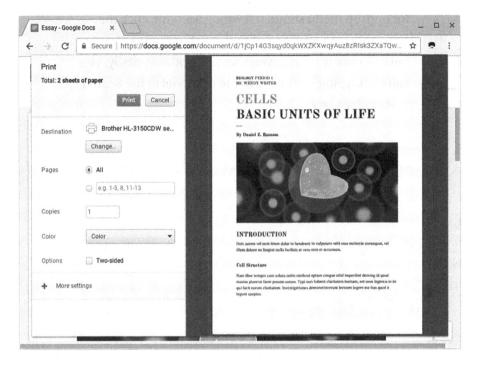

Figure 7-26. *The Print panel at first displays essentials, such as controls for setting the print destination, choosing which pages to print, and specifying the number of copies. Click the More Settings button to display further settings.*

Choosing Settings and Printing a Document

At first, the Print panel displays controls for three essential print settings: Destination, Pages, and Copies. Depending on the printer, other key settings may appear at first, such as Color and Two-sided for a color printer capable of two-sided printing.

- *Destination*: The Destination readout shows the current printing device—a printer or the Save as PDF service. To change the printing device, click the Change button and then click the printing device in the Select a destination dialog box (see Figure 7-27). If the Showing destinations

469

for pop-up menu shows the wrong account, click the pop-up button and then click the right account. If you have too many print devices set up to browse easily, you can start typing a printer's name or model in the Search destinations box.

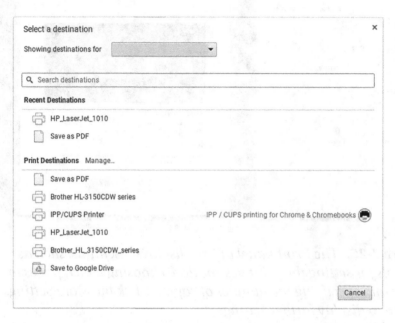

Figure 7-27. In the Select a destination dialog box, click the printing device you want to use

- *Pages*: Make sure the "All" option is selected if you want to print the whole document. Otherwise, click in the lower box (which selects the lower option button) and enter the details of what you want to print. You can enter individual page numbers, separated by commas, such as 1, 3, 5; a range, such as 1–5; or both, such as 1, 3, 5–8, 11.

- *Copies*: If you want to print more than one copy (the default), enter the number of copies in this box.

- *Color*: For a color printer, you can open this pop-up menu and choose the Color item (usually the default) or the Black and white item.

- *Two-sided*: Check this check box if you want to print on both sides of the paper rather than on one side.

If you need to choose other settings, click the More Settings button. Another section of the Print panel will appear, and you can choose further settings. Which settings are available depends on the printer, but the following list gives some examples of typical settings:

- *Paper size*: In this pop-up menu, choose the paper size, such as US Letter.

- *Margins*: In this pop-up menu, choose what type of margins to use on the page. Your choices typically include Default, None, Minimum, and Custom; if you choose Custom, you can drag the margins on the document preview to where you need them.

- *Quality*: In this pop-up menu, choose the print quality, such as 600 dpi.

- *Scale*: If you need to print the document at a larger or smaller size, increase or decrease the scale from 100%. For example, you may need to scale a document down to make it fit on a specific number of pages.

Once you have chosen suitable settings, click the Print button. Chrome OS will process the print job and send it to the print device.

"PRINTING" TO A PDF

As well as the printers you have set up, Chrome OS offers the Save as PDF print destination. This feature enables the user to create a PDF of the page and save it either to the Chromebook or to the user's Google Drive.

Saving a PDF can be a handy standby for capturing items when no printer is available, but you will still need to configure a printer on which to print those items later. If the user has a dedicated Chromebook, saving the PDF to the Chromebook is reasonable; if not, saving it to Google Drive is usually the better choice because the user will be able to print the PDF from any Chromebook (or other computer).

Canceling or Deleting a Print Job

Sometimes you may need to cancel or delete a print job you have sent to a printer.

If you need to cancel a print job you have just sent, you may be able to do so from the Printing notification, like this:

1. Click any icon in the notifications area (to the left of the status area) to display the current notifications.

2. Click the down-arrow button (which you can see on the second notification in Figure 7-28) to expand the notification. The top notification here is expanded.

Figure 7-28. *You may be able to cancel a print job by clicking the down-arrow button on its notification and then clicking the Cancel Printing button*

3. Click the Cancel Printing button.

Otherwise, to delete a print job, follow these steps:

1. Launch or activate Chrome.

2. Type chrome://devices in the omnibox and press the Enter key to display the Devices screen.

3. Click the Manage button for the printer to which you sent the job. The Google Cloud Print page for managing that printer appears.

4. Click the Show Print Jobs button. The list of print jobs appears.

473

5.   Click the entry for the print job you want to delete.

6.   Click the Delete button.

Casting Content to a Chromecast Device

As well as Chrome OS, the Chrome browser, Chromebooks, and Chromeboxes, Google also created the Chromecast family of devices. A Chromecast is a device that you plug in to the HDMI port on a TV or monitor and that enables you to play content from a computer or other device (such as an Android phone) on that TV or monitor. The Chromecast Audio, as its name suggests, is an audio-only device that you connect to regular (or "dumb"—not smart) speakers so that you can play audio on the speakers from a remote device.

Chromebooks make it easy to *cast* (send) content to a Chromecast device. Casting can be a great way to share information quickly with your whole class. You can cast content in three ways:

- *Chrome browser*: You can cast either a tab or the entire desktop.

- *Chrome OS desktop*: You can cast your Chromebook's entire desktop.

- *Video Player app*: You can cast videos stored on Google Drive.

The following sections will show you how to use these three ways of casting.

> ## UNDERSTANDING HOW CHROMECAST WORKS
>
> From the user perspective, casting to a Chromecast device appears to be straightforward streaming from the Chromebook. You cue the content you want to cast and then specify the destination Chromecast device—and the content will appear on the TV or monitor connected to the Chromecast.
>
> Behind the scenes, however, the implementation is more nuanced. When you cast a Chrome tab or the Chromebook's desktop, the Chromebook *does* stream that content to the Chromecast. But when you use the Video Player app to cast videos stored on Google Drive, the casting actually happens via remote control. The Video Player app causes the Chromecast device to connect to Google Drive and start streaming the video directly from there, so the stream is not being passed through the Chromebook.

Casting from the Chrome Browser

Starting from the Chrome browser, you can cast either a single tab or the Chromebook's entire desktop. To start casting, follow these steps:

1. Open a tab to the page you want to cast.

2. Click the More Actions button and then click the Cast item on the menu. The Cast to dialog box opens, showing a list of available Chromecast devices (see Figure 7-29).

Note   The Cast to dialog box casts the tab by default rather than the desktop. However, instead of the Cast to dialog box, you may see the Cast tab dialog box or the Cast desktop dialog box. As their names imply, the Cast tab dialog box indicates that Chrome OS will cast the tab, and the Cast desktop dialog box indicates that Chrome OS will cast the desktop. You can change the item to be cast by clicking the down-arrow button and using the Select source dialog box.

Figure 7-29. *The Cast to dialog box shows the available Chromecast devices*

3. To change the item that Chrome OS will cast, click the down-arrow button. The Select source dialog box will open (see Figure 7-30).

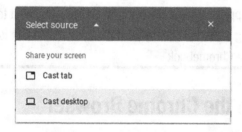

Figure 7-30. *In the Select source dialog box, click the Cast tab button or the Cast desktop button, as needed*

4. Click the Cast tab button or the Cast desktop button to specify what you want to cast. The Cast tab dialog box (see Figure 7-31) or the Cast desktop dialog box then opens, again showing the list of available Chromecast devices.

Figure 7-31. *In the Cast tab dialog box (shown here) or the Cast desktop dialog box, click the Chromecast device you want to use*

476

5. Click the Chromecast device you want to use. If you choose to cast your desktop, the Share your screen dialog box will open (see Figure 7-32). Check or uncheck the "Share audio" check box, as needed, and then click the Share button. A dialog box whose title is the Chromecast device's name will open, showing the Chrome Mirroring message and providing a volume slider and a Stop button (see Figure 7-33). The item you're casting then appears on the TV or monitor.

Figure 7-32. *In the Share your screen dialog box, check or uncheck the "Share audio" check box, as needed, and then click the Share button*

477

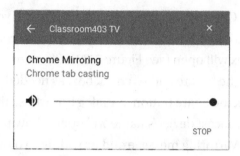

Figure 7-33. *This dialog box shows the name of the Chromecast device. Use the volume slider to control the volume and the Stop button to end the cast.*

6. Drag the volume slider as needed to adjust the output volume. You should also be able to adjust the volume on the TV, monitor, or speakers.

While the Chrome app is casting, the Display on another screen button appears to the right of the omnibox (see Figure 7-34). You can click this button to open the dialog box for controlling the cast.

Display on another screen

Figure 7-34. *The Display on another screen button appears to the right of the omnibox while the Chrome app is casting.*

When you are ready to end the cast, click the Stop button in the dialog box for controlling the cast.

Casting the Chrome OS Desktop

If you want to cast the Chrome desktop, you can start the cast from the status menu. To do so, follow these steps:

1. Open the app or apps you want to cast.

2. Click the status area to display the status menu (shown on the left in Figure 7-35).

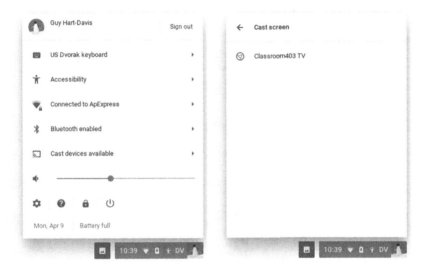

Figure 7-35. *On the status menu (left), click the Cast devices available button to display the Cast screen menu (right), and then click the Chromecast device to which you want to cast the desktop.*

3. Click the Cast devices available button to display the Cast screen menu (shown on the right in Figure 7-35).

4. Click the Chromecast device to which you want to cast the desktop. The Share your screen dialog box opens (see Figure 7-32, earlier in this chapter).

479

5. Check or uncheck the "Share audio" check box, as needed.

6. Click the Share button. The Chromebook's desktop will appear on the TV or monitor.

When you are ready to stop casting, click the status area and then click the Stop button to the right of the Casting screen item on the status menu (see Figure 7-36).

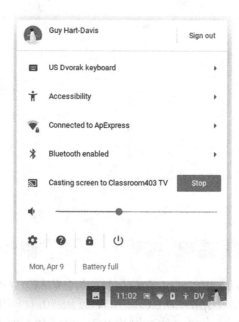

Figure 7-36. *To stop casting the Chromebook's desktop, open the status menu and click the Stop button to the right of the Casting screen item*

Casting from the Video Player App

You can also start casting files from the Video Player app, which you launch from the Files app. This works only for video files stored on Google Drive, not for files on the Chromebook itself or on external drives connected to the Chromebook.

To cast from the Video Player app, follow these steps:

1. Open the Files app. For example, click the Launcher button, click the up-arrow button, and then click the Files icon.

2. In the navigation pane on the left, display the folder on Google Drive that contains the video file you want to cast.

3. Double-click the video file to open it in the Video Player app (see Figure 7-37).

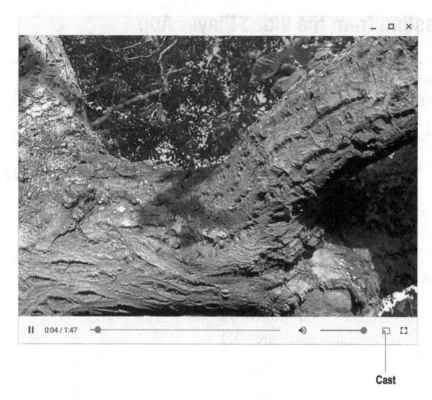

Cast

Figure 7-37. *Click the Cast button in the Video Player window to start casting the video to a Chromecast device*

4. Click the Cast button. The Cast Video Player dialog box opens (see Figure 7-38).

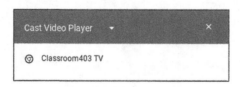

Figure 7-38. *In the Cast Video Player dialog box, click the Chromecast device you want to use*

5. Click the Chromecast device to which you want to cast the video. The video starts playing on the TV or monitor connected to that Chromecast device. On the Chromebook's screen, the video stops and displays a message giving the name of the Chromecast device on which the video is playing.

When you are ready to stop casting the video, click the Stop button on the Chromebook's screen.

Summary

In this chapter, you have learned how to connect Chromebooks to your school's network shares so they can access files locally as well as across the Internet. You also now know how printing with Google Cloud Print works, how to get your school's printers and Chromebooks to work together, and how to print and manage print jobs on Chromebooks. And you can display content from a Chromebook on a TV or monitor connected to a Chromecast device to share it with a class.

In the next chapter, we will examine how to organize your lessons with Google's Classroom app.

CHAPTER 8

Using Google Classroom

Google Classroom is a web service that enables teachers to set up and manage classes, organize class materials, and communicate easily with students. In this chapter, we will explore what Google Classroom is and how you can use it most effectively to organize classes in your school.

We will start by looking at how to sign in to Google Classroom and how to choose settings. We will then go through how to set up your classes, whether you are accepting provisioned classes or creating classes yourself. We will look at how to configure and manage classes, from adding materials all the way through archiving classes when you finish teaching them. On the way, we will dig into the details of how to communicate with students—setting and grading assignments, making announcements and posing questions, and contacting students via email.

Getting Started with Google Classroom

To get started with Google Classroom, go to `classroom.google.com` and sign in using your Google Education account.

The Classes page then appears, either showing a list of classes (if they are already set up for you) or a prompt to create or join your first class (see Figure 8-1).

© Guy Hart-Davis 2018
G. Hart-Davis, *Deploying Chromebooks in the Classroom*,
https://doi.org/10.1007/978-1-4842-3766-3_8

Classroom Main Menu   Create or join a class   Google apps   Notifications   Google Account

Figure 8-1. The Classes page shows either your list of existing classes or a prompt to create or join your first class.

The following list explains the key elements of the Classes page:

- *Classroom Main Menu*: Click this button to display the main menu, which enables you to navigate to your classes and calendar and access the Settings page.

- *Create or join a class*: Click this button to display a pop-up menu with a Join class item and a Create class item.

- *Google apps*: Click this button to display a pop-up panel showing icons for the various Google apps. You can click an icon to launch an app.

- *Notifications*: Click this button to display a pop-up panel showing your notifications.

- *Google Account*: Click this button to display a pop-up panel showing the name of the account under which you are signed in. This panel contains the following three buttons:

    - **My Account**: Click this button to display your account information in a new tab.

    - **Add account**: Click this button to start adding another account.

    - **Sign out**: Click this button to sign out of the account you are currently signed in to.

487

USING GOOGLE CLASSROOM ON OTHER PLATFORMS

Given that your school is using Chromebooks, its students and teachers will likely access Google Classroom mostly through the Chrome browser. However, Google Classroom also works with most major browsers and operating systems, so if your students or colleagues use PCs or Macs at home, they can access Classroom using browsers such as Microsoft Edge, Internet Explorer, Firefox, or Safari instead of Chrome.

Google Classroom is also available as an Android app and an Apple app. On Android, open the Play Store app and search for Google Classroom. On iOS, open the App Store app and search for Google Classroom. Verify that the result is from Google Inc.

Choosing Settings for Google Classroom

Google Classroom enables you to customize your profile picture and choose which notifications you receive. To do so, you work on the Settings page (see Figure 8-2), which you can display by clicking the Menu button in the upper-left corner of the Classes page and then clicking the Settings item on the menu.

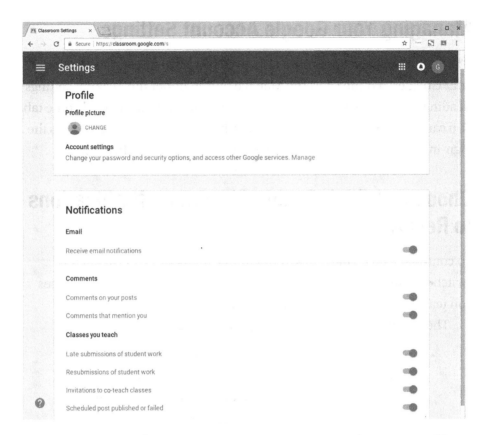

Figure 8-2. From the Settings page, you can customize your profile picture, manage your Google account settings, and choose which Google Classroom notifications to receive

Changing Your Profile Picture

To change your profile picture, click the Change button in the Profile box and then use the Select profile photo dialog box to select an existing photo or to take a new photo using the computer's webcam. This profile picture will appear across all the Google services you use, and it is visible to anyone, so make sure you are happy with the picture you select.

489

Managing Your Google Account Settings

The Settings page in Classroom also gives you access to the settings for your Google account. Click the Manage button under the Account settings heading to open the settings for your Google account in a new Chrome tab. You can then go to a category of settings by clicking a heading, such as the Sign-in & security heading or the Personal info & privacy heading.

Choosing Which Google Classroom Notifications to Receive

To control which Google Classroom notifications you receive, set the switches in the Email category, the Comments category, and the Classes you teach category on the Settings page.

The Email category contains only one setting:

- *Receive email notifications*: This switch is the master switch for email notifications. If you set this switch to Off, Google Classroom will hide all the other switches because those settings are not relevant.

The Comments category contains the following two settings:

- *Comments on your posts*: Set this switch to On to receive notifications for comments that students (or teachers) post in response to your posts. Receiving notifications for these comments is usually helpful—for example, the notifications may help you quickly resolve any issues the students raise regarding questions or assignments you have set. If you review your classes regularly and you receive too many notifications, you may prefer to turn notifications off.

- *Comments that mention you*: Set this switch to On to receive notifications of comments that mention you by your email address.

The Classes you teach category contains the following four settings:

- *Late submissions of student work*: Set this switch to On to receive a notification when a student submits work after the due date and time.

- *Resubmissions of student work*: Set this switch to On to receive a notification when a student resubmits work. These notifications can help you avoid spending time marking the work that the student had previously submitted.

- *Invitations to co-teach classes*: Set this switch to On to receive a notification when a teacher invites you to co-teach a class.

- *Scheduled post published or failed*: Set this switch to On to receive a notification each time Google Classroom publishes one of your scheduled posts or fails to publish one. If you schedule many posts, you will receive a lot of notifications, but you may find them helpful as a reminder of what is current in the class. Notifications of failed posts are especially helpful, giving you a heads-up that there is a problem you need to fix.

When you finish choosing settings, return to the Classes page by clicking the Menu button and then clicking the Classes item on the menu.

491

Note   For configuring notifications, students also have the Receive email notifications master switch, the Comments on your posts switch, and the Comments that mention you switch. In place of the Classes you teach category, students have the Classes you're enrolled in category, which contains four switches: the Work and other posts from teachers switch, the Returned work and grades from your teachers switch, the Invitations to join classes as a student switch, and the Due-date reminders for your work switch.

Setting Up Your Classes

Classes are the central component of Google Classroom. In this section, we will first examine how you accept provisioned classes, how you create classes manually, and how students join classes using class codes.

Accepting Provisioned Classes

If your school has set you up with provisioned classes, these classes will appear as class cards on the Classes page. You will need to accept each class by clicking the Accept button on its card, checking the details of the class on the page that appears, and then clicking the next Accept button.

Creating a Class

If your school has not set up all your classes for you, you can create classes manually. To create a class, follow these steps:

1. Click the Create or join a class button on the toolbar to open the pop-up menu.

2.   Click the Create class button. The Create class dialog box will open (see Figure 8-3).

Note   If you are signed in to a Google account that is not a G Suite for Education account, the Using Classroom at a school with students? dialog box will open the first time you click the Create class button. If you are using Classroom privately (for example, for practice or evaluation), check the "I've read and understand the above notice, and I'm not using Classroom at a school with students" check box, and then click the Continue button. If you are at a school, click the Go Back button, sign into the G Suite for Education account, and then start creating the class.

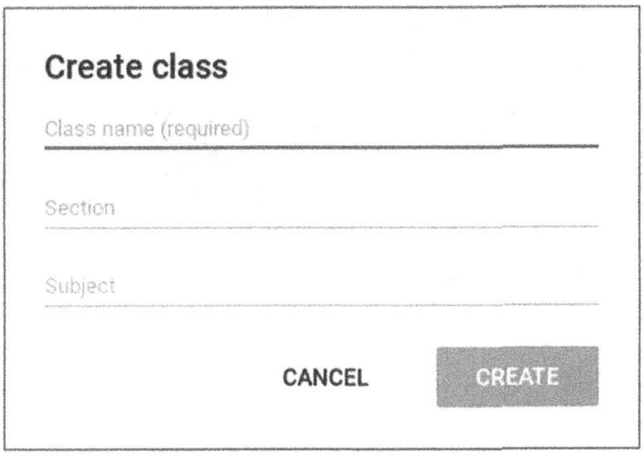

Create class

Class name (required)

Section

Subject

CANCEL   CREATE

Figure 8-3. *In the Create class dialog box, type the class name, the section, and the subject and then click the Create button*

3.   Type the class name in the "Class name (required)" field.

4.   Click the "Section" field and type the section, if necessary.

5.   Click the "Subject" field and start typing the subject.
     A pop-up menu will open showing predefined
     subjects. You can then select the appropriate subject
     if it appears in the list; if not, finish typing the subject.

6.   Click the Create button. Google Classroom creates
     the class, and the page for the class appears in the
     Chrome tab. This page has three tabs: the Stream
     tab, which is displayed first (see Figure 8-4); the
     Students tab; and the About tab.

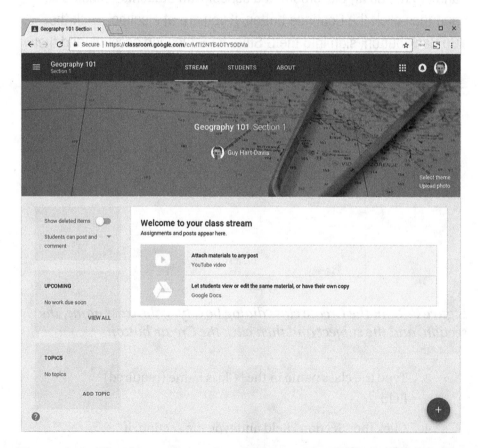

Figure 8-4. *The class appears in a Chrome tab. The Stream tab is
normally displayed at first.*

Joining a Class

If you are a student rather than a teacher, you can join a class by using the class code that identifies the class. Normally, your teacher will give you the class code.

Note   As a teacher, you can use this procedure for joining a class as a student—for example, if a colleague invites you to her class to try the student experience.

To join a class, follow these steps:

1. Click the Create or join a class button on the toolbar to open the pop-up menu.

2. Click the Join Class button. The Join class dialog box will open (see Figure 8-5).

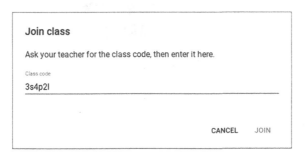

Figure 8-5. *In the Join class dialog box, enter the class code provided by your teacher*

3. Type the class code in the "Class code" field.

4. Click the Join button. The page for the class then appears, with the Stream tab displayed.

Note   For a student, the page for a class has three tabs: the Stream tab, the Classmates tab, and the About tab.

Navigating and Reorganizing Your Classes

From the page for a class, you can return to the Classes page by clicking the Classroom Main Menu button and then clicking the Classes item at the top of the menu (see Figure 8-6). The Classroom Main Menu also contains an entry for each class, which you can click to go straight to the page for that class.

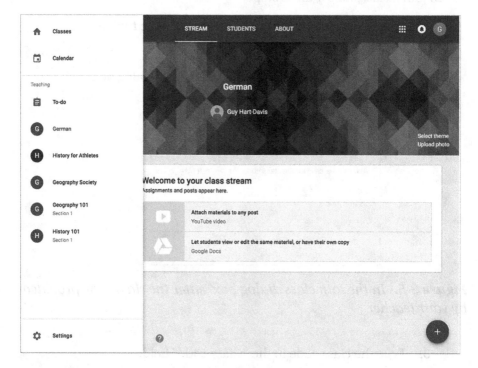

Figure 8-6.   *Click the Classes item at the top of the Classroom Main Menu to return to the Classes page. You can click a class name in the Teaching section of the Classroom Main Menu to go straight to that class' page.*

Each class appears as a class card on the Classes page (see Figure 8-7). You can rearrange the order of the cards in two ways:

- Drag a class card to where you want it to appear.

- Click the More Actions button (the three vertical dots) on the card you want to move and then click the Move item on the pop-up menu. In the Move class dialog box that opens (see Figure 8-8), click the To beginning button, the To end button, or the class after which you want to position the class.

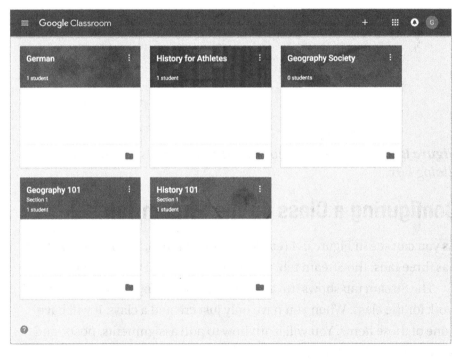

Figure 8-7. *Each class appears as a card on the Classes page. You can drag the class cards into your preferred order.*

Figure 8-8. *You can also move a class card by using the Move class dialog box*

Configuring a Class on the Stream Tab

As you can see in Figure 8-4 (earlier in this chapter), the page for a class has three tabs: the Stream tab, the Students tab, and the About tab.

The Stream tab shows the assignments, posts, topics, and upcoming work for the class. When you have only just created a class, it will have none of these items. You will learn how to add assignments, posts, and topics later in this chapter.

Setting the Theme for the Class

Across the top of the Stream tab is the theme picture or pattern, with the class name, the section name, and your name and photo superimposed on the middle of the picture or pattern. You can change the theme by applying a preset picture or pattern or by uploading a photo of your own (or of your school's).

To apply a preset picture or pattern, follow these steps:

1. Click the Select theme button in the lower-right corner of the theme picture or pattern to display the Gallery dialog box (see Figure 8-9).

Figure 8-9. *In the Gallery dialog box, click the Gallery tab or the Patterns tab, click the picture or pattern you want to use as the class theme, and then click the Select class theme button*

2. Click the Gallery tab if you want to use a picture for
   the theme, or click the Patterns tab if you want to
   apply a pattern.

3. Click the picture or the pattern. A blue circle
   containing a white check mark appears on it.

4. Click the Select class theme button. The picture or
   pattern appears across the top of the Stream tab.

To customize the theme with a photo you upload, follow these steps:

1. Click the Upload photo button in the lower-right
   corner of the theme picture or pattern to display the
   Gallery dialog box. In this case, the Gallery dialog
   box contains only the Upload tab.

2. Upload your photo in one of these ways:

   • Drag a photo from the desktop or a file-management
     window to the Drag a photo here placeholder.

   • Click the Select a photo from your computer button
     to display the Select a file to open dialog box.
     Navigate to the photo, click the photo, and then
     click the Open button.

3. Click the Select class theme button. The photo
   appears across the top of the Stream tab.

Showing and Hiding Deleted Items

You can control whether deleted items appear in the class stream for you
by setting the Show deleted items switch to On or Off.

Note   The Show deleted items switch works only on the teacher's view of the class. Google Classroom does not display deleted items for students, even when this switch is set to On.

Normally, you will likely find it best to hide deleted items to keep the class stream looking as clean and uncluttered as possible. However, sometimes you may find it helpful to display deleted items to get a view of what has been removed.

Viewing Upcoming Items

The Upcoming box shows the list of upcoming assignments and questions for which you have set due dates. A teacher or student can click one of the links in the Upcoming box to display the assignment or question.

If you have just created the class, or if there are no date-bound items set for the near future, you will see the message "No work due soon" in the Upcoming box.

You can click the View All button to display the full list of assignments for the class.

Viewing and Managing the Topics List

The Topics box shows the topics the class contains so far. If you have just created the class, the message "No topics" will appear in the Topics box instead.

You can add a topic by clicking the Add topic button, typing the name in the Add topic dialog box that opens (see Figure 8-10), and then clicking the Add button. The topic will then appear in the Topics box.

Figure 8-10. *To add a topic manually, type its name in the Add topic dialog box and then click the Add button*

Once you have added a topic, you can rename the topic or delete it by moving the pointer over it, clicking the More Actions button (the three vertical dots) that appears, and then clicking the Rename item or the Delete item on the menu.

Organizing Your Class Stream

Google Classroom automatically arranges the posts in your class stream in descending date order, so the newest posts appear at the top. Descending date order works pretty well as a default, but you will often need to reorganize items to make sure students see the most important items rather than just the newest items.

You can organize the class stream in the following ways:

- Move a post to the top of the stream

- Delete unneeded posts

- Filter the stream by topics

Moving a Post to the Top of the Stream

Your main tool for reorganizing the stream is the Move to Top command, which lets you move an item to the topmost position in the stream. To give this command, click the More Actions button (the three vertical dots) for the post and then click the Move to Top item on the pop-up menu.

Caution   Use the Move to Top command only when necessary because—unless students have turned off notifications—Google Classroom automatically sends each student a notification when you move a post to the top of the stream. Moving multiple items to the top, and shuffling them into your desired order, will launch a salvo of notifications.

Deleting Unneeded Posts

Another means of reorganizing the stream is to delete any posts that are no longer needed. Before deleting any item, make sure that it contains no associated items—such as comments or files—that it would be a better idea to keep.

Filtering the Stream by Topic

By adding topics to your posts, you enable students—and yourself—to filter the stream to make it easier to navigate. You can filter by topic in either of these ways:

- *Topics box*: In the Topics box on the left, click the topic you want to view.

- *Topic button*: Click the topic button on a post.

Whichever of these actions you take, Google Classroom will then display only the posts that are tagged with that topic (see Figure 8-11). You can then click another topic in the Topics box if necessary to switch to that topic.

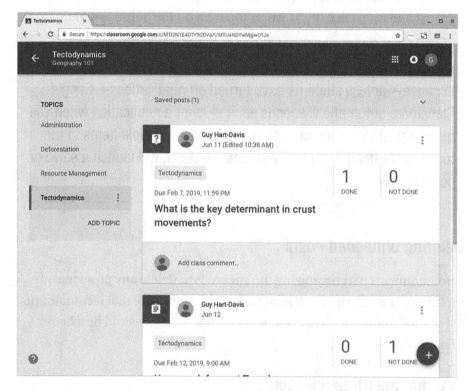

Figure 8-11. *Filtering by topic enables you to view only the posts tagged with the topic. You can switch to a different topic by clicking it in the Topics box, or click the Back button in the upper-left corner to return to the full stream.*

Note   You can rename a topic by clicking the More Actions button (the three vertical dots) to its right in the Topics box and then clicking the Rename item on the pop-up menu. In the Rename topic dialog box that opens, type the new name and then click the Rename button. You can also delete a topic by clicking the More Actions button, clicking the Delete item on the pop-up menu, and then clicking the Delete button in the Delete topic? dialog box.

When you are ready to return to the Stream tab, click the Back button (the left-arrow button) in the upper-left corner of the screen.

Working on the Students Tab for a Class

If students have already been assigned to your class by a management system, they will appear on the Students tab. Otherwise, the Students tab will be blank at first (see Figure 8-12).

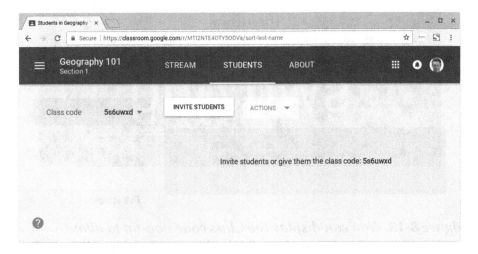

Figure 8-12.   *The Students tab shows the students assigned to the class. If you have just created the class, it will have no students, as shown here.*

Taking Actions from the Class Code Pop-Up Menu

The Class code pop-up menu appears in the upper-left corner of the
Students tab. From this pop-up menu, you can take the following actions:

- *Display*: Click the Display item to display a pop-up
  showing the class code at a large size (see Figure 8-13).
  This is helpful for showing your students the class code
  so they can join it; you can also click the Full screen
  button to switch the pop-up to full screen for even
  easier viewing. Click the Close (X) button in the upper-
  right corner of the pop-up or the upper-left corner of
  the full-screen display to hide the class code again.

Full screen

Figure 8-13. *You can display the Class code pop-up to allow
students to see the class code and join the class quickly. Click the Full
screen button to switch the class code to full screen to make it even
easier to see.*

- *Copy*: Click the Copy item to copy the class code to the Clipboard so that you can paste it elsewhere.

- *Reset*: Click the Reset item to reset the class code—in effect, to generate a new code for the class. The usual reason to reset the class code is if students are having difficulty joining a class.

- *Disable*: Click the Disable item to disable the class code, rendering it temporarily unusable. You might disable the class code once all the students have joined the class, and you want to make sure nobody else joins it. The word *Disabled* will appear in place of the *Class code* readout. When you are ready to re-enable the class code, click the Class code pop-up button and then click the Enable item on the pop-up menu.

Adding Students to the Class Using the Class Code

For the teacher, the easiest way of adding students to the class is by using the class code. If the students are physically present (for example, in the same room as you), you can open the Class code pop-up menu and click the Display item to display the class code at a large enough size for all to see; click the Full screen button if necessary. If the students are nearby, you can copy the class code and share it with them via a message.

Note   If students are unable to join the class using the class code, try resetting the class code. To do so, click the Class code pop-up menu and then click the Reset item.

Inviting Students to the Class

The other way to add students to the class is by inviting them via email. The invitation mechanism is based on Google Contacts, so each student you invite must already be one of your Google contacts. If your school has set up accounts centrally, your students should already be lined up for you to contact. If not, you will need to add the students manually in Google Contacts.

Once the students are set up as records in Google Contacts, you can invite them to classes by following these steps from the Students tab:

1. Click the Invite Students button to display the Invite students dialog box (shown in Figure 8-14 with one student added and a search underway).

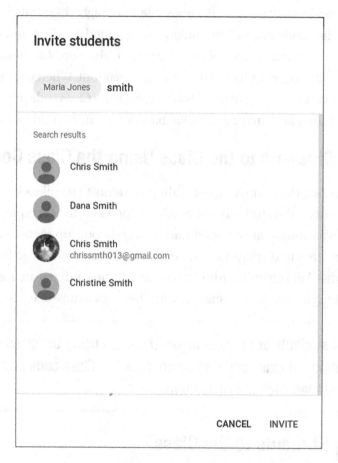

Figure 8-14. *In the Invite students dialog box, type the name or email address of each student you want to invite to the class. After assembling the list, click the Invite button.*

2. In the box at the top, start typing the name or email
    address of the first student you want to add. The
    Search results section of the dialog box will show
    matching contact records.

3. Click the appropriate record. It will then appear as a
    button at the top of the dialog box.

4. Repeat steps 2 and 3 to add the other students to
    the list.

Note   If you want other teachers to join your class as students, you
can invite them to the class by using the Invite students dialog box.
For example, you might want some colleagues to see how the class
looks from the student's perspective. However, if you want to invite a
teacher to join the class as a teacher, use the Invite Teachers button
on the About tab instead.

---

5. Click the Invite button. The Invite students dialog
    box closes. Classroom sends the invitations via
    email, and the names of the invited students appear
    in a list on the Students tab (see Figure 8-15).

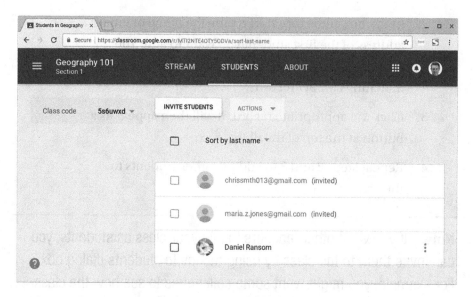

Figure 8-15. *The students you invited appear on the Students tab. Until a student accepts the invitation to join the class, the listing shows a generic icon instead of the student's picture, the email address rather than the name, and the status (invited).*

At first, each student's entry in the list appears in gray, showing the email address rather than the name, displaying a generic icon instead of the student's picture, and with the status (invited) to its right, as you can see on the first two items on the figure. When the student accepts the invitation, the student's picture replaces the generic icon, the student's name appears in black, the status (invited) disappears, and the More Actions button appears, as you can see on the third item in the figure.

By default, Classroom sorts the students' names by their last names. You can switch to sorting the students by their first names by clicking the pop-up menu above the list and then clicking the Sort by last name item.

To the left of each student's entry is a check box that you can check when you need to take an action on the student, such as emailing the student or removing the student from the class. You can check the master check box above the list to check all the individual check boxes at once—for example, when you want to take an action on all the students in the class.

How the Student Joins the Class

For the student, joining the class via your invitation is straightforward. The invitation appears as an email message in Gmail. The student clicks the Join button in the message to display the Join class? dialog box (see Figure 8-16), which displays the Google account the student is currently using. The student can then click the Join button to join the class using this account or click the Switch Account button to switch to a different account and join the class under that account.

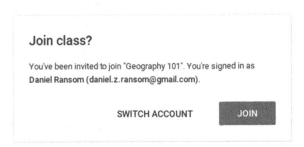

Figure 8-16. *The Join class? dialog box makes sure the student knows which Google account he is using. The student can click the Switch Account button to switch to a different account before joining the class.*

Taking Actions on the Students in a Class

After adding students to a class, you can take the following actions on them. To take an action, check the box for each student you want to affect, click the Actions pop-up menu, and then click the appropriate item:

- *Email*: Click this item to start an email message to the student or students in Gmail.

Note   You can also email an individual student by clicking the More Actions button (the three vertical dots) on the student's row and then clicking the Email student item on the menu.

- *Remove*: Click this item to remove the student or students from the class.

Note   Removing a student from a class does not remove the student's work (which remains in the class folders) or any comments the student has posted (which remain in the class stream).

- *Mute*: Click this item to mute the student or students. The Mute action is available only once the student has joined the class.

Working on the About Tab for a Class

From the About tab for a class (see Figure 8-17), you can add information about the class, manage resources and materials for the class, and invite teachers to the class.

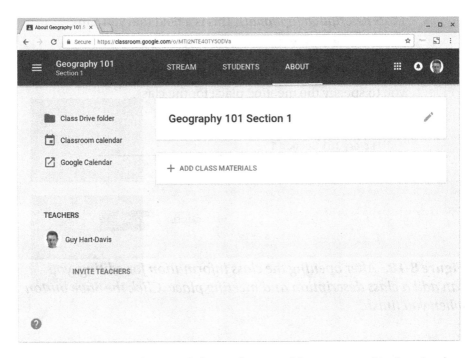

Figure 8-17. *The About tab for a class enables you to edit the class's information, manage resources and materials, and invite teachers*

Adding Information About the Class

The class name and section name appear at the top of the About tab, with an Edit button (a pencil icon) to their right. Click the Edit button to open the class information for editing (see Figure 8-18). You can then add or edit the following fields:

- *Class name and section*: The class name and section comprise the formal name under which the class appears in Classroom. Unless you entered the class name and section wrongly in the first place, you likely do not need to change them.

513

- *Class description (optional)*: This is a field that you can use to make clear what the class covers.

- *Where does the class meet? (optional)*: This field enables you to specify the meeting place for the class.

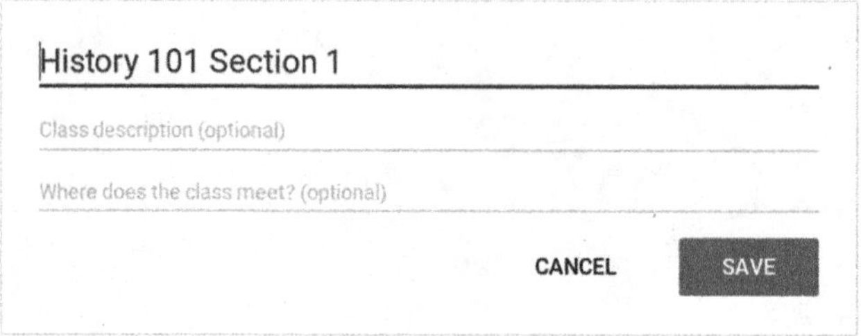

Figure 8-18. *After opening the class information for editing, you can add a class description and meeting place. Click the Save button when you finish.*

After making your changes to the class information, click the Save button to save them.

Adding Materials to a Class

From the About tab, you can quickly add four types of materials to the class:

- *Attachment*: You can attach a file by uploading it from your computer or by selecting it on Google Drive.

- *Google Drive*: You can insert a file from Google Drive.

- *YouTube videos*: You can add a link to one or more videos on YouTube.

- *Links*: You can add a hyperlink to a web page or a local page.

To add materials to the class, follow these steps:

1. Click the Add Class Materials button. The controls shown in Figure 8-19 will appear.

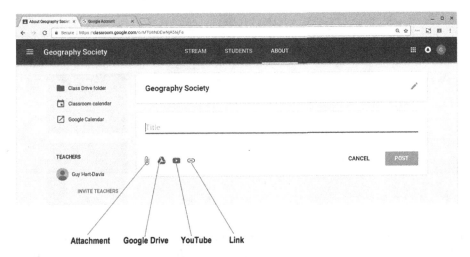

Figure 8-19. *Type the title for the item you are adding and then click the appropriate button to open a dialog box for specifying the item*

2. Type the title for the item in the Title box. Google Classroom then enables the Post button.

3. Click the appropriate button for the type of item you want to add:

   • *Attachment*: Click this button to display the Insert files using Google Drive dialog box. As you can see in Figure 8-20, this dialog box has four tabs: the Upload tab, which enables you to upload files from your computer; the Recent tab, which shows recently used files on Google Drive; the My Drive tab, which shows all your files on Google Drive; and the Starred tab, which shows files you have marked with a star on Google Drive. Identify the files and then click the Upload button or the Add button.

Figure 8-20. *The Upload tab of the Insert files from Google Drive dialog box enables you to upload files by either dragging them to the dialog box or clicking the Select files from your computer button and selecting them*

Tip   The Insert files using Google Drive dialog box enables you to search on the Recent tab, the My Drive tab, and the Starred tab. However, if you store many files on Google Drive, you may find it easiest to star those files you know you will need to work with frequently.

- *Google Drive*: Click this button to display the Insert files using Google Drive dialog box—the same dialog box as opens when you click the Attachment button. On the Recent tab (shown in Figure 8-21), the My Drive tab (shown in Figure 8-22), and the Starred tab, you can restrict the display to particular file types—such as to the Documents file type or the Spreadsheets file type—by clicking the File type pop-up button and then

clicking the appropriate item on the pop-up menu.
You can also switch between Grid view and List view
by clicking the Grid view button or the List view button
(these two buttons replace one another). Select the file
you want to add and then click the Add button.

Note   On the My Drive tab or the Starred tab of the Insert files using
Google Drive dialog box, you can change the sort method by clicking
the Sort options button and then clicking the Last modified item, the
Last modified by me item, the Last opened by me item, or the Name
item on the pop-up menu.

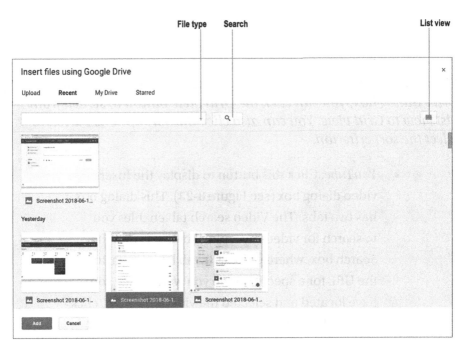

Figure 8-21. *On the Recent tab of the Insert files using Google Drive
dialog box, you can use the File type pop-up menu to display only
specific file types, such as PDF files. You can click the List view button
to switch from Grid view to List view.*

517

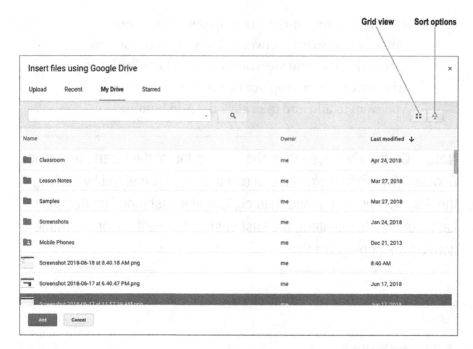

Figure 8-22. *On the My Drive tab of the Insert files using Google Drive dialog box, you can click the Grid view button to switch from List view to Grid view. You can also click the Sort options button to select the sort criterion.*

- *YouTube*: Click this button to display the Insert video dialog box (see Figure 8-23). This dialog box has two tabs: The Video search tab enables you to search for videos by typing keywords into the Search box, whereas the URL tab lets you paste in the URL for a specific video you want. Once you have located and selected the video you want, click the Add button to add it.

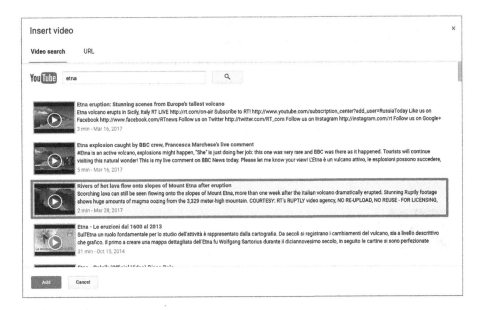

Figure 8-23. *On the Video search tab of the Insert video dialog box, type your search term and press the Enter key. You can then click a search result to select that video.*

- *Link*: Click this button to display the Add link dialog box (see Figure 8-24). Type or paste the link in the "Link" field and then click the Add Link button.

Figure 8-24. *To add a link, type or paste the URL in the "Link" field of the Add link dialog box and then click the Add Link button*

4. After you have selected the file or link, the details will appear on the About tab in a box that has the title you assigned. You can then add other materials as needed; you can also click the Delete (X) button on the right of an item to remove that item. Figure 8-25 shows two items added.

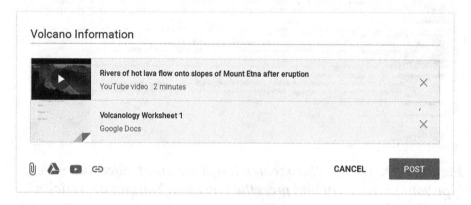

Figure 8-25. *After adding all the materials, click the Post button to post them*

5. When you have added all the materials, click the Post button. Google Classroom will post the materials to the class, where students (and teachers) can access them.

SHARING A WEB PAGE WITH YOUR CLASS

As you have seen in the main text, you can give students access to a web page by adding a link to that page to the materials on the About tab.

A handy and quick way to share a web page with your class is to use the Share to Classroom extension in Chrome. Once you have installed this extension from the Web Store, you can navigate to the appropriate web page, click the Share to Classroom button toward the right end of the Chrome toolbar, and then select the class with which you want to share the web page.

Editing and Deleting Materials for a Class

After adding materials for a class, you can edit them or delete them as needed.

To edit materials, follow these steps:

1. Click the More Actions button for the box of materials you want to change and then click the Edit item on the pop-up menu. The box of materials will open in a dialog box (see Figure 8-26).

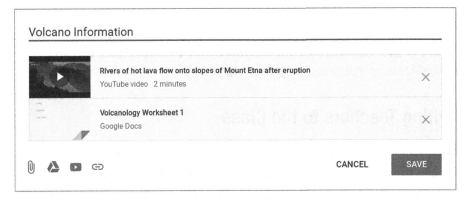

Figure 8-26. *You can edit the box of materials by changing its title, adding items, or removing items*

2. Edit the title if necessary.

3. To delete an individual item, click its Delete (X) button.

4. To add an item, click the appropriate button in the lower-left corner of the dialog box and then follow the procedure explained earlier in this chapter.

5. When you have finished making changes to the box of materials, click the Save button.

To delete a whole box of materials, click the More Actions button for the box and then click the Delete item on the pop-up menu. In the Delete? dialog box that opens (see Figure 8-27), click the Delete button.

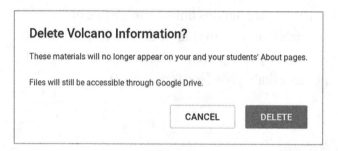

Delete Volcano Information?

These materials will no longer appear on your and your students' About pages.

Files will still be accessible through Google Drive.

CANCEL   DELETE

Figure 8-27. *Click the Delete button in the Delete dialog box to delete a whole box of materials from the class*

Inviting Teachers to the Class

When you want one or more other teachers to work with you on a class, you can invite the teacher or teachers to join the class. Inviting a teacher works in a similar way to inviting a student: The teacher must be one of your Google contacts, and Classroom sends the invitation to the teacher via Gmail.

Note   Each teacher you add to the class has the same privileges as you for that class.

To invite one or more teachers to the class, follow these steps:

1. Click the Invite Teachers button in the Teachers box on the About tab for the class. The Invite Teachers dialog box will open.

2. At the top of the dialog box, start typing the name or email address of the first teacher you want to invite. The Search results list will show matches.

3. Click the appropriate match. A button for the teacher will appear at the top of the dialog box.

4. Repeat steps 2 and 3 to add more teachers as needed.

5. Click the Invite button. The Invite Teachers dialog box will close, and Classroom will send the invitations via Gmail.

Classroom adds the teacher or teachers to the Teachers list on the About tab. At first, each teacher's entry appears as a generic icon and the email address, with a More Actions button to the right of it. When the teacher accepts the invitation by clicking the Join button in the "Invitation to co-teach" message she receives, her picture and name will replace the generic icon and the email address in the Teachers list.

Note   To remove a teacher from the class, click the More Actions button to the right of the teacher's entry in the Teachers box and then click the Remove from class item on the menu.

Viewing Class Calendars

Google Classroom automatically maintains a calendar for each class. The class calendar data is shared between Google Classroom and Google Calendar:

- *Google Classroom calendar*: Assignments and questions for which you have set due dates appear in the calendar in Google Classroom.

- *Google Calendar*: Assignments and questions for which you have set due dates also appear in the class calendar in Google Calendar. You can also add other class-related events to the class calendar in Google Calendar. For example, you might add the dates of exams or special activities.

Viewing the Google Classroom Calendar

To view the Google Classroom calendar for a class, click the Menu button and then click the Calendar item. The Calendar page appears (see Figure 8-28), showing the assignments and questions for which you have set due dates.

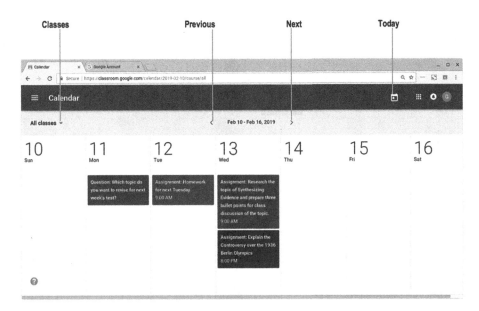

Figure 8-28. *The Calendar page in Google Classroom provides an easy-to-read reference to the questions and assignments for which you have set due dates.*

To control which classes appear, click the Classes pop-up menu under the Calendar heading and then click either the All classes item or the item for the class you want to view.

To choose the week shown, click the Previous button or the Next button as needed. You can click the Today button to jump to the week containing the current date.

Adding Class Events via Google Calendar

As you saw in the previous section, Google Classroom automatically adds assignments and questions that have due dates to the Calendar in Classroom. These date-bound assignments and questions also appear in your My calendars list in Google Calendar, which picks up calendars for your classes from Google Classroom. Figure 8-29 shows Google Calendar, with several class calendars appearing in the My calendars list on the left.

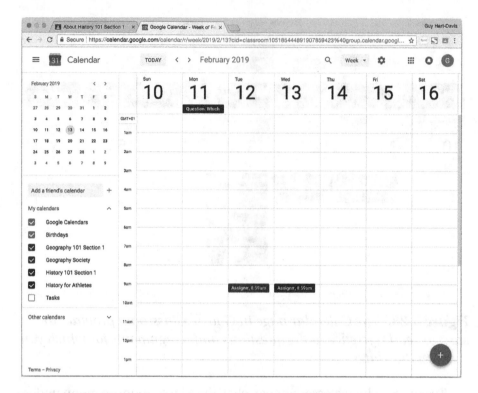

Figure 8-29. *Your class calendars appear in the My calendars list in Google Calendar, which also shows date-bound assignments and questions. You can create a new event and assign it to a class calendar to share the event with the class members.*

To share other types of events with your students, create a new event in the appropriate class calendar in Google Calendar. As usual, click the Create event button (the red circle containing a white + sign) in the lower-right corner of the Google Calendar window, specify the details on the page that appears (see Figure 8-30), and then click the Save button.

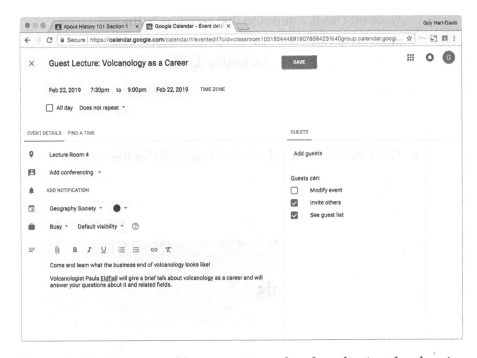

Figure 8-30. *You can add an event to a class by selecting the class in the Calendars list in Google Calendar*

Communicating with the Students in Your Classes

Google Classroom makes it easy to communicate with the students in your classes. You can communicate with the students via three kinds of posts:

- *Announcement*: An announcement is information that you post for the students. For example, you might announce an upcoming class trip.

- *Assignment*: This is a task that you allocate to the students. For example, you might assign reading or homework.

- *Question*: This is a question that you pose to the students—for example, to check their understanding of a particular point or to get feedback on a lesson.

Each type of post can contain items such as file attachments, links to files on Google Drive, links to videos on YouTube, or links to internal or external URLs.

Google Classroom uses largely similar interfaces for these three types of posts. To avoid unnecessary repetition, the first of the following subsections will show you how to use the post controls in detail. The following subsections will explain how to create the different kinds of posts, assuming you already know how to use the post controls.

Using the Post Controls

This section will show you how to use the post controls that Google Classroom provides for working with announcements, assignments, and questions and will show examples of each.

Starting a Post

To start creating a post, follow these steps:

1. On the Classes page, click the card for the class. The Stream tab for the class appears.

2. Click the Add (+) button in the lower-right corner to display the pop-up menu (see Figure 8-31).

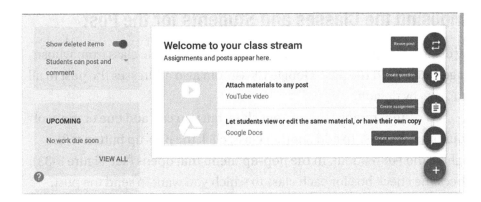

Figure 8-31. *To start creating a post, click the Add (+) button in the lower-right corner of the Stream tab and then click the appropriate button on the pop-up menu*

3. Click the appropriate item on the pop-up menu to display the corresponding dialog box. For example, click the Create assignment item to display the Assignment dialog box (see Figure 8-32).

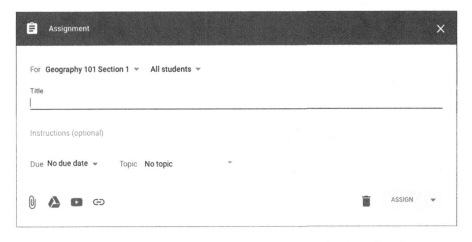

Figure 8-32. *Google Classroom displays the dialog box for the type of post you want to create—for example, the Assignment dialog box shown here*

Choosing the Classes and Students for the Post

By default, Google Classroom addresses the post to the class from whose page you started the post. Google Classroom also addresses the post to all students by default.

You cannot remove the current class, but you can add one or more of your other classes. To add another class, click the pop-up button to the right of the *For* readout. In the pop-up menu that opens (see Figure 8-33), check the check box for each class to which you want to send the post.

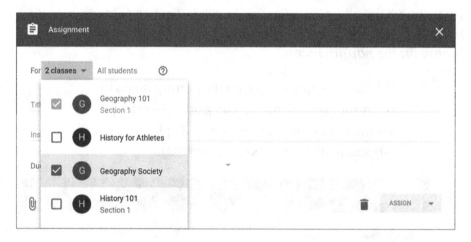

Figure 8-33. *Click the pop-up button to the right of the For readout and then check the box for each class that is to receive the post*

As long as you are posting to only one class, you can choose which students within the class receive the post. To do so, click the right pop-up button on the For line. In the pop-up menu that opens, check or uncheck the "All students" check box as needed. You can then check or uncheck the check box for each individual student. If you need to post to only a few students, unchecking the "All students" check box and then checking the check box for each of those few students is usually quickest. If you need to post to most students, check the "All students" check box and then uncheck the check box for each student you want to omit.

Note   If you are posting to multiple classes, you can only post to all the students in those classes; you cannot post to individual students.

Entering the Title and Instructions for the Post

Each post has what is effectively its title, although the Google Classroom interface gives this field a different name depending on the type of item you are creating. For an assignment, the field is indeed called "Title"; for an announcement, the field is called "Share with your class"; and for a question, the field is called "Question." The "Title" field or equivalent field appears in the list on the Stream tab and identifies the post.

Click the "Title" field or equivalent field for the post and type the title you want to appear. If the post includes an "Instructions" field, enter any instructions to help the students grasp what you want.

Note   The "Instructions" field is optional, but you will usually find that students benefit from clear instructions—even if the "Title" field seems to explain everything.

Entering the Due Date and Topic for the Post

Next, enter the due date for an assignment or a question, plus the topic for any post.

To enter the due date, click the pop-up button to the right of the *Due* readout. In the Due date & time pop-up panel that appears (see Figure 8-34), click the "Date" field and then click the due date on the calendar panel that appears; alternatively, you can click the Delete (X) button to delete the date that currently appears. To add a due time to the due date, click the "Time (optional)" field and then type the due time; here, too, you can click the Delete (X) button to delete the time that currently appears.

531

Figure 8-34. In the Due date & time pop-up panel, click the "Date" field and then click the due date on the calendar panel that appears. To set a due time, click the "Time (optional)" field and then type the due time.

To add the topic to any post, click the pop-up button to the right of the Topic readout, which typically is set to the No topic item by default. The pop-up menu lists each topic you have already added to the class, the default No topic item (which you can apply to remove the current topic), and the Create topic item, which you can click to enter a new topic.

Note   If you use the Create topic feature to create a new topic, Google Classroom will add the topic to the Topics list for the class.

Adding Materials to the Post

Next, you can add any necessary items to the post. These are the same types of items that you can add to the class from the About tab:

- *Attachment*: You can attach a file by uploading it from your computer or by selecting it on Google Drive.

- *Google Drive*: You can insert a file from Google Drive.

- *YouTube videos*: You can add a link to one or more videos on YouTube.

- *Links*: You can add a hyperlink to a web page or a local page.

As you would expect, the controls for adding the items to a post work in much the same way as the controls for adding items to a class. For example, to add a YouTube video link to an assignment, you would click the YouTube button in the lower-left corner of the Assignment dialog box (see Figure 8-35) and then follow the usual procedure for selecting the file.

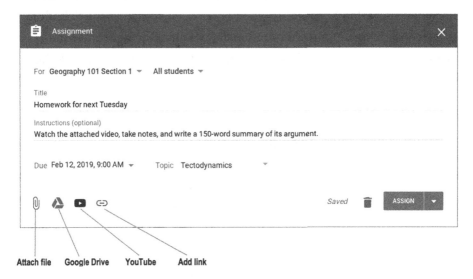

Figure 8-35. *To add materials to a post, click the Attach file button, the Google Drive button, the YouTube button, or the Add link button in the lower-left corner of the Assignment dialog box*

Posting the Post, Scheduling the Post, or Saving It as a Draft

When you have finished entering the details for a post, double-check that everything is correct and then post it by clicking the main command button in the dialog box—for example, click the Ask button for a question or the Assign button for an assignment.

Note   If you find you need to delete the post, click the Delete button (the trash icon) to the left of the main command button in the post's dialog box.

Instead of posting the post, you can schedule it to be posted later or save the post as a draft so you can finish it at another time.

To schedule the post, click the pop-up button to the right of the main command button and then click the Schedule item on the pop-up menu. The Schedule dialog box for this type of post opens, such as the Schedule assignment dialog box shown in Figure 8-36. Select the date and time at which you want Google Classroom to post the post and then click the Schedule button.

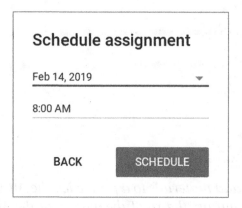

Figure 8-36. In the Schedule dialog box for the post, such as the Schedule assignment dialog box, choose the date and time for posting the post and then click the Schedule button

To save the post as a draft, click the pop-up button to the right of the main command button and then click the Save draft item on the pop-up menu. Google Classroom saves the post as a draft and closes the dialog box.

When you are ready to resume work on a draft announcement, click the Saved posts button below the theme picture on the Stream tab. The Saved posts area expands, showing the Drafts box. Click the draft you want to reopen.

Adding a Class Comment to a Post

After posting a post, you can add a class comment to it. A class comment is a text comment that is shared with the teacher (or teachers) and the class members. You can control who can post and comment by clicking the pop-up button below the "Show deleted items" switch on the Stream tab and then clicking the appropriate item on the pop-up menu:

- *Students can post and comment*: This is the default setting. If necessary, you can prevent individual students from posting and commenting by muting them.

- *Students can only comment*: Choose this setting if you need to prevent all students from posting. You can prevent individual students from commenting by muting them.

- *Only teachers can post or comment*: Choose this setting if you find that allowing students to post or comment generates too much traffic in the class. Choosing this setting has the same effect as muting all students.

To add a class comment, click the Add class comment button, type the comment in the text field that appears, and then click the Post button.

Replying to Student Comments

If you let students post class comments, you will likely need to reply to some of them. To reply to a class comment, follow these steps:

1. Move the pointer over the class comment to which you want to reply. The Reply button (a left-curling arrow icon) and the More Actions button (the three vertical dots) appear.

2. Click the Reply button. The reply field appears (see Figure 8-37). Google Classroom automatically includes the commenter's email address.

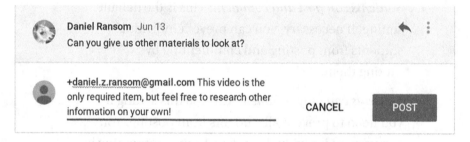

Figure 8-37. *To reply to a class comment, move the pointer over the comment, click the Reply button, type the reply, and then click the Post button*

3. Type your reply to the comment.

4. Click the Post button. Your reply will appear underneath the related class comment.

MENTIONING A TEACHER OR STUDENT IN A POST

Google Classroom includes a feature for mentioning someone by name in a post or comment. To do so, type + or @ in the comment field and then start typing the person's name. In the list of email addresses that appears, click the appropriate address and then finish the post or comment as usual.

When you mention someone in a post or comment, that person will receive an email notification of the mention unless they have turned off notifications.

Dealing with Private Comments

As well as posting class comments (if you permit students to do so), a student can also send you a private comment after you assign an assignment or a question. The student sends a private comment by opening the assignment or question, clicking the Add private comment link, typing the comment in the text field that appears, and then clicking the Post button.

A private comment appears in the Private comments box on the Student Answers tab for a question and the Student Work tab for an assignment. You can respond to the private comment by clicking the Add private comment link below it, typing your response, and then clicking the Post button.

Deleting Students' Posts and Comments

As the teacher, you can delete the posts and comments that students make. To delete a post or comment, move the pointer over it, click the More Actions button (the three vertical dots) that appears, and then click the Delete item on the menu. In the Delete comment? dialog box or the Delete post? dialog box that appears, click the Delete button.

Muting a Student

If a student posts or comments to a class too frequently, you may want to mute that student rather that prevent all the students in the class from posting or commenting. Muting a student has three main effects:

- The student cannot comment or post.

- The student cannot reply to classmates' work.

- Other students cannot see the work that the muted student submits.

To mute a student, follow these steps:

1. Move the pointer over a post or comment from the student. The More Actions button (the three vertical dots) appears on the right of the post or comment.

2. Click the More Actions button to open the menu and then click the Mute item on the pop-up menu. The Mute item includes the student's name—for example, Mute Bill Smith. The Mute? dialog box then opens, also showing the student's name (see Figure 8-38).

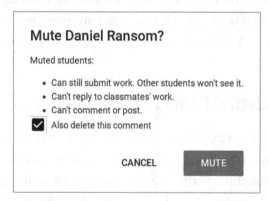

Figure 8-38. *In the Mute? dialog box, check the "Also delete this comment" check box or the "Also delete this post" check box if necessary, and then click the Mute button*

3. Check the "Also delete this comment" check box or the "Also delete this post" check box if you want to get rid of the comment or post.

4. Click the Mute button.

When you are ready to unmute the student, follow these steps:

1. Move the pointer over a post or comment from the student. The More Actions button (the three vertical dots) appears on the right of the post or comment.

2. Click the More Actions button to open the menu and then click the Unmute item on the pop-up menu. The Unmute? dialog box then opens (see Figure 8-39), showing the student's name in its title.

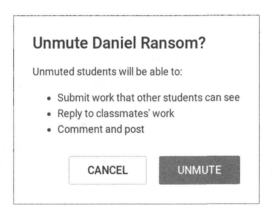

Figure 8-39. *Click the Unmute button in the Unmute? dialog box to enable the student to participate fully in the class again*

3. Click the Unmute button.

Editing a Post

To edit a post, click the More Actions button (the three vertical dots) on the post's card on the Stream tab and then click the Edit item on the pop-up menu. The post opens for editing in the same dialog box you used to create it—for example, the Announcement dialog box for an announcement. Make the changes needed and then click the Save button to save them.

Reusing a Post

Google Classroom makes it easy to reuse one of your earlier posts. Often, reusing a post is the quickest way of creating a new post, as you can pick up most of the existing settings—such as the classes, the students, and the topic—rather than having to set them up again from scratch. You can also change any of these items when reusing a post.

To reuse a post, follow these steps:

1. On the Stream tab, click the Add (+) button to display the pop-up menu.

2. Click the Reuse post item. The Select class dialog box opens (see Figure 8-40).

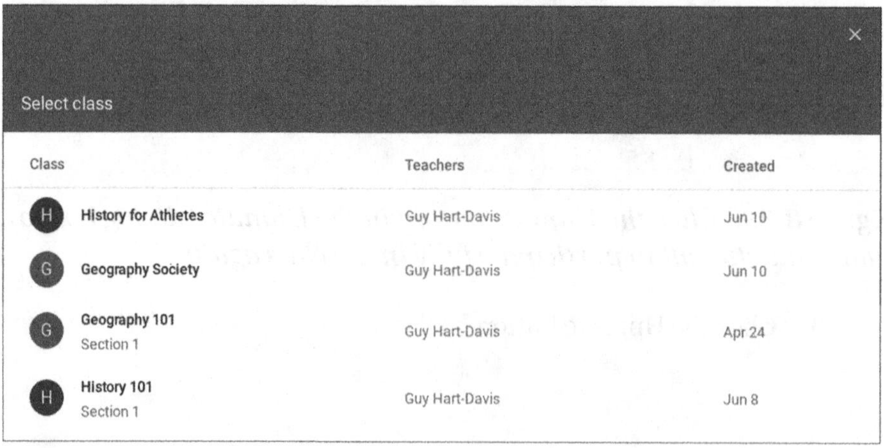

Select class		
Class	**Teachers**	**Created**
H History for Athletes	Guy Hart-Davis	Jun 10
G Geography Society	Guy Hart-Davis	Jun 10
G Geography 101 Section 1	Guy Hart-Davis	Apr 24
H History 101 Section 1	Guy Hart-Davis	Jun 8

Figure 8-40. *In the Select class dialog box, click the class that contains the post you want to reuse.*

3.   Click the class that contains the post you want to reuse. The Select post dialog box opens, showing the posts in that class (see Figure 8-41).

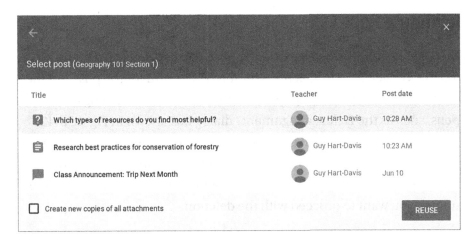

Figure 8-41. *In the Select post dialog box, click the post you want to reuse, check the "Create new copies of all attachments" check box if appropriate, and then click the Reuse button.*

4.   Click the post you want to reuse.

5.   Check the "Create new copies of all attachments" check box if you want to include the attachments.

6.   Click the Reuse button. The item then appears in the corresponding dialog box. For example, a question appears in the Question dialog box.

7.   Edit the item as needed, using the techniques explained earlier in this chapter.

8.   Set a new due date for the item if appropriate.

9. Click the main command button, such as the Ask
    button for a question. Google Classroom posts the
    item.

Deleting a Post

When you no longer need a particular post, you can delete it. On the
Stream tab, click the More Actions button on the card for the post and then
click the Delete item on the pop-up menu. In the Delete? dialog box that
opens, such as the Delete assignment? dialog box shown in Figure 8-42,
read the information to make sure you are aware of any associated items
that will be deleted; for example, deleting an assignment also deletes
any grades or comments added to the assignment. Then, click the Delete
button if you want to proceed with the deletion.

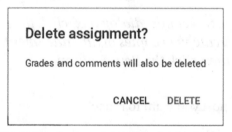

Delete assignment?

Grades and comments will also be deleted

CANCEL   DELETE

Figure 8-42. *When deleting a post, make sure you know which
associated items will be deleted, such as any grades and comments
added to an assignment.*

Making Announcements

In Google Classroom, an *announcement* is a post that does not include
an assignment. An announcement can contain materials—such as files,
YouTube videos, and links—if necessary.

Announcements are easy to communicate with students because they are hard to miss. First, announcements appear prominently at the top of the class stream. Second, each student automatically receives an email notification for each announcement by default; students can disable this notification if they want.

Note   This section assumes that you have read the previous section, "Using the Post Controls," and that you therefore know how to use the standard controls for working with posts.

To create an announcement, follow these steps:

1. On the Stream tab for the class, click the Add (+) button in the lower-right corner to display the pop-up menu.

2. Click the Create announcement item. The Announcement dialog box opens (see Figure 8-43).

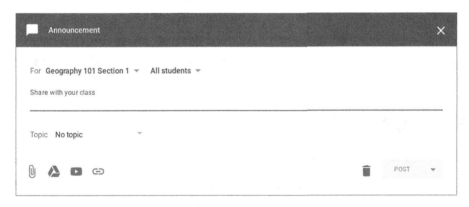

Figure 8-43. *In the Announcement dialog box, enter the announcement's title in the "Share with your class" field, choose the topic in the Topic pop-up menu, add any materials needed, and then click the Post button.*

3. By default, the For pop-up menu is set to the current class. Add other classes if necessary.

4. By default, the second pop-up menu is set to All students. Change the recipients if necessary.

5. In the "Share with your class" field, type the title for the announcement.

6. Click the Topic pop-up menu and choose the topic. You can create a new topic if necessary.

7. Add any materials needed to the announcement.

8. Click the Post button to post the announcement.

Setting, Grading, and Returning Assignments

Google Classroom gives you tools that make it easy to set, collect, and manage assignments for your students. You can create an assignment either with or without a due date, provide the materials the students need to complete the assignment, and monitor how many students have submitted the assignment. Once a student has submitted work, you can grade it and return it.

Creating an Assignment

Follow these steps to create an assignment:

1. On the Stream tab for the class, click the Add (+) button in the lower-right corner to display the pop-up menu.

2. Click the Create assignment item. The Assignment dialog box opens (see Figure 8-44).

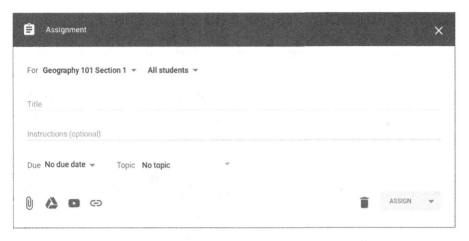

Figure 8-44. *In the Assignment dialog box, you can optionally include instructions as well as the assignment title and any materials the students need to complete it*

3. By default, the For pop-up menu is set to the current class. Add other classes if necessary.

4. By default, the second pop-up menu is set to All students. Change the recipients if necessary.

5. In the Title box, type the title for the assignment.

6. In the Instructions (optional) box, type any instructions to help the students understand exactly what you want them to do.

7. To give a due date for the assignment, click the Due pop-up menu and then specify the date—and, if necessary, the time—in the Due date & time pop-up panel.

8. Click the Topic pop-up menu and choose the topic. You can create a new topic if necessary.

9. Add any materials needed to the assignment.

10. Click the Assign button to post the assignment.

Tracking Students' Progress on an Assignment

After you post the assignment, it appears on the Stream tab (see Figure 8-45). If you assigned a topic, that appears as a button at the top, above the due date (if you assigned one). The *Done* readout and *Not Done* readout in the upper-right corner of the assignment's box show the number of students who have and have not submitted the assignment.

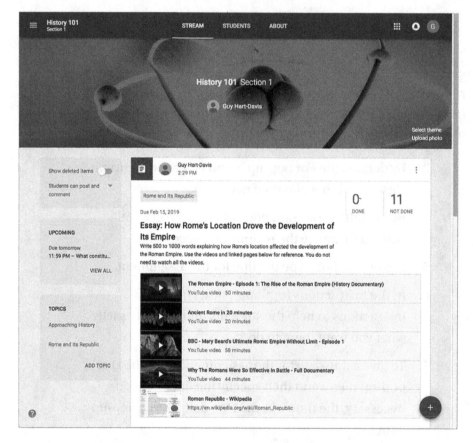

Figure 8-45. *After you set an assignment, it appears on the Stream tab. The Done and Not Done readouts give you a quick reference to students' progress on the assignment.*

To see more detail, click the assignment's name or click either the *Done* readout or the *Not Done* readout. The Student Work tab for the assignment appears (see Figure 8-46), showing the *Done* readout and the *Not Done* readout, plus the following controls:

- *Select all*: Click this check box to select the check boxes for all the students.

- *Email selected students*: Click this button to start an email message in Gmail to the selected students. Gmail places the assignment's name in the Subject field of the message.

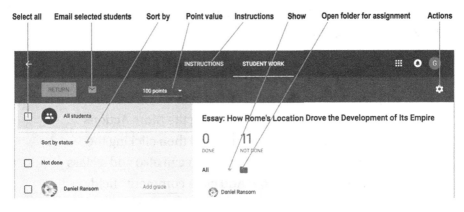

Figure 8-46. *The Student Work tab for an assignment shows details of which students have and have not submitted the assignment*

- *Sort by*: To control how Google Classroom sorts the students, click this pop-up menu and then click the Sort by last name item, the Sort by first name item, or the Sort by status item, as needed.

- *Point value*: To change the number of points for the grading, type the new number in the text field, press the Enter key, and then click the Update button in the

Update point value dialog box that opens (see Figure 8-47). To change the assignment to being an ungraded one, click the pop-up button, click the Ungraded item on the pop-up menu, and then click the Update button in the Update point value dialog box.

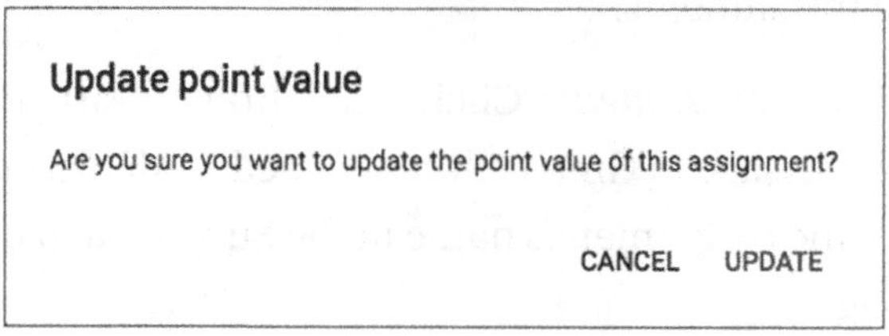

Figure 8-47. *Click the Update button in the Update point value dialog box to change the point value of the assignment*

- *Instructions*: Click this tab to display the Instructions page for the assignment (see Figure 8-48). Here, you can edit the assignment by clicking the More Actions button (the three vertical dots) and then clicking the Edit item on the pop-up menu. You can also add a class comment by clicking the "Add class comment" field, typing the comment, and then clicking the Post button.

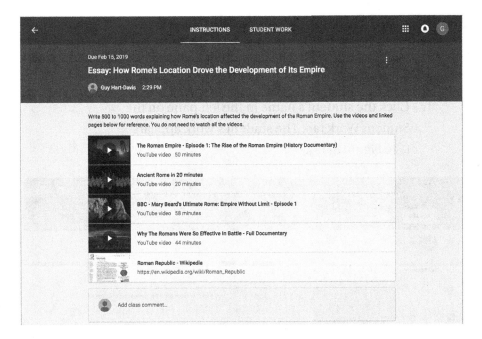

Figure 8-48. On the Instructions tab, you can review the assignment, edit it if necessary from the More Actions button, or add a class comment

- *Show*: To change which students' assignments are displayed, click this pop-up button and then click the All item, the Done item, the Not done item, or the Returned item, as needed.

- *Open folder for assignment*: Click this button to open the folder for the assignment.

- *Actions*: Click this icon to display the pop-up menu, and then click the Copy all grades to Google Sheets item, the Download all grades as CSV item, or the Download these grades as CSV item, as needed.

Grading and Returning an Assignment

Once a student has submitted an assignment, you can grade it and return it. Follow these steps:

1. Click the student's name in the left pane on the Student Work tab. The student's work appears (see Figure 8-49).

Figure 8-49. *Click the student's name in the left pane on the Student Work tab and then click the item you want to view.*

2. Click the item you want to view. The item opens in the appropriate app—for example, a Google Docs document opens in a Google Docs tab in the Chrome app.

3. Once you have viewed the item, close its tab. The Chrome app returns you to the Student Work tab.

Note   You can add a private comment to the student by clicking the Add private comment button at the bottom of the Student Work tab, typing the comment, and then clicking the Post button.

---

4. Click the Add grade box to the right of the student's name and type the grade. You can use two decimal places if necessary; if you use more decimal places, Google Classroom will round the number to two decimal places.

5. When you are ready to return the assignment, make sure the student's check box in the left column is checked and then click the Return button. In the Return work? dialog box that opens (see Figure 8-50), look through the marks to make sure all looks well, type a private comment if necessary, and then click the Return button.

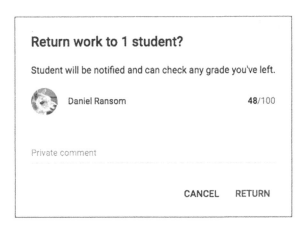

Return work to 1 student?

Student will be notified and can check any grade you've left.

Daniel Ransom   48/100

Private comment

CANCEL   RETURN

Figure 8-50. *In the Return work? dialog box, type any private comment needed and then click the Return button.*

Working with Questions

Google Classroom's Questions feature enables you to pose either open-answer questions or multiple-choice questions to the students in your classes. Questions can be a great way both to check students' knowledge and understanding of material and to get feedback on what is working well, what is not working well, or what students would find helpful in your classes.

Creating a Question

Follow these steps to create a question:

1. On the Stream tab for the class, click the Add (+) button in the lower-right corner to display the pop-up menu.

2. Click the Create question item. The Question dialog box opens (see Figure 8-51).

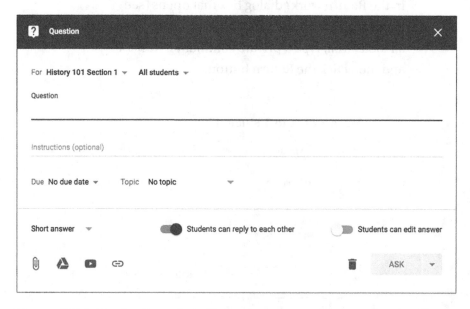

Figure 8-51. *In the Question dialog box, enter the question itself, enter any instructions needed, and choose between a short answer and multiple choice. You can also control whether students can reply to each other and whether students can edit their answers.*

3. By default, the For pop-up menu is set to the current class. Add other classes if necessary.

4. By default, the second pop-up menu is set to All students. Change the recipients if necessary.

5. In the Question box, type the text of the question.

6. In the Instructions (optional) box, type any instructions to help the students understand the context for the question and the types of responses you are looking for.

7. To give a due date for the question, click the Due pop-up menu and then specify the date—and, if necessary, the time—in the Due date & time pop-up panel.

8. Click the Topic pop-up menu and choose the topic. You can create a new topic if necessary.

9. Click the pop-up menu below the Due pop-up menu and then click the Short answer item or the Multiple choice item as needed.

10. For a short-answer question, set the two switches that appear:

    • *Students can reply to each other*: Set this switch to On if you want students to be able to discuss the question.

    • *Students can edit answer*: Set this switch to On if you want to allow students to edit their answers.

11. For a multiple-choice question, click the Add option line and type each answer needed (see Figure 8-52), then set the "Students can see class summary" switch to On or Off as needed.

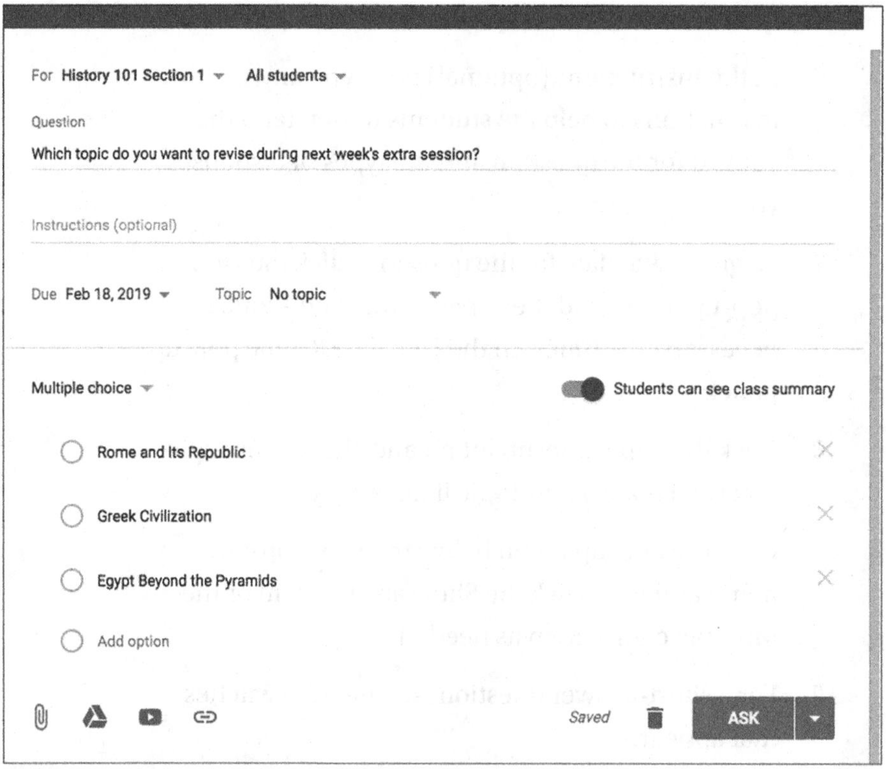

For History 101 Section 1 ▾   All students ▾

Question

Which topic do you want to revise during next week's extra session?

Instructions (optional)

Due Feb 18, 2019 ▾   Topic   No topic   ▾

Multiple choice ▾   ⬤ Students can see class summary

○   Rome and Its Republic   ✕

○   Greek Civilization   ✕

○   Egypt Beyond the Pyramids   ✕

○   Add option

📎   ▲   ▶   🔗   Saved   🗑   **ASK**   ▾

Figure 8-52. *Enter the answers for a multiple-choice question by clicking the Add option line and typing each answer. Set the "Students can see class summary" switch to On or Off as required.*

12.   Add any materials needed to the assignment.

13.   Click the Ask button to post the question.

Viewing and Grading Responses to a Question

You can view the responses to a question—and, if necessary, grade the responses and return them to the students—by using the same techniques as for an assignment:

- *View the responses*: Click the question on the Stream tab to display the Student Answers tab for the question.

The Student Answers tab (see Figure 8-53) works in a
similar way to the Student Work tab for an assignment.

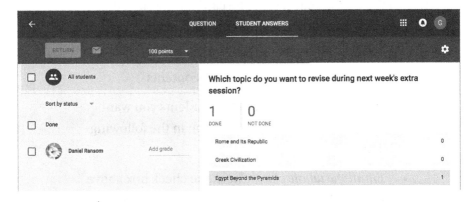

Figure 8-53. *On the Student Answers tab for a question, you can
view the answers to the question. You can also grade and return the
answers if necessary.*

- *Grade an answer*: In the left pane, click the "Add
  grade" field for the appropriate student and then type
  the grade.

- *Return an answer*: In the left pane, check the check box
  for the student or students and then click the Return
  button. In the Return work? dialog box, type any private
  comment needed and then click the Return button.

Emailing the Students in the Class

As long as Gmail is enabled, Google Classroom enables you to email an
entire class of students or one or more individual students within the class.

To send email messages to students, you work through the class. Follow these steps:

1. On the Classes page, click the card for the class that contains the student or students you want to email. The page for the class appears.

2. Click the Student tab to display its contents.

3. Depending on which student or students you want to email, take the appropriate action in the following sublist:

   - *Email the whole class*: Check the check box above the list of students, then click the Actions button and click the Email item on the pop-up menu.

   - *Email multiple students*: In the list of students, check the check box for each student you want to email. Then, click the Actions button and click the Email item on the pop-up menu.

   - *Email a single student*: In the list of students, click the More Actions button (the three vertical dots), and then click the Email item on the pop-up menu.

4. In the Gmail tab that Google Classroom makes Chrome open, type the subject and text of the message.

5. Optionally, attach files, links, or other items to the message.

6. Click the Send button to send the message.

Archiving and Unarchiving Classes

When you have finished teaching a class, such as when a semester or the school year comes to its end, you can archive the class to move it to safe storage and remove it from your home page and your students' home pages. When you need the class again, you can restore the class and start using it once more. If it turns out that you will never need an archived class again, you can delete it instead.

Note   Only teachers (including co-teachers) can archive classes; students cannot archive classes.

Understanding What Happens When You Archive a Class

Before you start archiving classes, it is a good idea to understand what archiving does and does not do. Here are the details:

- *The class and its materials are stored separately from your current classes*: Classroom keeps the materials you have added to the class, the work the students have done, and the posts made to the class.

- *The class disappears from home pages*: Classroom removes the class from the list of active classes on your home page and the students' home pages.

- *The archived class is viewable but not usable*: All teachers and students who were members of the class can view the archived class, but they cannot use the class unless a teacher unarchives it.

- *Class materials remain accessible in Google Drive*: Any files that were added to the class remain accessible in Google Drive. For example, students can still retrieve assignments for archived classes.

Archiving a Class

To archive a class, follow these steps:

1. Click the Classroom Main Menu button and then click the Classes item to display the Classes page.

2. Click the More Actions button (the three vertical dots) on the card for the class you want to archive and then click the Archive item. The Archive? dialog box opens (see Figure 8-54).

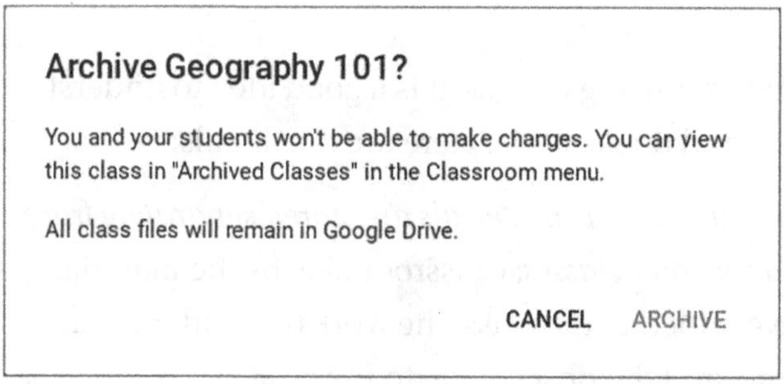

Archive Geography 101?

You and your students won't be able to make changes. You can view this class in "Archived Classes" in the Classroom menu.

All class files will remain in Google Drive.

CANCEL   ARCHIVE

Figure 8-54. *In the Archive? dialog box, verify that you have chosen the right class and then click the Archive button*

3. Make sure that you have chosen the right class to archive.

4. Click the Archive button. Classroom archives the class and removes it from the Classes page.

Unarchiving a Class

When you need to use an archived class again, follow these steps to unarchive it:

1. Click the Classroom Main Menu button and then click the Archived Classes item toward the bottom. The Archived Classes page appears.

2. Click the More Actions button (the three vertical dots) on the card for the class you want to unarchive and then click the Restore item. The Restore class? dialog box opens (see Figure 8-55).

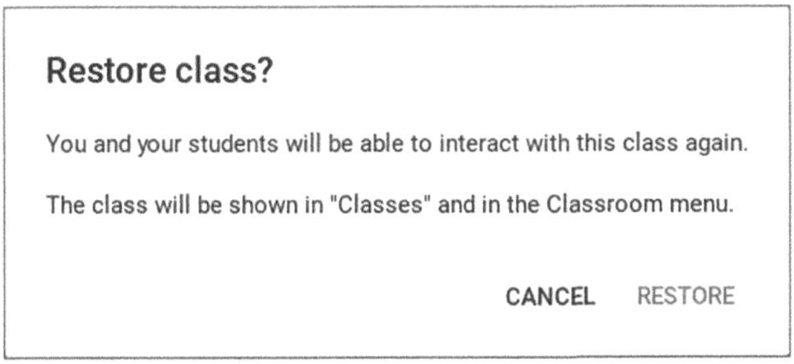

Restore class?

You and your students will be able to interact with this class again.

The class will be shown in "Classes" and in the Classroom menu.

CANCEL   RESTORE

Figure 8-55. *Click the Restore button in the Restore class? dialog box to restore the class from the archive to the Classes page and to active use*

3. Click the Restore button. Classroom restores the class and removes it from the Archived Classes page.

To start using the class, go back to the Classes page by clicking the Classroom Main Menu button and then clicking the Classes item.

Summary

In this chapter, you have learned how to use Google Classroom to organize classes in your school. You now know what Google Classroom is, what it enables you to do, and how to configure settings for the service. You can accept provisioned classes or create classes from scratch, add materials to the classes as needed, and communicate with your students via assignments, announcements, questions, and email messages.

In the next chapter, we will examine how to troubleshoot common problems with Chromebooks and keep your digital classrooms running.

CHAPTER 9

Troubleshooting Chromebooks in the Classroom

This chapter will show you how to troubleshoot the problems you are most likely to experience with Chromebooks in the classroom.

As you will know from your experience with computers and students, many different things can go wrong with hardware, software, wetware, and where the three 'wares meet. Some problems have quick and easy fixes, while other problems—even if they initially appear trivial—can require involved steps and plenty of time to troubleshoot.

This chapter assumes that you will be troubleshooting Chromebooks deployed in your school's classrooms and that your priority is to keep the Chromebooks running and your classrooms functioning smoothly. This means that you likely won't have time to dig into the specifics of each problem the moment it occurs; instead, you will want to work around problems as far as possible and spend time troubleshooting only when you are free to do so. To this end, the chapter will begin by suggesting a troubleshooting approach that assumes you have extra Chromebooks that you can swap in and out of the classrooms as necessary.

© Guy Hart-Davis 2018
G. Hart-Davis, *Deploying Chromebooks in the Classroom*,
https://doi.org/10.1007/978-1-4842-3766-3_9

After setting out this approach, the chapter will walk you through three key troubleshooting moves: resetting a Chromebook to clear up minor problems, running a Powerwash to get rid of major problems, and recovering the Chromebook to resolve intractable problems. Following that, the chapter will present separate sections on troubleshooting issues with networking, performance, and storage; keyboards, touchpads, and touchscreens; batteries; and Bluetooth, cameras, and audio.

Two Moves to Streamline Troubleshooting Your School's Chromebooks

When something goes wrong with a desktop computer in the classroom, you will normally need to troubleshoot it soon—if not immediately— in order to keep the classroom functioning usefully. But you will normally have much greater flexibility in troubleshooting your school's Chromebooks. This means that you may be better off using a restart-and-replace approach to troubleshooting any problem you can't instantly resolve. You can then use other troubleshooting moves—such as resetting the Chromebook, running a Powerwash on it, or using the Chromebook Recovery Utility—to resolve the problem when you have time.

Restarting as a Troubleshooting Move

As you no doubt know from experience, you can clear up many problems with end-user electronics—from smartphones and tablets to laptops and desktops—simply by restarting them. The same goes for Chromebooks. The speed and simplicity of restarting a Chromebook means that a restart is often a sensible place to start troubleshooting any problem that does not have an immediate fix. A restart usually takes less than a minute, and any student can perform it.

You will find that many of the sections in this chapter suggest restarting the Chromebook either as a first move in troubleshooting a problem or as a subsequent move if other options fail.

Tip   The quick way to restart a Chromebook is to hold down the Reload key and press the Power key or the Power button. It is best to sign out before using this keyboard shortcut because Chrome OS does not give you the chance to save any unsaved data. Otherwise, the normal way to restart a Chromebook is to give the Shut down command, either from the status menu when you are signed in or from the sign-in screen; after the Chromebook shuts down, press the Power key or Power button to restart it.

Replacing a Chromebook as a Troubleshooting Move

If a restart does not clear up a problem that will prevent the Chromebook from functioning as needed in the classroom, your best move is to replace the Chromebook with a spare—as long as you have a spare.

If possible, plan and maintain your Chromebook fleet so that you have one or more spare Chromebooks that you can swap in when one of your regular Chromebooks suffers problems or gets broken.

Resolving Problems by Resetting and Powerwashing Chromebooks

Chrome OS provides two moves for resolving intractable stability or configuration issues on a Chromebook:

- *Reset*: You can reset all the settings to factory defaults. Resetting leaves all the user accounts on the Chromebook and does not delete any user files.

- *Powerwash*: You can remove all user accounts and user files and reset the Chromebook to its original condition.

Caution   Because a Powerwash removes all user accounts and user files from the Chromebook, make sure you have backed up any content stored only on the Chromebook before starting a Powerwash. Given that Chromebooks are designed to store almost all content online, such a backup is usually not a problem.

The following subsections will explain how to perform a reset and a Powerwash.

Note   If even a Powerwash cannot restore the Chromebook to health, you may be able to recover it by using the Chromebook Recovery Utility and a recovery device. See the section "Recovering a Chromebook Using a Chrome OS Recovery Device" later in this chapter for details.

Displaying the Reset Screen in the Settings Window

To reset or Powerwash a Chromebook, first display the Reset screen in the Settings window. Follow these steps:

1. Click the status area at the right end of the shelf to open the status menu.

2. Click the Settings icon to display the Settings window.

3. Click the Navigation button on the left to display the Navigation panel and then click the Advanced section to expand its contents.

4. Click the Reset button to display the Reset screen (see Figure 9-1).

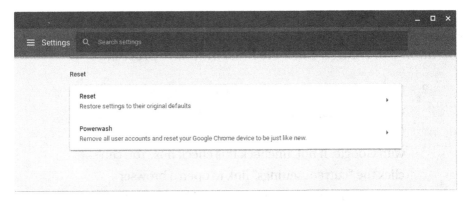

Figure 9-1. *From the Reset screen in the Settings window, you can reset a Chromebook's settings to their factory defaults or Powerwash the Chromebook to remove all user accounts and reset the settings*

Resetting a Chromebook to Factory Default Settings

To reset a Chromebook to factory default settings, follow these steps from the Reset screen in the Settings window:

1. Click the Reset button. The Reset dialog box opens (see Figure 9-2).

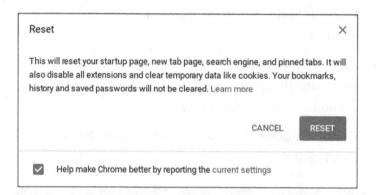

Reset	×
This will reset your startup page, new tab page, search engine, and pinned tabs. It will also disable all extensions and clear temporary data like cookies. Your bookmarks, history and saved passwords will not be cleared. Learn more	
	CANCEL RESET
☑ Help make Chrome better by reporting the current settings	

Figure 9-2. *In the Reset dialog box, read the details of what the reset operation will change. Click the Reset button to proceed.*

2. Check the "Help make Chrome better by reporting the current settings" check box if you are happy for Chrome OS to share the details of the Chromebook's settings with Google. If not, uncheck this check box. You can click the "current settings" link to open a browser window showing the settings you will be sharing.

3. Click the Reset button. Chrome OS will reset the Chromebook's settings.

When resetting the Chromebook, Chrome OS closes your current tabs, but Chrome OS does not sign you out of the device, and the Chromebook does not restart, so you may find the experience underwhelming.

Nevertheless, see if the problem you were experiencing has been resolved. If not, you may want to run a Powerwash, as explained in the next section.

Powerwashing a Chromebook

To Powerwash a Chromebook, removing all user accounts and returning the device to its original state, follow these steps from the Reset screen in the Settings window:

1. Click the Powerwash button. The Restart your device dialog box opens (see Figure 9-3).

Note   If the Powerwash setting does not appear on the Reset screen, your Chromebook is a managed device. You will need to have an administrator reconfigure it for you.

Figure 9-3.   *Click the Restart button in the Restart your device dialog box to start the Powerwash reset process.*

2. Click the Restart button. The Chromebook restarts. The Reset this Chrome device dialog opens.

567

3. Click the Powerwash button. The Confirm
    Powerwash dialog box then opens, warning you that
    all user accounts and local data will be removed.

4. Click the Continue button. The Powerwash in
    progress screen appears, showing the progress of
    the Powerwash process.

When the Powerwash is complete, the Welcome! dialog will open, and
you can set up the Chromebook again from scratch.

Recovering a Chromebook Using a Chrome OS Recovery Device

The ultimate troubleshooting step for a Chromebook is to recover it by
using a recovery device, which is a USB flash drive or an SD card with a
copy of Chrome OS on it. This section will explain when to use a recovery
device, how to create the recovery device, and how to use it.

Understanding When to Use a Recovery Device

Normally, you would use a recovery device if the Chromebook displays the
message *Chrome OS is missing or damaged* when you power the device on.

You can also use a recovery device when all other troubleshooting
moves have failed. Usually, you would try a reset first; a Powerwash next,
if the reset did not help; and then recovery with a recovery device, if the
Powerwash did not fix the problem either.

Creating a Recovery Device

To create a recovery device, you can use either a Chromebook or a
Windows PC or a Mac that has the Chrome browser installed on it. On this
Chromebook, PC, or Mac, you install the Chromebook Recovery Utility as

an app in the Chrome browser. You then run the Chromebook Recovery Utility, which downloads a suitable copy of Chrome OS for the Chromebook and creates the recovery device on a USB flash drive or an SD card.

The following subsections will take you through the details of what you need to do.

Installing Chrome on the PC or Mac

If you are using a PC or Mac to create the recovery device, it must have the Chrome browser installed on it because the Chromebook Recovery Utility runs as a Chrome app.

If the PC or Mac already has Chrome, skip this section. If not, steer your current browser to the Chrome website (`https://www.google.com/chrome`) and then download and install Chrome.

Installing the Chromebook Recovery Utility

Next, install the Chromebook Recovery Utility as an app in Chrome on the Chromebook, the PC, or the Mac. Launch Chrome and go to the following page in the Chrome Web Store: `https://chrome.google.com/webstore/detail/chromebook-recovery-utili/jndclpdbaamdhonoechobihbbiimdgai`.

Tip   The URL for the Chromebook Recovery Utility is a challenge to type—for me, anyway. You can also locate the Chromebook Recovery Utility by going to `http://google.com/chromeos/recovery` and then clicking one of the Recovery app links in the Step 2 section. In theory, another way to locate the Chromebook Recovery Utility is to go to the Chrome Web Store and search for "Chromebook recovery utility," but this search currently returns only results for other Chrome extensions, not for the Chromebook Recovery Utility.

When you reach the web address for the Chromebook Recovery Utility, a pop-up window will open showing information about the utility (see Figure 9-4). Read the details to double-check you have found the right utility and then click the Add to Chrome button.

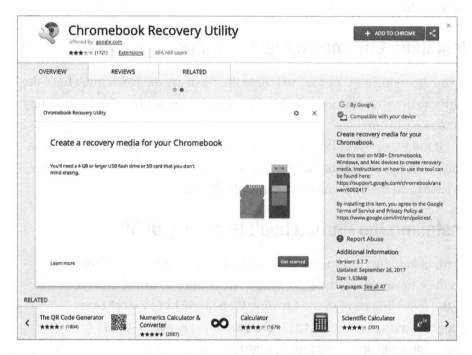

Figure 9-4.   *When you find the Chromebook Recovery Utility, click the Add to Chrome button at the top to add it to the Chrome browser*

In the Add "Chromebook Recovery Utility"? dialog box that opens (see Figure 9-5), click the Add app button.

Figure 9-5. *Click the Add app button in the Add "Chromebook Recovery Utility"? dialog box*

Once Chrome has added the Recovery app, it will display the Apps screen, which now includes the Recovery icon (see Figure 9-6).

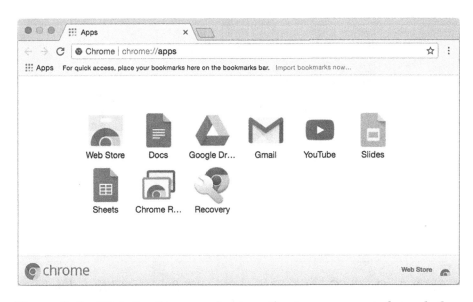

Figure 9-6. *Click the Recovery icon on the Apps screen to launch the Recovery app*

Running the Chromebook Recovery Utility and Creating the Recovery Device

You are now ready to run the Chromebook Recovery Utility and create the recovery device. To do so, follow these steps:

1. Click the Recovery icon to launch the Recovery app. The Chromebook Recovery Utility window then appears, showing the Create a recovery media for your Chromebook screen (see Figure 9-7).

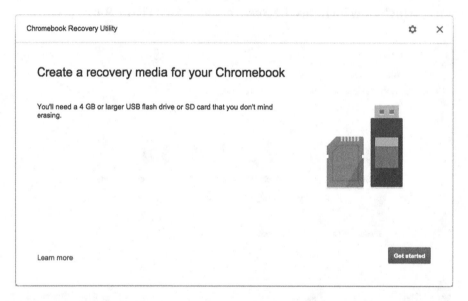

Figure 9-7. *On the Create a recovery media for your Chromebook screen of the Chromebook Recovery Utility, click the Get started button.*

2. Click the Get started button. The Identify your Chromebook screen appears (see Figure 9-8).

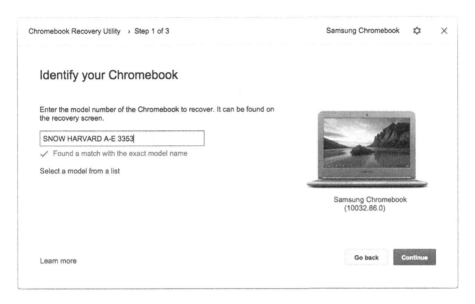

Figure 9-8. *On the Identify your Chromebook screen, either type the Chromebook's model number in the text box or click the Select a model from a list link and then use the Select a manufacturer pop-up menu and the Select a product pop-up menu to enter the details*

3. Type the model name and number in the text box, and make sure the *Found a match with the exact model name* readout appears; an image of the Chromebook and its description should appear too. Alternatively, click the Select a model from a list link to display the Select a manufacturer pop-up menu and the Select a product pop-up menu, and then use these pop-up menus to identify the model.

4. Click the Continue button. The Insert your USB flash drive or SD card screen appears (see Figure 9-9).

573

Figure 9-9. *On the Insert your USB flash drive or SD card screen, open the Select the media you'd like to use pop-up menu and click the USB flash drive or SD card item. You can also take other actions, such as erasing the recovery medium or using a local image of Chrome OS.*

5. Connect the USB flash drive or SD card to the computer if it is not already connected.

6. Open the Select the media you'd like to use pop-up menu and then click the menu item for the USB flash drive or SD card.

Note You can click the Settings icon (the gear icon) toward the right end of the title bar of the Chromebook Recovery Utility window to take three actions: Click the Erase recovery media menu item to erase the contents of the recovery media. Click the Use local image menu item to open a dialog box for selecting a Chrome OS image from your computer so that the Chromebook Recovery Utility does not have to download the image. Click the Send feedback menu item to open the Tell Us What's Happening dialog box, which enables you to send details of problems you experience using the Chromebook Recovery Utility to Google.

7. Click the Continue button. The Create a recovery image screen appears (see Figure 9-10).

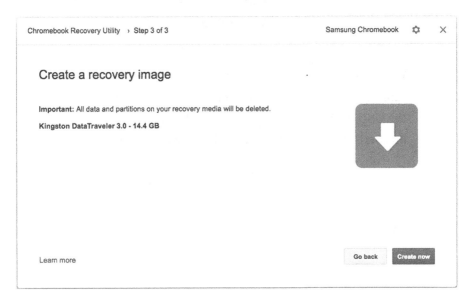

Figure 9-10. *On the Create a recovery image screen, verify that you have chosen the correct USB drive or SD card and then click the Create now button*

8. Double-check the device name to verify that you have chosen the correct USB drive or SD card.

9. Click the Create now button. The Chromebook Recovery Utility downloads the Chrome OS image, verifies the download, and then unpacks it. The Chromebook Recovery Utility then erases the USB

flash drive or SD card, repartitions it, and installs the Chrome OS image on it. When this process is complete, the Chromebook Recovery Utility will eject the USB flash drive or SD card from the computer's file system.

Note   On the Mac, the authopen process may request permission to "make changes" after unpacking the downloaded image. The changes are erasing the USB flash drive or SD card. Type your password and then click the OK button to proceed.

---

10.   When the Success! Your recovery media is ready screen appears (see Figure 9-11), you can remove the USB flash drive or SD card and click the Done button to close the Chromebook Recovery Utility.

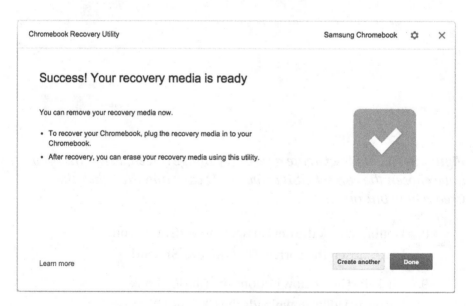

Figure 9-11.   *When the Success! Your recovery media is ready screen appears, remove the USB flash drive or SD card and click the Done button*

Recovering the Chromebook with the Recovery Drive

You can now recover the Chromebook using the recovery drive, like this:

1. Put the Chromebook into Recovery mode:

    -   If the Chromebook puts itself into Recovery mode when you press the Power key or Power button, you are all set.

    -   If the Chromebook boots to the sign-in screen, click the Shut down button to shut it down. Then, hold down the Esc key and the Reload key while you press the Power key or Power button. The Chromebook boots to Recovery mode.

2. Plug the USB flash drive or SD card into the Chromebook. The Chromebook automatically reads the drive or card and begins the process of reinstalling Chrome OS from it.

3. Wait while the recovery takes place. First, the Chromebook verifies the integrity of the recovery media. Next, you see the message "System recovery is in progress..." as the Chromebook reinstalls Chrome OS from the recovery media.

4. When the message "System recovery is complete" appears, remove the USB flash drive or SD card from the Chromebook. The Chromebook then restarts automatically.

5. When the Welcome! screen appears, set the Chromebook up from scratch, as discussed in Chapter 3.

Troubleshooting Network Issues

Chromebooks are designed to spend most of their lives connected to the Internet and to perform almost all tasks online, so you will need to make sure your network connections are working. In this section, we will look at how to troubleshoot network issues, starting with checking the essentials, moving along to resolving two specific network-connection errors, and then covering how to update the password for a Wi-Fi network.

Checking the Essentials

First, check the essentials:

- *Verify that Wi-Fi is enabled*: Look at the Wi-Fi icon in the status area at the right end of the shelf. If the Wi-Fi icon has a line through it, Wi-Fi is disabled. To enable Wi-Fi, click the Wi-Fi icon, click the Wi-Fi button (which will say No network) on the status menu, and then set the "Wi-Fi" switch at the top of the Network status menu to On.

- *Check whether the Chromebook is connected to a network*: See whether the Wi-Fi icon in the status area is showing connection bars (the arcs that indicate the signal strength).

- *See if the Chromebook is connected to the right network*: Click the Wi-Fi icon in the status area to display the status menu and then look at the Wi-Fi button. If the Chromebook is connected to a network, the Wi-Fi button shows *Connected to* and the network's name.

Note If the Chromebook has connected to the wrong network, make sure that the right network is available. If the Chromebook has multiple known networks, it works its way through them until it finds one that is available.

- *Make sure the Wi-Fi network is available*: If you find that the Chromebook is not able to connect to the Wi-Fi network it is supposed to connect to, make sure the network is available. For example, see if one of the other Chromebooks has connected successfully to the network, or check whether your phone or tablet can see the network. If you find the network has disappeared, you probably need to restart the Wi-Fi access point (or have a colleague restart it) rather than chastise the Chromebook.

Resolving Network-Connection Errors

When Chrome OS is unable to connect to a network, it returns a network-connection error. This section will explain how to troubleshoot two network-connection errors that you are likely to encounter with your school's Chromebooks:

- *Failed to Connect to Network: DHCP Lookup Failed*
- *Out of Range*

Resolving the "Failed to Connect to Network: DHCP Lookup Failed" Error

The message *Failed to Connect to Network: DHCP Lookup Failed* indicates that the Chromebook is able to connect to the Wi-Fi network, but the Dynamic Host Configuration Protocol (DHCP) service is not available. Unless you specify an IP address and other network details manually for the Chromebook, it will be unable to use the Wi-Fi network.

This error message typically indicates a problem with the Wi-Fi network with which the Chromebook is trying to connect. When you encounter this error, you would usually need to restart the Wi-Fi access point or have a colleague restart it.

Resolving the "Out of Range" Error

As you would expect, the message *Network Connection Error: Out of Range* typically occurs when the Chromebook is too far from the Wi-Fi network; in this case, the remedy is to either bring the Chromebook within range of the network or switch to another network that's available. But this error can also occur when the Chromebook is well within range of the network. If this happens, try the following steps to troubleshoot it:

- *Connect to another network and then reconnect to this network*: If another Wi-Fi network is available, try connecting the Chromebook to that network. If the Chromebook connects successfully, try switching back to the problem network. If the Chromebook cannot connect to the other network either, try restarting the Chromebook.

- *Restart the Chromebook*: Restarting clears out any glitches that have occurred in the network settings, so it can often resolve the problem.

- *Forget the Wi-Fi network and connect again*: Forgetting the Wi-Fi network removes the network settings; connecting to the network again replaces them. Follow these steps:

  1. Click the Wi-Fi icon in the status area to display the status menu.

  2. Click the Wi-Fi button to display the Network status menu.

  3. Click the Network settings icon (the gear icon) in the upper-right corner to open the Settings window.

  4. Click the button for the current network to display the Wi-Fi screen.

  5. Click the right-arrow button on the right of the button for the current network to display the Settings screen for the network.

  6. Click the Forget button. Chrome OS forgets the network, and the Wi-Fi screen appears again.

  7. Click the network you just made the Chromebook forget. The Join Wi-Fi network dialog box opens.

  8. Type the password for the network.

  9. Check the "Share this network with other users" check box if necessary.

  10. Click the Connect button.

- *Change the name servers*: Follow these steps:

  1. Click the Wi-Fi icon in the status area to display the status menu.

  2. Click the Wi-Fi button to display the Network status menu.

  3. Click the Network settings icon (the gear icon) in the upper-right corner to open the Settings window.

  4. Click the button for the current network to display the Wi-Fi screen.

  5. Click the right-arrow button on the right of the button for the current network to display the Settings screen for the network.

  6. Click the Network heading to display the fields in the Network section.

  7. Click the Name servers pop-up menu and choose a different setting. For example, if the current setting is Automatic name servers, you might try Google name servers or Custom name servers.

Updating the Password for a Wi-Fi Network

When you try to connect to a Wi-Fi network whose password has changed, Chrome OS will display the Join Wi-Fi network dialog box, prompting you to enter the password. However, if Chrome OS attempts to connect to the Wi-Fi network automatically, when the connection fails because of the password problem, Chrome OS will then connect to the next known network—assuming one is available—without telling you that it was unable to connect to the first network. This behavior makes good sense for ensuring the Chromebook has an Internet connection, but it can mean that some of the networks on the known list are not usable.

So, if you know that a Wi-Fi network's password has changed, it is a good idea to update the password on your Chromebooks to ensure they can connect to the network. The easiest way to do this is simply to connect manually to the network, forcing the Join Wi-Fi network dialog box to open so you can enter the password. You can also connect in the following, more roundabout, way:

1. Click the status area to open the status menu.

2. Click the Settings icon to open the Settings window.

3. In the Network section, click the right-arrow button on the right of the Wi-Fi button to display the Wi-Fi screen.

4. Click the right-arrow button on the right of the network whose password you want to update. The configuration screen for the network appears.

5. Click the Configure button. The Join Wi-Fi network dialog box opens.

6. Type the new password in the Password box.

7. Click the Connect button.

Troubleshooting Performance Issues

This section will tell you how to deal with the two performance issues you are most likely to experience with Chromebooks:

- The Chromebook runs too slowly.

- The Chromebook freezes, crashes, or spontaneously restarts itself.

Troubleshooting a Chromebook Running Too Slowly

If a Chromebook is running too slowly, try closing any tabs or windows that you no longer need. If performance improves, it is likely that the Chromebook was running out of memory. Unless the Chromebook is a model with expandable RAM, and you can add more RAM to it (preferably as much as it will hold), your best bet is to limit the number of tabs and windows you have open at any given time. Restarting the Chromebook may provide temporary relief, but the problem is likely to recur once you start overtaxing its resources.

If the Chromebook is temporarily slow, but performance then improves, apparently of its own accord, check to see whether there is a problem with the Internet connection.

Note   Look at the status area to see if the System Update icon (an arrow) appears. If so, apply the update to see if it delivers any performance improvement.

Troubleshooting a Chromebook Freezing, Crashing, or Restarting

If a Chromebook freezes when a Chrome window is active, try pressing Ctrl+Shift+R to force a refresh of the page. A refresh may be enough to unfreeze the Chromebook.

If the Chromebook is still frozen, try restarting it by holding down the Reload key and pressing the Power key or the Power button. If the Restart shortcut does not work, power down the Chromebook by pressing the Power key or Power button and then start it again.

If the Chromebook continues to freeze after the restart, or if it crashes, try uninstalling the most recently installed apps or extensions:

- *Uninstall an app*:

    a.   Click the Launcher button to open the Launcher.

    b.   Click the up-arrow button to display the Launcher screen.

    c.   Right-click the app to display the shortcut menu.

    d.   Click the Uninstall item on the menu. The Remove dialog box for the app opens.

    e.   Click the Remove button.

- *Uninstall an extension*:

    a.   Open or activate a Chrome window.

    b.   Click the More Actions button (the three vertical dots) to display the menu.

    c.   Click or highlight the More tools item to display the More tools submenu, and then click the Extensions item to open a Chrome tab displaying the Extensions screen.

    d.   Click the Delete icon (the trash icon) to the right of the extension you want to remove. The Remove dialog box for the extension opens.

    e.   Click the Remove button.

If a Chromebook restarts spontaneously, you will normally need to run a Powerwash to recover it.

Troubleshooting Storage Issues

Even though Chromebooks typically store most data on the Internet, you may sometimes find Chromebooks run out of storage, especially if one or more of the following factors applies:

- The Chromebook has a small amount of storage, such as 16 GB.

- Multiple user accounts have been set up on the Chromebook.

- The Chromebook's users have downloaded many files or large files (such as videos) for local use.

Note   As with most computers, Chromebooks have less storage than their nominal capacity. Part of the difference is Chrome OS and its apps, which occupy several gigabytes between them. The other reason is that Chromebook manufacturers use decimal (base 10) numbers rather than binary (base 2) numbers for measuring storage capacity. In decimal, a gigabyte has 1,000,000,000 bytes of storage—1000 x 1000 x 1000. But in binary, a gigabyte has 1,073,741,824 bytes—1024 x 1024 x 1024—or 7.4% more; technically, this is a gibibyte, or 1 GiB, but few people use the term. So, when a manufacturer claims a Chromebook has 16 GB of storage, that means it has 16,000,000,000 bytes, which translates to 14.9 GB in binary.

See How Much Storage Is Available on a Chromebook

Follow these steps to see how much storage is available on a Chromebook:

1. Click the status area to display the status menu.

2. Click the Settings icon to open the Settings window.

3. In the Device section, click the Storage management button to display the Storage management screen (see Figure 9-12).

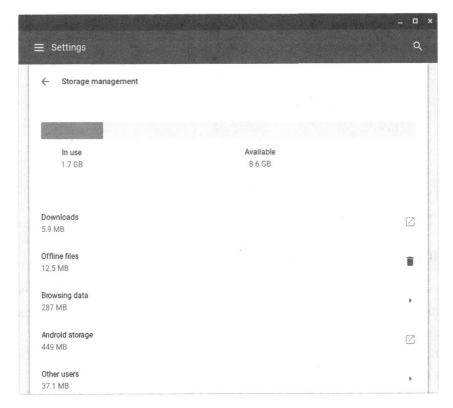

Figure 9-12. *Look at the histogram at the top of the Storage management screen in the Settings window to see how much space is free on the Chromebook and what categories of items are consuming space*

587

4. Look at the histogram at the top, which shows a blue
    In use bar and a gray Available bar.

Tip   You can also see how much storage is available in the
Files app. Click the Downloads folder (because it is stored on the
Chromebook), and then click the More Actions button and look at the
readout at the bottom.

Free Up Storage on a Chromebook

When you find a Chromebook has run low on space, you can free up space
in the following ways:

- Remove any extra user accounts.

- Delete downloaded files and offline files you no longer
  need.

- Clear your browser cache.

- Uninstall any apps you do not need.

See the following subsections for details of these moves.

Remove Any Extra User Accounts

Usually, the best place to start recovering space on a Chromebook that has
multiple users is by removing any user accounts that are no longer needed.
Each user account can contain downloaded files, offline files, and files
cached by the browser, so for a Chromebook shared by many users, space
may disappear quickly.

Note   You cannot remove the owner account from the Chromebook this way. To remove the owner account, first run a Powerwash, restoring the Chromebook to factory settings. You can then set up the Chromebook again using the account you want to have as the new owner account.

To remove a user account from a Chromebook, follow these steps:

1. If you are signed in to the Chromebook, click the status area and then click the Sign out button on the status menu. The sign-in screen appears.

2. On the sign-in screen, click the user account. The Password field appears.

3. Click the pop-up menu button on the selected user account. The pop-up menu opens.

4. Click the Remove this user item. A warning appears, telling you that the user's files and local data will be removed from the Chromebook.

5. Click the Remove this user button. Chrome OS removes the user account.

Delete Offline Files and Downloaded Files

After removing any extra user accounts, you can recover further space by deleting offline files and downloaded files from within your own user account. To delete these files, take the following steps:

1. Click the status area to display the status menu.

2. Click the Settings icon to open the Settings window.

3. In the Device section, click the Storage management button to display the Storage management screen (shown in Figure 9-12, earlier in this chapter).

4. To delete the offline files, click the Offline files button, and then click the Delete Files button in the Delete offline files? dialog box that opens (see Figure 9-13).

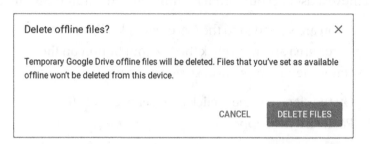

Figure 9-13. *Click the Delete Files button in the Delete offline files? dialog box to remove all your offline files from the Chromebook*

5. If you want to delete downloaded files, click the Downloads button to open a Files window showing the contents of the Downloads folder.

6. Delete any downloaded files you no longer need. To delete a file, select it and then click the Delete button (the Trash icon) on the toolbar. You can also delete a file by right-clicking it and then clicking Delete on the contextual menu, or by selecting the file and then pressing Alt+Backspace.

Note   If you need to check the contents of a file before deleting it, get a preview by selecting the file and pressing the spacebar. Press the spacebar again to close the preview.

---

7.   When you finish working with the downloaded files,
     go back to the Storage management screen if you
     want to clear your browser cache.

Clear Your Browser Cache

Your next step in reclaiming precious space on a Chromebook is to clear
the browser cache—the images and data that Chrome has stored to enable
you to browse more quickly and return to sites you have previously visited.

To clear the browser cache, follow these steps from the Storage
management screen:

1.   Click the Browsing data button to open the Clear
     Browsing Data dialog box.

2.   Click the Basic tab or the Advanced tab as needed.

Note   See the section "Clearing Browsing Data" in Chapter 4 for full
details on the categories of data you can clear in the Clear browsing
data dialog box.

---

3.   Uncheck the check box for each category of data
     you do not want to clear. (All the check boxes are
     checked by default.)

4.   Click the Clear Data button.

Troubleshooting Keyboard Issues

In this section, we will examine how to troubleshoot keyboard issues that occur with Chromebooks. Usually, keyboard issues fall into the following two categories:

- The keyboard does not respond.

- The keys produce the wrong characters.

Troubleshooting the Keyboard Not Responding

If the keyboard on a Chromebook stops working, your best bet is normally to restart the Chromebook. If the pointer is still working, shut down the Chromebook by clicking the Shut down button on either the status menu (if you or another user are logged in) or on the sign-in screen. Otherwise, press and hold the Power key or Power button to power off the Chromebook. After the Chromebook shuts down, press the Power key or Power button again to restart the Chromebook.

If the keyboard now works, try signing in using the same account that had the keyboard problem. If the keyboard now works fine in that account, the Chromebook is back in business. But if the keyboard problem recurs, sign out of the account and restart the Chromebook again. If the account exhibiting the problems is not the owner account for the Chromebook, delete that account from the Chromebook and then add it back again. But if the problem account is the owner account, reset the Chromebook as explained in the section "Resolving Problems by Resetting and Powerwashing Chromebooks" earlier in this chapter.

If the keyboard still does not work after restarting the Chromebook, you will need to contact the Chromebook's manufacturer. For a short-term fix, you can try connecting a USB keyboard and see if that works.

Troubleshooting the Keys Producing the Wrong Characters

If pressing the keys on the Chromebook's keyboard produces the wrong characters on the screen, most likely the keyboard layout has been changed. To find out, click the status area and then look at the Input method item near the top. If this item shows the wrong keyboard layout, click the item to display the Input methods status menu and then click the right keyboard layout, such as US keyboard.

If the keyboard layout you need does not appear on the Input methods status menu, click the Settings icon to display the Languages and input section of the Settings window. You can then click the Input method button to expand the Input method controls and use them to configure the input method.

Troubleshooting Touchpad Issues

If the touchpad on a Chromebook stops registering touches, check to see whether the touchpad has accumulated dirt or dust. If so, use a soft, lint-free cloth to remove the dirt or dust.

If—or when—the touchpad is clean enough but is still not responding, try pressing the Esc key several times. Next, try drumming your fingers on the touchpad for several seconds to see if it starts registering.

If the touchpad is still not responding, you will need to resort to two of the three standard moves. First, try restarting the Chromebook by powering it off and then on again. If restarting does not solve the problem, run a Powerwash.

If the touchpad problem persists after the Powerwash, sign in to the Chromebook (or have someone else sign in) using a different user account than the one that was having the trouble. If the touchpad works correctly for this user account, delete the other user account from the Chromebook and then add it again.

If none of these moves cures the problem, contact the Chromebook's manufacturer for advice. In the meantime, consider plugging in a USB mouse if you need to keep the Chromebook operational.

TROUBLESHOOTING UNWANTED TOUCHPAD CLICKS

If you find a user complains that the touchpad clicks things by itself, first turn off the tap-to-click feature. Open the Settings app, click the Touchpad button in the Device section to display the Touchpad screen, and then set the Enable tap-to-click switch to Off.

If the Enable tap-to-click switch is already set to Off, or if the problem persists after you set it to Off, the culprit is most likely the Automatic clicks accessibility feature, which automatically clicks following a short delay after the pointer is moved. To turn this feature off, click the status area, click the Accessibility button on the status menu, and then click the Automatic clicks item on the Accessibility status menu.

Troubleshooting Touchscreen Issues

If the touchscreen on a Chromebook stops responding to touch, your first move should be to clean the screen to remove any dirt or dust that may be preventing it from reading touches correctly. Normally, the best thing to use is a soft, lint-free cloth moistened slightly with water. If you need heavier-duty cleaning, consult the Chromebook manufacturer's website for recommendations on cleaners that are safe for the screen; do not reach for the contents of the janitorial closet.

Beyond cleaning the touchscreen and checking for any obvious damage, try restarting the Chromebook, resetting it, and Powerwashing it. If these standard moves do not resuscitate the touchscreen, contact the manufacturer for advice.

Troubleshooting Battery Issues

The battery in a Chromebook should last several years, but you may need to troubleshoot issues along the way.

The problem you are most likely to see is the battery not charging even though the charger is plugged into the Chromebook and connected to a socket. When this happens, start by checking the obvious points of failure:

- *Verify that the charger cable is connected securely to the charger*: The cables may have become loose.

- *Verify that the charger cable is connected correctly to the Chromebook*: Chromebooks use various types of power ports, and you may find a student has plugged the power connector into the wrong port. If this has happened, check that the assaulted port has survived the experience.

- *Verify that the charger cable is intact and fully connected to the socket:* Replace the cable if it has been damaged.

- *Verify that the power socket is providing power*: If the charger, the cable, and the connections are fine, try a different socket.

- *Try replacing the charger*: If you have other Chromebooks of the same type, borrow a working charger from one of them and see if it works for the problem Chromebook.

After you have checked the obvious, try disconnecting and reconnecting the Chromebook, then charge it for 30 minutes. Follow these steps:

1. Disconnect the charger from the socket.

2. Disconnect the charger from the Chromebook.

3. Reconnect the charger to the Chromebook.

4. Reconnect the charger to the socket.

5. Leave the Chromebook to charge for 30 minutes.

If the Chromebook still will not charge after 30 minutes, try resetting the Chromebook, as explained in the section "Resolving Problems by Resetting and Powerwashing Chromebooks" earlier in this chapter. If the reset does not get the Chromebook to start charging, you will need to contact the manufacturer for further steps to fix the problem.

Troubleshooting Bluetooth Issues

Bluetooth on Chromebooks can be highly useful for connecting devices such as headphones, speakers, and mice, but it seems to produce more problems than on Windows PCs and Macs. While Chrome OS does support many widely used Bluetooth devices, there are many other devices that it does not support.

This section will show you how to troubleshoot typical problems using Bluetooth devices.

Make Sure the Bluetooth Device Is Close Enough to the Chromebook

Start by making sure that the Bluetooth device is close enough to the Chromebook for Bluetooth to work. If the device works intermittently with the Chromebook and is located more than a few yards away, try moving the device closer to see if a stronger connection solves the problem.

Note   The range at which a Bluetooth device can sustain a connection depends on the device's class and its hardware. There are three classes: Class 1 devices transmit at 100 mW and have an intended range of 100 meters (328 feet); Class 2 devices transmit at 2.5 mW and have an intended range of 10 meters (33 feet); and Class 3 devices transmit at 1 mW and also have an intended range of 10 meters (still 33 feet). These intended ranges are not absolute. If there are walls or other obstructions between the Bluetooth devices, the effective range will be less. But Bluetooth should normally work well within a typical classroom.

Verifying That Bluetooth Is Enabled

First, verify that Bluetooth is enabled on the Chromebook. To do so, click the status area and look at the Bluetooth readout on the status menu (shown on the left in Figure 9-14). If the readout says `Bluetooth disabled`, click the menu item to display the Bluetooth status menu (shown on the right in Figure 9-14) and then set the switch at the top to On.

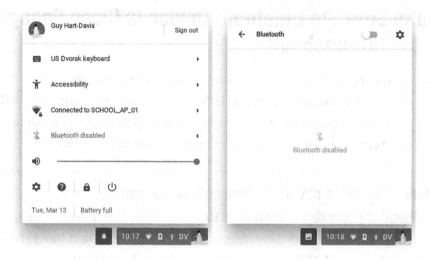

Figure 9-14. *If the Bluetooth item on the status menu (left) shows Bluetooth disabled, click the menu item to display the Bluetooth status menu (right) and then set the switch at the top to On*

The Bluetooth status menu then displays the list of Bluetooth devices within range. As you can see in the left screen in Figure 9-15, the Paired devices list appears at the top of the Bluetooth status menu, with the Unpaired devices list below it. You may need to scroll down to see all the devices in the Unpaired devices list, as in the right screen in Figure 9-15.

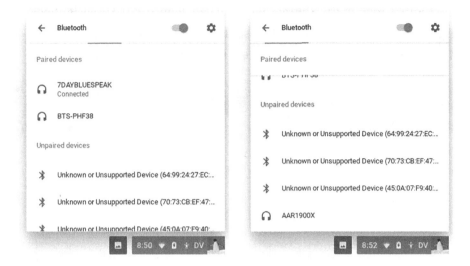

Figure 9-15. *The Bluetooth status menu shows the Paired devices list at the top and the Unpaired devices list below it. Scroll down if necessary to locate the device you are trying to connect.*

ADDING BLUETOOTH TO A CHROMEBOOK THAT LACKS IT

If the Bluetooth item (which displays Bluetooth enabled or Bluetooth disabled) does not appear on the status menu, the Chromebook does not support Bluetooth. If you need the Chromebook to have Bluetooth capabilities, you may be able to add them by plugging in a USB Bluetooth adapter. To reduce the risk of the Bluetooth adapter getting broken, look for a small adapter that will protrude only a short distance from the socket.

Seeing If the Bluetooth Device Is Compatible with Chrome OS

Next, see if Chrome OS lists the Bluetooth device as being compatible. To do this, turn the Bluetooth device on and look either at the Bluetooth status menu or the Bluetooth screen in the Settings window. Usually, the

599

Bluetooth screen in the Settings window (see Figure 9-16) is easier because it gives you more space to see the list of Bluetooth devices and the full MAC addresses of any devices that are unknown or unsupported.

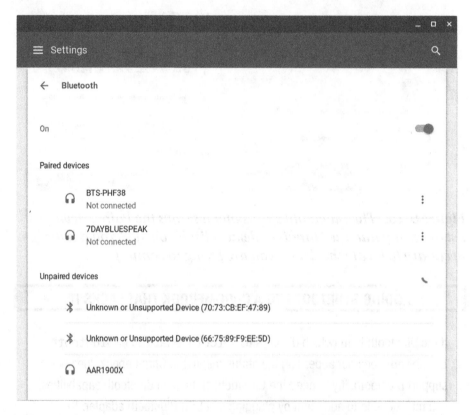

Figure 9-16. *The Unpaired devices list on the Bluetooth screen in the Settings window shows "Unknown or Unsupported Device" for any Bluetooth device Chrome OS cannot recognize or does not support*

Look at the Unpaired devices list to see whether Chrome OS can handle the Bluetooth device. If the device appears by name with a category icon, like the AAR1900X audio receiver (an honorary headphone) shown in the figure, Chrome OS recognizes the device and supports it. If the device appears as Unknown or Unsupported Device and its MAC address, with the generic Bluetooth icon, Chrome OS does not recognize the device and most likely does not support it.

FINDING OUT WHICH MAC ADDRESS BELONGS TO WHICH DEVICE

Looking at Figure 9-16, you have likely spotted a problem: To know *which* Bluetooth device Chrome OS does not recognize or support, you need to be able to identify the device by its MAC address. Most Bluetooth devices do not have the MAC address printed on them, so identifying a device from its MAC address can be a challenge—especially because the Chromebook may list Bluetooth devices in neighboring rooms, or even neighboring properties, as well as the ones you can physically control. The resulting plethora of Bluetooth devices renders useless the old standby of turning on a Bluetooth device and identifying it by the new entry on the list of devices.

One option is to open a browser window, search for a MAC address lookup tool (the search `mac address lookup` usually produces plenty of results), and then enter the MAC address of the unknown or unsupported device that Chrome OS is reporting. The lookup tool may return the manufacturer's name, which may give you enough information to identify the device. However, the manufacturers of many devices are not listed, so this approach works only sometimes.

A more promising way to learn a Bluetooth device's MAC address is to use a Windows PC or a Mac, as both Windows and MacOS have much wider Bluetooth support than Chrome OS. You can either use a Bluetooth scanner app to find information about nearby Bluetooth devices or pair the Bluetooth device with the PC or Mac and then look at the device's information. For example, on MacOS, choose Apple ➤ About This Mac to open the About This Mac window, click the System Report button to launch the System Information app, and then click the Bluetooth item in the Hardware section of the sidebar to display details on paired and connected Bluetooth devices.

Verifying That the Bluetooth Device Is Working

If the Bluetooth device worked before with Chrome OS, but you cannot get it working with Chrome OS now, double-check that the device is working. First, try a different Chromebook to see if the device will work with it. If not, use a computer or device running a different operating system, such as an Android phone, to verify that the device is working. You will usually need to pair the Bluetooth device with the computer or device in order to get it working, and you will normally need to unpair the Bluetooth device again in order to pair it with the Chromebook afterward.

Disabling and Reenabling Bluetooth on the Chromebook

Assuming the Bluetooth device proves to be working, try disabling and re-enabling Bluetooth on the Chromebook. The easiest way to do this is by using the status menu:

1. Click the status area to display the status menu.

2. Click the Bluetooth button to display the Bluetooth status menu.

3. Set the switch at the top to Off.

4. Set the switch back to On.

After re-enabling Bluetooth, try connecting to the device again. If you still cannot get the Bluetooth device to work, and you are sure it is compatible, try restarting the Chromebook to reload the operating system.

Troubleshooting Camera Issues

If the camera on a Chromebook stops working, the problem will usually be pretty obvious: Either an app (such as the Camera app built into Chrome OS or Google's Hangout app) displays a black rectangle where a smiling face should be, or Chrome OS displays the message "No camera found"— or both.

Once you have checked that the camera has not been physically removed or otherwise suffered terminal trauma, power the Chromebook down and then power it back on. If, once you have signed in using the same account, the camera works in the app with which the problem occurred, you are back in business. If not, try running another app that uses the camera. If that app works, but the problem app does not, try uninstalling and then reinstalling the problem app.

If the camera is still not working, try resetting the Chromebook. If a reset does not solve the problem, try a Powerwash. Beyond that, you will need to contact the Chromebook's manufacturer for advice on fixing the camera or getting it fixed.

Troubleshooting Audio Issues

When using Chromebooks in classrooms, usually the main audio problem you experience is difficulty in keeping the volume down. But as you already know the solution to this problem, this section will explore three other audio issues your school's Chromebooks may exhibit:

- The Chromebook produces no sound.

- The Chromebook produces distorted or stuttering sound.

- The Chromebook plays audio in mono rather than stereo.

Troubleshooting No Sound

If a Chromebook is producing no sound, first look for obvious problems with any speakers, headphones, or other audio hardware connected to the headphone port. For example, speakers may be muted, disconnected from a power source, or set to zero volume; and headphones may simply be broken. If necessary, disconnect any audio hardware so you can troubleshoot the problem using the Chromebook's internal speaker.

Next, make sure that the audio is not muted and that the volume level is not set to zero. Either simply press the Volume Up key on the keyboard until the pop-up volume control shows a moderate volume, or click the status bar to display the status menu and then drag the Volume slider to set a moderate volume.

Tip Keep the volume down when troubleshooting a lack of audio output. You may find that the Chromebook is sending the audio to a remote device, such as a Bluetooth speaker in another classroom.

If there is still no sound, find out where the Chromebook is sending the audio. Click the status bar to display the status menu (shown on the left in Figure 9-17) and then click the right-arrow button at the right end of the Volume slider to display the Audio settings status menu (shown on the right in Figure 9-17). Then, look at the Output section to see which audio output device bears a white check mark in a green circle. If the audio is going to the wrong output, click the right output, such as the Speaker (internal) item.

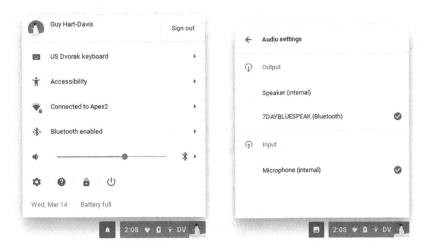

Figure 9-17. *Click the right-arrow button on the right of the Volume slider in the status menu (left) to display the Audio settings status menu (right), whose Output section shows you the current audio output device*

These steps are normally enough to restore audio playback. If not, try as many of the three standard troubleshooting moves as needed:

- Restart the Chromebook.

- Reset the Chromebook.

- Powerwash the Chromebook.

Troubleshooting Distorted Sound or Stuttering Playback

If a Chromebook is producing distorted sound, first look for a physical cause, such as the following:

- *The volume is too high for the internal speakers*: Chromebooks tend to have small speakers that are not capable of producing the volume of sound that some students prefer. External speakers may be a solution.

- *There is a poor connection to external speakers or headphones*: Make sure the speaker or headphone cable is plugged securely into the Chromebook's headphone port. Check the cable for damage. Check the headphone port for damage or for what medical professionals call "foreign bodies," such as lint, gum, or insects.

- *A teenager is listening to emo*: The immediate solution is headphones. The longer-term solution is the passage of several years.

Another possibility is that two Chrome apps are trying to output audio at the same time. When this happens, you will normally hear one app's output with interruptions rather than some output from each app. Look through the open apps and close any audio-capable apps other than the one whose output you want to hear. If this does not solve the problem, try restarting the Chromebook. If a restart does not help either, reset the Chromebook.

If a Chromebook's audio stutters when playing to a Bluetooth device, see if a restart helps. However, anecdotal evidence suggests that Chrome OS is prone to stuttering when playing audio to some Bluetooth devices. If the problem persists, try using another Bluetooth device or (preferably) a wired device instead.

Troubleshooting Audio Playing in Mono

If the Chromebook plays audio in mono when it should be in stereo, the problem is usually that the Mono audio accessibility setting has been enabled. To turn it off, follow these steps:

1. Click the status area to display the status menu.

2. Click the Accessibility button to display the Accessibility status menu.

3. In the Additional settings section, see if the Mono audio item bears a green circle with a white check mark. If so, click the Mono audio item to remove the check mark.

Note If the Mono audio setting is not enabled, make sure that the cable for external speakers or headphones is fully inserted in the Chromebook's headphone port. A partial connection may cause only one channel to play, giving a mono-like effect.

Summary

In this chapter, you have learned to deal with a wide variety of the problems you are most likely to encounter when running a fleet of Chromebooks in a school's classrooms. Armed with extra Chromebooks and the restart-and-replace approach, you can keep your classrooms fully computerized and resolve problems when you have time. You know how to perform the three major problem-solving moves: resetting a Chromebook, running a Powerwash, and recovering a Chromebook using

a recovery device. You have also learned how to troubleshoot a wide range
of issues, ranging from networking and performance to hardware issues
involving the keyboard, touchpad, touchscreen, and other Chromebook
components.

Index

A

© Guy Hart-Davis 2018
G. Hart-Davis, *Deploying Chromebooks in the Classroom*,
https://doi.org/10.1007/978-1-4842-3766-3

Y, Z